Nineteenth-Century British Music Studies
Volume 3

Nineteenth-Century British Music Studies

Volume 3

Edited by

PETER HORTON AND BENNETT ZON

ASHGATE

Published by
Ashgate Publishing Limited
Gower House
Croft Road
Aldershot
Hants GU11 3HR
England

Ashgate Publishing Company
Suite 420
101 Cherry Street
Burlington, VT 05401-4405
USA

Ashgate website: http://www.ashgate.com

British Library Cataloguing in Publication Data
Nineteenth-century British music studies
    Vol. 3. – (Music in nineteenth-century Britain)
    1. Music – Great Britain – 19th century – History and
    criticism – Congresses
    I. Horton, Peter II. Zon, Bennett III. Biennial Conference on
    Music in Nineteenth-Century Britain (3rd : 2001 : Royal
    College of Music, London)
    780.9'41'09034

Library of Congress Cataloging-in-Publication Data
Nineteenth-century British music studies/edited by Bennett Zon.
    (Music in Nineteenth-Century Britain)
    Papers deriving from the third biennial conference of the Society for the
    Study of Music in Nineteenth-Century Britain, held at the Royal College of
    Music, London, July 2001.
    Includes index.
    ISBN 0-7546-3614-3 (hc.)
    1. Music – Great Britain – 19th century – History and Criticism.
    I. Zon, Bennett. II. Society for the Study of Music in Nineteenth Century
    Britain. III. Series.

    ML285.5.N56   1999
    780'.941'09034—dc21   98-54371
                                                                                                              CIP
                                                                                                              MN

ISBN 0 7546 3614 3

Typeset in Sabon by Bookcraft Ltd, Stroud, Gloucestershire and printed in Great Britain by MPG Books Ltd, Bodmin, Cornwall.

Contents

List of Figures

List of Tables and Music Examples

Tables

Music Examples

Notes on Contributors

Duncan James Barker read music at St Edmund Hall, Oxford, before moving to the University of Durham where he completed a Ph.D. on the music of Sir Alexander Campbell Mackenzie (1847–1935) in 1999, under the supervision of Dr Jeremy Dibble. He now works as Development Manager for the Royal College of Music in London, having previously worked for Making Music. He is still an active freelance writer on music, having provided articles for the *New Grove*, second edition, and programme notes for leading London orchestras and artists. He is currently researching for a book on Mackenzie.

George Biddlecombe is a Lecturer in the Academic Studies Department and Chair of the York Gate Research Events Committee at the Royal Academy of Music. His research concentrates on operatic issues in nineteenth-century Britain. His publications include *English Opera from 1834 to 1864 with Particular Reference to the Works of Michael Balfe* (New York and London, 1994) and numerous contributions to the new *Dictionary of National Biography*, the *New Grove*, second edition, and the *Oxford Companion to the Romantic Age: British Culture, 1776–1832*. His recent work has focused on the reception of the soprano Jenny Lind, and he is currently engaged in a study of the representation of women singers in Britain in the nineteenth century.

G.W.E. Brightwell was educated at Harrow School and the University of Durham, where he was Organ Scholar at Durham Cathedral. He graduated BA in Music in 1995 and subsequently wrote a history of the National Training School for Music for an MA; he is completing a doctorate on the history of the Royal College of Music, 1883–1948. He is currently University Organist and Director of the Chapel Choir at the University of Glasgow.

Peter Campbell is currently completing a Ph.D. at the University of Melbourne. An accomplished choral singer, he has devoted the past ten years to researching the rich and largely undocumented history of Australia's choirs. He has been commissioned to write entries for the *New Grove*, second edition, the *Oxford Companion to Australian Music* and the *Currency Companion to Music and Dance in Australia*, and has published histories of the Australian Intervarsity Choral Movement and the Canberra Choral Society, as well as co-authoring a bio-bibliography of the composer Larry Sitsky (Westport, Conn., 1997).

Barbara Eichner studied musicology, German and Scandinavian literature at the Ludwig-Maximilians-Universität Munich, earning her MA in 2001.

In 1997–98 she spent an exchange year at the University of Southampton and she has also worked as a music journalist and literary editor. In 2002 she began doctoral work at the University of Oxford on German compositions from the second half of the nineteenth century dealing with Nordic mythology, Germanic sagas and medieval history and their relation to the shaping of a German national identity. Further fields of interest include Ethel Smyth and nineteenth-century popular music.

Peter Horton has made a particular study of the music of Samuel Sebastian Wesley (1810–76), editing his complete anthems for *Musica Britannica*. He has recently completed a study of Wesley's life and works (Oxford, forthcoming). He has contributed to previous volumes of *Nineteenth-Century British Music Studies* and is Reference Librarian and Research Co-ordinator at the Royal College of Music.

Valerie Langfield is a freelance musician and currently a Ph.D. student at the University of Birmingham. Her primary research interest is the music and context of the British Musical Renaissance, and in particular the work of Roger Quilter (1877–1953); she is the author of *Roger Quilter, His Life and Music*, published by the Boydell Press in 1992. She is a contributor to the *New Grove*, second edition, and the new *Dictionary of National Biography*.

Thomas Muir read history at Oxford University and taught history and politics for 20 years at Stonyhurst College. In 1997–2000 he read music at the University of York and he is currently researching Catholic Church music in England 1903–62 for a Ph.D. at the University of Durham under the supervision of Bennett Zon. This article represents the first fruits of that research, which includes the construction of a database mapping out the Catholic musical repertoire of that period. A second article, 'From Sight to Sound: Archival Evidence for English Catholic Music 1829–1962', outlining the contents of some of the major Catholic music collections, will be published in the forthcoming issue (no. 22) of *Catholic Archives* by the Catholic Archives Society. In addition he has published various articles on English Catholic and Jesuit history, and his book *Stonyhurst College: 1593–1993* (London, 1993) is the standard history of that institution.

Grant Olwage is a Ph.D. candidate at Rhodes University in South Africa. His research interests include musical colonialism in South Africa, Victorian music, film music, and 'the voice'. He has articles forthcoming on late Victorian hymnody and gender, and on colonialism and the politics of race in Victorian England and colonial South Africa.

Fiona M. Palmer is Lecturer in Music at Queen's University, Belfast. Her monograph *Dragonetti in England 1794–1846: the Career of a Double*

Bass Virtuoso (Oxford, 1997) has provided a springboard for her current research project – a critical biography of Vincent Novello (1781–1861), planned for completion in 2004. Novello's vision and industry in the context of the marketplace and the social circles within which he worked will provide the focus of the book. She continues to work as a professional double bassist and plays with the Ulster Orchestra on a regular basis.

Charlotte Purkis is Principal Lecturer in Drama and Performing Arts at King Alfred's College, Winchester. She has published on German dance history, Austro-American opera and *fin-de-siècle* literature, is a contributor to Sophie Fuller and Nicky Losseff (eds), *The Idea of Music in Victorian Fiction* (Aldershot, 2004), and is currently preparing interdisciplinary work on music and film for a forthcoming publication.

Julian Rushton, West Riding Professor of Music at the University of Leeds (1982–2002), is Chairman of *Musica Britannica*, for which he has edited a symphony by Cipriani Potter. He has also edited four volumes of the New Berlioz Edition. His books include Cambridge handbooks on Mozart's *Don Giovanni* and *Idomeneo*, Berlioz's *Roméo et Juliette*, and Elgar's *Enigma Variations*; *The Musical Language of Berlioz* (Cambridge, 1983); *Classical Music: A Concise History* (London, 1986); and *The Music of Berlioz*, published by Oxford University Press in 2001. He was President of the Royal Musical Association from 1994 to 1999, and in 2000 was elected a Corresponding Member of the American Musicological Society.

Derek B. Scott is Chair of Music at the University of Salford and researches into music, culture and ideology. He is author of *The Singing Bourgeois* (Milton Keynes, 1989, rev. edn Aldershot, 2001) and editor of *Music, Culture, and Society* (Oxford, 2000). His latest book, *From the Erotic to the Demonic: On Critical Musicology*, was published by Oxford University Press in March 2003. He is also a composer.

Nicholas Temperley, educated at Cambridge University, is Professor Emeritus at the University of Illinois. He is the author of *The Music of the English Parish Church* (Cambridge, 1979) and *The Hymn Tune Index* (Oxford, 1998) and the editor of *The London Pianoforte School 1766–1860* (20 vols, New York and London, 1982–85), *Music in Britain*, vol. 5: *The Romantic Age 1800–1914* (London, 1981) and *The Lost Chord: Essays on Victorian Music* (Bloomington, Ind., 1989). He is now at work on a study of British composers who migrated to the United States in the late eighteenth century.

Susan Wollenberg is Reader in Music at the University of Oxford, Faculty of Music, and Fellow and Tutor of Lady Margaret Hall, as well as College Lecturer in Music at Brasenose College. She is the author of *Music at Oxford in the Eighteenth and Nineteenth Centuries* (Oxford, 2001).

Editors' Foreword

It is the inevitable consequence of increased popularity that *Nineteenth-Century British Music Studies* 3 comprises only a very small proportion of the papers given at the third biennial conference on Music in Nineteenth-Century Britain. The conference, held at the Royal College of Music in July 2001, was attended by roughly 130 people from all over the world, with some 70 delegates offering papers. The attendance figures represent an increase of some 35 per cent on the previous conference held at Durham in 1999 (about 95 delegates), and over a 50 per cent increase on the first conference held at Hull in 1997 (about 65 delegates). What started, at Hull, as a small – but select – minority interest has in fact become a major concern in today's musicological world. One reason for this, cited in the previous volume in this series, is undoubtedly the death knell of the 'land without music' mindset amongst scholars. Today's musicologists simply do not have to make apologies for being interested in what previous generations deemed inferior. Quite the contrary, for with the erosion of this particular intellectual prejudice scholars now engage freely with the topic, and they do so in a way which reflects, stimulates and contributes to the diversity of currently prevailing methodologies. The effect of this is not only to reinforce cumulatively the legitimacy of the topic within the musicological community at large, but also to attract interest from scholars working in other areas of the arts. It is, arguably, this interdisciplinary interest which most characterises nineteenth-century British music studies. Likewise, it is in this particular emphasis that its real influence lies, for unlike many other fields of research, it is premised on situating music broadly within the culture of its time and place, as is apparent in the title of the conference from which the papers derive – Music in Nineteenth-Century Britain.

Nineteenth-century British music studies is, nevertheless, in its infancy as a topic, and although steeped in an inherently interdisciplinary ethos, much of the work being carried out today is done at the strictly musical coalface. This combination – of the interdisciplinary and the disciplinary, if you will – is clearly represented in the essays of this volume. Julian Rushton's keynote address, 'Learning in London, Learning from London', probes the historiographical implications of London's musical hegemony and asks what methodological ramifications this has for nineteenth-century British music studies. 'What is the nineteenth century?' 'what is British music?' and 'did London influence the Continent?' are just some of his questions. From these questions, and his thought-provoking answers to them, the volume proceeds to issues of gender. Charlotte Purkis discusses the significance of

Rosa Newmarch in turn-of-the-century music appreciation, and re-evaluates her position in gendered music criticism. Grant Olwage deals with concerns of masculinity and church music, with close readings of Victorian hymn texts and tunes, and George Biddlecombe discusses the iconisation (and demonisation) of Jenny Lind.

Music appreciation, Victorian hymns and iconisation also play into the topic of church music. Thomas Muir assesses English Catholic church music, with particular emphasis on the construction of *The Westminster Hymnal* of 1912. Nicholas Temperley discusses issues, ancient and modern, in the music of John Stainer, and Peter Horton assesses the musical factors underlying the perception of S.S. Wesley as church composer. Many of these same general concerns – that of appreciation, repertoire and the construction of identity – also feature in the section 'National Identity'. Derek Scott deals with British national identity and Gilbert and Sullivan's comic operas. Peter Campbell looks to the empire in his work on the Australian flag as representation of patriotism and nationalism, and Barbara Eichner introduces the German music of Johann Rupprecht Dürrner and his influence in the musical life of Edinburgh. The volume ends with a section concerning national and local institutions. Duncan Barker considers Alexander Mackenzie's work as conductor of the Philharmonic Society and principal of the Royal Academy of Music and Fiona Palmer investigates the role of Vincent Novello, also within the Philharmonic Society. Susan Wollenberg delves into the Oxford Commemorations and their relationship to nineteenth-century British festival culture, and Giles Brightwell provides an in-depth examination of the issues surrounding the rise of the Royal College of Music. Valerie Langfield concludes this section with an essay on the emergence and significance of the von Glehns as a family 'institution' in the context of musical London.

We would like to offer special thanks to the Royal College of Music for hosting the third biennial conference on Music in Nineteenth-Century Britain. The conference was a spectacular organisational accomplishment, and it goes without saying that its success was in no small part due to the commitment, dedication and support which the college provided. We would also like to thank Rachel Lynch and her team at Ashgate for their continued help in the preparation of this volume, and for their expertise in all matters editorial.

Peter Horton and Bennett Zon

INTRODUCTION

Learning in London, Learning from London

Julian Rushton

What is the nineteenth century? It is an arbitrary division of time, only to
be preferred to traditional periodization – Baroque, Classical, Romantic –
because the measurement of time in centuries is, at least in theory, neutral,
implying nothing interpretative. If only it were so simple. Such measure-
ments, once established, set in place interpretative processes we can
hardly avoid. In reality, each end of the nineteenth century slices in two
the lives of Samuel Wesley and Edward Elgar, to name only obvious
examples: so are they nineteenth-century composers? The monarchy is
hardly more useful. The Georgian period (if we forget William IV) merges
into the Victorian, the Victorian into the Edwardian, and the Edwardian
into the new Georgian.

What, for that matter, is British music? Reception studies at the
London 2001 conference on nineteenth-century music in Britain referred
not to music written in Britain, still less to music of British composers, but
to Bach and Mozart, an emphasis which unfortunately tends to support
the ancient libel 'das Land ohne Musik'. For if that term ever had cause to
exist, it was because of a prevailing image of an imperial nation thriving
largely on imported music, and music imported from Europe at that.
While the sun never set on the Empire, music from more distant climes
was perceived mainly as exotic, quaint, and no part of mainstream
musical life. The music relished in nineteenth-century London came from
neighbours, friends and Imperial rivals in Europe. Was this pronounced
xenophilia, as Nicholas Temperley has called it, confined to the capital?
To what extent should we question both the hegemony of London culture
over British, as well as the hegemony of European music in these offshore
islands? The questions are emphatically worth asking; but as scholars, we
must sometimes be prepared to accept unpalatable answers.

London, inescapably, was the capital of a vast trading empire. At the
heart of the century, it gathered the culture, artistic and scientific, of the
world – not just the British Empire – into the Crystal Palace. London was
at the centre of a culture which loved to purchase artefacts, including
music, from abroad. Put positively, and topically, we may say that British
musical life, and especially that of London, was enriched by immigration.
The musicians were more often economic migrants than political

refugees, and some were birds of passage who came for a season or two. This phenomenon simply continues the practice of the eighteenth century, which was marked by the impact of migrant and immigrant musicians from Handel and Pepusch, through J.C. Bach and Abel, to Salomon and Haydn; but then internationalism was the norm throughout most of European musical culture in the eighteenth century, whereas one of the striking features of the nineteenth was musical nationalism.

To take London first, we need only recall that *Elijah* was first performed in Birmingham to question whether even the migrant musicians confined their significant activities to the capital. Haydn had visited Oxford and Cambridge; Spohr, Chopin and Liszt went further afield; Mendelssohn on his first visit made an unusual north-western extension of the Grand Tour, and its traces are to be found not only in his letters and pictures but also, when emotion was recollected in tranquillity, in music. Among the vast repertoire of musical works on British themes – British queens misread by Schiller, Shakespeare, Walter Scott – it is refreshing, in Mendelssohn's case, to find in *Die Hebriden* and the *Scottish Symphony* something poetically more authentic than Ossian and topographically more authoritative than the setting of *Emilia di Liverpool* in the mountains overlooking that city. Some musicians, notably Hallé, settled outside London. If Berlioz and Wagner confined their activities to the capital, it was not because there was nothing in the provinces to attract a serious musician. It was a condition of their contracts. All musicians passed through London; many stayed, for London had money, and the largest concentration of musicians and resources devoted to music – not least educational resources such as the Royal Academy and Royal College of Music.

Migration studies, in some circumstances exile studies, form a growing musicological field of the highest interest, understandably concentrated on the politically enforced migrations of the twentieth century. The norm for musicians in earlier times was to go where the money was, or where they needed to go for education. This vigorous and productive immigration is arguably a sign of vigorous and productive musical activity; but it isn't a sign of vigorous and productive musical creativity, and I mean that in the wider sense in which not only British composers, but also British performers of international distinction remained relatively uncommon. The influence of the Continent on British musical life is inescapable. Composers and performers arrived in Britain with baggage in the form of compositions, playing experience and performing styles; whereas when British composers went to Europe, it was usually to study, so that they also brought Continental notions back home.

But was it impossible for the traffic in music and musical ideas to proceed in the reverse direction? Among Continental musicians, quite a number made their careers here; in this Costa and Hallé were part of a long tradition. Those who were birds of passage, and returned home to the Continent, certainly left enough behind to have a permanent effect on the musical life of Britain. But did they take nothing British home, by way of souvenir? Was the transfer of musical thought all in one direction? And did migrant British musicians leave nothing behind on the Continent? Only a few British musicians in the nineteenth century actually settled abroad: besides Field, working mainly in Russia, there was Henry Hugh – or Heinrich Hugo – Pierson, an Old Harrovian and student of Mozart's student Attwood, defined by Nicholas Temperley in *The New Grove* as a 'German composer of English origin', rather than a Briton who settled in Germany – where, perhaps ironically, he taught Hubert Parry. There is thus a circularity in connections between musicians which may be no less significant where some of those involved are not of British origin.

The dearth of British composers of international repute is usually considered to have extended over the 200-odd years between the death of Henry Purcell and maturity of Edward Elgar in the very last years of the nineteenth century. This formulation overlooks Handel, but even if he is considered British – and why should he not be? – this deficit is only reduced to 140 years, and still includes practically the whole nineteenth century. Today we may query this critical position by references, more or less scornful, to the dead hand of a nineteenth- and twentieth-century 'high culture', which crams musical achievers into an imaginary museum of Great Works, exposing the select in glass cases and relegating the swarming mass to filing cabinets in a damp basement. We cannot, however, deny canon formation as a historical, and also a living, phenomenon, nor the absence within the various canons of any British composer between Handel and Elgar – if, that is, Elgar is indeed canonical, which might be disputed. British musical culture clearly differed in significant ways from that of France, Germany or Russia (to name only the major imperial powers). A land that possessed music, therefore, was a land with great big composers who were natives. By this criterion, some Scandinavian and Iberian nations were equally deprived in the nineteenth century; but they were not rival imperial powers, and the deficit is accordingly less glaring.

Much is being achieved to demonstrate the richness of musical life in the previously unregarded corners of Britain, for example at the conference on music in the English provinces earlier in 2001, under the auspices of the Leeds University Centre for English Music. But while music in the English provinces may be unique, its existence is not. Despite the very different socio-economic and political situations of other countries in the nineteenth century, their provinces are surely differently but no less historically interesting than those of Britain. What some of those other nations supplied, and what Britain lacked, was musical nationalism. London in certain respects continued the culture of the eighteenth century while other nations, under the stress of war and revolution, were changing their own. In the mid- to late eighteenth century internationalism was the norm. It was consciously promoted by Gluck, and – at least until the French Revolution fulfilled and corrupted ideals of the Age of Enlightenment – few musicians, even in France, would have regarded national distinctiveness in music as a worthy objective. How different was the nineteenth century, where nationalism became a cause in the struggle to end continental empires!

Nationalism is a dog with a bad name, for it goes with xenophobia, fascism and other loathsome phenomena. Perhaps patriotism is a safer word; to take pride in the achievements of one's country is patriotic, but it does not preclude appreciation of the achievements of others. But nationalism is the word normally employed in music-historical studies. Nationalism is pernicious only when combined with purity: something which in cultural and political terms is nearly always pernicious, and leads to blinkered vision, xenophobia and ultimately ethnic cleansing and the Holocaust.

The patriotic nationalist, if the oxymoron may be permitted, assimilates from other cultures what is needed to make a distinctive statement which may well have a powerful national accent, flavour or style, but which may nevertheless find appreciation elsewhere. Late nineteenth-century Britain took Dvořák to its heart, and he had considerable impact on Elgar. A few years later, the nationalism of Vaughan Williams – who grew to a mature age, if not to musical maturity, in the nineteenth century – is not sullied by the fact that, as a student at the Royal College of Music, he composed a piano quintet whose stylistic ambience is broadly that of Brahms – as indeed was the ambience of his less national-minded teachers. Vaughan Williams subsequently studied with Ravel, while his colleague Gustav Holst was a passionate Wagnerian. But these men did as much as any to lay the foundations for a nationalist movement in English – rather than British – music in the early to mid-twentieth century. Elgar was not formally a nationalist, and he was no less eclectic than Vaughan Williams, yet he could claim with some justice that certain of his melodies, like some of Parry's, have the right to be considered folk music (most obviously Elgar's 'Land of Hope and Glory' and Parry's 'Jerusalem').

The activities of composers at work well into the twentieth century cannot themselves answer the accusation that for most of the nineteenth century Britain did not deliver to the world the chief ornaments of the musical culture it shared, but rather exchanged them for coal and iron and steel and technological innovation. Why is it that a sense of national identity in music – obvious in Italy, which had dominated so much of European music in the eighteenth century, apparent in Germany early in the nineteenth century, in Russia, Bohemia and Poland by mid-century, and in France in the latter half of the nineteenth century – was relatively so weak in Britain until the twentieth? The historical position of Britain was undeniably peculiar. Unlike the rest of Europe, notably France, Britain was neither losing wars, nor suffering invasion, nor undergoing political revolutions. For France, the long nineteenth century is defined by revolutionary upheaval, and by international and civil wars: 1789, 1814–15, 1830, 1848, 1870–71; even the relative stability of the Third Republic was threatened by the Dreyfus case and 1914. Yet there can be no doubt of the intensity and liveliness of French culture, including music, during the nineteenth century, even though these events took place largely on French soil; and upheavals scarcely less disorientating occurred in other Continental nations, whereas the British Isles, notoriously, have not been successfully invaded since 1066, and the last devastating civil war was over by 1650.

The promotion of the British as a musical nation, or group of nations, need not be a problem if we pick the right terms of debate. Against the battalions of classical, romantic, and modernist composers, we must admit that we cannot compete. The battle is to be fought, as it were, not on the playing fields of Eton, but in the parishes of Bolton; less in the repertoire of the Philharmonic Society of London than in that of the Hallé; and less in the choral splendours of the Crystal Palace than in the choral societies and festivals of Halifax, Hanley, Leeds, and in the world of the brass band. An interest in the musical life of nineteenth-century Britain forces us to find strategies for dealing with a vast amount of surviving music. History has not yet caused unregarded works to disappear, while forming others into a recognisable canon. Until comparatively recently, most British nineteenth-century music has languished in a state of neglect outside the choral foundations which remained devoted to Stanford, Walmisley and S.S. Wesley. But with such vast quantities of material to explore, little of it widely available in modern publications, the task is both exciting and daunting.

It is peculiarly difficult, in our self-conscious age, to address the task of establishing in retrospect some kind of system of values. How to judge the symphonies of Samuel Wesley, Potter and Macfarren? On the one hand, we may wish to right historical injustice, and restore fine music to regular performance; on the other, we tend to disapprove of the implied result, which would be to retain, while stretching, existing canonic patterns. The musicology of nineteenth-century Britain can proceed with confidence to consider context, reception, popular music and the application of historically based ethnomusicological principles. It is far more difficult to address equally important questions of a critical nature. We may argue that as far as the eighteenth century is concerned, British musical culture probably did not suffer from the lack of any great composer of British origin, although it certainly did suffer from the early deaths of some of its most promising composers such as Linley junior, Storace and Pinto. Even in the nineteenth century, although the lack of major British composers was noticed abroad, as we learn from Schumann, that sense of deprivation might not have been much felt. But we have lived through the twentieth century; and our efforts to recreate the sense of a past time through the most scientific musicological methods cannot extinguish the reception history of nineteenth-century British music since that time as long as great men have social and cultural cachet: while there exist the Beethovenhaus, the New Berlioz Edition and all the other editions including those of our own composers Purcell and Byrd, other monuments like Bayreuth, and cultural manifestations such as modern Salzburg. At every turn, we are confronted by the giants of European musical culture – performers along with composers; and we are surely not wrong in feeling a special predilection for their work. The syndrome of the great composer cannot be wished away. Indeed, the sense of a canon is arguably more alive in our culture than ever before. Nor will the British case be helped by combating the hegemony of the dead white European male. More performances of Maude Valérie White and Ethel Smyth are much to be desired; but to add even a female composer to an existing canon will not weaken the pre-eminence of Brahms, Strauss or Elgar, among Smyth's contemporaries, or the separation of Great from less great, established from marginal composers. Given the qualities of Fanny Mendelssohn and Clara Wieck, whose music richly deserves more exposure, the reputation of Britain is hardly going to be affected by the removal of the M from DWEM.

Many of the most intriguing questions posed by what is variously called new, critical, or interpretative musicology are necessarily concerned with composers of established reputation – if only because nobody would otherwise be very interested in the answers. Such musicology often tends to reinforce the canonical status of Great Composers precisely by focusing on their personal weaknesses or on previously unobserved significations in, say, the symphonies of Beethoven and the songs of Schubert. Such studies have yet to be made of the symphonies of Wesley and Potter, or the songs of Henry Bishop and Liza Lehmann. Much the same can be said of another form of modern musicology which is sometimes, simplistically, considered the antithesis of interpretative and contextual study, namely analysis. The difficulties that discipline tends to experience with vocal music, which have led to its neglect of Bach cantatas, or Handel operas, in favour of keyboard music, means that quantities of British music are likely to be neglected by analysts because they require engagement with the poetry of Tennyson or Longfellow – or the Bible. But there are few, if any, deep analyses of Potter's or

Macfarren's symphonies, Sterndale Bennett's and Mackenzie's chamber music, or works in either genre by Parry and Stanford. Only Elgar seems likely to suffer the rod of analytical discipline in the near future, and that mainly in connection with music composed after 1900. We must face the fact that repertoires of British nineteenth-century music are not yet well enough established for the scalpel of music analysis, or the more chemical, sometimes acidulated, penetration of postmodern musicology. The true pioneers in this field, therefore, are not musicologists but enterprising performers, broadcasters and record companies which are giving us the sound of Parry, Stanford, Wallace, Smyth and others.

What foreign musicians most obviously got out of Britain, of course, was money. They were surely drawn here in part by the political and economic stability which created an atmosphere in which national pride in cultural achievements appeared unnecessary. The musical importance of London was based on its wealth, but the lesser wealth of the most promising native composers was either inherited or earned by hackwork, like being Professor of Music at Cambridge and Principal of the Royal Academy. Foreign musicians could more easily find a paymaster, even if the tune called was not one they might have chosen; Berlioz might have preferred not to conduct Donizetti, and Wagner to conduct Potter. In the context of the 1850s, these two were unusual in that major performances of their own works were not what called them to London, but rather their abilities as conductors, whereas Verdi came over to attend to large-scale works of his own; but then Italian opera was already well established in London.

The movement of musicians matters less, in any case, than the movement of musical ideas. That Continental ideas affected the music of nineteenth-century Britain is clear, but what of the reverse process? Certainly in the eighteenth century British musical life had considerable effect on the Continent: besides Mozart, who learned much while in London, if mainly from the immigrant J.C. Bach, Gluck claimed to be affected by Handel, as was Haydn in his oratorios. The English piano affected Haydn's last and greatest works for keyboard (including the trios). Moreover, his English canzonets are markedly different from his earlier German songs, and not only sowed the seeds for nineteenth-century English song, but are also an overlooked influence on the development of German Romantic song, for, the language of the poetry aside, several of them are true Lieder. The question of transmission of musical ideas is never simple, and those who influenced British composers were themselves under the spell of diverse musical styles, not always from compatriots. The Anglo-Irish Field studied with an Italian master, Clementi, who is rightly cemented into the concept of the London Pianoforte school; in turn, Field affected more than the development of Chopin's nocturnes and concertos. As Nicholas Temperley hints, it may be worth investigating further the possible effect of Pierson on German vocal and orchestral music, at least by the more original Kleinmeister whose output, interesting and varied as it is, is hardly to be considered superior to the products of contemporary Britons. One of the most intriguing of the little-known migrants of the time, Pierson was surely the model European citizen, composer of pieces called 'Germania' and 'O Deutschland hoch in Ehren', but also of 'Hurrah for Merry England'.

Another matter worth investigating is the effect upon European composers of adapting to London's peculiar methods of concert-giving and the musical tastes, even achievements, of Londoners. What was the effect of London on their renewed approach to the publics of Paris, Berlin or Düsseldorf? Ferdinand Ries spent eleven years in England; he wrote English songs, published quantities of piano music, and wrote half a dozen symphonies for the Philharmonic Society, a tally of performances comparing favourably with that of Potter. On his return to Germany, Ries performed some of his London symphonies at the Lower Rhine Festival, with revisions no doubt intended to adapt them to local taste, but without radically altering their nature. Ries was notoriously accused, by the Meister himself, of imitating Beethoven; but it is open to investigation whether his creative misunderstanding was more or less creative and more or less a misunderstanding than were those of, say, Schubert, Cherubini, Spohr, Mendelssohn, Potter or Macfarren. But it is likely, at least, that his London symphonies result from his adapting his musical inclinations to local taste, and coming up with something which then played a modest role in the development of the nineteenth-century symphony on the Continent. After Ries came Weber, who unfortunately never left London alive. The usual critical response to *Oberon* is to admire what is Weberish and deplore what is English. More fairly, and positively, we may consider it a late flowering of English semi-opera, although Weber's main characters actually sing. If it now seems over-complicated in plot, and over-dependent on the machinery of spectacle, it nevertheless struck Berlioz, never uncritical even of his idols, as 'a masterpiece, pure, radiant, unified'. We cannot say that in the 1820s London was suffering a bout of seriously bad taste; after all, it appreciated the genius of Beethoven and Weber and just at this time was developing a taste for Mozart. Transferred back to the Continent, *Oberon* readily conforms to contemporary German styles evidenced in Hoffmann, Spohr and Marschner, and its rich mixture of elements could even have affected Berlioz's predilection for mixed genres, or what Daniel Albright calls 'Berlioz's Semi-operas' – the English-sourced *Roméo et Juliette*, and *La Damnation de Faust*, which Berlioz planned to rewrite as an opera for Drury Lane.

Mendelssohn may have been a net contributor to the musical culture of Britain. However, the circulation of influence continues in that *Elijah*, or

Elias, was actually composed to a German text; had Mendelssohn lived longer it would surely have been a staple part of his festival repertoire in Germany, like *St Paul*. But Mendelssohn's British connections went back nearly twenty years before *Elijah*. No doubt he studied the taste of English audiences, and no doubt that taste was founded on Handel. But did he gain nothing from his close involvement with such British musicians as Wesley, Attwood and Hullah? It was not only Moscheles, surely, with whom he exchanged ideas in London. Two years after the premiere of *Elijah*, the older Berlioz arrived in London at a significant point in his career. He admired Mendelssohn more than Handel; perhaps, however, the concept of an oratorio in the vulgar tongue, like *Elijah*, which he heard in 1847, may have affected his decision, in the early 1850s, to compose *L'Enfance du Christ*. Berlioz's fugal overture, following an introductory recitative, matches the pattern of *Elijah* precisely. A more concrete example of London's influence on this composer occurs in his Te Deum, completed shortly after his return to Paris in 1849. When he returned to London as a judge of musical instruments during the Great Exhibition in the Crystal Palace, he, like Haydn before him, experienced the massed voices of the Charity Children in St Paul's Cathedral. As a result, he added choruses of children to the celestial music of *La Damnation de Faust* and in parts of the Te Deum. The same effect would not be obtained by an additional chorus of adult voices. Berlioz was one of the most colour-conscious of composers, and in his Te Deum it is this sound – reproduced from something unique to London – which tips certain passages from the merely monumental into the sublime. While we cannot expect to unearth anything as significant as the effect of the 'contenance angloise' in the fifteenth century, or the brilliance of the Elizabethan school, which gave new impetus to keyboard music in the Netherlands and Germany, there is surely scope for further investigation of the effect of Britain, so potent in the other arts as well as in commerce and industry, on the musicians of nineteenth-century Europe.

PART ONE
Issues of Gender

CHAPTER ONE

'Leader of Fashion in Musical Thought'

The Importance of Rosa Newmarch in the Context of Turn-of-the-Century British Music Appreciation

Charlotte Purkis

In 1911 an article in the *Musical Times* surveyed the career of Rosa Newmarch (1858–1940), then in her early fifties. It indicated three key reasons for her attainment of 'distinction' and 'recognition' in the contemporary musical world. The author, 'M', praised Newmarch first for 'the eloquence, penetration and lucidity of her programme notes', secondly, for her abilities as a 'critical biographer and historian', and last but not least, for the way she brought 'a poetic temperament to bear on all her literary tasks'.[1] Newmarch's contributions to British cultural life had been received with enthusiasm for some years. Between 1900 and 1904, for example, on the occasions of presentations of her papers on 'The Development of National Music in Russia', the Vice-President of the Musical Association Charles Maclean had described her not only as 'so complete a mistress of her subject' but had also commented how 'her services to our English musical literature' were 'becoming very consider-able'.[2] Today Rosa Newmarch's name continues to feature significantly in biographical studies of late nineteenth-century musical personalities, for example, in Arthur Jacobs's work on Henry Wood and David Brown's on Tchaikovsky.[3] There have been several calls for a substantial biography, for example, by Alfred Boynton Stevenson, the author of a recent article,

---

1   M, 'Mrs. Rosa Newmarch', *Musical Times*, 52 (1 Apr. 1911), p. 225. Judging from the pose in the accompanying photograph and the lack of other sources, the article appears to have been based on a personal interview.

2   *Proceedings of the Musical Association, Twenty-Sixth Session, 1899–1900* (London: Novello & Co., 1900), p. 72; *Thirtieth Session, 1903–1904* (1904), p. 71.

3   Arthur Jacobs, for example, in *Henry J. Wood: Maker of the Proms* (London: Methuen, 1994), commented how Newmarch became 'the great educator of the British public in Russian music', calling her a 'pioneer British musicologist' and citing the 'authoritative' nature of her writings (p. 58) as well as her 'versatility' (p. 304).

'Chaikovski and Mrs Rosa Newmarch Revisited'.[4] In 2001 four of her books were reissued by Best Books.[5] In spite of this resurgence of interest, there has been little scholarly evaluation of Newmarch in her own right. Although she features significantly in a number of biographical studies of those great male contemporaries whose musical careers she dedicated considerable time and effort to promoting, the full range of her achievements continues to be obscured.

In recent decades a 'traditional' evaluation of Newmarch's work has become established which continues to reinforce the assessment made at the time of her death. In 1940 obituaries had presented her predominantly as what we recognise today as a musicologist. The *Monthly Musical Record* simply records: 'Newmarch, Rosa Harriet. Translator and writer on Russian music.'[6] The *Musical Times* lists a selection of her books, editions, translations and articles within its brief appreciation but in such a way as to separate this body of work from the rest of her output, which it then further subdivides by distinguishing what it terms her 'utility writings' (programme notes for the musical public) from her poetry 'at the other end of the scale'. Concluding comments again foreground her more academic work, which it calls 'authoritative' and reflective of 'specialized knowledge'.[7] Although H.C. Colles and Peter Platt in their 1980 *New Grove* article highlight her 'analytic' work as official programme writer to the Queen's Hall orchestra from 1908 until 1927 for the way it demonstrated her 'great sympathy with every kind of high artistic aim',[8] by the 2001 edition of *New Grove* the sense of a creative individual at work has effectively been bypassed. Greater emphasis falls on her academic work, for example by the use of such expressions as she 'did much to further', she was 'a source of information', she 'took up the cause' and 'showed great insight and sympathy with'.[9] Although there is mention of the impact of Newmarch's work on musicians and on composers, there is no explicit reference either to her approach to the interpretation of music or to her role in the formation of British musical taste.

In short, far greater emphasis has been placed on Newmarch's importance as a facilitator than on her role as original thinker. This works to the detriment of furthering understanding of late nineteenth-century British musical culture because it is in and through her own words and the

---

4   *Inter-American Music Review*, 14/2 (Winter–Spring, 1995), pp. 63–78.

5   *The Russian Opera; Jean Sibelius; Tchaikovsky: His Life and Works*; and *Henry J. Wood* (Living Masters of Music).

6   70 (May 1940), p. 90.

7   81, no. 1162 (May 1940), pp. 233–34.

8   *The New Grove Dictionary of Music and Musicians*, ed. Stanley Sadie (London: Macmillan, 1980), vol. 13, p. 165.

9   *The New Grove Dictionary of Music and Musicians*, 2nd edition, ed. Stanley Sadie and John Tyrrell (London: Macmillan, 2001), vol. 17, pp. 807–8.

method and context through which she shaped these that her creative ideas were expressed, rather than in those translations and editions of the words of others in which she merely mirrored the talents of composers, conductors and other authors. This is not to imply that Newmarch's knowledge and expertise – demonstrated, for example, in her role as 'midwife' of Russian culture for British audiences – is in any way unimportant, or that there was no connection between the spheres in which she worked, but rather that her 'artist-critic' persona is as deserving of attention as is her 'musicological-academic' writing.

In this connection, it is highly significant that several of Newmarch's contemporaries attributed her critical talents and her popularity amongst her audience to a thoroughly creative mind. Although the closest she got to musical performance was to accompany song recitals with lectures and to have several translations from the Russian set to music by Elgar,[10] in the 1904 discussion at the Musical Association meeting her new book on Henry Wood was applauded as 'a very brilliant performance'.[11] Much later Henry Wood's own comment, that 'Mrs. Newmarch's analytical notes still attract me, for they are not merely a synopsis of the works she treats, but are beautiful specimens of English literature', is also indicative of how her work was considered to be intrinsically creative.[12] Furthermore, in summarising her life story in the Musical Times of 1911, 'M' commented how 'she was ... always moving in a musical atmosphere, both executive and critical', and this contextual observation strengthened the remark that 'poetic temperament' pervaded all forms of her writing.[13] Moreover, in the brief overview of her overseas connections in the same article, 'M' quotes from an interview with Newmarch conducted by M. Charles Chasse in May 1908 in the Bulletin Français de la Société Internationale de Musique. Referring to her poetry – she published two volumes: Songs to a Singer and Other Verses (1906) and Horae Amoris, Songs and Sonnets (1903) discussed here – 'M' stated: 'the role of interpreter has not been enough for her; for she also has her own song, and the sorrowful cadence of "Horae Amoris" has revealed to the public a soul which "sees life through the curtain of music, and music through the curtain of life"'.[14]

---

10 1914 choral songs: 'Death in the Hills', 'Love's Tempest' and 'Serenade'.
11 Discussion following Rosa Newmarch's lecture 'The Development of National Opera in Russia (Fourth Paper)', in Proceedings of the Musical Association, Thirtieth Session, 1903–1904 (London: Novello & Co., 1904), p. 71.
12 Henry J. Wood, My Life of Music (London Victor Gollancz, 1938), p. 232.
13 M, 'Mrs. Rosa Newmarch', p. 225.
14 Ibid., p. 226. Almost the same compliment is paid by James Douglas in his review of Songs to a Singer and Other Verses in Throne, cited in an advertisement at the back of Newmarch's Poetry and Progress in Russia (London: John Lane, The Bodley Head, 1907), p. 271: 'Her temper is rare. She is one of those who see life through the veil of music, and music through the veil of life.'

By the time of the appearance of *The Russian Opera* (1914) Newmarch was heralded by the *Daily Sketch* for occupying 'a peculiar position with regard to music in this country' because 'she finds herself to be quite a leader of fashion in musical thought'.[15] The originality of her contributions, both to thinking about music and to thinking musically, was perceived to lie in a set of interconnected approaches to listening. These created appreciation as an art form and can be summarised as follows. First, just as performers and conductors are interpreters whose actions construct musical meaning, so listeners are themselves involved in a chain of response to the musical conceptions which originate with composers; secondly, music should be responded to with one's whole being; thirdly, technical analysis can be unhelpful if it serves to inhibit the development of such reception. While it is fair to say that Newmarch herself might not have thought of the style of music appreciation she exhibited in her programme notes and review articles as either particularly innovative or aesthetically 'primary', that is, as itself art, her many references to the critical act and to the responsibility of the inter-preter vis-à-vis the audience's response are acutely self-aware. As such these references, which are woven into every different type of commentary on music which she practised, reveal her aims to be inseparable from her inter-pretative approach to music in performance and are crucial to understanding her unique way of approaching the appreciation of music as a listener, placing her as an equal amongst the audience of her readers.

Newmarch's view of her writing, specifically with regard to programme notes, as quoted in the *Musical Times* 1911 article, provides clear evidence of her aim to stimulate an appreciation of contemporary music:

> In writing of a new work, I make it a principle to avoid *criticism* of a kind which might in the smallest degree check or cool the enthusiasm of the public who are not yet familiar with it. On the other hand I think the 'programmist' is more than justified in pointing out what strikes him, or her, as characteristically beautiful in a work. This may seem one-sided, but in reality it effects the right kind of balance. Most people are capable of some sort of carping criticism for themselves. But to point – with due discrimination – to the things which seem last-ingly beautiful in a work can do no harm, and must do good. I think the lack of balanced appreciation is one of our worst faults as a musical nation. I only mention this because, little as I concern myself with the ephemeral criticism which withers during the day – or the night – according to whether it appears in a morning or an evening paper, I have noticed a tendency to fall foul of some of my programmes because I have tried to set some details in a poetic rather than prosaic light.[16]

---

15 Advertisement for *The Russian Opera* in the back pages of Rosa Newmarch's *The Russian Arts* (1916).
16 M, 'Mrs. Rosa Newmarch', p. 227.

Observations that Newmarch made elsewhere about audience expand the picture of her emerging motivation and provide evidence of her reputation as an authority on public taste. In a 1928 retrospective, *A Quarter of a Century of Promenade Concerts at Queen's Hall*, she discussed how, at the time of the opening season of 1895–96:

> there was a growing public which, deprived of operatic nourishment and satiated with what the Handelian legacy provided, desired something more adventurous and sensational in music. An omnivorous and uncritical generation, perhaps, but one which craved for living forms, energetic movement. colour and passion, and the genius of race. Only in modern orchestral music could this awakening hunger for a vital, secular art, find satisfaction at that juncture.[17]

Rather than blowing her own trumpet as programme-note writer, Newmarch laid the laurels implicitly at the feet of the programmer-conductor, Henry Wood, by going on to say: 'the first series of Promenade Concerts comprised forty-nine concerts, and if anyone doubts the rapid education of public taste effected by these Concerts, let him compare the programmes of 1895 with those of two or three years later.'[18] Earlier in the book's introduction she had commented that: 'It is hardly too much to claim for these concerts that they have been the greatest educative power in music that we have had in this country.'[19] There is no doubt that, although her modesty prevented explicit mention, readers of this commemorative booklet would have associated Newmarch's own widely acclaimed 'analytical programme notes' with this observation.

More can be gleaned of her attitudes to the critical act from the introductions she furnished to her translated and edited biographical studies as well as her many journalistic pieces. In 1912, for example, in a review article of recently published British writings on music aimed at the encouragement of British composition, entitled 'Chauvinism in Music', which discussed Hubert Parry's *Style in Musical Art* and Cecil Forsyth's *Music and Nationalism* among others, there are significant subtextual references to the effect that not all criticism is useful to 'the public' – a group at whose door blame is most consistently laid for lack of appreciation of native composition at the turn of the century, and the people at whom she is targeting her work:

> Loud are the complaints that native work is neglected in our concert-rooms, and still more in our homes, yet when a novelty of British manufacture is produced the criticism it evokes ... is often of a very

---

17 Rosa Newmarch, *A Quarter of a Century of Promenade Concerts at Queen's Hall* (London: Baines & Scarsbrook, 1928), pp. 7–8.
18 Ibid., p. 8.
19 Ibid., p. 5.

perfunctory kind, and fails entirely to help the public to form any
sound criteria as to the national music about which they are expected
to show increasing enthusiasm.[20]

She went on to propose that 'the critical energy, which is largely wasted in
worshipping one artist and advising another, might be very helpfully
employed in laying before the public some clearer and more definite
conclusions as to where we actually are moving, and where we can move,
in the matter of a national school of music'.[21]

Newmarch's preoccupation, however, was not the promotion of native
British music, but the elevation of the profile of foreign music in Britain. A
crucial aspect of this process was the cultivation of British taste to respond
to the humanity in all music, however unknown and unusual, regardless
of cultural-political boundaries. Time and again in her writings she
commented that her work was not geared towards the needs of the music
profession, but to those of a wider public. For example, in her 1906
edition and translation of Modeste Tchaikovsky's *Life and Letters of
Peter Illich Tchaikovsky*, she wrote 'not so much [for] the needs of the
specialist' as for 'those of that large section of the musical public whose
interest in Tchaikovsky has been awakened by the sincerely emotional
and human elements of his music', disengaging thereby, by implication,
those listeners who were more susceptible to their subjectivities from
music 'specialists' who were not.[22] Furthermore, in her foreword to her
1910 translation of Vincent d'Indy's *César Franck*, she discussed admir-
ingly and at length the critical practice of the French writer Camille
Mauclair, in whose work 'so many aspects of the art are treated with such
delicate perception and from a standpoint all too rare – from that of the
worshipper of Music rather than Musicians', a comment which again
revealed her advocacy of the listener as enthusiastic pleasure-seeker.[23] By
1914, in her own book, *The Russian Opera*, she disclosed her admiration
for the writers on, rather than the analysts of, the music she had been
translating and editing: 'Too much technical analysis has been intentionally avoided in this volume. The musician can supply this deficiency by the
study of the scores mentioned in the book ... the average opera-goer will
be glad to gain a general view of the subject, unencumbered by the monotonous terminology of musical analysis.'[24]

---

20 Rosa Newmarch, 'Chauvinism in Music', *Edinburgh Review*, 216/441 (July 1912), pp.
95–96.
21 Ibid., p. 97.
22 Modeste Tchaikovsky, *The Life and Letters of Peter Illich Tchaikovsky*, ed. and trans.
Rosa Newmarch (London: John Lane, The Bodley Head, 1906), p. xi.
23 Vincent d'Indy, *César Franck*, trans. Rosa Newmarch (London: John Lane, The Bodley
Head, 1910), p. 6.
24 Rosa Newmarch, *The Russian Opera* (London: E.P. Dutton & Co., 1914), p. x.

Yet, in keeping with her wide knowledge and the increasing sense of authority accorded her by other commentators (such as those who discussed her Musical Association lectures), Newmarch could not avoid speaking – and being seen, as her career developed – as a specialist. This is particularly noticeable in the forewords to her books, which reveal a guiding, prescriptive attitude towards the development of public taste. In the foreword to her edition and translation of Karel Hoffmeister's *Antonín Dvořák* (1928), for example, she referred to the problematics of reception in surveying public and critical reaction to Dvořák in England since the 1880s. Her remarks make clear her attitude to a responsible didacticism, which should be a feature of the contemporary critic-impresario's make-up:

> The decrease in Dvořák's popularity is not easily explained. There seems no reason for such a distinct reaction. With every composer, even the greatest, a wholesome and necessary process of elimination is bound to set in after the first indiscriminate acceptance by the public of almost everything he wrote. Our ways with music are the ways of the satiated owl with a mouse. But they are not so perfectly regulated, being a matter of chance rather than digestion. In modern life there are too many arbiters of the composer's destiny: the shifting taste of the public and the critics, commercial considerations, sometimes even the lack of a powerful patron to see him safely established. Too often it happens that the few works which 'draw' are kept bright by use, the rest of a musician's lifework is arbitrarily consigned to the scrap-heap.[25]

It is noteworthy that, despite her consistent rejection of the need for technical skills to appreciate music, Newmarch intentionally introduced musicological knowledge. In the way that she presented much as fact, particularly when discussing the composer's intentions, she remained bound to the problem of how to balance author-centred with reader-centred meaning, a topic which dominated late nineteenth-century debates about the nature of musical criticism, specifically the power of the critic and his or her attitude to the composer's intentions. Three key attitudes lay at the root of established critical practices. The first was that ethics and aesthetics were interconnected, as expressed, for example, in the Revd Hugh Reginald Haweis's *Music and Morals* (1871). The second was that critics were educated and thus more capable than amateurs not only of describing compositional methodology in technical terms but also of evaluating performance on behalf of other listeners; this view characterised the majority of contemporary reviews and guidebooks to musical understanding. The third was that the meaning of musical works, and

---

25 Karel Hoffmeister, *Antonín Dvořák*, ed. and trans. Rosa Newmarch (London: John Lane, The Bodley Head, 1928), p. xii.

therefore their interpretation, had been inscribed by the composer. Examples of this are W.J. Henderson's comment in *What is Good Music: Suggestions to Persons Desiring to Cultivate a Taste in Musical Art* (1901), where he explained how the composer 'says to the hearer, "Listen to my music and feel what I have felt"',[26] and Edward Baughan's insistence that, in spite of new tendencies being pursued by 'gushing' amateurs, 'the spectator in musical composition is the composer'.[27]

During the 1890s writers became interested in foregrounding the role of listening in the construction of meaning. Gertrude Hudson and John Runciman, both of whom contributed articles to *The Dome* and *The Chord* – journals which Newmarch may have read because of their interdisciplinary scope – discussed and demonstrated the power of the critic and his or her relationship to the composer's intentions.[28] In a provocative article in the *Fortnightly Review* of 1894 Runciman set out the current debate about 'Old' and 'New' criticism, defining 'Old' as 'impersonal' and 'New' as 'avowedly personal'. Following another writer from the *Magazine of Music* the previous year, Runciman went on to declare that 'since all criticism is at bottom expression of our own thoughts and feelings, let us frankly talk about ourselves!'[29] He stated his own summary of this position thus:

> Here I am, endowed with certain faculties, cultured to a greater or less [sic] extent; the question for me to decide is not whether the artist I am criticising produces a result the same as or different from that produced by certain dead-and-gone worthies, whom you call authorities, 'standards of taste,' and what-not, and for whom I care not one jot, but whether the result gives or does not give me pleasure! ... In the case of the new method, everything depends upon the critic ... all genuine criticism ... is autobiographical.[30]

In his *Old Scores and New Readings* (1899) Runciman stated that what he valued most of all was 'the record, the impressions of a fully-endowed man, with full technical knowledge and a most sensitive aesthetic sense, in the presence of great music'. Such criticism would, he said, 'open a new world to our view'.[31] In other words, it was the human qualities exposed in the music by the nature of the listener's response which made such criticism 'new'. Writing about the shortcomings of Schumann as

26 (London: John Murray, 1901), p. 116.
27 (London: John Murray, 1901), p. 116.
28 For further information on Gertrude Hudson see my forthcoming essay in Sophie Fuller and Nicky Losseff (eds), *The Idea of Music in Victorian Fiction* (Aldershot: Ashgate, 2004).
29 John F. Runciman, 'Musical Criticism and the Critics', *Fortnightly Review*, 62 (July–Dec. 1894), p. 173.
30 Ibid., pp. 173–74, 175.
31 John F. Runciman, *Old Scores and New Readings: Discussions on Musical Subjects* (London: At the Sign of the Unicorn, 1899), pp. 12–13.

critic in *The Dome* in the same year, Runciman further clarified that 'the highest kind of criticism, the only criticism which has a permanent value and does not die with its subject ... is the criticism in which ... the writer ... recounts the effect of the subject upon his own soul ... The critic holds himself as a kind of mirror'.[32] This self-reflexivity had been linked by Clifford Harrison in *The Lute of Apollo* (1896) to Walter Pater's influential 'Conclusion' to *The Renaissance* (1873), with its recognition of critical temperament as 'that strange, perpetual, weaving and unweaving of ourselves'.[33] Harrison's formulation was that music 'not only speaks to us, but it is, in a sense, our own voice. We find in it a perpetual self-expression.'[34]

Newmarch's desire to foreground individual response and foster the listener's own sense of individuality, either through the encouragement of moments of contemplative silence – at least in the mind – or by assuming empathy between herself and her reader, illustrates the key trait of this new critical position. For example, in *The Concert-Goer's Library of Descriptive Notes*, a compilation of her analytical programmes for the Queen's Hall concerts between 1908 and 1927, there are many asides in the descriptive passages about the music which exemplify this new critical thinking, such as the comment on Sibelius's *Oceanides*, Op. 73, that the work 'needs no musical analysis'.[35] Moreover, with regard to William Walton's overture *Portsmouth Point* she expressed the view that music appreciation need not depend on extra-musical notions or a technical analytical approach, but the music might simply 'be enjoyed as pure music': 'Nor is there any need to dissect its form; it is better to swallow it in one exhilarating draught.'[36] And in her note on Debussy's *Prélude à l'après-midi d'un faune* she declared that 'Each individual listener will make his own interpretation of the symbolical meaning of the work.'[37]

At the time of Debussy's death in 1918 Newmarch reflected on her experience of listening to his *Pelléas et Mélisande* in Paris in 1902, presenting in the *Contemporary Review* a very personal perspective. Although she admitted she had not appreciated the work as music-drama,

---

32 John F. Runciman, 'Robert Schumann: An Impertinence', *The Dome*, 3/9 (July 1899), p. 234.

33 Cited in Eric Warner and Graham Hough (eds), *Strangeness and Beauty: an Anthology of Aesthetic Criticism 1840–1910*, vol. 2: *Pater to Symons* (Cambridge: Cambridge University Press, 1983), p. 31.

34 *The Lute of Apollo* (London: A.D. Innes, 1896), p. 153.

35 Rosa Newmarch, *The Concert-Goer's Library of Descriptive Notes*, vol. 5 (London, New York, Toronto: Oxford University Press, 1938), p. 91.

36 Ibid., p. 97.

37 Ibid., p. 26.

she depicted a self-revelatory moment which had come over her while listening: 'I remember that I sat night after night letting this cool, silvery liquid music slide over me, often without once opening my eyes upon the stage ... The music was like the voice of a friend telling me an old romantic tale in subdued accents.'[38] Significantly making reference to a contentious topic of her time – the reception of programme music[39] – she manifested her predilection for the listener's sensuous abandonment to their own reverie by saying that, although the work 'appealed to me as a kind of vocal and instrumental symphonic poem', she had 'no further use' for the programme 'once visualised', perhaps because 'I knew Moussorgsky's music long before I heard Debussy's opera.'[40] Broadening out to an observation on the *Prélude à l'après-midi d'un faune*, she consciously drew her readers into her frame of mind, referring to Debussy's secret spell 'to which we gladly yield ourselves', attempting surreptitiously to match the creative process by which such a spell is cast with the use of a carefully chosen quotation from a scholarly source: 'No definite and rigid forms are imposed upon our will, but the music acts as a mediating power, leading us almost imperceptibly to a revelation of nature's mysteries, until the listener', to quote M. Albert Bazailles, '"sees himself in soughing woods" and "hears himself on winds that pass", and is lost in ecstatic reverie'.[41]

In Newmarch's literary style her subjective response to music sometimes incorporates visual images, such as this citation from Bazailles. Not only was it a tendency of the time to invoke the experience of music in paintings, but marrying verbal depiction to image provided a means of enhancing programmatic reading of the music concerned.[42] Such moments in Newmarch's writing recall another manifestation of her creative nature, since she had been a student of painting for two years from the age of nineteen and in 1897, after her marriage, she had travelled to Russia, where she had worked under the art critic Vladimir Stasov at the Imperial Public Library.[43] Her developed artistic sense continued to reveal itself in her subsequent musical writings, where cross- and interdisciplinary connections between the aural and the visual senses operated

---

38 Rosa Newmarch, 'Debussy', *Contemporary Review*, 113 (May 1918), p. 539.

39 See, for example, William Wallace, 'The Scope of Programme Music', *Proceedings of the Musical Association, Twenty-Fifth Session, 1898–1899* (London: Novello & Co.), pp. 139–56.

40 Newmarch, 'Debussy', p. 539.

41 Ibid., pp. 540–41.

42 See Suzanne Fagence Cooper, 'Aspiring to the Condition of Painting in Britain 1860–1900', in Jeremy Dibble and Bennett Zon (eds), *Nineteenth-Century British Music Studies*, vol. 2 (Aldershot: Ashgate, 2002), pp. 252–77.

43 'Obituary', *Musical Times*, 81, no. 1162 (May 1940), p. 233.

from both directions: painting to music and music to painting. In her 1906 study, *The Russian Arts*, she highlighted in several of her analyses of paintings how images seem to 'perform', and peppered her reading with suggestive remarks to assist her readers' perception. Thus music became a key to the appreciation of painting and informed its conceptualisation as a sensual act.[44] Although her impressionistic appreciation of, for example, Vladimir Makovsky's 'Roussalkas' is not musical as such, she did comment on the image as if it were performed to the viewer, emphasising thereby a physiological response. Not only did she observe its 'wild and wayward procession of white, nude bodies, interlaced in almost frenzied movement, moving like a mist-wreath over the surface of a moonlit mill pond', but she concluded with the comment that the Roussalkas figure in operas as well as other art forms.[45] Later she used the concept of improvisation to convey an impression of Ivan Aivazovsky's 'The Ninth Wave': 'It is difficult indeed to believe that these stirring plein air performances are merely memorizings of hoarded themes rather than improvisations.'[46] The Roussalkas reappeared in her vision of Ivan Shishkin's 'A Birch Grove', where she developed an anthropomorphic reading:

> The charm and mystery of the forests; the serried ranks of pines in all their gothic grace; the fretted canopy of birch branches, casting dancing shadows, and letting through glittering flecks of light upon the pearly whiteness of their trunks; the moist mossy patches beneath the trees, where here and there a vivid red fungus shows like an elfin light; eerie pools where once Roussalkas disported in the moonlight – these are the only allurements it has to offer. But then it is endlessly fascinating to watch the gradual transformation of the birch woods, throwing off their nunlike veils of silver-grey, as spring advances, for one of misty green, and shedding their summer beauty in spangles of palest gold, during the brief glory of a Russian autumn. And all this coquettish robing and unrobing is carried on amid the unchanging, dignified sobriety of the pine forests. What wonder that these two kinds of trees – eternal types of masculine and feminine beauty – are endowed in the folk lore of the North, with almost human attributes and individualities?[47]

This kind of visualised physical, even erotic, response revealed how her mind worked, and the approach was carried into some of her musical notes, where the aural and the visual combine very effectively. Her way of asking questions of her audience, as at the end of the last quotation,

---

44 For further reference to contemporary contextual discussions of 'Musicology through the Arts' see Bennett Zon, *Music and Metaphor in Nineteenth-Century British Musicology* (Aldershot: Ashgate, 2000), pp. 25–69.

45 Rosa Newmarch, *The Russian Arts* (London: Herbert Jenkins Ltd., 1906), p. 141.

46 Ibid., p. 193.

47 Ibid., p. 197.

served to draw readers in as if she herself were performing her interpretation and inducing the audience to join in with her suggestions, which is why some of the observations seem deliberately titillating. A musical example of this is her reading of Sibelius's *Oceanides*, which according to her 'records sensitive, individual impressions of an awakening sea stirring under the cold lips of the wind at dawn ... Oceanus stretches his night-benumbed limbs, tingling with returning remembrance of his potency, and the music swells to a grand climax ...'.[48] Further evidence of erotic associations with music are revealed in her comment on the changing nature of popular taste effected by Wood, in which she emphasised the pleasure involved in the act of consumption, associating food and sex with Wood as the generous host: 'At last the "ideal model" has changed. A young and hot-headed generation has asked for new sensations in music ... The Queen's Hall Concerts furnished a banquet, and Mr Wood has been our Amphitryon. We have had our reaction, or, as some consider, an orchestral orgy.'[49]

Another method of encouraging the listener/reader's personal engagement can be seen in her tendency to assume universalising qualities in the music. This is shown in the passage about Tchaikovsky's *Pathetic Symphony* which was cited in the 1911 *Musical Times* article with the comment that she sought 'to lay bare the underlying poetic bases of the music':

> Tchaikovsky gives utterance to thoughts and problems that lie deep down in every thinking mortal ... The experiences which inspired Tchaikovsky in this Symphony are identical with our own; even if we rarely allow them to ripple the surface of our life, they agitate its depths in a blind, unconscious way. Therefore when we hear them expressed with such piercing and intimate feeling, Tchaikovsky's music seems to us less a revelation than a startling emanation from our own innermost being.[50]

In praising Henry Wood as a conductor Newmarch embarked on a long discussion of the importance of interpretation, making a number of remarks that would be surprising in a male author of the time. Her comments are applicable as much to a listener trying to understand music as to Wood's role as a conductor:

> I confess I do not understand the attitude of those people who see a danger to their art in this question of individual interpretation. Their case seems to be this: that the world now goes to hear the virtuoso, not the composer. But since it is an absolute condition of musical art

---

48 *The Concert-Goer's Library of Descriptive Notes*, vol. 5, p. 91.
49 Newmarch, *Henry J. Wood* (London: John Lane, The Bodley Head, 1904), p. 16.
50 M, 'Mrs. Rosa Newmarch', p. 227.

that it must reach us through two mediums of communication – the instrument and the performer – how can it be otherwise? A musical work without a performer has the same half-reality of existence as an unborn infant. Some one must bring it into the world – must compel it to utter those sounds which are the proclamation of life itself.[51]

Further on in the discussion she returned to this birth metaphor, making the interpretative act bodily, like a mother's role; but in talking about the act of breathing interpretation into music, her emphasis may have been rather to construct the male – in this case, Henry Wood – as God-like:

So, whatever pedants and conscientious objectors may say to the contrary, the really great interpretive artist is the one who can infuse the most of his soul's fire and his heart's blood into the silent and inanimate body of an unperformed score. He must wake it to existence with his own life, and urge it to fulfilment with his own breath until it palpitates and responds, 'Be thou, spirit fierce, My spirit! Be thou me, impetuous one!'[52]

Several uniquely feminine aspects to Newmarch's discourse suggest that her gendered response to music may have been more witting than unwitting, since earlier she had by implication criticised male commentators, saying: 'As a rule, the complaints against individual interpretation in music come from those whose emotional gamut is very limited in compass, and whose emotional tone is of the thinnest quality. Such people are as out of place in the concert-room as those of low physical vitality are in the football field.'[53] In 1904 women would not have been on a football field, so her use of the metaphor appeared to point to the inadequacies of male listeners. Another more flippant example is her comment on Wagner in the preface to *César Franck*, where she referred to the way he 'knitted up the Beethoven traditions and wedded symphony to the drama'.[54]

Newmarch's approach to music was not merely recreative or investigative, it was concerned with making the intuition, feeling and imagination of the music resound in the listener. These aspects are associated more with the artistic side of music-making than with the reception of music in twentieth-century thinking, but in her writing, although she was in many key respects 'scholarly', Newmarch shunned the notion that musicality could be trained and that it should be based on knowledge rather than instinct. In a sense her work resisted the discipline of musicology as it was developing by the end of her life, into what Suzanne Cusick has recently described as 'a hierarchy of musical thought over the various musical practices ... with

---

51 Newmarch, *Henry J. Wood*, pp. 94–95.
52 Ibid., p. 47.
53 Ibid., p. 45.
54 *César Franck*, p. 7.

musicology at its apex, controlling through an objective approach to musical knowledge the subjective experience of music as creation, physical and social practice, emotional and sensual pleasure'.[55] For Newmarch, although music in her experience and recommendation was sometimes above or beyond analysis or discussion, it was never 'autonomous', since it was the sensual power of the music and its ability to speak to the listener which characterised its human qualities. Writing of Elgar's Symphony in A flat in a programme note, she commented: 'there is hardly a spiritual or mental condition which music cannot echo and reflect, the musician who continued to write that kind of purely geometrical and objective music that expressed nothing but itself would be in the position of the painter who still clung to the limitations of the Byzantine iconographers'. Her response to composers, such as Elgar in this work, who, 'admitting ... the futility of writing music which does not set its hearers seeking for any inner meaning at all', did not write consciously programmatic works, was to turn to psychology for explanation, and here, still writing about Elgar, she clarified that the sense that words cannot express the music is not due to 'autonomy', but 'the utterance of thoughts and feelings for which words seem inadequate ... the work now before us seems to have a clear, but wordless, psychological programme'.[56]

Similarities between Newmarch's preoccupations with musical meaning and the European critical scene are worth pursuing in order more fully to appreciate the radicalism of her position with regard to 'embodied' reception,[57] notably Hanslick's concerns in *The Beautiful in Music* (1854), translated and published in English in 1891. Although Newmarch's linguistic skills would have enabled her to go to the original source, she may also have known the writings of Violet Paget, who, writing under the pseudonym Vernon Lee, contributed a review article on Hanslick's music entitled 'The Riddle of Music' to the *Quarterly Review* in January 1906, in which she traced its response in Edmund Gurney's *The Power of Sound*. Hanslick's antipathy to the destruction of musical beauty by analysis rings a bell in the work of Newmarch, and although his work has been most consistently championed for its rejection of feeling-based theories of music, many moments in his discourse acknowledge 'the role of psychological states in music and also [imply] that these states may be associated with something like a body'.[58] As

55 Suzanne G. Cusick, 'Gender, Musicology, and Feminism', in Nicholas Cook and Mark Everist (eds), *Rethinking Music* (Oxford: Oxford University Press, 1999), p. 480.
56 M, 'Mrs. Rosa Newmarch', p. 228.
57 See also Suzanne G. Cusick, 'Feminist Theory, Music Theory', *Perspectives on New Music*, 32/1(Winter 1994), pp. 14–26.
58 Fred Everett Maus, 'Hanslick's Animism', *Journal of Musicology*, 10 (1992), p. 280.

Fred Everett Maus has suggested, passages like the following seem to be 'at odds with the author's explicit assertions' but 'can lead to many important insights' about understandings of music in the late nineteenth century which should not have been ignored for so long: 'Thoughts and feelings run like blood in the arteries of the harmonious body of beautiful sounds. They are not that body; they are not perceivable, but they animate it.'[59]

Ultimately Hanslick regarded the agent of music as the composer, not the listener. According to Lee, Hanslick demonstrated that 'whatever its coincident powers of suggesting human emotion, the genius of a composer is manifested in the audible shapes, the musical monuments which he builds up in the soul of the listener'.[60] Newmarch, interested as she was in the composer's autobiographical resonance in his music, proposed rather that the listener assume the active role of endowing music with the power of expression so that within the listening experience emotional suggestiveness is at one with the music and its meaning. Whether music was, as for Hanslick, independent from material nature, or a matter, as for Newmarch, of interpretation which the listener/reader alone could really 'give birth to', it was Newmarch rather than Vernon Lee who was perhaps the more radical thinker. She never appeared intimidated by the power of music and she did not share Lee's fear of the penetrating force of the demonic power of music, which, it could be argued, afflicted Hanslick too. Where Newmarch is useful, then, is in providing contextualisation for accounts of musical experience grounded in the social realities of listening; where Lee is useful is to trace links between these points of view through focusing on psychological aesthetic questions and their physiological impact. Addressing the concerns of both these women writers on music enables Hanslick's arguments to be revealed in greater complexity, in terms of contemporary debates in Britain, thus adding a gendered dimension to the retrospective speculation and justification which Maus's rereading generates.

Newmarch's 'musical thought' has suffered from critical neglect in the decades since 1940: her gendered critical voice and the subjectivity embodied in her personal responses to music as well as her dedication to musical appreciation for the general public have largely been ignored. As the 1911 *Musical Times* article on Newmarch makes clear, before the First World War she was a serious force in British musical life. Moreover, by 1915, according to Edmondstone Duncan in *Ultra-Modernism in Music*, prejudice against women's involvement in the arts was 'fast

---

59 Ibid., and Eduard Hanslick, *On the Musically Beautiful*, trans. Geoffrey Payzant (Indianapolis: Hackett Publishing Company, 1986), p. 82.
60 Vernon Lee, 'The Riddle of Music', *Quarterly Review*, 406 (Jan. 1906), p. 209.

becoming obsolete'. Although he saw a composer, Ethel Smyth, as the leader in what he calls 'this category', his comments could be applied to the growing band of women writers on music:

> In every department of music there are signs that women's ability is gradually gathering to a great issue. All honour then to those pioneers who carve a fresh outlet for such energy, familiarising the public with a new idea, thus making the efforts of generations to come, easier and more acceptable.[61]

Yet late nineteenth-century women's contributions to the reception history of contemporary music have received little attention to date from music historians, even from those specifically concerned with the participation of women in musical culture of that time. It is surprising that women were not recognised for their critical abilities when they were fully appreciated for their abilities as performers, since both activities involve interpretation.[62] The work of British female critical writers on music has been notably absent from discussions of that interconnected 'musicological' field comprising aesthetics, theory, history and criticism, which circumscribes the 'creative' one of composition and performance. Over the same period of time there has been an assumption that music appreciation is lightweight compared with technical and therefore more scholarly musical analysis and theoretically informed criticism. The case of Rosa Newmarch informs and complicates historical investigations of music and gender and music criticism because the nature of her writing, her sphere of interest, and the attitude she, and others, adopted with regard to the purpose of her work involves historians in the interrogation of their own intellectual premises.

In the last two decades a postmodern fluidity has affected the boundaries of musicology, informing, for example, Bennett Zon's recent decision to use this modern term to connote all the disciplines involving writing about music.[63] In this context opportunities have opened up for reappraising the roles all forms of writing play in the historical understanding of music. Central to any reassessment of the application of literary modes of expression to the comprehension of musical meanings is the recovery of a fuller understanding of the creative dimension of such

---

61 Edmondstone Duncan, *Ultra-Modernism in Music* (London: Winthrop Rogers, 1915), p. 113.

62 See, for example, Havelock Ellis's discussion in *Man and Woman* (1894, p. 326): 'there can be no doubt whatever that if we leave out of consideration the interpretive arts, the artistic impulse is vastly more spontaneous, more pronounced, and more widely spread among men than among women', cited in Talia Schaffer and Kathy Alexis Psomiades (eds), *Women and British Aestheticism* (Charlottesville, Va. and London: University Press of Virginia, 1999), p. 34.

63 *Music and Metaphor in Nineteenth-Century British Musicology.*

expressions and their significance both in late nineteenth-century and in late twentieth-/early twenty-first-century 'postmodern' contexts. The role of writings such as Newmarch's in challenging the dominant nineteenth-century view that verbal interpretations of music were secondary in importance to other forms of creative involvement and self-expression may prove vital in this connection.

CHAPTER TWO

Hym(n)ing: Music and Masculinity in the Early Victorian Church

Grant Olwage

Two things in particular are striking about Victorian historiographic practice: its opportunistic (ab)use of 'history' for an agenda of the present, and its awareness of the possibilities for reading discursive changes as evidence of cultural process. Take, for example, an anonymous review of *The Hymnary* that appeared in 1873: 'From time to time the popular style of words varies largely, hence a sketch of the history of hymns, would be also a sketch of the history of contemporary religious thought, and to a very great extent to trace the variations of style in hymn *tunes* would lead up to the same point.' Just as the tantalising project was mooted, however, it was withdrawn; it was simply 'far too large a question'.[1] Others, though, were less daunted, and where the imperative prevailed to find in hymn tunes the state of society at large, the 'evidence' of history was sure to have something to say about the matter.

These concerns dovetailed nicely in the work of John Heywood, minor tune writer and major polemicist (now almost completely forgotten). In a tract of 1881, Heywood sounded an alarm, issuing a call to action that would later impel the revisionary programmes of late Victorian and early Edwardian hymnals: contemporary hymnody was in a 'sickly condition', it had 'nearly reached a very *bathos* of degradation'. The doctor-critic proposed the following cure: 'Now as knowledge of the cause and progress of disease will frequently guide the physician to the treatment necessary to ensure restoration to health and vigour, so a brief sketch of our progress in this branch of church music during the present century may, perhaps, conduce to a similar result.'[2] The rhetoric of pathology clearly places Heywood's text, as he in turn had placed late Victorian hymnody, in a 'degenerationist' paradigm, and throughout

---

1 Anon., 'Reviews: The Hymnary', *The Musical Times and Singing-Class Circular*, 16/354 (June 1873), p. 115.
2 John Heywood, *Our Church Hymnody: an Essay and Review* (London: Simpkin, Marshall & Co., 1881), pp. 7, 27. All nineteenth-century texts are first referenced in footnotes, and thereafter cited in the text.

the tract 'disease' is only the most explicit of metaphors for hymnody's general decline. Degeneration, we know, had no single referent in Victorian England. If its mid-century provenance has been located in medico-psychiatric discourse, its application across a range of disciplines was, by the 1880s, facilitated by its status as common sense; knowledge about degeneration was assimilated into the vocabularies of the everyday, so that the biological, national and aesthetic were perceived to be mutually implicated in their respective declines.[3] It was precisely by drawing on the charged language of degeneration's analogical logic that Heywood's analysis received its force. After all, a degenerate hymnody was but a symptom of societal malaise.

There are other dynamics of the 'logic' of degeneration at work in Heywood's analysis: certain tune 'types' were marked as deviant, and, amongst other strategies of disavowal, gendered feminine (a story for another time), and a programme for hymnody's recuperation was put forward. Heywood's remedy for hymnodic health, recall, was to be found in lessons from the recent past; more precisely in reforms around the beginning of Victoria's reign. Here, he found some kindred spirits. For the early reformers too had pinned their hopes for reform on the premise of a decline.[4] An exemplary case in point is John Antes La Trobe. Bemoaning the 'low state of Ecclesiastical music' in 1831, La Trobe, with recourse to the 'testimony' of history, argued that 'a neglect of the art [of church music] keep[s] pace with the decline of the nation'. Left unchecked, then, the 'degraded art' of pre-Victorian hymnody was offered as a mirror to the nation of its looming 'corruption'. Like Heywood, La Trobe turned to history for hymnody's salvation. That he should have found this in the Reformation, that greatest of all English tales of renewal, might seem unremarkable.[5] Perhaps more surprising is that the early Victorian reforms were written as a story of cultural (re)masculinisation.

---

3   See, for example, the chapter titled 'Contexts' in Daniel Pick, *Faces of Degeneration: a European Disorder, c.1848–c.1918* (Cambridge: Cambridge University Press, 1989); and Stephen Arata, *Fictions of Loss in the Victorian Fin de Siècle* (Cambridge: Cambridge University Press, 1996), esp. the introduction.

4   The discourse of national decline seems to have been (and continues to be?) something of a hallmark of English self-analysis. For a discussion of opera's entanglement in this discourse in early eighteenth-century England, see Suzanne Aspden, '"An Infinity of Factions": Opera in Eighteenth-Century Britain and the Undoing of Society', *Cambridge Opera Journal*, 9/1 (1997), pp. 1–19.

5   John Antes La Trobe, *The Music of the Church, Considered in its Various Branches, Congregational and Choral: an Historical and Practical Treatise for the General Reader* (London: L.B. Seeley and Sons, 1831), pp. 6, 29; also pp. 16–17.

(Ef)feminising tactics

The 'othered' tunes of early Victorian hymnody reforms embraced a diverse range of contemporary compositional practices; it seems that the only thing they had in common was a certain 'secularity', and to reformist minds this was cause enough for their undoing.[6] Significantly, the construction of 'the secular' was premised on a politics of class, though seldom made explicit.[7] On the one hand, tunes of a 'vulgar and secular character' included, for example, 'popular ballads and the productions of the stage' and 'jigs or love-sick airs'.[8] On the other, and to class-ify the stage productions more precisely, tunes were identified with, and on occasion as, operatic airs. For the early nineteenth-century middle-class reformers the offensive taint of secularity was figured as an attribute of either lower- or upper-class musical culture. I want to elaborate briefly by focusing on aspects of 'aristocratic culture'.

Like most nineteenth-century reformers, the influential editor of *The Parish Choir*, Robert Druitt, sought to prescribe a specifically sacred style for church music. This was founded on the idea that church music was to have 'no affinity with the secular or theatrical music of the day'. In matters of musical style the directive translated thus: 'all superadded embellishment, any phrase introduced for mere effect, should be rigidly excluded'.[9] Indeed, 'the ornamental' became the most persistent marker of musical secularity. While the insistent qualification of ornament as secular in reform literature reveals the work necessary to maintain the construction, it also served to establish the equivalence of secularity and musical ornament as a truism. Thus La Trobe warned against 'burden[ing] a sacred composition with *secular ornaments*', which he listed as 'turns, flourishes, interludes, shakes,

---

6   A caveat: the 'reforms' were by no means a unified project, embracing often quite different, even opposing, programmes. Some, for example, sought the revival of the choral service, either exclusively choral or predominantly congregational; others sought a revival of chant, in its various forms; while still others were more interested in the reformation of congregational psalmody; often there were varying degrees of accommodation and intersection between these. Nicholas Temperley's *The Music of the English Parish Church*, vol. 1 (Cambridge: Cambridge University Press, 1979) remains the best account of the diverse aims that constituted the reforms; see chaps. 7 and 8.

7   It was also premised on a politics of denominationalism; aspects of Methodist and Roman Catholic musical practice in particular were productive sites for the construction of the secular. I will not, however, here consider the implications of denominationalism for my argument. I should also point out that almost all my sources issue from the Church of England, and that, unless specified otherwise, I am referring to Anglican hymning.

8   Anon., 'On the Objectionable Character of Many Psalm Tunes in Common Use', *The Parish Choir* (May 1846), p. 31.

9   Robert Druitt, *A Popular Tract on Church Music, with Remarks on its Moral and Political Importance, and a Practical Scheme for its Reformation* (London: Francis & John Rivington, 1845), pp. 35, 38.

trills, appoggiaturas, and', just to be thorough, 'other expletive notes' (pp. 136–37; my emphasis). While he was referring specifically to the improvisatory practices of church organists here, the same 'ornamental flourishes' were routinely discovered in vocal psalmody (p. 219). The crux of the matter was that melodic ornamentation recalled, for La Trobe and the other early reformers, the music and performance of another type of singer: the opera star. What is more, in reform texts opera and its ornamental 'liberties' became prime agents in the story of hymnody's decline (pp. 134–35, 141).

This location of hymning in the opera house, I suggest, provided middle-class reformers with a space in which to fashion a counter-masculine poetics, in a move that entailed, in the first instance, the feminising of aristocratic cultural products such as opera. It is well known that the opera in England was *perceived* to be an aristocratic haunt. True, middle-class resistance, both discursive and financial, to Italian opera was on the wane by the beginning of the nineteenth century.[10] Still, the association lingered long enough to be restated at the end of the century. In his magisterial history of the musical life of nineteenth-century England J.A. Fuller Maitland remarked that 'Italian opera was the typical amusement of the upper classes of society' for the first half of Victoria's century.[11] My purpose in rehashing the kinship between aristocrat and opera is to highlight the complex of discourses in which musical ornament was implicated, and thereby potentially gendered. First, and as is well known, the middle classes came to figure the aristocracy under the general sign of 'effeminacy' from the eighteenth century on.[12] Likewise, the English opera house, or rather the Italian opera in England, occupied a feminised space. As late as 1889, for example, an article on 'Manliness in Music' laid the blame for perceptions of musicianly effeminacy firmly at the opera star's dressing-room door.[13]

Labelling a hymn-tune style ornamental in early Victorian England at the same time marked it as classed and gendered, in a twofold inscription

---

10   See Theodore Fenner, *Opera in London: Views of the Press, 1785–1830* (Carbondale and Edwardsville, Ill.: Southern Illinois University Press, 1994), pp. 66–67, 271, and 80, 93.

11   J.A. Fuller Maitland, *English Music in the XIXth Century* (London: Grant Richards, 1902), p. 46.

12   Eve Kosofsky Sedgwick, for example, writes of 'the feminization of the aristocracy as a whole [which] came to be seen as ethereal, decorative, and otiose in relation to the vigorous and productive values of the middle class'; *Between Men: English Literature and Male Homosocial Desire* (New York: Columbia University Press, 1985), p. 93.

13   See Anon., 'Manliness in Music', *The Musical Times and Singing-Class Circular*, 30/558 (Aug. 1889), pp. 460–61. In lieu of any work on the gendering of the genre in early Victorian England, the feminising of Italian opera in England seems to have assumed the status of a somewhat transhistorical myth. For the early eighteenth-century origins of this myth, see Thomas McGeary, 'Gendering Opera: Italian Opera as the Feminine Other in Britain', *Journal of Musicological Research*, 14 (1994), pp. 17–34; and Aspden, '"An Infinity of Factions"'.

that drew hymn-tune criticism into the complex process of middle-class self-definition. That self-fashioning, we know, found an exemplary counter-image in aristocratic identities, amongst others, and this was especially true for the (re)making of middle-class manhood.[14] But if, for Thomas Carlyle in 1831, the 'old ideal of Manhood ha[d] grown obsolete, and the new [was] still invisible', one, and perhaps *the*, defining feature of middle-class masculinity was firmly in place by the 1830s: self-discipline.[15] Much has been said about this technique of the self, some of which will be relevant later, but for now I want to explore the implications of this normative thinking for the practices of the 'undisciplined'.

James Eli Adams has related the regime of ascetic self-government to a new conception of the male subject. Under the conjoint authority of Evangelical faith and Romantic subjectivity an ideal of essential selfhood was imagined, which, importantly for my purposes, repudiated self-consciousness as a mark of 'theatricality'.[16] Theatricality was a loaded word for the early Victorians. Functioning as a trope of the false, as a misrepresentation of reality that was equally applicable to music as to the dramatic stage, it relied for its effect on the insertion of distance between people, and within the person, typically casting the relationship as one of performer and spectator, true self and represented self.[17] The disjunction between the new middle-class ideal of the real and the theatrical relied not simply on excessive display but on a display of 'excess', which, as we will see, was always gendered.

In early Victorian reform texts, where the theatrical became a prominent music-critical concept, that excess was figured as ornament. This logic was clearly in operation in an anecdote told by an anonymous urban traveller who had ventured into a Roman Catholic chapel in London some time in the mid-1840s. *The Parish Choir* reported the reminiscence:

> Well does the fair young scion of aristocracy remember that wondrous voice [singing High Mass]! She had heard its tones the

---

14 Narratives of the 'rise' of the English middle classes typically write the early Victorian era as a time of arrival. For a classic study of this position, see Leonore Davidoff and Catherine Hall, *Family Fortunes: Men and Women of the English Middle Class, 1780–1850* (London: Hutchinson, 1987). Note especially their confident assertion that 'by the middle of the nineteenth century, these disparate elements [of middle-class culture in the late eighteenth century] had been welded together into a powerful unified culture', p. 23.

15 Quoted in James Eli Adams, *Dandies and Desert Saints: Styles of Victorian Masculinities* (Ithaca, NY and London: Cornell University Press, 1995), p. 1. Adams traces this ascetic self-discipline to the secularisation of the puritan strain within Evangelical thought as it converged with the discourse of a political economy in which the capitalist's profit was the reward for his abstinence, pp. 110–11.

16 Ibid., p. 10.

17 See Alison Byerly, *Realism, Representation, and the Arts in Nineteenth-Century Literature* (Cambridge: Cambridge University Press, 1997), p. 52.

preceding night at the opera. It is the celebrated *prima donna*, who is now warbling the inspired strains of Mozart, in his matchless Kyrie. But in what way? As the deprecatory strain proceeds, the splendid singer revels in a series of roulades and shakes, that are sadly out of place in a prayer for mercy and forgiveness.[18]

In an impressive array of correspondences, the false Roman Church's false church music – 'It is the opera over again for a shilling!' (p. 14) – provided the setting for a narration of the theatrical: the female aristocratic spectator, as opposed to the congregant (p. 6) is 'entrance[d]' by the prima donna's ornamental singing in a falsification of the prescribed church-going experience (p. 14). Significantly, the writer's analysis of the theatrical hinged on the melodic ornaments. It was in the excess of melody that the music and church were theatricalised.

Readings of the ornamental, furthermore, typically rely on the assumption of a distinction between surface decoration and structural essence, a logic which similarly structures the ideology of the theatrical. By putting this logic into play, discourses of the theatrical and the ornamental mutually reinforce what one might call the surface as negativity. This much is clear from the final evidence that *The Parish Choir* offered for constituting the Roman chapel as a 'modern theatre' (p. 6): amidst the splendour of the musical Mass, 'a fine old hymn may be heard (with embellishments)' (p. 15). The literal bracketing off of tune and ornament implies a structural hierarchy in which ornament, like – and hence – its parenthesising, denotes the superfluous; the hymn tune, by contrast, is complete in its autonomy. Reformist thinking, however, did not confine the elaboration of ornament as surface to musical matters. More insidious, musical ornament was not infrequently figured as subversive of the very essence of Anglican worship itself. As *The Parish Choir* noted elsewhere: 'exaggerated and effeminate melodies' expressed 'religious excitement' rather than 'the deep-seated energy of a calm but influential devotion'.[19] It should not surprise us that

---

18 Anon., 'Church Music and Romanism', *The Parish Choir*, 2 (1847), p. 14.

19 Anon., 'Value of Tallis's Harmonies', *The Parish Choir* (Feb. 1846), p. 4. A very minority position, though one that surfaced throughout the nineteenth century, argued that music per se was an ornament to worship. For example, 'the organ of the high-church section of Toryism', the *Standard*, suggested that the non-musical sections of the service were 'so eloquent, so full of masculine dignity … that *music, or any other added ornament, cannot fail to deform them*'. Establishing the '*intellectual*' service as the norm, the paper proceeded to pose the following to its readers: 'What needs there then the aid of music? We had almost said, what justification is there for exposing men to the danger of mistaking animal sensation for a masculine devout conviction?' (2 Apr. 1834); quoted in Edward Hodges, *An Apology for Church Music and Musical Festivals, in Answer to the Animadversions of the Standard and the Record* (London: Rivington, 1834), pp. 7, 9. The *Standard*, of course, was trading in the well-worn binarism of musical sensuality and the rationality of the word. That binary, as we well know, and as the *Standard* demonstrated, typically came gendered.

ornament's unruly tactics of the superficial are gendered as unmanly here. To sum up, the reading of ornament as surface and excess enabled reformers to configure early Victorian hymnody within discourses of the theatrical; discourses which, as Alison Byerly has shown, gendered theatricality as feminine, and which in turn, as we have seen, were antithetical to the ruling idea of manly self-discipline.[20]

The intersections of class and gender in tune criticism that I have outlined are nowhere more in evidence than in the label 'effeminate'. For if effeminacy's role in gender politics seems obvious, we should not forget that, well into the nineteenth century, effeminacy operated also in an older discursive regime as a sign for 'luxury', and more particularly the excess of aristocratic luxury.[21] As the Carlylean new man positioned himself against luxury as feminine, so did the masculine poetics of hymnody reform. Before I get to that story, though, I want to pursue how another set of discourses provided further ground for the gendering of hymn tunes.

The sublime Crotch

By all accounts, William Crotch was an academy man. Oxford don and first principal of the Royal Academy of Music, he is credited with having set the study of music on the path to gaining credibility in the universities. In part, this was achieved through his regular professorial lectures, later collected as *Substance of Several Courses of Lectures on Music* (1831). The most influential of these was titled 'On the Three Styles of Music'. Here, Crotch delineated a threefold typology of the Sublime, the Beautiful, and the Ornamental, summoning the pronouncements of aesthetic sages such as Joshua Reynolds and Edmund Burke,[22] and herein lay the lecture's power: the application of neoclassical aesthetic thought solely to music. Music critics now had their own aesthetic bible.

For my purposes, Crotch's *Lectures* affords the opportunity to pursue further an archaeology of the musical ornament, for which, as Naomi

---

20 Byerly, *Realism, Representation, and the Arts*, p. 55.
21 For particular views of the *effeminatus* and luxury, see Linda Dowling, *Hellenism and Homosexuality in Victorian Oxford* (Ithaca, NY and London: Cornell University Press, 1994), chap. 1; and Alan Sinfield, *The Wilde Century: Effeminacy, Oscar Wilde and the Queer Moment* (New York: Columbia University Press, 1994), chap. 2.
22 For an extremely brief discussion of Crotch's debt to eighteenth-century aesthetics, and a more thorough analysis of his view of the sublime, see Bennett Zon, 'History, Historicism and the Sublime Analogy', *Nineteenth-Century British Music Studies*, vol. 1, ed. Bennett Zon (Aldershot: Ashgate, 1999), pp. 23–29.

Schor would add, 'the sexism of rhetoric is of crucial significance'.[23] Admittedly, Crotch did not explicitly gender his styles. Nevertheless, they were elaborated in a discourse of 'normative aesthetics' which, in Schor's feminist reading, 'carr[ied] into the field of representation the sexual hier-archies of the phallocentric cultural order'. More importantly, as I show below, Victorian tune criticism's reception of Crotchean aesthetics did indeed gender his categories. If neoclassical aesthetics developed the sublime as a masculinist aesthetic, then 'the ornamental [was] inevitably bound up with the feminine, when it [was] not the pathological';[24] Western culture has of course had a problem in distinguishing between the two. Clearly, Crotch fits this scenario. Not only was the ornamental 'the lowest and least estimated' style, but its 'undue prevalence ... [was] a sure indication of the decline and decay of any art'.[25] The ordering of historical time by the rhetoric of pathology, a ploy with which we are by now familiar, was given a now equally familiar twist: the sublime was exemplified by the 'grandest style in music ... the sacred style – that of the church' (p. 32). But as the reform literature laid bare, church music was not necessarily 'sacred'. Crotch's basic argument, then, was this: the rebuke of present-day (church) music's secularisation/decay was its ornamentalness. A glimpse at Crotch's editorial practice confirms this, for like Heywood's use of 'history', Crotch's aesthetics was but a pretext for compositional reform.

Nearing the end of his life, the Oxford polymath edited a volume of *Psalm Tunes* (1836) that set the trend for early Victorian hymnody; the production of psalters became a fashionable pastime.[26] But, archaeology always being ideological, there was more involved than simply the recu-peration of Reformation tunes. For Crotch, and other reformers, the restoration of the old psalm tunes was an act of both reinstatement and purification, involving in turn, and very broadly, the attempt to sideline a certain repertoire of largely eighteenth-century tunes and the clean-up of

---

23 Naomi Schor, *Reading in Detail: Aesthetics and the Feminine* (New York and London: Methuen, 1987), p. 45. My analysis is indebted to Schor's reading of 'reading detail'.
24 Ibid., pp. 4, 45.
25 William Crotch, *Substance of Several Courses of Lectures on Music* (London: Longman et al., 1831), pp. 38, 66. Just to clarify, Crotch does not trace the prevalence of ornament to the rise of opera. He does, however, provide a framework for the reading of (aspects of) opera as ornamental.
26 The labours of two reformers come to mind: John Hullah's *The Psalter, or Psalms of David in Metre* (London: John W. Parker, 1843) and *The Whole Book of Psalms* (London, 1844), and both William Henry Havergal's *A Reprint of All the Tunes in Ravenscroft's Book of Psalms* (London: J.A. Novello, 1845) and *Old Church Psalmody* (London: J. Hart, n.d. [1847]). I should perhaps point out that I am not using the terms psalmody and hymnody in any strict sense; the Victorians themselves often used them interchangeably.

the psalm tunes 'themselves'. The sublime and ornamental loomed large in this project.

Crotch identified the 'most sublime Psalm Tunes [as] the most ancient we have – those used by the Reformers'. Against this, he opposed a 'bad style',[27] which, as reported by *The Parish Choir*, meant 'psalms made out of Songs, Glees, and Quartetts, in drawling, whining, minuet-like strains, with two or three notes to each syllable, full of modern or chromatic discords, with interludes, symphonies, introductions, shakes, flourishes, cadences, appogiaturas [*sic*]' and so on. This style, to 'be denounced and utterly abolished', was none other than the ornamental.[28] But the sublime tunes could not simply replace the bad ones, as they too had become ornamentalised; they had, thus, to be resublimated. One reformer who certainly thought of his work in these terms was the failed composer, Dickens collaborator, and influential educator John Hullah, who, lamenting that the 'noble melodies' of psalm tunes had become 'wretchedly corrupted, encumbered with endless passing notes, turns, and shakes', set himself the task of restoring 'this style of music to its original purity' (*The Psalter*, p. viii).

Schor has argued that in neoclassical aesthetic writings it is not only the traditional gendering of male form and female matter by which detail, or ornament, is marked as feminine, but as much by the process of '*mal*formation', by which ornament supposedly operates.[29] It is in these terms, I suggest, that we should understand Hullah's conviction in the corruptibility of ornament for an essential, 'pure' tune form. For the Reformation psalm tunes were not only exemplars of the hymnodic sublime, but also of manliness; the tunes of a 'solid, manly, Church-like character', in *The Parish Choir*'s words.[30] If the manliness of the psalm tunes, or more correctly of the 'original' tunes, became a commonplace of early reform texts, the quest for their purification was an essay also in remasculinisation.

One instance of tune criticism that shows nicely how the characteristics of the sublime coincided with the attributes of early Victorian hegemonic masculinity is a rare, muted critique of the reform project proffered by one Edward Young at the outer edge of early Victorian time. With a good dose of irony Young provided a definition for what was going as the sacred at the time, what he called 'the "no-excitement," "no-sentiment," "didactic gravity" Canon': 'the language ... that is not everywhere sober, self-restrained, and abstinent of all excitement of what are called the "animal

---

27 William Crotch, *Psalm Tunes, Selected for the Use of Cathedrals and Parish Churches* (London, 1836), pp. 1, 3.

28 Anon., 'Dr. Crotch on Psalm Tunes', *The Parish Choir* (Feb. 1846), p. 8.

29 Schor, *Reading in Detail*, p. 17.

30 Anon., 'Practical Hints on Congregational Psalmody', *The Parish Choir* (July 1847), p. 152.

spirits" cannot be properly a sacred language'.[31] Crucial for the musical realisation of this language was 'the *non-florid* principle', where florid 'denote[d], in certain quarters, a style of music un-churchlike, un-sacred'. More musically specific, it described a 'licentious variety' in the length, or rather 'shortness', of the notes, 'indeed any use whatever of notes below a certain rank' (p. 163). What Young meant by this, of course, was the preference for notes of 'longer' duration, or 'white notes'; those few enthusiasts of reform psalters will nod in recognition at his observation of 'the all but absolute non-appearance of any black [note] below a crotchet' (ibid.). There are several issues here. First, we should remember that in the conservative world of Victorian church music note duration signified an absolute duration independent of tempo; in theory, longer notes were truly sung long in time, which in part explains the recurring complaint against slow singing. Crotch, for one, conflated tempo and duration in his valorisation of the long–slow: 'Very slow notes belong to sublimity, and very rapid ones to ornament' (*Lectures*, p. 50). For Young, however, the non-florid principle of white-note predominance had less to do with tempo than with 'uniformity' of rhythm, 'the monotonous, mechanical pendulum swing ... of form and formalising' (p. 164).

Ex. 2.1   Old Hundredth: (a) 'equal note' version; (b) William Henry Havergal's 'standard' version

31 Edward Young, *The Harp of God: Twelve Letters on Liturgical Music. Its Import, History, Present State, and Reformation* (London: James Nisbet & Co., 1861), pp. 140, 132. Young, in short, argued that the sacred should be passion*ful*, in an overtly emotional and bodily way.

As an extreme case of rhythmic uniformity/monotony the example of the Victorian Old Hundredth, in both of its standard nineteenth-century incarnations, serves well (see Ex. 2.1); again, both are part of Crotch's legacy (see *Psalm Tunes*). The equal-note version speaks for itself, but probably the most familiar – at least I grew up with it – is no less uniform. I do not want to venture into the dubious source-studies scholarship of the reformers here, save to point out that of the many rhythmic variants of late fifteenth- and early sixteenth-century Old Hundredths available to the pioneering scholars, the one canonised as the 'true English version' had a sublime (pun intended) uniformity to it. Perhaps no one invested more in authenticating, and standardising, Old Hundredth than the crippled parish priest turned music antiquarian William Havergal. In his *History* of the tune he delighted in revealing at length its symmetrical structure. He began thus: 'Each of its four strains comprises four long and four short notes, uniformly but peculiarly disposed ...'.[32] What I want to emphasise is the symmetrical uniformity of this *particular* version. What was it about uniformity that made it the litmus of authenticity; a principle, as Young so perceptively observed, of the musical sacred? We might do well to take a lead from the commonplace that the appeal to authenticities of various kinds reveals as much about the present as the past.

It will come as no surprise, then, to learn that uniformity had a kinship with the sublime.[33] In its Crotchean formulation, '[u]niformity is not only compatible with the sublime, but is often the cause of it' (*Lectures*, p. 33). If, as Young noted, the sameness of uniformity had to do with 'form and formalising', variety was but another variation on the pathology of ornament theme. Again, Crotch said it best: 'The ornamental style is the result of ... abrupt variations', 'rapid, broken, and varied rhythm' (pp. 35–36). In other words, rhythmic variation broke up, or deformed, the sublime's uniformity, or unity of form. More than an aesthetic category for the classification of musical objects, the sublime functioned rather, and more powerfully, as an editorial principle of textual disciplining in the production of a masculine tune poetics that came to dominate the first decades of Victoria's reign.

It is time to bring together a few preliminary threads. The coincidences, chronological and other, between the language of the sacred sublime and constructions of bourgeois manliness are striking. If both were animated by the will to self-regulation, of sexual energies and ornamental excesses amongst others, they also animated each other. And if the male reformers fashioned a poetics of hymnody, an instance of

---

32 William Henry Havergal, *A History of the Old Hundredth Psalm Tune* (New York: Mason Bros., 1854), p. 17.
33 See Schor, *Reading in Detail*, p. 18.

artistic manhood, after a normative model of masculinity, this model, at the same time, was shored up by that hymnody.[34] The point at which practices of the self end and aesthetic praxis takes off is, potentially, a vanishing point, and one that I will not pursue here. But there was at least one idea of self whose practices were themselves thought of as aesthetic acts. I am of course referring to the dandy, a figure of no small importance to Victorian tune criticism.

The ridiculous dandy

The dandy has always been a heavily textualised figure.[35] A fundamentally theatrical being, he was readily accommodated in constructions of aristocratic manhood but rejected by bourgeois masculinity. An early account of the dandy makes this clear. In his 'philosophy of clothing', *Sartor Resartus*, that great apologist for the new manliness, Thomas Carlyle, satirised the dandy as 'a grotesque icon of an outworn aristocratic order'.[36] As we know, the dandy's theatricality was most spectacularly, though by no means solely, a function of costume. By way of contrast, that staple of Victorian male dress, the dark suit, was soon to become normative. As Elizabeth Eastlake, in a moment of transsexual ventriloquism, noted in 'his' essay on the social politics of dress: 'In this age, however, it would be difficult to impugn us for any over-indulgence of this propensity [for sartorial extravagance], – the male costume being reduced to a mysterious combination of the inconvenient and the unpicturesque, which, except in the light of a retribution, it is puzzling to account for.'[37] To think of the black suit as an act of punishment was perhaps not that far off the mark if we remember

---

34 For similar arguments on the interplay between artistic and social masculinities, see, for example, Herbert Sussman, *Victorian Masculinities: Manhood and Masculine Poetics in Early Victorian Literature and Art* (Cambridge: Cambridge University Press, 1995); and Adams, *Dandies and Desert Saints*.

35 The classic modern study of the English dandy is Ellen Moers's *The Dandy: Brummell to Beerbohm* (London: Secker & Warburg, 1960). Adams's *Dandies and Desert Saints* is a superb critical account, and Rhonda K. Garelick's *Rising Star: Dandyism, Gender, and Performance in the Fin de Siècle* (Princeton: Princeton University Press, 1998) is an interesting view of the dandy's influence on twentieth-century popular culture. My account of the dandy is drawn largely from these works.

36 See Adams, *Dandies and Desert Saints*, p. 21; and the chapter titled 'The Dandiacal Body' in Thomas Carlyle, *Sartor Resartus: the Life and Opinions of Herr Teufelsdröck* (London: Chapman & Hall, 1871; originally serialised 1833–34), pp. 188–99.

37 Anon. [Elizabeth Eastlake], *Music, and the Art of Dress* (London: John Murray, 1852), pp. 65–66.

that Evangelical ideology was a foundational constituent of Victorian bourgeois culture; Eastlake found the male wardrobe 'as ugly as the staunchest Puritan could have desired' (p. 66). Whatever the case may be, it is, and has always been, common to find in the new clothes the disciplinary imperative of early Victorian manliness. Eastlake, for example, viewed the waistcoat, though mind you only 'if a straight one', as an 'excellent restraint' (p. 67). The dandy's flouting of this sartorial discipline was variously transgressive. On the one hand, his ornamental costume suggested a performance of self that seemed antithetical to the new idea of a 'true' self that I discussed earlier. On the other, and perhaps more disturbing, if the 'performance' turned out to coincide with the true self, its very public display defied that social proscription against disclosure of personality that Richard Sennett has famously charted in 'the fall of public man'.[38] All in all, then, the theatrical dandy occupied a social space typically reserved by Victorian discourse for the feminine.[39] What does this have to do with hymns?

In 1836 the *Musical World* featured a caricature of that most popular of psalm tunes, the Old Hundredth (see Ex. 2.2). The brief, and (but for a couple of didactic epigraphs) only, textual commentary explained as follows: 'The 100th Psalm harmonized on the principles of the "Dandy-Sublime," and dedicated, with every appropriate feeling, to those "profound musicians" who consider bold progressions and daring harmonies – in plain English, unnatural modulations and extravagant discords, as the only tests of fine composition.'[40] As the blurb noted, the tune's dandiness was located in its harmony; the melody, in both rhythm (or lack thereof) and contour, was the standard Victorian version, and the same melody, we have seen, that constituted the tune as an epitome of the manly sublime. In this harmonic garb, then, the tune was quite literally a hybrid 'Dandy-Sublime'.[41] But perhaps the scare quotes caution against too hasty a reading. So let me backtrack.

The introductory blurb not only identified harmony as the dandifier, but specified the culprit as chromaticism: 'bold progressions and daring harmonies'. And in case the reader-listener missed the point, the arrangement's chromatic harmonies are underlaid with a rising chromatic bass in the first line. The first thing to mention about the arrangement is that it is a caricature; Havergal labelled it as such when he reproduced it in his *History* (pp. 49–50). Caricatures, of course, are grotesque exaggerations,

---

38   See Richard Sennett, *The Fall of Public Man* (New York: Alfred A. Knopf, 1977), chap. 8.
39   See Adams, *Dandies and Desert Saints*, p. 186.
40   Thomas Adams, arr., no title (20 May 1836), p. 156.
41   I acknowledge here a debt to Bennett Zon for making me think further about the 'Dandy-Sublime'.

Ex. 2.2   Thomas Adams's 'Dandy-Sublime' Old Hundredth

by definition unnatural. And the harmonisation is 'unnatural', and in two senses: first, in the language of functional harmony, a context within which the nineteenth-century hymn tune operated unequivocally, the musical syntax is gibberish; second, contemporary music theory (for the most) confidently located diatonic harmony in 'Nature' itself, through an appeal to the acoustic phenomenon of overtones. Against this naturalisation of diatonicism, chromaticism was generally figured as, if not unnatural, then certainly less natural. It was only at the very end of the nineteenth century, for example, that one of the most popular late Victorian manuals, Ebenezer Prout's *Harmony*, refuted this Enlightenment insight; even then, Prout could not quite fully escape old, deeply ingrained habits.[42] But we need not rely on the evidence of music theory; 'in plain English', the commentary to the arrangement itself named the harmony's *unnatural* modulations'. The 'Dandy-Sublime', then, bolstered its 'message' against harmonic excess by constructing that harmony as artificial, at odds with the natural order, just as was that most spectacular of signifiers of artifice, the dandy.[43]

There is a more explicit link, though, that ties the dandy still more firmly to the arrangement: the immediate context of its production. An account of this was given in Havergal's *History*, where not only did the score make the second of its (at least) three Victorian print appearances but its own very brief story was recounted. Here, then, was the 'Dandy-Sublime's' *raison d'être*: 'The caricature was well-timed, for Mr. Adams [the arranger] well knew that nowhere is psalmody so disgraced by the freaks and fancies of piano-forte organists, as it is in and about the metropolis' (pp. 49–50). If Havergal's slippage between tenses betrays the almost two decades that separate his *History* and the arrangement's original publication, we have no reason (here) to suspect him of doctoring the past. After all, admonishments of the organist were a stock of the reform literature; Crotch, for instance, cautioned the organist against 'chromatic shifting of chords ... no modern discords or effects should be produced' (*Psalm Tunes*, p. 4). Again, though, the problem involved more than just the harmonic excess itself. Rather, what was at stake was the role harmony played in the context of scripting a theatrics of contemporary hymning; harmony was the musical excess made manifest of overtly performative practices. In this

---

42 At least twice Prout referred to the minor key, which he defined primarily through its minor third, as 'more artificial' than the major; see *Harmony: its Theory and Practice* (London: Augener, 1903; rev. 16th edn, 1901), pp. 123, 208. Prout's 'abandonment of the harmonic series as the basis on which the system [of harmony] is founded' was articulated in the preface to the 16th edn, p. vii; cf. the preface to the 1st edn of 1889. Stainer was somewhat radical in 'founding' his *A Theory of Harmony* (London, Oxford and Cambridge: Rivington, 1871) on 'the tempered scale', rather than on the harmonic series.

The minor third had, of course, proved persistently problematic for music theory because of its intractable upper partials. Crotch dispensed the wisdom of his age when he pronounced the minor third, and chromaticism, as not of nature: 'The major key is more agreeable to the ear than the minor, and the diatonic scale and discords than the chromatic ... The triads of the major key are the same with the perfect chords formed by any note with its five principal harmonics, and are therefore as much a part of nature as light itself ... But the minor key consists partly, and sometimes wholly, of minor thirds. Now, the minor triad is not, like the major, a part of nature'; *Lectures*, pp. 47–48.

43 An early analysis of the (admittedly *fin-de-siècle*) dandy highlighted his relationship to 'the artificial'; see Holbrook Jackson, *The Eighteen Nineties: a Review of Art and Ideas at the Close of the Nineteenth Century* (London: Grant Richards, 1913), chap. 6, 'The New Dandyism'.

critique of display, La Trobe led the way. He ranted that 'the organist degrade[d] the church into a concert-room' (p. 124), and attributed the 'ostentation in the act of performance' to 'unsuitable harmony' (p. 122). This became the formula for discussions of contemporary organ performance in reform texts: the organist-performer displayed through harmony. In short, the organist's performance recalled that of the dandy. Just as the dandy's ornamental dress put him on display, so did the organist's harmonic ornament.

In one sense, though, harmony per se was thought of as an ornament. The popular metaphorisation of melody as 'clothed' in harmony relied, I suggest, on a paradox in the philosophy of dress: clothes both concealed and expressed an essential subjectivity; either way, however, they were performative, and, at base, ornamental, external to the true self. If, as I have shown, the editorial energy of the reformers was driven by the chimerical quest for authenticity, the reformers themselves were under no illusion that their critical editions of psalters were not always already compromised. Again, Havergal is exemplary. Confronted by an inchoate mass of source material, he must have been only too aware of the difficulties involved in reviving Reformation psalmody in anything like its 'original' incarnation(s). The confessions of an editor testify as much:

> We cannot use the old tunes, in their earliest forms, either as to their melodies, or as to the manner in which they were harmonized ... Hence, the utter uselessness of talking, in all cases, of original versions of tunes. There are no such versions for certainty to be had; and if we really had them, we most likely should decline using them. (*Old Church Psalmody*, pp. 6–7)

Surely there could be nothing more honest than this, a frank admission as to the uncertainty of the very nature of the project? But Havergal's practice tells a different story. The trade-off, it transpires, was more clearly circumscribed: harmony itself was the compromising element, just as it was to be easily compromised by the reformers. The extraordinary undertaking to fix an authentic melody for Old Hundredth in its *History* is only the extreme case of Havergal's attitude to psalm-tune melody in general. After all was done and contrary to what was said, it seems that true melodies did exist, as the reform discourse of corrupt and pure texts bears out.

This assumption of a melodic essence, I think, provided the reformers with a rationale for their harmonic interventions. In other words, locating a tune's authenticity in its melody made credible the practice of giving it a new harmonic identity without jeopardising the critical project. Thus, while Havergal does not, cannot, claim authorship of the tunes in *Old Church Psalmody*, he does not hesitate to point out that all but two of the harmonisations are his own (p. 8). All this suggests that harmony in general was non-essential to a tune's 'true' identity, an idea perhaps nowhere more apparent than in the clothes-like ability of harmony to mask that melodic identity. So an editor who disliked a particular melody might take Henry Smart's lead: 'I thought it best to admit them [the melodies, of which Smart did not 'approve'] – clothed, however, in such a style of harmony as might, in some degree, compensate for their original meanness or triviality of character'.[44] If a tune was to be metaphorised as a dandy, then, its dandiness was likely to be located in its harmony. Nowhere were the connections between self and appearance, melody and (wrong) harmony made more explicit than in this late Victorian restatement of an old idea: 'A fine old tune when modernized and clothed in weak, inappropriate harmony loses its character, as a noble and venerable-looking man would appear very strange if he were attired in the dress and jewels of a fop.'[45]

Finally, to return to the 'Dandy-Sublime', and to the organists who had occasioned the arrangement. As I mentioned, the anti-organist rhetoric almost always centred on the problematics of display and its relationship to the ornamental. But the ornamental excess so decried by the reformers lends itself to another reading: as a misreading of the sublime. Needless to say, Crotch's sublime was far more complex than I made out earlier. For instance, while 'simplicity' was a sure sign of the sublime, so was its 'opposite, intricacy, when on a large scale' (*Lectures*, p. 33). Similarly, a 'uniform succession of major chords, the most agreeable of all sounds', and an 'unintelligible combination of extra-neous discords' were equally aspects of the sublime (p. 34). And while in delineating the musical sublime Crotch had quite specific events in mind – large-scale intricacy meant largely vocal counterpoint, for example – the potential for alternative interpretations of 'intricacy, when on a large scale', and 'unintelligible ... discords', and so of the sublime, should not be overlooked.[46] Crotch, moreover, was well aware that his three styles were seldom distinct in practice (p. 36). For the organist, and like other

---

44 Henry Smart, *A Choral Book Containing a Selection of Tunes Employed in the English Church Newly Harmonized for Four Voices and Organ* (London: Boosey & Sons, n.d. [1855]), unpaginated.

45 R.B. Daniel, *Chapters on Church Music* (London: Elliot Stock, 1894), p. 19.

46 Not to press too hard, but the original eighteenth-century and dominant Burkean notion of the sublime emphasised dark, gloom, pain, horror, even the grotesque. The Crotchean sublime diluted this 'aspect', and on the whole privileged the grand, high, lofty, elevated aspect of the sublime (p. 32). While the differences between the two aspects might be finessed in perception aesthetics, I suggest that this was less easily done in compositional practice. Perhaps it was an awareness of this that led Crotch, the church music composer, to privilege one aspect of the sublime over another in his attempt to sacralise the category for reform(ed) composition.

early Victorian producers of church music under the sway of the reform ethos, the pressure to produce the sublime was no doubt great. But, as the 'Dandy-Sublime' suggests, things could go wrong: in the organist's hands the sublime could become ornamentalised, it could be dandified.

At the end of the century, when the dandy had made something of a public comeback, Adams's arrangement was reprinted in the *Musical Times*, which glossed it with the following quip: "'Tis but one step from the "Dandy sublime" to the "Dandy ridiculous".'[47] But I think the venerable journal missed the point. For the dandy was already a sign of the ridiculous, a *prêt-à-porter* caricature, so that the 'Dandy-Sublime' *was* the sublime made ridiculous. Whatever the case, one thing is certain about the arrangement: its style, as one of the epigraphs made clear, was to be avoided – perhaps because it wasn't the 'true' sublime?[48]

Hym(n)ing

The 'problem' of the 'Dandy-Sublime', then, was its collusion with an ethics of performance as display, and part of that dilemma can be ascribed to the prevalence of improvisation in early nineteenth-century hymning: the gallery band, the soloist mimicking the opera star and, of course, the organist misreading the sublime all come to mind. No doubt the melodic and harmonic excesses I have outlined were in part a function of improvisation; the relation between 'the ornamental' and improvisation in a range of musical contexts is very well known. While it would be disingenuous to argue that pre-Victorian hymnody existed only as an oral culture that facilitated ornamentalised improvisation – the four weighty volumes of the recent *Hymn Tune Index* stand as an incontrovertible challenge to any such myth – it would be less controversial to say that the sheer magnitude of the textualisation that English hymnody underwent in the wake of the reforms (is it any wonder that the *Hymn Tune Index* leaves off just before the Victorian age begins?) was a rearguard action: as much an attempt to discipline an improvisatory-based performance tradition as it was to fix a canon

---

47 Anon., no title, *The Musical Times*, 40/679 (1 Sept. 1899), p. 604.
48 Junius to the Duke of Grafton (apparently): 'I do not give you to posterity as a pattern to imitate, but as an example to deter.'

of tunes.[49] Compare, for example, the improvisatory excesses that the 'Dandy-Sublime' burlesqued and Smart's harmonic strait-jacketing; hence the subtitle to his book, *Tunes ... Newly Harmonized for ... Voices and Organ.*

What more precisely was the correct(ed) harmonic clothing that the reformers sought to impose, the harmonic style of the masculine poetics that I am exploring? Again, the fortunes of Old Hundredth provide a clue. And again, I turn to its tireless chronicler, Havergal, who, writing towards the end of the early Victorian period, reflected, with a tinge of regret, on the triumph of the reform initiatives:

> The harmony which used to be set to the tune, was far more varied and elaborate than any which is now used. Hardly a company of singers can now be found who sing the tune, as to its harmony, in more than one way; whereas, our forefathers were accustomed to harmonize and sing it in many ways. (*A History*, pp. 37–38)

He went on to detail the current practice:

> The ordinary mode in which the tune is now harmonized in England, has been justly censured for its monotonous effect. According to that mode the initial and terminal note of each strain, excepting in only one instance, is set to the tonal harmony. The old masters studiously avoided such sameness. (p. 39)[50]

---

49 Of course, notated music by no means guarantees fidelity in performance. Nevertheless in most instances it does presume, and encourage, a 'correct' reading. Conversely, unnotated music does not imply interpretative licence. Victorian church musicians' interest in music literacy, I think, emphasises my point. Since the Reformation, psalters had functioned secondarily as music literacy primers: prefaces provided the 'theory' and the psalms themselves the exercises. With the secularisation of (music) education in Victorian England, hymnals were no longer required to, and rarely did, serve this function. Still, the keen interest taken in music literacy by church musicians continued, perhaps even intensified. Clearly, the new skill was intended to enable congregations to read the tunes as written – not to encourage ad-libbing.

Vic Gammon has read the mass-produced Victorian hymnal as a will to standardise and control both repertoire and performance practice in the context of church reforms in general; see '"Babylonian Performances": The Rise and Suppression of Popular Church Music, 1660–1870', in E. and S. Yeo (eds), *Popular Culture and Class Conflict, 1590–1914* (Brighton: Harvester, 1981), pp. 62–88. I will not pursue here the possibility of reading textualisation itself as a gendered activity.

50 Given Havergal's own harmonic practice it is somewhat ironic that he lamented harmonic monotony, which was precisely what a later generation of reformers praised about his compositions. John Spencer Curwen, for example, regarded Havergal as 'the prophet of the purists', whose 'strict style' gloried in 'severe but pleasing simplicity', and commented in particular on his 'diatonic harmonies'; see *Studies in Worship Music, Chiefly as Regards Congregational History*, 1st ser. (London: J. Curwen & Sons, 1888), pp. 257, 261.

Certainly no sign of any harmonic dandy here. There are two things to note about this generic style. First, it was based on a highly selective reading of Reformation harmonic practice; Crotch's dictum of 'new Church music, but *no new style*' (quoted in Havergal, *A Reprint*, p. xx) was often invoked to rationalise the 'borrowings'. Second, and like the Reformation and its products in general, the new-old style was gendered masculine. These twin concerns indeed informed Havergal's work, and as there is a relatively neat fit between his theory and practice, it is time to turn to his own harmonisation of Old Hundredth, which held pride of place as the first tune in *Old Church Psalmody* (see Ex. 2.3).

Ex. 2.3   Havergal's *Old Church Psalmody* harmonisation of the Old Hundredth

Perhaps the only thing that would strike us about the harmony in Example 2.3 is that there is nothing particularly striking about it; that no doubt was the point. For example, there is not a single seventh chord, the absence of which, we are told, was one of the 'peculiarities' of the old psalmody. And if a 'succession of fundamental chords [was] a main characteristic' of the old style, then root positions certainly predominate; only three first inversions prevent a full house (*A Reprint*, p. xiv; *Old Church Psalmody*, pp. 4–5). This 'plain' harmonic style was articulated within a verbal discourse of now familiar catchwords such as chaste, severe, simple, sober, earnest: a legacy, to be sure, of Evangelical discourse but one which, as historians of Victorian masculinity have argued, had a particular resonance for middle-class manliness.[51] Elsewhere, Havergal's gendering of style was made explicit. For instance, the cadential 6/4,

---

51 For La Trobe these discourses were one and the same. In his discussion of Reformation psalmody he spoke of 'manly simplicity', 'chaste tunes … and manliness of expression' (pp. 190, 199).

'which the old worthies used by every contrivance to avoid' but which characterised 'modern tunes', was feeble, mawkish and secular.[52] In the old style, '[e]verywhere the more masculine combination of 5/4 resolved into 5/3 [was] observable', and Havergal dutifully followed suit; see the 4–3 suspension in the penultimate bar (*A Reprint*, p. xv; *Old Church Psalmody*, pp. 5–6).

There are other features of Havergal's gendered reading of Reformation practice for a masculine poetics that I could explore, but I prefer to return to narratives of history, and especially ones that gendered history. Havergal had appended to his *History* a selection of 'specimens' of the tune. Broadly chronological, it began with the 'original' Old Hundredths and concluded with his own harmonisation of the tune; the story, it seems, had come full circle: the second reformation had fulfilled the promise of the first that the intervening centuries had reneged on.

So far I have been concerned largely with what one might call a masculinity of the imagination, with a gendered criticism and a masculine style of composition that traded in metaphor. True, those metaphors may have had actual bodies as distant referents. But 'masculinity', of course, has as much (perhaps more?) to do with the male body and its practices as with the discursive constructs that attend and are inseparable from that body. This was no less the case for the reformers, for whom an interest in the imaginary masculine was also an interest in actual, mostly male, bodies. In other words, manly hymns and men were implicated in each other's fortunes. In the arena of gender (and class, nationality, and later race) identities, musicality *tout court* has stood on the side of the 'other' in England since at least the early modern period. That this ideology took a particularly strong form in the nineteenth century has become a critical commonplace, and its implications for the lack of, or at least rigorously circumscribed, male middle- and upper-class participation in performance are well known.[53] La Trobe, for one,

---

52 Notice that Havergal did not merely set a higher value on, and masculinise, an 'old' style, but did so by devaluing current practice. He did this, I suggest, because of the 'secularity' of the cadential 6/4, which had become a harmonic trope for melodic ornament in the aria; Havergal's attitude to melodic ornament was exemplified in his praise of the old style's 'utter abhorrence of everything *appogiatural* [sic] in the melody' (*A Reprint*, p. 5). That 'cadence' per se had been hijacked by, and so equated with, ornamental practice is evident from its regular place on the list of proscribed ornamentalisms.

53 The most recent discussion of this much-rehearsed scenario occurs in Phyllis Weliver, *Women Musicians in Victorian Fiction, 1850–1900: Representations of Music, Science and Gender in the Leisured Home* (Aldershot: Ashgate, 2000), chap. 1. For a discussion of the racialising of musicality in Victorian South Africa, see chap. 1 of my 'Music and Post/Colonialism: the Dialectics of Choral Culture on a South African Frontier' (Ph.D. diss., Rhodes University, 2003).

attributed the reason for music being 'so little cultivated, in this country, by men' to 'the frivolous prejudices, which denounce the art as unmanly' (p. 403). As might be expected, the church was not immune to this 'knowledge', and as a powerful obstacle to the reforms it became a recurring concern in an already packed programme. The fall-out of male musical reticence seems largely to have affected the congregation: the reluctance to sing in church was due to 'the cold, artificial tone of fashionable English society, self-wrapped, apathetic, which repudiates all show of feeling … which teaches that a gentleman should never seem moved'.[54] It is worth noting here that while the object of Druitt's analysis appears to be the congregation at large, ultimately he is concerned with the men in the congregation. Indeed, this was at the heart of efforts to revive congregational singing: to get the men, above all, to sing again. Leading the way, *The Parish Choir* declared that 'it is the *man's* voice that we want. Women and children do sing already; but the congregational chorus wants the body, volume, and richness, which the man's voice alone can give' (1847, p. 127). And here, I think, is the crux of the matter: just as the reformers endeavoured to masculinise hymn tunes, so they desired to remasculinise the congregational body by putting men's voices back into it.

I emphasise *re*masculinise, because again the reformers found historical precedent – in the Reformation, as always – for male congregational song: 'In an age when Psalms were sung with great energy by large masses of people, the men's voices, predominating by their power, would engross the ear, and clearly sustain the melody' (Havergal, *A Reprint*, p. ix). We may sceptically ask how Havergal came by this sort of information: what contemporary listeners did he cite; what were their agendas? As it turns out, he cited no one, for the 'truth' of whether sixteenth-century English*men* sang loud and proud was of no particular importance to him. Rather, it was an assumption, at once evidence for and a by-product of the manliness of Reformation tunes. Let me explain. The Reformation psalm tune, of course, had its melody in the 'tenor', and for the reform critic this proved felicitous. Here, as voice part was conflated with sexed voice, was incontrovertible evidence of psalmody's original manliness; by the nineteenth century the melody had long moved to the top voice in multi-part arrangements, easily sung by women or children but apparently too 'high' for the average male congregant. If, as I argued earlier, a tune's essence was its melody, the sex of the melody's first singers was significant for a gendering of the tune. The 'authentic' manly melodies were originally sung by men.

Such force did this coincidence assume that it was sufficient to 'excuse' the early psalm tune's contrapuntal excesses: 'though the

---

54 Druitt, *A Popular Tract*, p. 22.

Tenor, as the air or tune for the adult male voices of the congregations, is always plain and equal, and though the Bass, also, is generally of the easiest mould, yet the other parts are often learnedly ornate' (Havergal, *A Reprint*, p. ix). Havergal's analysis brings into play a range of binarisms which line up something like this: 'male' voice – by which is meant tenor and bass – and plain melody as essence; 'female' voice – or 'unmanly' voice, as the maleness of the countertenors and boy trebles is side-stepped (pp. x–xi) – and florid counterpoint as ornament. The gendering of structural essence and ornament, of melody and harmonic accompaniment that I explored earlier, is ultimately 'naturalised', then, by the presence of real (though only gendered, not sexed) bodies. Not to put too fine a point on it, the old psalm tune was in essence masculine, because written for men.

Objections will no doubt be raised: surely the women in the congregation also sang the melody; what has become of their voice in all of this (male analysis of men)? I would argue that Havergal would simply reply that the 'mass of plain Tenor voice' overwhelmed them, as the tenor's range was then able to hold – *tenere* – the tenor melody. Besides, he might add, the female voices in the congregation would be lost amongst the upper parts of the choir. In Havergal's time the converse might be argued: the melody was written for the soprano-treble, and the male singing it in his range, even if it wasn't, as was usually claimed, too high for him, would be in competition with the lower parts of the choir. Either way, *he* was now silenced. Which leads me to return finally to the singing men and harmony of my reform period.

As has been mentioned, the gendering of musicianship in Victorian England no doubt had something to do with, as John Spencer Curwen put it, men 'making melody in their hearts' while standing silent during hymn time.[55] But other, 'musical' reasons were also put forward, and I want to examine these briefly by focusing on a series of articles titled 'Practical Hints on Congregational Psalmody' that appeared in *The Parish Choir* in 1847. The first constraint against male participation was that the melody was too high for most men to sing (p. 127). Deprived of the melody, men were forced elsewhere for vocal succour. This they found in the bass, but again there were problems:

> To most of the commonest tunes there is a great variety of harmonies. The organist can play any of these that he chooses; he can alter, vary, and combine them, or can invent new ones. No person who wishes to sing the bass of the Old Hundredth in church, knows which of the thousand harmonies in existence will be used.

---

55 *Studies in Worship Music*, p. 329.

And so we are presented with a very different story: instead of not singing for fear of being unmanned, men, checked at every turn, simply could not sing; the 'music' prevented them from singing. *The Parish Choir* proposed the following solution: 'The tunes must be fixed, with definite harmonies, which must not be departed from' (p. 128). Here, I think, is part of the reason for that rush towards textualisation that I spoke about earlier: the desire to discipline harmony, both to fix and to simplify (or masculinise) it, was the same desire to revive congregational, and especially male congregational, singing, to wrest church music from the show-off organists and choirs, to re-*form* the tunes.

The story of the gendered life of Victorian hymnody does not stop here. If Havergal and company could temporarily settle a tune's 'gender' they had little control over its fortunes at large. As a reading of mid- and late Victorian hymn criticism reveals, the masculinisation plan, put simply, did not work: as tunes increasingly came to be labelled unmanly, so did men withdraw even more from the congregational body. All of which points to, and as the gender gurus have for a long time been telling us, the extraordinary amount of work expended in the name of constructing and maintaining dominant identities. The flip side, of course, is the always precarious nature of that project. And so, to bring my own story full circle. When Heywood, and the late Victorian reformers, turned to 'history', to their early Victorian forebears, for their own dose of hymnodic Viagra, they too would find 'the past' to be a bit of a limp cure.

Thanks to supervisors present and past, Christine Lucia and Roger Parker, and to Phyllis Weliver for their comments on early drafts of this essay, and to Undine Weber for a proofing eye.

CHAPTER THREE

The Construction of a Cultural Icon

The Case of Jenny Lind

George Biddlecombe

Thanks to reports of her German triumphs, Jenny Lind, already known as 'the Swedish Nightingale', was a celebrity even before she first arrived in London in April 1847. Soon the 'Jenny Lind' steam engine of the London and Brighton Railway, 'Jenny Lind' gloves, statuettes, photographs, prints, decorated boxes, sheet music songs, and, perhaps less flatteringly, an elephant testified to her fame. But this celebrity was accompanied by a process constructing her as a personification of important cultural values to the point that a new iconic persona was invented. This essay sets out to uncover how and why the myth of Jenny Lind was created during her earliest years in London, focusing in particular on the theatrical politics of the period and various ideological pressures that contributed to the construction of Lind as a cultural icon. It then concentrates on the immediately posthumous phase of the 1890s, specifically investigating how the authors of the first book-length biography dealt with an event that threatened to throw the myth into crisis.

To understand the creation of this iconic figure we first need to consider the impression of Lind that was received in Britain before her actual arrival in terms of establishing certain core components of her mythical persona that would subsequently be developed here. Having left Stockholm, where her career had hitherto been based, under the aegis of Meyerbeer, then Generalmusikdirektor at the Prussian Court, Lind made her triumphant Berlin debut in December 1844. During the following two years she consolidated her reputation with engagements in Vienna and in various German cities, including, in August 1845, singing in the concerts given on the Rhine by King Friedrich Wilhelm IV of Prussia, amongst whose exalted guests were Queen Victoria, making her first visit to the Continent since acceding to the throne, and Prince Albert.

The Times first referred to Lind in December 1844 with a report on her first appearance in Berlin. Within weeks the same paper noted that Alfred

Bunn, the manager of Drury Lane Theatre, had engaged Lind to make her British debut at his theatre.[1] She soon received a rival offer from Benjamin Lumley of Her Majesty's Theatre, setting in train a sequence of events involving contractual and legal matters that was closely followed in the London press and to which we shall return. Further information reached Britain from London musical journalists visiting the Continent. In 1845 J.W. Davison reported to the *Musical World* that he was disappointed by Lind's singing, but the anonymous correspondent of the *Illustrated London News* and, the following year, Henry Chorley in the *Athenaeum* waxed lyrical over her talents and personality. Both critics drew on the image disseminated by what was effectively Lind's German publicity machine, the underlying aim of which was to appropriate this Scandinavian as a German, endowed with a 'simple and genial and earnest personality', to quote Chorley, whose opportunity to gain such an apparently profound personal knowledge of Lind was limited to two short and stilted meetings. Nevertheless, for all that they originated in appeals to German nationalistic pride, such remarks would later not be lost on Lind's British supporters.[2]

Lind's personal popularity was also drawn to the attention of the British public. *The Times* related that, when she sprained an ankle, the Prussian king immediately 'despatched one of his private surgeons to attend upon the celebrated cantatrice, and had frequently sent to inquire after the patient. Upwards of 1000 cards were daily left at the residence of the favourite by private individuals of distinction.'[3] More boisterous manifestations of Lind mania also became known, such as a case in 1846 when the enthusiasm of a group of German students left an ageing Englishman terrified. In 1847 this story was told to Charles Dickens, who relayed it to his friend Douglas Jerrold. Soon afterwards Dickens's account appeared in *Douglas Jerrold's Weekly Newspaper* and, a week

---

1   *The Times*, 25 Dec. 1844, p. 5; 20 Jan. 1845, p. 5.
2   *Musical World*, 20 (9 Oct. 1845), pp. 482–83; *Illustrated London News*, 7 (11 Oct. 1845), pp. 232–33; *Athenaeum*, no. 990 (17 Oct. 1846), pp. 1074–75. The *Illustrated London News* article, including its portrait, was based on an anonymous German biography, *Jenny Lind, die schwedische Nachtigall. Eine biographische Skizze. Mit dem Portrait der Künstlerin* (Hamburg: B.G. Berendsohn, 1845). Chorley's opinions on Lind's character and suitability for certain roles are noticeably close to assertions made in the same publication. On his two visits to Lind, each lasting only ten minutes and 'so ceremonious that I sit on the edge of my chair & make speeches', see Robert Terrell Bledsoe, *Henry Fothergill Chorley: Victorian Journalist* (Aldershot: Ashgate, 1998), p. 156. Chorley owed these meetings to an introduction from Mendelssohn (ibid., p. 155). The *Illustrated London News* article was possibly written by George Hogarth, who certainly attended the Beethoven Festival (see *Musical World*, 20 (28 Aug. 1845), p. 410).
3   *The Times*, 6 Apr. 1846, p. 2.

before Lind's arrival, in George Hogarth's *Musical Herald*.[4] Hogarth was, of course, Dickens's father-in-law.

By now interest surrounding the soprano had reached an extraordinary pitch. It was heightened by rumours as to whether she would indeed come, by continuing press reports of legal conflicts, and by two burlesques, which opened on rival stages only days before Lind finally set foot in London.[5] Shortly afterwards a full-page eulogistic biographical article, complete with a portrait and a Swedish song supposedly composed by Lind herself, appeared in the *Illustrated London News*,[6] and a range of other commercial interests swiftly exploited her fame.

A crucial role in the early phase of the construction of Lind as a cultural icon was played by Rumsey Forster, the music critic of the aristocratic daily newspaper the *Morning Post*. The ecstatic reception that greeted Lind on her debut at Her Majesty's Theatre as Alice in Meyerbeer's *Roberto il diavolo* on 4 May 1847 (all operas were produced in Italian at Her Majesty's) was vividly reported in the London press. But Forster's accounts exceeded all others. Within a matter of days he had not only told his readers of Lind's 'serenity and earnestness ... elevation of intellect ... deep sensibility ... [and] Rafaello-like delicacy'; he insisted that when she performed her next role, Amina in *La sonnambula*, what the audience witnessed was not a theatrical illusion but a revealing of her innermost self: 'the saint-like purity of her mind and heart'.[7]

---

4   The event took place in the autumn of 1846. Having accompanied Lind's carriage to the gates of the unspecified city where she had been performing, the students returned to her hotel, rushed into her bedroom, and tore the bed linen into strips, which they then wore as decorations. In fact they had gone into the Englishman's room by mistake, and he was convinced that they were politically motivated. See Dickens's letter to Douglas Jerrold dated 14 Feb. 1847 in *The Pilgrim Edition: The Letters of Charles Dickens*, ed. Madeline House and Graham Storey (Oxford: Clarendon Press, 1965–) (hereafter *The Letters of Charles Dickens*), vol. 5, pp. 27–29; *Douglas Jerrold's Weekly Newspaper*, 27 Feb. 1847, pp. 253–54; and the *Musical Herald*, 2 (10 Apr. 1847), p. 48.

5   A.B. Reach's *Jenny Lind at Last. or, The Swedish Nightingale*, which opened at the Lyceum on 14 April, and H.R. Addison's *Jenny Lind; or, The Northern Star*, premiered at the Adelphi on the following night, just two days before Lind's arrival on 17 April. A third burlesque, A.L.V. Campbell's *More Ethiopians; or Jenny Lind in New York*, was first performed at the Grecian Saloon on 13 May.

6   *Illustrated London News*, 10 (24 Apr. 1847), p. 272. The biography and the song (with an English translation) were taken from a recent Viennese biographical pamphlet by A.J. Becher, *Jenny Lind. Eine Skizze ihres Lebens ... vermehrte Auflage* (Vienna: Jasper'schen Buchhandlung, 1847). The portrait was adapted from that used in 1845.

7   *Morning Post*, 19 Apr. 1847, p. 5; 14 May 1847, p. 5. There is no evidence that when Forster wrote the former report he had ever seen Lind from a close distance. For an example of the eulogistic reaction to Lind's debut, see the *Illustrated London News*, 10 (8 May 1847), p. 301. See also the humorous account of 'Mr. Straggles', who is caught in the crush at Lind's performances, in the same issue, p. 298.

Even now this statement is extraordinary. Hans Christian Andersen, an ardent champion of Lind, had described her as making him 'sensible of the holiness there is in art',[8] and possibly Forster was taking a hint from this, as well as from opinions such as Chorley's; but surely no singer had ever been portrayed in Britain in such extreme terms. Forster was collapsing the fictional into the real – a process which, as we shall see, was central to the mythologizing of Lind. Certainly the melodramatic nature of the roles of Alice and Amina facilitated this view, for both are heroines of exemplary virtue who bring about the Manichaean triumph of Good-ness; but Forster made it clear that neither this, nor Lind's superlative performances, could fully explain her saint-like character: this went beyond stage performance and was seen as emanating from within her. It was the first assertion of Lind's virtual sanctification, which would last well into the twentieth century.

But behind this lies an intriguing point. Whereas other reviewers, however enthusiastic, had discussed Lind's performances at length, only Forster had discerned this saintliness. The explanation for this lies in the bitter politics of the London opera world. After nearly a century and a half as the only home of Italian opera in London, Her Majesty's Theatre, directed by Benjamin Lumley, was facing enormous competition from the newly established Royal Italian Opera company at Covent Garden, which had opened barely a month earlier, with the great soprano Giulia Grisi as the jewel in its crown. Lumley had a personal as well as a commercial reason to seek the downfall of this rival camp: Grisi and other key figures – above all Fanny Persiani, the soprano who had created the eponymous part of *Lucia di Lammermoor* and other major roles, and the tenor Giovanni Matteo Mario, widely regarded as Giovanni Battista Rubini's successor – had performed at Her Majesty's until their recent well-publi-cised secession to Covent Garden. Of this company, described as 'a set of the finest singers ... the world ever heard',[9] only the astonishing bass Luigi

---

8 'One feels as she makes her appearance on the stage, that she is a pure vessel, from which a holy draught is presented to us ... Through Jenny Lind, I first became sensible of the holiness there is in art: through her I learned that one must forget oneself in the service of the Supreme.' Hans Christian Andersen, *The True Story of My Life* (London: Longmans & Co., 1847), pp. 202–4. Andersen's translator, Mary Howitt, dedicated the volume 'To Jenny Lind ... in admiration of her beautiful talents and still more beautiful life'. Howitt's words seconded Forster's picture of Lind. Though the translation was not published until after Forster's initial reviews (Howitt's preface is dated 26 June 1847), he could well have been given advance information by such a committed supporter of both Andersen and Lind. Lind's daughter hinted that Andersen vainly hoped to form a relationship with Lind (see Mrs Raymond Maude, *The Life of Jenny Lind* (London: Cassell, 1926), pp. 25–27); if true, this would suggest another motivation for his adulatory comments.

9 *Musical World*, 19 (18 Apr. 1844), p. 13.

Lablache had remained with Lumley. The manager was relying on the appeal of Lind as a fresh new star to entice audiences, just as he first hoped that Mendelssohn would provide an extra draw by supplying a new opera based on *The Tempest* with Lind as the prima donna, and then, after that fell flat, he relied on the premiere of Verdi's *I masnadieri* to re-establish his theatre's fortunes.

The stakes were indeed high. Even allowing for exaggeration, Emanuele Muzio, Verdi's factotum, may not have been far wrong when he said that by the end of Lind's first season Lumley's takings would equal the income of an entire small Italian state.[10] In the modern marketing sense, Forster was promoting Lind's image. But his columns were recognized as the mouthpiece of Her Majesty's Theatre and he himself was nicknamed 'Jenkins' by his disparagers amongst London music journalists. The musical press was deeply divided by recent events. The *Musical World*, which had already poured scorn on 'the hyperbolical and fawning Jenkins' (easily identified by 'the regard of blank stupidity, which is his characteristic', and ever ready to extol Her Majesty's Theatre 'in return for his nightly boxes' – an insinuation, if not of outright bribery, at least of a quid pro quo),[11] criticized Lumley and Lind while praising Grisi and her colleagues in terms that made the reviews of Charles Gruneisen, critic of the *Morning Post*, appear models of restraint, despite the fact that he had a vested interest in the Covent Garden company and therefore portrayed it to best advantage. Chorley asserted the *Athenaeum*'s impartiality by continuing to admire Grisi while often, though not always, praising Lind, and castigating Lumley for his exploitation of the star system. *Punch*'s contributors had previously held 'Jenkins's' verbose style up to ridicule, but ceased these attacks when they themselves chose to support the Nightingale. The *Illustrated London News* seems to have had two music critics on its staff, one a supporter of Lind and Her Majesty's, the other of the Royal Italian Opera company. Of these two protagonists – possibly Hogarth and

---

10 See Muzio's letter dated 4 June 1847 to Antonio Barezzi in *Giuseppe Verdi nelle lettere di Emanuele Muzio ad Antonio Barezzi*, ed. Luigi Agostino Garibaldi (Milan: Fratelli Treves, 1931), p. 325. Muzio stated that Lumley's predicted income would be six million francs, or £240 000, at the then current exchange rate of 25 francs to the pound sterling (see the *Illustrated London News*, 10 (23 Jan. 1847), p. 54). To put this figure into perspective, in 1846 the income of the Duchy of Cornwall was £50 395, expenditure £44 921, and balance £5474; for the Duchy of Lancaster, the income was £40 915, expenditure £34 527, and balance £6388 (*The Times*, 27 July 1847, p. 3). Meanwhile, in 1847 'the usual Board Wages of Servants' were 12s. or 13s. per week (*Illustrated London News*, 10 (1 May 1847), p. 278), and in 1848 the average annual income of a government clerk was about £300 (*Morning Chronicle*, 23 Feb. 1848, p. 3).

11 *Musical World*, 19 (22 Aug. 1844), pp. 275, 277–78. Personal enmity had flared over Sterndale Bennett's unsuccessful attempt to be appointed Reid Professor at Edinburgh University in 1844 (J.W. Davison strongly supported his candidature).

Gruneisen – the former was more powerful, as is reflected in the size and scope of the reviews and illustrations favouring Lind and her camp.[12]

It may have been simply an aggrieved member of the public who wrote to *The Times* under the pseudonym 'Democritus' protesting that calls for a testimonial 'in token of ... admiration of this lady's talents as a singer and purity as a woman', as appreciation that she 'has made 5,000*l*. this season, and not violated propriety in the course of the entire two months she has passed in London', were blatant propaganda.[13] But clearly there was some substance to the claim that such adulation of Lind was not driven solely by aesthetic appreciation. In the event she received a massively expensive statue from Lumley – nearly three feet of solid silver, topped with the figure of Genius. Its description in *The Art-Union* was clearly the work of a Lind–Lumley supporter. The statue was not only 'perhaps the purest work of Art of its class that has ever been produced in England' but also 'one of the many proofs received by the accomplished lady that her estimable character and high moral worth, as well as her lofty genius, have been appreciated in England'. After referring to 'the cordiality of the English people' and Lumley's 'continued courtesy and liberality', the author concluded with the hope that this 'liberal gift' would 'induce her again to visit a country to which she expresses herself fervently and gratefully attached'.[14]

Experienced theatre people such as the actor William Macready and his friend Charles Dickens would have been well aware of what lay behind such grandiose gestures. Deeply versed in the politics of the London theatre and implacable enemies of Lind's adversary Alfred Bunn, both were so enthusiastic about the Nightingale as to visit her on the morning after her

---

12 As an example of the attitude of the *Musical World* towards Lind and her advocates, see its response (22 (31 July 1847), p. 491) to Hans Christian Andersen's claim that Mendelssohn had said to him 'There will not in a whole century ... be born another being so gifted as she' (*The True Story of My Life*, p. 202): 'We need scarcely say that Mendelssohn (upon whom it has become the fashion to father all sorts of unimaginable absurdities) never could or did utter anything so ludicrously wide of the truth. Mr. Hans Andersen, the "Danish Poet" (*romancer* would be better) ought to be ashamed of himself thus to trifle with the name of the most renowned composer of his age.' The most balanced view of the conflict between the rival companies came from 'Morgan Rattler' (i.e. Percival Weldon Banks) in his retrospective article 'Of the Two Italian Operas', *Fraser's Magazine*, 35 (Jan.–June 1847), pp. 728–38. *Punch*'s items on Lind were probably written by one or more members of the team of Douglas Jerrold, Mark Lemon and Gilbert à Beckett. I am grateful to Dr Leanne Langley for identifying Gruneisen as, possibly, the pro-Covent Garden critic of the *Illustrated London News* and for other observations concerning the London musical press.
13 *The Times*, 25 June 1847, p. 8. 'Democritus' continued: 'Should we not have [a testimonial] to Prince Albert, to reward him for marrying our queen and refraining from outraging public decency?'
14 *Art-Union*, 9 (1 Sept. 1847), p. 334. The statue was also described and illustrated in the *Illustrated London News*, 11 (1 Sept. 1847), p. 176.

debut, and they later met her socially.[15] Queen Victoria knew of the operatic infighting from her singing teacher Lablache, but it did not prevent
her from being one of Lind's most committed admirers, to the point of
ordering a State Visit to her performance of *Norma*, which she found
enthralling.[16] Within a short span of time, such was the momentum of the
Lind image that, in Henry Chorley's words, 'Mdlle. Lind's character stands
high before the curtain for delicacy, modesty, an innocent undervaluation
of her own genius – in short, for goodness unprecedented.'[17]

As we have seen, some of this perception could be traced back to
reports emanating from Germany, including Chorley's own earlier
comments. But Rumsey Forster had done his work well. At breakneck
speed and with unerring judgement he had defined the image of Lind in
terms of the essential desiderata of bourgeois Victorian womanhood:
saint-like purity allied to attributes such as serenity and sensibility.

Forster's key strategy in creating this image was to define Lind in opposition to Grisi, focusing on the core issue of 'purity' versus sexual immo-
rality where theatrical women were concerned. The example of John
Ruskin's mother is telling: he was refused permission to invite Jenny Lind
for supper, clearly on the assumption that women of her profession must
be of dubious morals.[18] Yet Lind had apparently led a blameless life,
whereas it was well known that Grisi had been married, that a duel had
been fought over her, that she had separated from her husband, and was
now living with Mario, with whom she had had a child.[19] Other voices
took up the cause. Within months of Lind's arrival an anonymous
pamphlet portrayed her as the moral saviour of the theatre, in contrast to

---

15 See Dickens's letter to Miss Burdett Coutts of, probably, 26 May 1847, in *The Letters of
Charles Dickens*, vol. 5, pp. 71–72, including the reference to the dinner party given for Lind
by Macready on 30 May 1847 at which Dickens and his wife Catherine were present.
16 See the entry for 6 May 1847 in Queen Victoria's Journal, the Royal Archives, Windsor
Castle (hereafter RA VIC/QVJ) regarding Lablache's support for Lind and his opinion that
Lumley's 'awkwardness & mismanagement' were the cause of the recent operatic upheavals.
Queen Victoria and Prince Albert attended Lind's debut on 4 May and numerous
performances thereafter. Following the State Visit to *Norma* on 15 June the Queen noted
that 'Jenny Lind's acting & singing exceeded all I have ever heard' (RA VIC/QVJ/1847: 15
June). Quotations from RA VIC/QVJ are by permission of Her Majesty Queen Elizabeth II.
17 *Athenaeum*, no. 1050 (11 Dec. 1847), p. 1279.
18 See *The Works of John Ruskin*, ed. E.T. Cook and Alexander Wedderburn, 39 vols
(London: G. Allen, 1903–12), vol. 1, p. xlvii. Ruskin's mother seems to have been more
concerned than his father, gauging from Ruskin's remark in his letter to his father probably
of 31 January 1849 that 'my mother ... was horrified' at the thought of social contact with
Lind, for 'she seems to look upon her just as on an ordinary actress' (*The Works of John
Ruskin*, vol. 36, p. 93).
19 There is no indication in RA VIC/QVJ that Queen Victoria was disturbed by this. Grisi
had, of course, long been her favourite until the arrival of Lind, and the Queen praised Grisi
in later years (see RA VIC/QVJ/1850: 11 April; RA VIC/QVJ/1857: 6 June).

women 'whose lives were passed in open and notorious sin of the blackest and most offensive nature – when their lovers of the stage were their paramours of the boudoir': targets that obviously included Grisi, she who portrayed Norma as 'black, swarthy, and savage'.[20]

Polemics about sexual morality went side by side with a geographic-ethnic factor. Andrew Winter, a contributor to the periodical the *People's Journal*, pressed into service Lind's German style of acting, more restrained than the Italian. He insisted that 'the character of her acting partakes of all the qualities which mark the differences between the northern and southern races. Simple, pure, and earnest, her passions assume not the vehement tone of Grisi, but they are none the less intense.' Again, Lind's performance was being read as an index of her moral character, its distinguishing features now defined as exclusive to the northern race – doubtless comfortably including Britain. He went so far as to describe Lind, the well-known Swede, as 'our ideal of the Teutonic maid. She is the loving, earnest creature, German authors so delight in depicting.'[21] It is a clear example of the well-known phenomenon of Germanophilia, in this case doubly validating Lind by identifying her supposed racial characteristics with German literature. But let us remember that this was also a time of cultural awareness of Scandinavia. One of Chorley's first reactions to Lind had been to see her as an example of Nordic culture,[22] while her own Swedish songs reinforced this. The Lind persona was now located within a broad Germano-Nordicism, also, of course, predominantly Protestant, whereas the southerner was Catholic. If Grisi was definitively the Other, Lind could be made to embody familiar cultural values. Another author, Hargrave Jennings, reinforced this from a different perspective when he reported that Lind stayed encloistered at home, that she liked nothing better than tending her garden, and she dressed as simply as a shepherdess. These were, of course, the traditional credentials of pastoralism, but Jennings was making a further point; at a time of qualms

---

20 *A Review of the Performances of Mademoiselle Jenny Lind, during her Engagement at Her Majesty's Theatre and their Influence and Effect upon our National Drama; with a Notice of her Life* (London: J. & L. Dickinson, 1847), pp. 7, 25.

21 Andrew Winter, *People's Journal*, 3 (1847), pp. 317–18. The *People's Journal* appealed to the same intellectual constituency as the *Athenaeum*. Its other contributors included Mary Cowden Clarke, Chorley and Mary Howitt. Winter's phraseology recalls Chorley's allusion in October 1846 to Lind's 'simple and genial and earnest personality' (see above, n. 2).

22 See, for instance, Chorley's words in his first article on Lind (see above, n. 2): 'Will anyone understand me if I say, that there seems to me in Mdlle. Lind's art a touch of the same northern depth of feeling, combined with sweetness and elegance, as I find (with all its dignity) in Thorwaldsen's sculpture, and (with all their homeliness) in Frederika Bremer's novels, and (with all its voluptuousness) in Andersen's 'Improvisatore,' and (with all their unpretending simplicity) in the songs of Lindblad? If I have been tedious, it has been from a wish to illustrate the most interesting expression of this northern spirit in Art with which we have been yet visited' (p. 1075).

about the respectability of the professional woman, they would have been seen as additional proofs that, despite all the publicity attached to her, Lind herself happily subscribed to accepted social values.[23]

The author Rose Ellen Hendricks – and the fact that this was a woman suggests the extent to which women felt they could identify with the Lind persona – took the Lind iconization a significant step further when she wrote a novel that used the plot of La figlia del regimento, another of Lind's successful roles, as a springboard to moralize on a range of issues – acceptance of socially tainted motherhood, the morally ambiguous position of an oriental courtesan, the perverted religion of a Roman Catholic priest. Significantly, the impeccable heroine of the opera, Maria, is renamed 'Jenny Lind', and indeed this is the title of the novel: Jenny Lind. Clearly we have here another example of the practice of utilizing the demonized features of various cultural Others (fallen women, diabolical Catholics) as a means of constructing the Lind persona. Beyond this, however, we are faced by an astonishing confusion of the fictional and real Lind that far exceeds that promoted by Foster in the Morning Post. The eponymous character explains that the soldier Suplizio (another role, of course, in the opera) 'gave me the Swedish name of Jenny Lind, in memory of a favourite deceased sister'. The heroine of George Sand's recent novel Consuelo had been inspired by the soprano Pauline Viardot-Garcia, but this publishing of a fiction under the name of a living musician may well be unique. The iconic figure has achieved totally independent existence as a collection of signifiers; the name 'Jenny Lind' has become a metonym for a whole complex of ideological desiderata.[24]

How far Lind herself colluded in the process of mythologization may be inferred from a statement she sent to a Swedish newspaper following a

---

23 Hargrave Jennings, 'Sketch of the Life of Jenny Lind', People's Journal, 4 (1848), p. 131. Compare Hans Christian Andersen's assertion that 'a peaceful, quiet home, is the object of her thoughts' (The True Story of My Life, p. 203). Charlotte Brontë, deeply concerned about publicity for women, recommended Lind as a role model: 'I believe that, for a woman [publicity] is degrading if it is not glorious. If I could not be a Lind – I would not be a singer' (letter to W.S. Williams dated 19 December 1849, in The Letters of Charlotte Brontë, ed. Margaret Smith (Oxford: Clarendon Press, 1995–), vol. 2, p. 312).

24 Jenny Lind: a Tale, 2 vols (London: E. Churlton, 1848). The novel's dedication makes clear its debt to the opera. The full explanation of the naming of the heroine is as follows (vol. 1, p. 37): '"I am the Daughter of the Regiment," began the singular girl; "the 21st Regiment of the Grand Army of Napoleon has adopted me ... Suplizio ... called me his child, and gave me the Swedish name of Jenny Lind, in memory of a favourite deceased sister ... [p. 97] she has been dead for many years".' The courtesan is Greek (here deemed oriental) and is seduced by a married aristocrat. The demonization of a Roman Catholic priest brings to mind Lewis's famous gothic novel The Monk. The priest is shown as guilty of perverting religion for his own ends. All three – the Greek mistress, her keeper and the priest – meet their deaths. Sand's novel, in which Haydn and Porpora appear, was published in 1843.

row at the Berlin Opera three years earlier. In order to exonerate herself, Lind cast herself as a real-life melodramatic heroine: 'I am a poor, sensitive, lonely girl, in a foreign land, surrounded by cabals and intrigues.'[25] If she attempted to manipulate public opinion here, surely she would barely have refrained from doing so in London.

Lind's decision to withdraw from opera in 1849, widely perceived as the result of deepening qualms born of a highly moral and religious nature, and as being influenced by the views of the Bishop of Norwich, an opponent of the theatre, added the element of piety to her persona. In particular, the anti-theatre public could now see her as a glowing convert to their cause.[26] This aura of chaste piety was enhanced by the well-publicized charity concerts which she had already begun. The combination of piety and charity was further strengthened when, in the case of *Elijah*, her oratorio performances combined Protestant fervour with a lament for the revered Mendelssohn, whose support for Lind had been well known. It was a perception with which an astute politician such as Disraeli was happy to associate himself. Couched in powerful rhetoric, the speech he gave in 1849, recalling Lind's charity concert for the Brompton Hospital for Consumption the previous year, encapsulates these features of the Lind icon:

> I look upon the conduct of this lady as one of the most remarkable features of the age we live in. I know nothing in classic story, or in those feudal epochs when we are taught that the individual was more

---

25 See Lind's letter to Lars Hierta dated Berlin, 25 November 1844, quoted in Henry Scott Holland and W.S. Rockstro, *Memoir of Madame Jenny Lind-Goldschmidt: Her Early Art-life and Dramatic Career, 1820–1851*, 2 vols (London: John Murray, 1891) (hereafter Holland and Rockstro), vol. 1, pp. 207–209. The row concerned the allocation of the main soprano role in the premiere of Meyerbeer's new opera *Ein Feldlager in Schlesien* to Leopoldine Tuczek, the resident prima donna.

26 See *Punch*, 16 (1849), p. 68. Lind became a close friend of Bishop Stanley's family. Privately she had contemplated leaving the theatre for some years: see, for instance, her letter to her Berlin friend Amalia Wichmann dated 4 July 1846 in *The Lost Letters of Jenny Lind*, translated from the German and edited with commentaries by W. Porter Ware and Thaddeus C. Lockard, Jr. (London: Victor Gollancz, 1966) (hereafter Porter Ware and Lockard), p. 34. The value placed upon female piety is clear from J.W. Lake's recently published poetic vision of the ideal woman, predicated on the view that 'the utmost of a woman's character is contained in domestic life; first, her piety towards God; and next, in the duties of a daughter, a wife, a mother, and a sister' (*London Literary and Musical Observer*, no. 6 (29 Apr. 1848), p. 94). The issue was heightened by awareness that Lind had not withdrawn from opera in order, for example, to acquiesce in the wishes of a prospective husband, for at this same period she broke off an engagement to marry a Captain Harris, who had insisted that she should cease all connections with the theatre. Both her marriage plans and the breaking of her engagement were reported in the press (see *Punch*, 16 (1849), pp. 78, 81, 219, and the *Morning Chronicle*, 21 May 1849, p. 4, which specified Harris's insistence). Her decision to leave the theatre threw Lumley and his supporters into consternation: see the first *Punch* article cited in this footnote, and Forster's discussion, focusing on Lind's 'religious scruples and moral objections', in the *Morning Post*, 30 Apr. 1849, p. 5.

influential, when character was more forcible – I know nothing to be compared with the career of this admirable woman. Why, gentlemen, it almost reaches the high ideal of human nature when we portray to ourselves a youthful maiden, innocent and benignant, in the possession of an unparalleled and omnipotent charm, alternately entrancing the heart of nations, and then kneeling at the tomb of suffering, of calamity, and of care ...

And, gentlemen, I, for one, honour Jenny Lind above all things, because she has shown that she comprehends her position, and that a great artist, sustained by virtue, upheld by self-respect, and full of the magnificence of her mission, ranks in the highest class of human beings and human benefactors.[27]

The process of romantic sanctification was only intensified by Lind's death. If her performances at Her Majesty's had become enshrined in nostalgic memory, her later life, encompassing all the values of domesticity and motherhood, let alone an intense religiosity, and overlapping with the public vision of Queen Victoria, was of no less powerful appeal. The earliest posthumous biography of Lind put the finishing touches to the myth whose construction was begun forty years earlier. The names of the well-known musician W.S. Rockstro and Canon Holland of St Paul's Cathedral would swiftly have occurred to Otto Goldschmidt, Lind's husband, when he selected her biographers. They combined the required musical and personal adulation with the social status that would give their work the stamp of authority. Dedicated to Queen Victoria, their quasi-official biography, *Memoir of Madame Jenny Lind-Goldschmidt: Her Early Art-life and Dramatic Career, 1820–1851*, was published in 1891, four years after Lind's death.

The extent to which Holland and Rockstro carried forward the cultural tropes noted earlier is a sign of how firmly embedded these had become. Holland and Rockstro's rhetoric exceeded even Rumsey Forster's. They portray the young Lind traversing a perilous path 'in the security of the pure in heart, with such sure feet as those with which, on Raphael's canvas, St Margaret passes, without an effort, or a fear, in maiden gentleness, over the writhing Dragon and through the gate of Hell'. Later, the role of Alice in *Roberto il diavolo*, in which she made her London debut, 'drew on her own vivid personality, with its intensity of faith, with its horror of sin, with its passionate and chivalrous purity'. In sum, throughout her life she 'retained, without even an effort, all her inherent and native simplicity, her freshness, her undaunted sincerity ... Swept up, in the

---

27 Holland and Rockstro, vol. 2, pp. 232–33.

sudden rush of an overwhelming success, out of obscurity into the company and friendship of princes and kings, this girl, in her simple-hearted virginity, kept a conscience as true and fine as steel. No illusion bewildered her: no worldly splendour ever succeeded in beguiling her.' These iconic elements are overlaid with the Lisztian Romantic ideology, so easily linked to the Parable of the Talents, that the Artist was at the service of God and Man: Lind's was a 'divine endowment', and she perceived the use of her abilities as a 'holy privilege'.[28]

But Holland and Rockstro had to deal with an unpleasant truth that threatened to undermine this sanctification. In order to begin her triumphant career at Her Majesty's Theatre, Lind had broken a previous contract to sing at Bunn's less prestigious and certainly less lucrative Drury Lane Theatre. Mendelssohn had helped draw up her new contract with Lumley, by which, for her first season alone, she received what must have been one of the highest fees ever paid to any soprano: the massive sum of £4800 plus valuable extras in kind – probably more than three and a half times as much as she would have gained from Bunn's contract, and over a third more than Lumley had paid Grisi at Covent Garden.[29] Bunn took Lind to court and she lost the case, which was reported at length in

---

28 Ibid., vol. 1, pp. 47–48, 58, 81, 99. Lind's tour in America, largely organized by the renowned impresario P.J. Barnum, and during which she married her accompanist Goldschmidt, was portrayed as one more opportunity to discharge this sacred responsibility.

29 Lind's contract with Bunn stipulated that she would give a total of twenty performances of Vielka in The Camp of Silesia (an adaptation of Ein Feldlager in Schlesien) and, should Bunn require it, Amina in La Sonnambula, inclusive. She would receive 50 louis d'or, or approximately £40, per performance, plus half of the receipts of a benefit performance (Holland and Rockstro, vol. 1, pp. 234–35). Lind would therefore have received about £800 for the twenty contractual performances. Given that in 1833 Malibran received £1000 from, apparently, the full receipts of a benefit performance under the terms of her contract with Bunn (ibid., p. 235), Lind might have received £500 from her benefit, which would have brought her total sum to approximately £1300. (Bunn paid Malibran £80 per performance, twice his offer to Lind.) On 21 November 1846 Lumley wrote to Mendelssohn reporting that he told Lind that Grisi received 80 000 francs and that 'I will give you the same, or even more', and that he would compensate Lind for loss of earnings caused by her wish not to accept payment for concerts (ibid., vol. 2, p. 12). On the basis of 25 francs to the £ (see n. 10), this means Grisi was receiving £3200. To this she would have added the income from concerts, estimated by Lumley at 20 000 francs, i.e. £800. Thus Lumley was paying Lind the total of £4000 Grisi earned, plus a further £800, let alone supplying a house and horse and carriage. Mendelssohn ensured that Lind's contract allowed her to sing at concerts ordered by Queen Victoria, and at private parties where she might receive a cadeau (ibid., vol. 2, pp. 8–9, 13). Also, at this stage there was still the possibility of creating the soprano role in Mendelssohn's projected opera. Mendelssohn alluded to this in his letter to Lind of 12 October 1846 (ibid., vol. 1, p. 433). Had the opera come about, it would have been a wonderful coup for Lind.

the press.[30] The aggrieved manager, whose tenure of Drury Lane had now been brought to an end, largely, he claimed, owing to Lind's actions, published his own seventy-three-page account of the saga, accusing 'the innocent, the simple, the friendless, and unprotected Jenny', that 'dear, unsophisticated creature', of being, in reality, totally 'adept in worldly ways'. Bunn was attempting to puncture Lind's iconic reputation, focusing on the tendency to bestow upon her the status of an operatic heroine. Indeed, he used this very term.[31] No one knew the genre better than he; also a librettist, he had created several such ideal women, including the classic example in Balfe's *The Bohemian Girl*.

We have seen that when Lind had been embroiled in a dispute at the Berlin Opera she had evoked this very image of a virtuous melodramatic heroine caught in a web of intrigue. Now, in the letters she exchanged with Bunn in attempting to extricate herself from the contract, she relied fundamentally on the same approach. The correspondence was read aloud in court when the case was heard at the Court of Queen's Bench, Guildhall, London, in February 1848, after delays for which each side blamed the other. The letters constituted the only direct statements heard from the plaintiff and defendant, for neither was called to give evidence, and Lind was not even in the country.

Lind first pleaded that she could not comply with the contract on the flimsy grounds that she was unable to learn English adequately (operas were translated into English at Drury Lane), that she needed to rest, and that the contract was not binding because her Swedish guardian had not given his prior agreement. She then strove to overwrite the professional basis of the case with a personal appeal. Bunn, who was 'entitle[d] to my gratitude and my highest esteem', would act 'not as a *directeur*, but as a gentleman *par excellence*', just as she, incapable of 'chicanery', was not to be judged as any other soprano: she had neither 'the personal advantages, nor the assurance, nor the charlatanism of the other prima donnas' ('I

---

30   See, for instance, the account of the court proceedings in *The Times*, 23 Feb. 1848, pp. 7–8. The development of the case, prior to coming to court, had also been extensively reported. For reports during 1847 see, for example *The Times*, 15 June, p. 7; 17 June, p. 8; 18 June, p. 7; 3 Sept., p. 7; 16 Sept., p. 6; 25 Oct., p. 7; 4 Dec., p. 8; 22 Dec., p. 8; and during 1848, 4 Feb., p. 7. For the recollections (of doubtful reliability) of the case of the librettist Edward Fitzball, who gave evidence, see his *Thirty-five Years of a Dramatic Author's Life*, 2 vols (London: T.C. Newby, 1859), vol. 2, pp. 239–42. Regarding the influence of the case on the subsequent legal proceedings of *Lumley* v *Gye* (1853), see S.M. Waddams, 'Johanna Wagner and the rival Opera Houses', *Law Quarterly Review*, 117 (2001), pp. 431–58 (pp. 445, 447–48).

31   Alfred Bunn, *The Case of Bunn versus Lind, Tried at the Court of Queen's Bench ... February 22nd, 1848 ...* (London: W.S. Johnson, 1848) (hereafter *Bunn versus Lind*), pp. 72–73. See p. 73 for Bunn's reference to 'the lady who is the heroine of [the case]'.

think that slap in the face of "other prima donnas" might well have been spared', Bunn's lawyer observed wryly in court: 'I wonder what Grisi would say if she heard it'). As for signing the contract, she claimed she had been 'persuaded, not to say surprised, into a step so contrary to my interests' by Meyerbeer, who stood to gain from her appearing in an English version of his opera *Ein Feldlager in Schlesien*. But now Meyerbeer had apparently abandoned this plan and with it Lind herself, leaving her 'in the most isolated position', with 'no other resource than to beg you ... to disengage me from an unconsidered promise'.

All this was dismissed by Bunn as 'downright hypocrisy ... in the garb of *naiveté*'. Not only was there 'no more honourable man in existence' than Meyerbeer, but also he had negotiated the contract on Lind's behalf with every care for her 'proper remuneration and professional protection'. According to Bunn, Lind was transparently trying to divert attention from a professional transaction so that she could take up a better contract at Her Majesty's Theatre.[32]

But if Lind's version of events had no effect on Bunn, the emotive power of her plea was not lost on Sir Frederick Thesiger, the then Attorney General and by far the most unscrupulous of the lawyers in the court, who led her defence team. Issues of contract law, comparisons with Lind's illustrious predecessor Malibran, and barbed comments about the rivalry between Her Majesty's Theatre and the Royal Italian Opera at Covent Garden were all raised, but Thesiger's most extraordinary ploy was to portray Lind as an abandoned, persecuted heroine, basing his material on her own words. Even Bunn's counsel, who had foreseen attempts to play on Lind's gender and personal charisma,[33] seems to have been caught unawares by the extent to which Thesiger exploited this theme. Lind, he repeatedly claimed, was an orphan: 'a young person, fatherless and motherless ... a young person, without parents'; she was of tender 'age and inexperience', 'unacquainted with the ways of the world', yet nonetheless imbued with an unsurpassable sense of fairness and candour in her dealings with Bunn. Thesiger identified Bunn as the culpable party – predictably, since he was the plaintiff. Bunn had probably misled Lind about the London operatic world, Thesiger insisted, and had then so pressed her that she had overlooked the ridicule to which she could be exposed by 'her ignorance of the language and of the country, where she was unknown and where she had no protector' – and had signed the contract. It was this fear

---

32 For the above quotations see *Bunn versus Lind*, pp. 6, 7, 9, 11. Inexplicably, on 13 February 1847, only shortly before the court case was heard, Lind had asserted to Amalia Wichmann (see above, n. 26) that Bunn had threatened her with imprisonment if she arrived in London while his contract was still in force (Porter Ware and Lockard, p. 47).

33 *Bunn versus Lind*, pp. 19–20, 28.

of a professional debacle, he maintained, that was her 'just excuse' for with-
drawing from the agreement. But Bunn 'stands upon the letter of the law,
and asks for his bond, and what by law he is entitled to'.[34] The allusion to
Shylock was as far as Thesiger could go in vilifying Bunn in court. He had
good reason not to refer to Meyerbeer's involvement, for it was essential
to his case to draw a veil over the actual events surrounding the drawing
up and signing of the contract.

It was a farcical argument. Yet Thesiger clearly considered the effect this
fictional representation of Lind would have on the susceptibilities of the jury
to be of major importance in limiting the damages that would inevitably be
awarded against her. In this he was not mistaken. Whereas Bunn had
claimed £10 000, the jury awarded £2500, not so much more than the £2000
Lind had earlier offered for an annulment of the contract.[35] In due course,
Holland and Rockstro, though they passed over the blatant lie that Lind was
an orphan (both her parents had been very much alive), built upon Thesiger's
ploy in order to exonerate Lind from any taint of guilt and restore her saintly
image in their readers' minds. Heightened prose was used to amplify yet
further the emotional power of her imagined plight. Our heroine 'stood in
urgent need of an experienced and impartial adviser, but where was she to
look for one? She stood alone. A mere child, whose interest was pitted
against that of one of the most acute and enterprising speculators in the then
theatrical world.' Unable to 'guard herself against the brutalities of manag-
ers', the bewildered Jenny signs the fatal document, 'trapped into the engagement before she knew what she was doing'. Such dramatization of the fateful
moment cannot but bring to mind the Act II finale of *Lucia di Lammermoor*,
which Lind had performed to great acclaim. Bunn is cast as the full-blown
melodramatic villain. Darkly we learn that 'no one knew better than he how
… to tempt an aspiring *debutante*' ('vile seducer: how many poor girls has he
ruined?' we are surely invited to wonder). Once the evil deed has been done
he is full of 'vulgar insolence'.[36]

---

34   Ibid., pp. 54, 58, 59, 61, 62, 65; *The Times*, 23 Feb. 1848, p. 8.
35   For Lind's prior offer, see *Bunn versus Lind*, p. 17. Bunn was convinced that Lumley had
agreed to pay the damages. In court Lind's solicitor, who, significantly, was also Lumley's
solicitor, denied this, but in fact Lumley had already promised Lind in writing that he would
do so. It is highly probable that he also paid for Lind's legal representation. Conversely,
Lumley claimed that Bunn was in a business relationship with the management of the Royal
Italian Opera (*Bunn versus Lind*, pp. 13, 33, 71–72; Holland and Rockstro, vol. 2, p. 29;
Benjamin Lumley, *Reminiscences of the Opera* (London: Hurst & Blackett, 1864), pp. 177,
209). On 15 April 1848 Thesiger sought to reduce the damages still further, calling for a new
trial on the grounds that those awarded were excessive. He now also pleaded that Lind had
been 'in ill health' as another excuse for her breaking the contract (*The Times*, 17 Apr. 1848,
p. 7). His application was rejected.
36   Holland and Rockstro, vol. 1, pp. 228–29; vol. 2, p. 199.

Again in the history of the Lind icon a complete fantasy was being propagated to great effect. Clearly Rockstro, who wrote this section, hoped sympathy for Lind, depicted as an innocent female in the scheming world of the theatre, would overwhelm the reader into naively accepting his version of events. But Lind was no novice: she had dealt with contracts throughout the seven years of her professional career. Moreover, she was never short of powerful protectors and advisers.

Lind later shifted responsibility for persuading her to sign the contract mainly to Lord Westmorland, the British ambassador in Berlin in whose opera box the contract was signed. Rockstro finessed this with a weak excuse: Westmorland, the highly placed diplomat and an important member of London musical society, was presented as being 'as ignorant of managerial business and managerial terms as she was, and ... an absolute stranger to the manifold intrigues which seem to be inseparable from the destiny of a "Child of Drama"'. Then, in no more than a footnote, Rockstro switched the blame again: 'The moving spirit was undoubtedly Meyerbeer.'[37]

Rockstro knew full well that Lind had initially identified Meyerbeer as responsible. What, then, motivated him almost to airbrush the composer out of the account and yet still insinuate it was he who pressurized Lind against her better interests? Partly, of course, Rockstro was following Thesiger's example in concentrating his attack on Bunn, thus diverting attention from inconvenient details; but once again we must also ask how the Lind iconization was being used to serve a personal agenda. Elsewhere, Holland and Rockstro constantly point to Mendelssohn, beloved teacher of both Rockstro and Otto Goldschmidt, as Lind's guardian angel. Plainly, however, Lind's mentor at the time was not Mendelssohn but his enemy Meyerbeer; and Meyerbeer's greatest English patrons were Lord and Lady Westmorland.[38] This would certainly explain why Rockstro left carefully worded implications about Westmorland's judgement and Meyerbeer's culpability.

The uniqueness and durability of Lind's place in the history of the British reception of musicians was dependent on the histories of the bourgeois values that were projected onto her persona – the values of female purity and matronly domesticity, the latter a feature that Holland and

---

37 Ibid., vol. 1, pp. 230–34.
38 Lady Westmorland retained a strong affection for Meyerbeer as a friend and was deeply saddened when he died. See her letter to Pauline, Countess of Neale dated London, 4 May 1864 (two days after Meyerbeer's death) in the MSS collection *Letters and papers of Lady Rose Weigall, her husband, the painter, Henry Weigall, and of her parents, Priscilla, Countess of Westmorland, and niece of the Duke of Wellington, and John, 11th Earl of Westmorland, a diplomat,* Centre for Kentish Studies, Maidstone, Kent.

Rockstro could add when they turned to her later life; Germano-Nordicism; and the concept of the outstanding professional female singer as a genius endowed with a divine vocation. Her musical declaiming of the Protestant creed in oratorio and her settling in England contributed to the ongoing re-formations of British national identity. That there was a strong racial element in this is evident from the now stunning remark of another late biographer, H. Sutherland Edwards, that because Lind 'had nothing Southern or Oriental in her nature[,] she cannot, ... like the Grisis, the Pastas, the Garcias, and ... Rossini, be claimed as of Jewish race'.[39]

Today we would repudiate at least some of the deep-seated cultural factors that constituted the Lind icon. Nevertheless, this myth continues to hold sway. We still encounter something akin to adoration in Porter Ware and Lockard's comments in their 1966 edition of Lind correspondence. It is even more sobering to find the pro-German, pro-Mendelssohn, anti-French, anti-Meyerbeer underpinning of the Lind idealization discussed here being replicated in Joan Bulman's biography of 1956. Since then Dahlhaus has merely alluded to the Lind cult without critically commenting on what generated it.[40] What the iconization of Lind demonstrates, above all, is that further work on operatic subjects in nineteenth-century Britain (and indeed elsewhere) needs to be alert to the ideological factors, theatrical politics, and other vested interests that shaped the sources to which we turn for our understanding of the past.

---

39 H. Sutherland Edwards, *The Prima Donna: Her History and Surroundings from the Seventeenth to the Nineteenth Century* (London: Remington & Co., 1888), p. 36. Sutherland Edwards now named six Jews she worked with: Meyerbeer, Moscheles, Mendelssohn, Lumley, Benedict and Otto Goldschmidt.

40 Porter Ware and Lockard; Joan Bulman, *Jenny Lind* (London: James Barrie, 1956); Carl Dahlhaus, *Nineteenth-Century Music*, trans. J. Bradford Robinson (Berkeley and Los Angeles: University of California Press, 1989), pp. 143, 184.

PART TWO
Church Music

CHAPTER FOUR

'Hark an awful voice is sounding'

Redefining the English Catholic Hymn Repertory: *The Westminster Hymnal* of 1912

Thomas Muir

The significance of *The Westminster Hymnal*

'Hark an awful voice is sounding' is a translation of the Latin hymn 'En clara vox redarguit' by Edward Caswall (1814–78). It is set to a tune by R.L. De Pearsall (1795–1856) and is the opening item of *The Westminster Hymnal*, first published in 1912 by R. and T. Washbourne, London.[1] The title page proclaims the volume to be 'the only collection authorised by the hierarchy of England and Wales'.[2] It was intended to impose new and uniform standards on Catholic hymn singing, which at that time had a poor reputation. So the choice of such a hymn at the beginning of the collection showed a shrewd disregard for its ironic potential.[3]

Nevertheless *The Westminster Hymnal*, precisely because it was official, exerted enormous influence on English Catholics. It ran through

---

1 Abbreviated as *WH*. References are by number unless a page is cited. Other abbreviations are as follows: *PH: The Parochial Hymn Book, Containing Prayers and Devotions for all the Faithful including Vespers, Compline and all Liturgical Hymns for the Year both in Latin and English* (London: Burns & Oates, repr. 1883 (date of original edition not supplied)). *EH: The English Hymnal*, ed. William Birkbeck, Percy Dearmer et al. (London: Oxford University Press, 1906). WDA: The Westminster Diocesan Archives.

2 However, James Britten states that one bishop had said that he never saw the collection until it appeared in print. Thus the phrase 'authorised by the hierarchy ...' 'I have good reason to believe was an unauthorised statement, or rather it was allowed by one of the five bishops who formed the committee' – almost certainly a reference to John Cuthbert Hedley, the committee chairman. James Britten, 'Letter to the Editor', 10 August 1912, in *The Tablet*, NS 88 (July–Dec. 1912), p. 222.

3 For instance, *The Tablet* in its review remarked that 'hitherto the efforts of our compilers and editors of Catholic hymns have not been very successful'. It went on to say that *The Westminster Hymnal* 'will be a collection almost beyond reproach and a musical setting which will satisfy the severest tests of scholarship' – an assertion it immediately undermined by subsequently identifying a number of shortcomings. Anon. review of *The Westminster Hymnal*, 26 June 1912, in *The Tablet*, NS 87 (Jan.–June 1912), p. 968. It should be noted that at that time, although always edited by laymen (in this case Ernest Oldshaw), *The Tablet* was owned by the Archbishop of Westminster.

numerous editions up till 1965, affecting the quality of singing and, just as importantly, through the sentiments expressed in its texts, the ideological mindset of the Catholic community.[4] This essay then looks at, first, the Catholic musical context in which it appeared; secondly, the functions it was expected to fulfil; thirdly, how the texts reflect the character of the English Catholic church at that time; and fourthly, the impact of Richard Runciman Terry (1865–1938). Throughout comparisons will be made with other Catholic hymnals. It will then be possible to measure how great a break *The Westminster Hymnal* made with its past and to assess what impact it had on congregational singing.

The Westminster Hymnal in its religious and musical context: 1849–1912

The Westminster Hymnal was one of several changes radically affecting the musical heritage of English Catholics early in the twentieth century. In 1903 Pope Pius X issued his famous 'Motu Proprio' decree asserting the primacy of Gregorian chant and, next to it, Renaissance polyphony.[5] More secular music, especially that of the 'Viennese School' headed by Mozart and Haydn, would be downgraded, if not excluded altogether.[6] The following year a second 'Motu Proprio' decree recommended Solesmes-style chant as revised by a special Vatican commission.[7]

These changes did not come out of the blue; for, as is well known, the Solesmes monks had been engaged in chant research for decades. Indeed, owing to French government persecution, they had just migrated temporarily to Appuldurcombe House on the Isle of Wight. Their fundamental premise, propounded by their founder Prosper Guéranger, of re-establishing connections between the contemporary church and its medieval past had particular resonance in England. Thus, just as Guéranger sought to bridge the comparatively narrow gulf created by the French Revolution, so

---

4   Except with the revision of 1940, a new 'edition' actually meant a reprinting. There is one exception, though. Unlike the first edition, subsequent reprints added an 'index of subjects' at the front.

5   Although usually referred to in this form, strictly speaking 'Motu Proprio' is the name of a type of papal document. Its true title, derived from the opening words, is 'Tra le sollecitudini'. Jan Michael Joncas, *From Sacred Song to Ritual Music* (Collegeville, Minn.: The Liturgical Press, 1997), pp. 1–2.

6   Pius X, trans. R. Terry, 'Motu Proprio', in *Music of the Roman Rite: a Manual for Choirmasters in English-Speaking Countries* (London: Burns, Oates & Washbourne Ltd., 1931), Appendix B, pp. 256–58.

7   Katherine Bergeron, *Decadent Enchantments: the Revival of Gregorian Chant at Solesmes* (Berkeley and Los Angeles: University of California Press, 1998), pp. 144–46.

English Catholics, especially members of the 'Downside Movement' headed by Edmund Ford and Aidan Gasquet, tried to cross a 250-year chasm between the Protestant Acts of Supremacy and Uniformity of 1559 and the Catholic Emancipation Act of 1829.[8] Inevitably the idea of recovering the past affected *The Westminster Hymnal*. Ford chaired the musical committee;[9] and it was Cardinal Vaughan, himself a Downside man, who had appointed Terry as music director at Westminster Cathedral. Indeed Vaughan had cherished schemes of having the Office chanted there by Downside monks based at Ealing or by Solesmes monks. Only when these schemes fell through did he accept a community of secular priests.[10] It should also be noted that versions of Gregorian chant had been sung by English Catholics throughout the recusant period – especially in the eighteenth and early nineteenth centuries.[11] Moreover the 1873 Westminster Synod had anticipated Pius X by calling for the restoration of the chant to its position of primacy. The text of this document was published and translated into English by none other than John Cuthbert Hedley (1837–1915), bishop of Newport, himself a Benedictine and chairman of the committee responsible for editing the text of *The Westminster Hymnal*.[12]

Reconnecting English Catholics with their cultural past also surfaced with the revival of Renaissance polyphony. In Germany this had been promoted by the Cecilian Society, founded in 1867, which was also active in England.[13] For instance, during the same period and earlier some Renaissance works were published by Novello.[14] Moreover from 1898 an enormous boost had been supplied by Terry's rediscovery, publication and performances of such works first at Downside, then at Westminster Cathedral.[15] In doing so he claimed that he was restoring to

---

8   Aidan Bellenger, OSB, 'The English Benedictines: the Search for a Monastic Identity, 1880–1920', *Monastic Studies: the Continuity of Tradition*, 1 (1920), 299–321.

9   Richard Terry, 'Musical Editor's Preface', in *WH*, p. xiii.

10   René Kollar, *Westminster Cathedral: From Dream to Reality* (Edinburgh: Faith and Life Publications Ltd., 1987), pp. 67–120.

11   See Bennett Zon, *The English Plainchant Revival* (Oxford: Oxford University Press, 1998), esp. pp. 9–47 for 'a general introduction to Post-Tridentine Liturgical Books in Europe'; pp. 72–103 for 'Plainchant in the English Catholic Church 1748–99'; pp. 104–40 for the contribution by John Francis Wade; pp. 169–215 for 'English Catholic Plainchant: the Beginning of the Nineteenth Century to the 1850s.'

12   Robert Guy, OSB, *The Synods in English, Being the Text of the Four Synods of Westminster, Translated into English* (Stratford on Avon: St Gregory's Press, 1886), pp. 185–95.

13   See, for example, the collection of bound volumes of Masses by Cecilian composers in the Ushaw College Music Room stamped with the signature of E. Bonney, choirmaster between 1898 and 1917.

14   Michael Hurd, *Vincent Novello – and Company* (London: Granada, 1981), pp. 28 and 69.

15   Hilda Andrews, *Westminster Retrospect: a Memoir of Sir Richard Terry* (London: Oxford University Press, 1948), pp. 34–41. 48–54, 61, 73–75, 83–89, 104–18.

English Catholics their cultural birthright.[16] Yet simultaneously he applied a particular twist. Up till then attention had been focused on Continental masters; so the revival of Renaissance polyphony amounted to a policy of bringing Roman values into England.[17] Terry, by drawing attention to English polyphonists, showed that composers like Tallis and Byrd were both English and part of an international Catholic scene. Roman and English native traditions were thus compatible. Such a revival would help bring English Catholics out of their insular backwater into the Catholic European mainstream.[18] It is no surprise, then, to see the same themes, albeit in different forms, appearing in *The Westminster Hymnal*, as will be shown.

The Westminster Hymnal thus appeared precisely at a time when a seismic shift was occurring in other areas of Catholic music. Its extent can be gauged by comparing publishers' lists. For instance, Alphonse Cary, at the back of Albert E. Tozer's *New and Complete Manual for Benediction* (1898), has only five of its 136 works by Renaissance and early Baroque composers;[19] the 1931 revision shows the exact obverse. There is no sign of the 'Viennese' style repertory promoted, for example, by John Egbert Turner, OSB (1853–97). Instead Cary's list is organised under such headings as 'Polyphonic Motets', 'Polyphonic Masses', 'Plainsong Masses' and 'Plainsong Motets'. Given, as will be argued, that *The Westminster Hymnal* was intended for use at Benediction, where Tozer's manual was standard fare, it is inconceivable that it was uninfluenced by the transformation.

It is also no accident that such changes occurred when they did; for by 1900 the English Catholic church had more or less completed its transformation from being a largely underground movement before 1829 to a fully public entity with a regular parish organisation – comprising churches (often in a flamboyantly Gothic style), schools and other buildings to match. The decree 'Sapienti Consilio', issued by the papacy in 1908, recognised this by removing the church from direct control by the Congregation of Propaganda. 'Missions' thus became 'Parishes' in name as well as in fact. Much greater attention could now be paid to cultural matters as distinct from the nineteenth-century

---

16   Richard Terry, *Catholic Church Music* (London: Greening & Co. Ltd., 1907), p. 198.

17   See, for example, *The Ecclesiastical Choir Book* (London: James Burns, 1848), consisting entirely of Continental works and dedicated to Henry Wiseman, the future Cardinal of Westminster and the promoter of Roman ideals.

18   See Terry, *Catholic Church Music*, pp. 187–91, where Tallis, Byrd and Philips are described as Catholic composers belonging to an international movement to which Englishmen had contributed since the time of Dunstable. See also his preface to Book 4 of his collection of *Downside Motets* (Stratton on the Fosse: Downside Abbey, 1898).

19   The composers are Tye, Arcadelt, Casali, Soriano and Richard Farrant.

emphasis on bricks, mortar and training enough priests[20] – though these remained important.[21]

This was also a time when Ultramontanism, emphasising uniform obedience to papal authority, was at its apogee. Papal infallibility had been formally asserted at the First Vatican Council (1870); but already, from the restoration of the episcopal hierarchy in 1850, it had been used systematically, and continued to be employed, by three successive Cardinal Archbishops of Westminster – Nicholas Wiseman (1850–65), Henry Manning (1865–92) and Herbert Vaughan (1892–1903) – to bring into line a Church that in recusant times had acquired considerable localised independence under Catholic gentry and religious orders.[22] Roman uniformity was the means for bishops to assert control over laity and clergy alike. The issuing of a hymnal by a bishops' committee that would be the 'only' authorised collection was the logical culmination of this process.

Uniformity also occurred through technological change. From the mid-nineteenth century onwards improved printing methods enabled publishers to mass produce music at a fraction of former costs. J. Alfred Novello was the first to take advantage of this; but others, like Burns & Oates and R. and T. Washbourne, quickly followed.[23] The effect of mass production – and distribution – was to standardise text and music. From the 1850s Catholic hymnals evolved from books with limited print runs aimed at small markets to works that had a truly national scope. For instance, Frederick Faber's hymnal was first produced at Derby in 1849 with a print run of only 1000 copies; however, in 1852 a new 10 000-copy edition appeared; and two years later it was revised and renamed *The Oratory Hymn Book*.[24] It had thus become fully associated with a religious order. The *St Dominic's Hymn Book* of 1881, starting at this point, shows how the process was taken further; for in 1886 Tozer turned it into *Catholic Hymns with Accompanying Tunes, Being a Musical Edition of St Dominic's Hymn Book*. Although containing only 79 items, the title exposes national Catholic pretensions, which were confirmed in 1898

---

20 See, for example, David Lannon's account of the work of Bishop Turner of Salford in 'William Turner, First Bishop of Salford, Pastor and Educator', *Recusant History* (The Catholic Record Society), 25/2 (2000), pp 192–217.

21 Sheridan Gilley, 'The Years of Equipoise. 1892–1943', in V. Alan McClelland and Michael Hodgetts (eds), *From Without the Flaminian Gate: 150 Years of Catholicism in England and Wales 1850–2000* (London: Darton, Longman & Todd, 1999), p. 34.

22 V. Alan McClelland, 'The Formative Years 1850–92', in McClelland and Hodgetts (eds), *From Without the Flaminian Gate*, pp. 4–10. Edward Norman, *The English Catholic Church in the Nineteenth Century* (Oxford: Clarendon Press, 1984), pp. 263–68, 273, 349–51, 362–63.

23 Hurd, *Vincent Novello*, pp. 49–54.

24 Frederick W. Faber, *Hymns by Frederick William Faber DD* (London: Burns & Oates Ltd., 1890), p. vii.

when it grew to 186 texts.[25] By this time, though, a number of hymnals with even greater scope had appeared. Henri Hemy's *Crown of Jesus Music*, published in 1864, was the first. Others included *The Parochial Hymnal* and *The Catholic Tune Book*.[26]

Arundel Hymns is a peculiar example. The title implies a localised connection with Arundel Cathedral. Moreover for Henry, Duke of Norfolk it was a work of piety, a point emphasised by the photograph of his Elizabethan ancestor St Philip Howard inside. Yet the preface states that

> the editors ... have gathered together the most representative anthology they could collect of popularly used Latin hymns, together with a large selection of English hymns by Catholic writers ... to illustrate the great truths of the Catholic faith ... The tunes represent, roughly speaking, the three great epochs of Catholic Church music – the plainchant period ... the polyphonic epoch; and the modern age, including Haydn, Mozart and the musicians of today.[27]

Musical continuity with the past was thus asserted – a theme picked up by later editions of *The Westminster Hymnal*.[28] The reference to Haydn and Mozart, though, must have damaged its prospects of becoming the national Catholic hymnal after the Motu Proprio, despite official endorsement by Pope Leo XIII and acceptance by Cardinal Vaughan for use in Westminster Cathedral.[29]

The Westminster Hymnal then fitted into a developing pattern – a tendency towards large print runs of more or less complete anthologies produced by private individuals or religious organisations claiming official sanction from the highest ecclesiastical authorities possible.[30] It was understandable that the bishops felt that they had to assert collective control. Thus, when in 1905 the Catholic Truth Society developed plans for a new hymnal, they created a committee to produce one of their own.[31]

---

25 *Catholic Hymns with Accompanying Tunes, Being a Musical Edition of St Dominic's Hymn Book*, ed. Albert Edmonds Tozer (London: Novello, Ewer & Co., 1886; 2nd and 3rd edns published in 1898 by Burns & Oates with Cary & Co. and Novello, Ewer & Co. respectively).

26 *Crown of Jesus Music, Parts I, II, III*, ed. Henri Hemy (London: Thomas Richardson & Son, 1864); *The Catholic Tune Book Containing a Complete Collection of Tunes in Every Metre to All English Hymns in General Use*, ed. John Storer (London: Alphonse Cary & R. Washbourne, 1892).

27 *Arundel Hymns*, ed. Henry Howard, Duke of Norfolk, and Charles T. Gatty (London: Boosey & Co. and R. and T. Washbourne, 1898 and 1901, repr. 1905), p. v.

28 David Matthew, 'Preface', in *The Westminster Hymnal: a New and Revised Edition Authorised by the Hierarchy*, ed. William Bainbridge (London: Burns & Oates Ltd., 1940), p. v.

29 *Arundel Hymns*, ed. Howard and Gatty (1905), p. iv.

30 For example, *The Parochial Hymn Book* cited letters of approbation from 14 bishops (no page number at this point).

31 WDA, *Bishops' Meetings 1888–1909*, p. 366. 'Low Week Acta' (1905), no. 6.

Table 4.1 Hymn texts from selected collections in *The Westminster Hymnal*

Author or editor	Title of collection	Total number of texts in collection	Number of texts from the collection in *The Westminster Hymnal*
H. Hemy (ed.)	*Crown of Jesus Music* (1864)	214[a]	64
F. Faber	*Hymns* (1861/R1890)	150	34[b]
Trans. and composed by E. Caswall	*Hymns and Poems*[c] (1849/R1873)	480 pp.	86 pp.
Anon. (ed.)	*The Parochial Hymn Book* (R1883)	633[d]	160
J. Storer (ed.)	*The Catholic Tune Book* (1892)	319	134
A.E. Tozer (ed.)	*Catholic Hymns* (1898)	186	91
H. Howard and C. Gatty (eds)	*Arundel Hymns* (1898/1901/R1905)	306	88

a The total excludes Benediction and Mass settings.
b *The Westminster Hymnal*'s own index (p. 411) lists 46 titles, suggesting that other Faber editions were drawn upon.
c First published as *Lyra Catholica Containing all the Breviary and Missal Hymns with Others from Various Sources* (London: James Burns, 1849). The expanded version, entitled *Hymns and Poems: Original and Translated,* was published in London by Burns & Oates in 1873.
d There are 79 other prayers and texts not intended for singing, producing a grand total of 712 items.

Evolution of this sort produced a standardisation of repertoire, as the number of hymn texts in *The Westminster Hymnal* from earlier sources shows (see Table 4.1). There is, however, one exception to this rule. *The Westminster Hymnal*, following earlier examples, has no fewer than 101 translations from Latin originals, 82 of them by Caswall.[32] Translation

---

32 *WH*, pp. 403–8, 411.

can subtly alter meaning, as becomes apparent when two versions are compared. *The Westminster Hymnal* shows this on seven separate occasions. For example, the anonymous translation of 'Ave maris stella' from *A Selection of Catholic Hymns* (1867) in no. 109 (1912) opens:

> Hail, thou resplendent star
> Which shinest o'er the main;
> Blest Mother of our God,
> And ever Virgin Queen.

Caswall's translation (no. 110) directly opposite reads:

> Hail, thou Star of ocean!
> Portal of the sky!
> Ever Virgin Mother
> of the Lord most High!

The difference lies not just in the meaning but also in the metre. Terry then had to write two different tunes of his own as well as edit J. Richardson's setting of Caswall's text. In effect, translation expanded the musical as well as the textual repertoire.[33]

Both Caswall and Faber were members of the Oratory, so their contribution to the evolution of Catholic hymnody deserves special attention (see Table 4.2). With *The Westminster Hymnal* this feature is even more pronounced, especially when another Oratorian's contribution, that of Henry, Cardinal Newman, is added (see Table 4.3). In this sense *The Westminster Hymnal* has not quite outgrown the status achieved by Tozer's *Catholic Hymns*, as it owes so much to contributions from one particular Order.

Inevitably such a development of repertoire produced a manipulation of texts. Indeed, with reference to other hymnals using his texts, the 1890 preface to Faber's *Hymns* complained that 'in one case the doctrine has been changed, and the author is made to express an opinion with which he is quite out of sympathy'.[34] Sometimes, though, *The Westminster Hymnal* restored the original. This happened with Caswall's 'O Jesu, Thou the beauty art', where Hemy supplied only a selection of verses, shuffled the order and added two others that do not come in the

---

33 For the other examples see *WH* 76 and 81 (Adoro te devote); *WH* 60 and 241 (Lux alma); *WH* 19, 45 and 67 (Jesu dulcis memoria); *WH* 4 and 75 (Verbum supernum prodiens); *WH* 48 and 48a (Veni Sancte Spiritus); *WH* 94 and 95 (Viva, viva! Gesu).
34 Faber, *Hymns*, p. v.

Table 4.2   Contributions of texts by
Faber and Caswall to selected Catholic hymnals

Title of hymnal	Number of texts	Number of texts contributed by Faber	Number of texts contributed by Caswall
Crown of Jesus Music (1864)	214	16	17
The Parochial Hymnal (R1883)	633	41	53
Catholic Hymns (R1898)	186[a]	32	23
Arundel Hymns (R1905)	306		

a   One of these is a translation of a Muzzarelli text and is referred to under his
name in *The Westminster Hymnal*, p. 411.

Table 4.3   The number of hymn texts contributed by
members of the Oratory to *The Westminster Hymnal*

Name	House	Number of texts contributed (out of 263)
F. Faber	London Oratory	46
E. Caswall	Birmingham Oratory	86
H. Newman	Birmingham Oratory	8
Total		140

original.[35] Similarly *The Parochial Hymnal* changed the opening line of
Caswall's 'O Christ, the glory of the angel choir!' to 'O Christ! The *beauty*
of the angel choir!' (*PH* 433; *WH* 167). In both cases *The Westminster
Hymnal* reverts to the original. Elsewhere, though, the position is more

---

35   *Crown of Jesus Music*, ed. Hemy, no. 170. WH 72.

ambiguous. Consider, for example, the liturgical implications of translating the 'Stabat Mater'. Caswall organises 'At the Cross her station keeping' – the Seven Douleurs of Our Lady – into six-line instead of three-line verses, as the Breviary specifies.[36] He also breaks the text up into three distinct hymns, corresponding to the services of the Office:

Verses	Liturgical use
1–5	Vespers
6–7	Matins
8–10	Lauds

The Westminster Hymnal by contrast restores the material as a single text on one page, retaining the six-line verses but supplying a melody to be sung twice round for each stanza (*WH* 28). Caswall's purpose is acknowledged in the subtitle; but the main contents' heading – 'Passiontide' – signifies a subtle alteration. It is no longer a Breviary text for the Office but something to be used as a complete entity, with a stronger association with the Good Friday service than the Feast of the Seven Douleurs (16–17 September).

Musical imperatives sometimes played a part in these processes. For instance, Faber's 'Joy of my heart, O let me pray' is grouped into two-line stanzas. Terry, because he uses music from the *Rottenburg Gesangbuch* (1865), reshapes them into eight-line verses.[37] A second example concerns Caswall's translation 'Hail, thou Star of ocean!' (see Ex. 4.1). Terry's own tune needs no alteration to the four-line verse pattern; Richardson's tune, containing 16 bars in 4/2 metre, produces four stanzas of eight lines each. To accommodate the last four lines the melody is therefore cut in half. Fortunately, the presence of a perfect cadence to the home key makes this feasible.[38]

Textual requirements, then, could affect pre-existing music, for it is unlikely in this instance that Richardson's tune was composed for the hymn. Musical and textual manipulation was therefore a two-way process that simultaneously interacted with liturgical demands. The business of putting hymns into the emerging context of a public parish liturgy after emancipation added further twists. The time, then, has come to see what function *The Westminster Hymnal* was expected to play.

---

36 Caswall, *Hymns and Poems* (London: Burns & Oates, 1873), p. 76; *Missale Romanum* (Mechelen: H. Dessain, 1896), 404 and 504; *Breviarum Romanum* (Mechelen: H. Dessain, 1913; repr. 1920, 1932), pp. 689–90, 701.

37 Faber, *Hymns*, no. 51; *WH* 120. The *Rottenburg Gesangbuch* tune is itself an adaptation of one from Vehe's *Gesangbüchlein* of 1537.

38 Caswall, *Hymns and Poems*, p. 105; *WH* 110(i) and (ii).

Ex. 4.1   'Hail, thou Star of ocean!' (tune by J. Richardson)

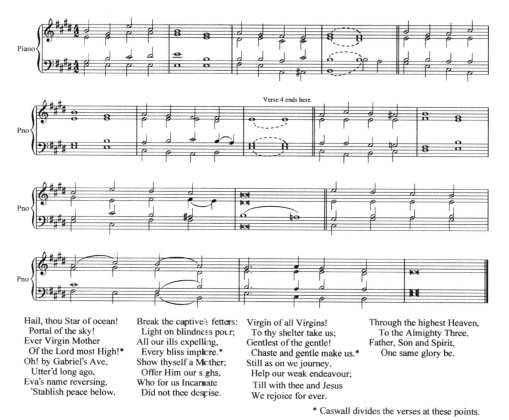

Hail, thou Star of ocean!	Break the captive's fetters:	Virgin of all Virgins!	Through the highest Heaven,
Portal of the sky!	Light on blindness pour;	To thy shelter take us;	To the Almighty Three,
Ever Virgin Mother	All our ills expelling,	Gentlest of the gentle!	Father, Son and Spirit,
Of the Lord most High!*	Every bliss implore.*	Chaste and gentle make us.*	One same glory be.
Oh! by Gabriel's Ave,	Show thyself a Mother;	Still as on we journey,	
Utter'd long ago,	Offer Him our sighs,	Help our weak endeavour;	
Eva's name reversing,	Who for us Incarnate	Till with thee and Jesus	
'Stablish peace below.	Did not thee despise.	We rejoice for ever.	

* Caswall divides the verses at these points.

The liturgical function of *The Westminster Hymnal* and its implications for Catholic congregational singing

The first point to observe is that *The Westminster Hymnal* was not primarily intended for the Mass. The 'Motu Proprio' declared that 'the language proper to the Roman Church is Latin. Hence it is forbidden to sing anything whatever in the vernacular in solemn liturgical functions.'[39] The most solemn liturgical function was High Mass; yet in the original *Westminster Hymnal* only 13 out of its 263 items are in Latin, two of which do not offer plainchant – a significant disqualification in a service where Gregorian chant was meant to reign supreme. Moreover 102

---

39 Pius X, in Terry, *Music of the Roman Rite*, Appendix B, p. 258.

English items were translations from Latin originals, confirming the impression that the hymnal was not intended for High Mass. It is true, though, that in later decades English hymns were sometimes sung at Low Mass. Most of the time, however, Low Mass was spoken; and before the introduction of the Dialogue Mass in the late 1940s congregational responses were usually uttered only by the server.[40]

This confined *The Westminster Hymnal* to public processions – early editions advertise band parts obtainable from Terry himself – and what Hedley refers to as 'extra liturgical worship and popular services', such as Sodalities, Confraternities, afternoon and evening services.[41]

Sodalities played an important part in Catholic education. Junior Sodalities were associated with Guardian Angels, so it is significant that *The Westminster Hymnal* devotes a section of nine items to this theme. Senior Sodalities focused on the Virgin Mary. There was also the cult of the Month of May, devotion to the Rosary and a large number of feasts dedicated to the same idea. Not surprisingly, *The Westminster Hymnal* has 35 hymns dealing with these subjects.

Confraternities are more problematical. Earlier hymnals, such as *The Catholic Hymnal*[42] or *The Parochial Hymnal*, devote space to the subject.[43] *The Westminster Hymnal* does not do this. On the other hand, the confraternities' association with particular saints meant that hymns in these categories of the contents page could be readily adopted for these purposes.[44]

The most popular afternoon or evening service was Benediction; and it was here that hymnals really came into their own. *The Westminster Hymnal* even has the service text on its back pages.[45] Its rivals were Vespers and Compline. Statistically, though, their challenge was negligible. MaGinty's analysis of the *Catholic Directory* for 1918 showed that Proper Vespers and Compline was celebrated in only 156 and 65 public churches

---

40 John Crichton, '1920–40: The Dawn of a Liturgical Movement', in John Crichton, Harold Winstone and John Ainslie (eds), *English Catholic Worship: Liturgical Renewal in England since 1900* (London: Geoffrey Chapman, 1979), p. 2. Hemy designated some of his English hymns as suitable for thanksgiving after communion, but does not say whether this applied to all types of Mass. If they were, then perhaps mid-nineteenth-century policy towards the use of the vernacular texts in music at High Mass was more flexible than was the case later. *Crown of Jesus Music*, e.g. nos. 20, 21, 22 and 44.

41 *WH*, p. v.

42 In the 1898 edition the Apostleship of Prayer, the Confraternity of the Holy Family and the Confraternity of the 'Bona Mors' are represented.

43 *PH* 615–45 and 633–701.

44 For instance, nos. 218, 225 and 226 are grouped in the contents page under 'The Holy Family'; *WH*, p. xiii.

45 Ibid., pp. 399–400. See also John Ainslie, 'English Liturgical Music before Vatican II', in Crichton et al. (eds), *English Catholic Worship*, p. 48.

on Sundays.[46] He argued that this was due to congregational unfamiliarity with plainchant – a clear sign that the 'Motu Proprio' had failed in this respect. Yet the 'Motu Proprio' insisted that 'In the Office of Vespers it should be the rule to follow the *Cerimoniale Episcoporum*, which prescribes the Gregorian Chant for the psalmody and permits figured music for the versicles of the *Gloria Patri* and the hymns.'[47] However, in greater solemnities choirs were allowed to alternate fauxbourdon with chant. Nevertheless 'the antiphons ... must be as a rule rendered with the Gregorian melody proper to each'.[48] Thus there was no scope to introduce new hymns, let alone those in the vernacular, and there was a marked tendency for the choir to do most of the singing anyway.[49] The only way round this was to provide English translations for the congregation to follow alongside the Latin as it was sung, as Adrian Fortescue attempted in *Latin Hymns Sung at the Church of St Hugh, Letchworth*. Here it was argued that if people had an English translation then 'first ... anyone who knows the tune may join the singers; secondly ... those who do not sing may be able to follow, to know what is being sung'.[50]

It is hardly surprising, then, that people voted with their feet, for it is arguable that one reason Benediction was popular was because they really could participate in the vernacular hymnody attached to it. *The Westminster Hymnal* then played a key role in consolidating this trend. There are, however, two objections. First *The Westminster Hymnal* has no musical settings for the central elements of the service – 'O salutaris', the Litany and 'Tantum ergo'. However, these were unnecessary because numerous settings were already available in Tozer's Benediction manual. Vernacular hymns were a penumbra around this central core, or linked two services together, as Tozer explains:

> The common practice among Catholics, hitherto, has been to look upon an English hymn as something of no great importance – a kind of 'stop gap' in the interval that exists between Vespers and the sermon, or while the Altar is being prepared for the rite of Benediction – and to pay no sort of heed to how it should be sung, or by whom.[51]

Here, though, lies the second objection, since the preceding argument about the popularity of Benediction depends on popular participation. If

---

46   Edward MaGinty, 'Vespers', *The Tablet*, NS 118 (July–Dec. 1927, 24 Sept.), pp. 395–96.
47   Pius X in Terry, *Music of the Roman Rite*, Appendix B, pp. 259–60.
48   Ibid., pp. 259–60.
49   That this was not always the case before is shown by the presence of English hymns listed under Vespers in *The Parochial Hymnal* (1883), p. x.
50   Transcribed and edited by Adrian Fortescue in *Latin Hymns Sung at the Church of Saint Hugh, Letchworth* (Cambridge: Cambridge University Press, 1913, repr. 1924), p. v.
51   *Catholic Hymns Original and Translated with Accompanying Tunes*, ed. Albert Edmonds Tozer (London: Cary & Co ; Burns & Oates, 1898), Preface, n.p.

Table 4.4   Types of music in Tozer's
New and Complete Manual for Benediction (1898)

Text	Number of settings using four-part harmony	Number of choral settings with an independent organ part	Number of four-part plainchant settings
O salutaris	10	1	1
Tantum ergo	10	1	—
Litanies	35	1	3[a]
Adoremus in aeternum	1	3	3
Totals	56	6	7

a Two have alternation between solo sopranos and the full choir, the other alternates between a solo singer and a unison chorus.

congregations did not sing, then this argument is undermined. To some extent, however, it can be finessed; for, as the quotation from Fortescue shows, participation can simply mean following the text. Nonetheless, as Tozer's statement immediately above reveals, a key point was the balance of power between choirs and congregations. In an age of Renaissance polyphony and chant choirs remained important; yet there were signs of change. For instance, there are only a small number of plainchant and choral settings alongside straight four-part harmony arrangements in Tozer's 1898 manual (see Table 4.4).

With *The Westminster Hymnal* the key feature concerns the melodic vocal range compared with that in other hymnals. For example, *The Parochial Hymnal* has 56 melodies rising (for men's voices) above *e'*. Terry tries to avoid this. Thus whereas *The Parochial Hymnal* melody for 'Christ the Lord is risen today' reaches an *f'*, neither of Terry's two tunes rises above *d'* (*PH* 121; *WH* 38). Elsewhere, with 'Ye sons and daughters of the Lord', the same tune is used in both hymnals; but Terry, by setting it in G rather than A minor, lowers the highest note from *e'* to *d'* (*PH* 119; *WH* 39).

The changing attitude is summed up by comparing Tozer's and Terry's prefaces. Tozer argued that:

> Some hymns are essentially suited for singing in unison with the whole body of worshippers ... Other Hymns, by their very structure, are utterly ruined and put out of place by such a mode of treatment: these should be sung by the choir alone with every attention to light

and shade which the words will naturally inspire in a truly artistic mind; they may then become veritable 'Sermons in music'.[52]

Terry, on the other hand, wanted every hymn to be available for congregational singing: 'Since vernacular hymns are essentially intended for the congregation rather than the choir, the first requisite is a strong and well defined melody which lends itself easily to unison singing.'[53] Here, though, some ambivalence appears: 'Experience has shown that the difficult tunes for a congregation are those in which the melody lies at a high pitch throughout, and not those which contain an occasional high note.' This, then, is his justification for very occasionally sending the melody above the e' for male voices.[54] Later he states: 'The keys chosen ... have been those which secured the requisite brightness, while placing the tune as a whole within the range of the average singer, to whom it would not cause strain or fatigue.'

There is, then, an element of special pleading here, as T.H. Knuckley noted in *The Tablet*, however correct the technical arguments about tessitura may be.[55] As a professional choir master Terry could not quite bring himself to embrace congregational hymn singing at the expense of the choir. Accompaniments in different hymnals show the changing background. Many items in the *Crown of Jesus Music* use three-part harmony, often with a rudimentary figured bass. Here unison singing seems to be implied, especially since so many hymns were meant for children. Other settings, though, such as Hemy's 'My God, grant by my tears', deploy four-part harmony.[56] At this point – in 1864 – Catholic hymnody seems to be in transition. The situation becomes more uncertain when one realises that the two upper parts could be sung chorally, the setting from Mozart of 'Sweet angel of mercy' being a case in point.[57] *The Parochial Hymnal* shows the same thing. In the vocal copy every tune except the plainchant items is set in at least two lines. Seventy-four specify a solo and chorus, seven a solo duet and chorus; 17 are laid out in three parts, 37 in four parts. There is even one in six parts. Taken with the high melodic lines referred to earlier, the choral, as distinct from the congregational, emphasis is plain.

Terry, following Tozer's *Catholic Hymns*, which he had helped edit, uses a different pattern. Two versions of *The Westminster Hymnal* were produced: a cheap 'text only' copy for the congregation and an expensive

---

52 *Catholic Hymns*, ed. Tozer (1898), Preface, n.p.
53 *WH*, p. ix.
54 See, for example, his own melody for no. 87, 'O Sacred Heart, all blissful light of heaven', which rises to an f' at bar 13.
55 T.H. Knuckley, 'Letter to the Editor', 26 June 1912, in *The Tablet*, NS 87 (Jan.–June 1912), p. 1022.
56 *Crown of Jesus Music*, ed. Hemy, no. 4.
57 Ibid., no. 7.

four-part version for the organist and choir.[58] In the latter there are no three-part figured bass settings. All hymns could now be sung using the choir and congregation together or separately. Thus people could opt out of singing simply to reflect on Tozer's 'sermons in music'. The same distinction applies to Tozer's Benediction manual, given that four-part harmony is mainly used there also. Its shape (170mm × 255mm) shows that it was intended for choirs. Congregations at best had access only to the text, as in *The Westminster Hymnal*. If all this is so, then meditation on the text could have been as important for Catholics in 1912 as singing it. Its didactic function, then, is what should be considered next.

The development and purpose of Catholic hymn texts in *The Westminster Hymnal*

Here, as with so much else, *The Westminster Hymnal* bears the imprint of earlier developments. Caswall and Faber were all-important, not least because the hymnal drew so extensively from their collections. Faber's purpose was threefold: 'first, to furnish some simple and original hymns for singing; secondly to provide English Catholics with a hymn book for reading'. Thirdly he refers to eleven hymns written for local schools, for at that time religious education was – and remained – a key issue.[59] More-over the link between indoctrination and musical training was well under-stood. As Hemy states: 'The people become familiarised with the music, and can use it to do their domestic devotions; the melody becomes associated and intertwined in the mind with the hymns, the tune suggests the hymn; the hymn calls to memory the tune.'[60]

The hymn 'I am a faithful Catholic' illustrates the technique. Classified as a children's hymn, it was set by Hemy to Papageno's tune from Mozart's opera *The Magic Flute*.[61] A catchy secular tune is thus associated with a religious idea in children's minds. Some hymns bridged the gap between childhood and adulthood. For example, 'This is the image of the Queen', where Hemy offers 'a Spanish air', a piece by Haydn and a melody of his own, is intended for the Month of May devotions.[62] On these occasions, especially in Jesuit schools, both pupils and staff were encouraged to offer poems before a statue of the Virgin, where Rosaries,

---

58 The text version cost between 2*d*. (just under 1 new penny) and 1/- (5 new pence). The full version was priced at 3/6 (17½ new pence) and 6/- (30 new pence).
59 Maurice Whitehead, 'A View from the Bridge: The Catholic School', in McClelland and Hodgetts (eds), *From Without the Flaminian Gate*, pp. 218–19.
60 *Crown of Jesus Music*, ed. Hemy, n.p.
61 Ibid., no. 62.
62 Ibid., no. 169.

Litanies and hymns might also be declaimed. Significantly, then, in *The Westminster Hymnal* the hymn appears under the heading 'The Blessed Virgin' instead of 'For Children'; so it is intended for people of all ages.[63] Along with the emphasis on Sodalities noted earlier this is another reason why so many items are associated with children, Mary and angels. Six out of the 13 texts classified in the hymnal as 'For Children' are about the relationship between Mary, the baby Jesus and infants.[64]

Faber's second purpose, the use of hymns 'for reading', was shared by Caswall; but although like Faber he wrote many original poems, elsewhere he gives a different twist by translating hymns from the Breviary for laymen as well as clergy. Thus in his preface he quotes 'The Catholic Choralist' with approval: 'The laity are not bound, like the clergy, to its [the Breviary's] recital, yet that portion of it which includes Hymns and Canticles might be frequently, if not daily, recited [note the choice of word] by them, with great spiritual benefit and truth.'[65]

The implications for singing were profound, for the private reading and recital of hymns confirmed the current separation between those who wrote hymns and those who composed music. *The Westminster Hymnal* has only two hymns where the author and composer are the same (*WH* 74 and 78). Thus Terry, like others before him, had no qualms about moving tunes around between hymns, altering both music and text in the process, as has been seen. It also explains why so many preferred to listen rather than perform. Caswall implicitly acknowledges this when he states, with reference to Breviary hymns, that 'the greater number of them appear to have been originally written, not with a view to private reading, but for the purpose of being sung to the beautiful ecclesiastical melodies by Monastic and other Religious Bodies at the Office in Chant'.[66]

In other words, because English Catholics had been a persecuted minority for so long, no tradition of hymn singing had emerged and a Counter-Reformation habit of private devotions had been substituted. Moreover the Oratory, of which Faber and Caswall were members, was an outward-looking missionary organisation whose clergy therefore often had to recite their prayers in private rather than a closed order like the medieval Benedictines, where life revolved around a daily Office chanted by the whole community. In the late nineteenth century what then followed was an attempt to restore music to hymn texts in the context of the parish church. *The Westminster Hymnal* marked a culmination of that process.

---

63 *WH*, pp. xiii–xiv.
64 *WH* 151, 152, 154, 155, 157 and 163. Nos. 154, 155 and 157 are by Faber.
65 Caswall, *Lyra Catholica* (London: James Burns, 1849), p. v.
66 Ibid., p. vii.

Table 4.5   The contents and organisation of
Caswall and Faber's hymnals (simplified)

Caswall (1849)	Faber (1852)
I: Hymns for the Week (Matins, Lauds, Vespers, etc.)	I: 'Hymns to God, his attributes and the Three persons of the Adorable Trinity'
II: Antiphons of the Blessed Virgin	II: 'Sacred Humanity of Jesus and the Mysteries of the Thirty-Three Years'
III: Hymns of the moveable feasts (Matins, Lauds, Vespers, etc.)	III: The Blessed Virgin Mary and the Holy Family
IV: Hymns belonging to the common of the Saints (Matins, Lauds, Vespers, etc.)	IV: Angels and Saints
	V: Sacraments, Faith and Spiritual Life
	VI: Miscellaneous: The World, Poor and Nature
	VII: 'Last Things'

The steps by which this was achieved can be shown from how various hymnals are organised in simplified tabular form. Table 4.5 reveals the difference between Faber's devotional structure and that produced by Caswall's adherence to the Breviary. Table 4.6 shows how, in 1873, they begin to be combined. Table 4.7 then demonstrates how the framework was modified to bring hymns to the parish, where, as has been suggested, Benediction rather than the Office was the norm. A parish hymnal had to cover the liturgical year, the principal feast days and a variety of other types of service or devotion. The similarity to Caswall in the early sections is clearly apparent. Moreover on the 47 occasions when Caswall's translation is used in *The Westminster Hymnal*, the name of the Office with which it was originally associated is provided. Nonetheless the table also shows how other sections more in keeping with Faber's methodology were added. There is also a straight progression from Tozer's basic 1886

Table 4.6   The contents and organisation (simplified) of
Edward Caswall's *Hymns and Poems: Original and Translated*
of 1873, showing how his original contributions are attached
to his earlier framework

The Roman Breviary

I.   Hymns for the Week (Matins, Lauds, Vespers, etc.)
II.   Antiphons of the Blessed Virgin
III.   Hymns of the Moveable Feasts (Matins, Lauds, Vespers, etc.)
IV.   Hymns of the Moveable Feasts (Matins, Lauds, Vespers, etc.)

These items are then added:

V.   Hymns and Sequences of the Roman Missal
VI.   Hymns from various Offices and other sources
VII.   Original Texts: Hymns and Meditative pieces
       'Masque of Angels' before Our Lady in the Temple
       The 'Minister of Eld'
       Odes
       Poems

---

model. This is hardly surprising given its pivotal status between a book
for a religious Order and one intended for general use across the whole
country.

In the process, as was demonstrated earlier, many texts, and with them
the music, had to be altered to suit the changed environment. By the same
token what was chosen – and, for that matter, left out – tells much about
the ideas the hierarchy wished to impose through *The Westminster
Hymnal*. A key watchword, as noted earlier, was 'uniformity'. This is
made manifest in a number of different ways.

One of these was Romanisation. 'Full in the panting heart of Rome' (*WH*
139), penned by none other than Wiseman, expresses the idea exactly. Verse 1
describes Rome itself – visited by admiring and loyal pilgrims:

> Full in the panting heart of Rome,
> Beneath the Apostle's crowning dome,
> From pilgrims' lips that kiss the ground,
> Breathes in all tongues one only sound:
> 'God bless our Pope, the great, the good'.

Table 4.7   The contents and organisation of
The Westminster Hymnal and three other collections

Section	Maher (d. 1877) and Trappes, *Liturgical Hymns* (n.d.) (70 items)	Tozer, *Catholic Hymns* (1886) (79 items)	Tozer, *Catholic Hymns* (1898) (150 items)	Terry, *The Westminster Hymnal* (1912) (263 items)
[1] Hymns for particular parts of the liturgical year	Nos. 1–48: Advent to Trinity Sunday (nos. 1–6: Hymns throughout the year)	Nos. 1–31: Advent to Corpus Christi	Advent to Corpus Christi	Advent to All Souls Day
[2] Hymns for the feast days associated with the Virgin Mary, Holy Family, Saints, Martyrs, Confessors, etc.	Nos. 49–55: Festival of 'Holy Housel or Eucharist'; nos. 56–57: Transfiguration; nos. 58–70: Festivals of the Virgin Mary, Saints, Confessors, etc.	Sacred Heart; Precious Blood; Virgin Mary; Festivals of Saints up to All Souls Day	Sacred Heart; Precious Blood; Virgin Mary; Festivals of Saints up to All Souls Day	'Holy Name'; 'The Blessed Sacrament'; 'The Sacred Heart', Precious Blood and Sacred Wounds; 'The Blessed Virgin', followed by 'The Church', 'Holy Angels', 'Heaven' and 'The Rosary'; 'The Holy Family'; Saints, Apostles and Martyrs, etc.;
[3] Hymns for children, retreats, morning and evening prayer, sacraments, confraternities and various other miscellaneous occasions	Nos. 68–69: Children's Mass	Missions and Retreats; 'Occasional'; 'Evening'	Missions and Retreats; General Hymns; 'Evening'; 'Confirmation'; Confraternities; Stations of the Cross; Children's Mass	Confirmation; Missions; Children; the Sea; General Hymns; 'Morning' and 'Evening'
[4] Latin hymns				Latin Hymns

Note: I have imposed the main subdivisions. Tozer's and Terry's hymnals, while in general following a numerical order, scatter some items across the book. The contents page is therefore, as the 1916 *Westminster Hymnal* put it, an 'Index of Subjects' (p. xiii).

By verse 3 Rome's message is being spread abroad:

> Then surging through each hallowed gate,
> Where martyrs glory, in peace, await,
> It sweeps beyond the solemn plain,
> Peals over Alps, across the main:
> 'God bless our Pope, the great, the good'.

Finally, in verse 5 the idea reaches the home and children:

> For like the sparks of unseen fire,
> That speak along the magic wire [electricity!],
> From home to home, from heart to heart,
> These words of countless children dart:
> 'God bless our Pope, the great, the good'.

Inevitably such a strong Roman stress affected particularist tendencies. It is remarkable, for instance, given the large number of Irish in Britain, that *The Westminster Hymnal* has only three hymns in honour of St Patrick, one of which – 'All praise to St Patrick' (*WH* 203) – was penned by Faber, an Englishman; and Terry himself composed the tune of 'St Patrick for our country pray' (*WH* 202). With English saints the signs are contradictory, especially when comparisons are made with earlier hymnals. *Crown of Jesus Music*, for example, is very much a northern hymn book, for Hemy taught at Ushaw College, just outside Durham. It testifies to that region's traditional importance for English Catholicism. So there are hymns and Benediction services in honour of St Cuthbert, the patron saint of Ushaw,[67] St Bede,[68] St Oswin[69] and St Wilfrid[70] – all of them northern saints. Only one of the Benediction services, however, has music by an Englishman – Charles Newsham, President of Ushaw. The others are set to tunes by Mendelssohn, Gluck and Beethoven, while St Cuthbert's hymn has a tune by Mozart. St Cuthbert also figures as 'Dear patron of the faithful north' in *The Parochial Hymnal* (no. 501); but in *The Westminster Hymnal* all references to him and St Oswin are eliminated.

On the other hand, there is evidence of continuing interest in native saints. The full name of the episcopal committee's chairman was John *Cuthbert* Hedley. His preface is dated 'St George's Day' and the hymnal itself has two items in honour of that saint, both set to tunes by

---

67 *Crown of Jesus Music*, ed. Hemy, nos. 109 and 260–62.
68 Ibid., nos. 100 and 233–35, by the Revd W.J. Maher, SJ and the Revd F. Stanfield.
69 Ibid., nos. 224–26.
70 Ibid., nos. 221–22.

Englishmen (nos. 198–99). There are also texts honouring St Bede (no. 249), St Winifrid – a Welsh saint (*WH* 209), St Andrew (*WH* 193), 'English Martyrs' (*WH* 136, 196–97 and 248) and 'English Saints' (*WH* 198–99 and 249), giving 9 out of 263 hymns in all.

The full complexity of the situation emerges when attempts were made to link English and Roman traditions together, much as Terry had tried to do with Renaissance polyphonists. Thus England's special relationship with Rome was emphasised by describing the parts played by St Augustine and Pope Gregory I in the conversion of England as told by Bede. Benedictines were particularly prone to do this. For instance, verses 1 and 2 of 'Lord receive our thankful homage' (*WH* 204), penned by the historian Dom Bede Camm (note the Christian name), state:

> Lord, receive our thankful homage,
> Who, from toils of error freed,
> Bless thee for the hand that saved us,
> And the heart that felt our need –
> For Saint Gregory our father,
> Vigilant in name and deed.
>
> For our own, our dear apostle,
> Gregory the Great, the Blest,
> Who, while England lay in darkness,
> Spared no labour, knew no rest;
> For the gracious love he bore us,
> Be thy holy name confessed.[71]

Verses 2 and 3 of 'Lover of Christ's immortal Bride' (*WH* 249), honouring St Bede and composed by Ambrose Burton, Hedley's colleague on the episcopal committee and who had worked in the north-east,[72] do the same thing:

> Thou toldest how from Rome a band
> of monks there came [a reference to
>   St Augustine], what souls they won,
> How kingdoms yielded, one by one,
> Till Christ was King o'er all the land.
>
> His empire stood a thousand years;
> For Peter is his chosen chief:

---

71 Camm sent the text of the hymn to Cardinal Bourne on 13 January 1903. WDA, Bourne Papers: Bo1/33 Church Music 1904–10. Bourne was therefore directly responsible for its insertion in *The Westminster Hymnal*.

72 WDA, *Bishops' Meetings 1858–1909*, p. 366: 'Low Week Acta: 1905', no. 6.

> And all were one in one belief,
> Till faith was quenched in blood and tears.

The sense of continuity with the past is palpable. Indeed Bishop
Matthew in his preface of 1940, following *Arundel Hymns,* regards *The
Westminster Hymnal* as a palimpsest of different eras in Catholic
hymnody from the earliest days to the present.[73] This was important ideo-
logically because the primacy of Rome argument depends on a continuous
line of Catholic belief under papal leadership going back to St Peter. In
reality the balance of material is rather uneven. As has been shown, there
are a large number of translations from medieval hymns; and eight out of
the nine Latin hymns are also medieval. At the other end of the spectrum
the substantial nineteenth-century input from Faber and Newman is
supplemented by texts from people like F. Stanfield (6 items), Edmund
Vaughan (4 items) and M. Bridges (6 items). However, only 11 items can
be clearly identified from the period 1500–1800.[74] In other words a
strong continuity is established with the medieval, as distinct from the
early modern, past.

Burton's hymn also brings out another aspect of uniformity, namely a
sense of exclusivity. Partly this is fostered by reminding people of past
persecutions, always a useful device for imposing discipline. The line 'till
faith was quenched in blood and tears' directly refers to the Reformation,
a theme continued in verse 4:

> Then from the vine the branch was torn,
> New teachers shaped the creed anew,
> And new-made treasons thinned to few
> The followers of a hope forlorn.

Notice how the first line describes a break in continuity. The implication
is clear. As with Guéranger and the Solesmes monks, links with the past
had to be re-established and, by the same token, papal authority and
Roman traditions reasserted. Just as with plainchant, hymnody is being
used with conscious ideological intent.

Such ideas appear in other hymns, like 'Tyburn's days are long
forgiven, unforgotten is the pain' by J. Reeks (*WH* 197) or 'Faith of our
fathers' by Faber (*WH* 138). The opening lines – 'Faith of our fathers,

---

73 Matthew, 'Preface', in *The Westminster Hymnal: a New and Revised Edition,* ed.
Bainbridge (1940), p. v.
74 'Adeste fideles' (no. 251), a text by St Francis Xavier translated by Caswall (no. 33), and
nine by St Alphonsus, one of which was translated by Caswall, the others by E. Vaughan
(nos. 26, 57, 65, 73, 90, 103, 104, 108, 231 in the *WH,* pp. 411–12).

living still, in spite of dungeon, fire and sword' – testify to the idea of continuity. Obedience surfaces in the refrain 'Faith of Our Fathers! Holy faith! We will be true till death!'

As can be seen, such hymns also evince a determination to recover England for the Catholic faith, inspired by the blood of martyrs and example of saints. Thus Reeks states:

> And the martyrs' cry for vengeance
>   rises before thy throne:–
> 'Save the land we love so well, Lord!
>   Claim its children for thine own.'

Such defiance also lies behind the emphasis on the cult of the Virgin Mary and of saints, so apparent in *The Westminster Hymnal*.[75] It is a conscious repudiation, dating from the Council of Trent, of Protestant criticism of these aspects of Catholic belief and not simply a result of following the Breviary.[76] Verse 3 of 'Faith of our fathers' opens:

> Faith of Our Fathers! *Mary's prayers*
> Shall win our country back to thee.

Yet behind such defiance lurks an element of fear – fear of Protestant contamination. Verse 2 of 'I am a faithful Catholic' states:

> I shun the haunts of those who seek
> To ensnare poor Catholic youth;
> No Church I own, no schools I know,
> But those that teach the truth.[77]

Here, then, was another reason for uniformity, and for the demand that *The Westminster Hymnal* be the only collection authorised by the hierarchy. Moreover it deliberately eschews all Protestant texts. Linked to this was the production of what James Britten described as 'the curiously illiterate preliminary list of approved hymns', published in full during 1910.[78] This is almost identical in content and layout with *The Westminster*

75 In addition to hymns in honour of the Virgin Mary and Holy Family there are 29 items honouring specific saints and 20 more under the categories of 'Apostles', 'Martyrs', 'English Martyrs' and 'English Saints'; WH (1916), pp. xiii and xiv.

76 John Elliott, *Europe Divided 1559–98* (London: Fontana/Collins, 1968, repr. 1977), p. 152.

77 *Crown of Jesus Music*, ed. Hemy, no. 62.

78 *The New (Complete) Catholic Hymn Book Containing the Hymns Prescribed and Arranged by the Catholic Hierarchy: with Latin Hymns and Benediction Service* (London: R. and T. Washbourne Ltd., 1910). This contains texts only.

Hymnal. Britten claimed that the policy was new.[79] In fact he should not have been surprised. The preface to *Arundel Hymns*, while admitting to the use of Protestant tunes, endorsed the policy as regards texts. There are also references to it as early as 10 October 1907 in the bishops' Acta.[80] The next logical step was to apply it to the music.

Terry's musical contribution to *The Westminster Hymnal*

The first thing to observe here is a difference in method; for whereas textually the hymnal was the product of a committee of bishops obsessed with doctrine and dogma, essentially the musical editing was the work of one man.[81]

Terry was born in 1865 at Ellington, Northumberland, but brought up by his uncle, the headmaster of Battersea Grammar School.[82] Thus, although retaining some northern contacts,[83] he epitomised the gradual southward shift in the centre of gravity within the Catholic community at that time.[84] Also, until 1895 he was an Anglican, which may explain the ambivalence behind the apparent certainty of some of his Catholic pronouncements.

At a tertiary level his musical training was practical. Between 1886 and 1888 he held an Organ scholarship at Oxford, where he matriculated, followed by a year's Choral scholarship at Cambridge; but in neither university did he take a degree. Scholarly skills were therefore picked up while reviving the English and Continental polyphonic repertoire, first at Downside (1896–1901), then at Westminster (1901–24). This has important implications for the quality of his editing in *The Westminster Hymnal.*

---

79   James Britten, 'Letter to the Editor', 10 August 1912, in *The Tablet*, NS 88 (July–Dec. 1912), p. 222.

80   WDA, *Bishops' Meetings 1864–1974*: folder marked 'Bourne 1903–08'. Hedley's preface also states that 'The hymns it [*The Westminster Hymnal*] contains are those that make up the book of hymns already approved by the bishops, with seven added to bring the number [of English hymns] up to 250'; *WH*, p. iii.

81   The presence of a musical editing committee is mentioned in the 'Music Editor's Preface'; but all accounts (e.g. *The Tablet*'s review, NS 87 (Jan.–June 1912), p. 968), including Hedley's introduction, emphasise the dominant role played by Terry. *WH*, pp. iii and xii.

82   The standard biography of Terry's career is still Andrews, *Westminster Retrospect*. For a more modern summary see T. Day, 'Sir Richard Terry and 16th-Century Polyphony', *Early Music*, 22 (1994), pp. 297–309.

83   In 1895 he was organist at St Dominic's, Newcastle.

84   Adrian Hastings, *A History of English Christianity 1920–85* (London: Collins, 1986), pp. 276–77.

Terry got the job not simply because he was at Westminster but through direct solicitation. In Cardinal Bourne's papers there survives a memorandum dated 31 March 1910 addressed to all the bishops. In it Terry stated that he had already set the bishops' hymnal to music, trying 'to give the correct version of each tune just as the composer wrote it'. His justification was an alleged general ignorance among English Catholics of their hymn repertoire and their inaccuracy in its rendition. Accordingly, he asked that the bishops give their imprimatur to his work as the authorised version and that diocesan inspectors enforce correct performances during their inspections of Catholic schools. On this basis he claimed that 'an important publishing firm' was willing to publish it at their own expense.[85]

The date of the memorandum, coinciding with the publication of the bishops' hymn texts, implies a good deal of haste on Terry's part, whatever subsequent revisions may have been undertaken by 1912; so the temptation to rely on his own judgement, rather than on objective factual research, must have been very strong. Moreover the separation between texts and music noted earlier gave Terry enormous latitude. However, there were two limiting factors: copyrights and traditional taste. Terry acknowledges both in his preface:

> The editor's original intention was to make the book an anthology of tunes by English composers. This was frustrated by the refusal of two proprietors of large collections of tunes to allow Terry to use their copyrights.[86]

> The collection includes all the popular tunes in common use amongst English-speaking Catholics. Some of these tunes are good, some indifferent; and some are bad. But it has been felt that since some of these of the last-named class have been – for one generation at least – bound up with the pious aspirations of so many holy lives, this is hardly the occasion for their suppression. They have therefore been retained ... Alternative tunes have been provided for most of them.[87]

The provision of alternative tunes was not unusual; but it does show how Terry tried to evade the problem. Twenty-one hymns in *The Westminster Hymnal* fall into the 'bad' tune category. Where Terry offers a tune of his own, or one by a favoured protégé, his preferences are fairly obvious. For example, Anselm Burge,[88] whose help Terry acknowledged in his preface, wrote the first tune of 'Ave Maria! O maiden, O mother' (*WH* 126). The

---

85 WDA, Bourne Papers: Bo1/33 Church Music 1904–10.
86 Britten identified one of these as the publishers of *Arundel Hymns*. These were R. and T. Washbourne and Boosey & Co. Since the former published *The Westminster Hymnal*, the latter must be the culprit. *The Tablet*, NS 88 (July–Dec. 1912), pp. 222–23. Given the way in which Terry secured the job of editor in the first place, this attitude is hardly surprising.
87 *WH*, pp. ix and v respectively.
88 Always referred to in the hymnal as 'Laurence Ampleforth'.

second tune is called 'Alta trinita beata' and is of medieval Italian origin. Given Terry's penchant for raiding Continental sources – of which more later – one suspects that here he made no allowances for traditional taste.

On two out of eight occasions when Terry offered a tune he put his own first (WH 38 and 107); but even when in second position his intention is clear, as shown with 'Hail thou star of ocean' (WH 110). Obviously Richardson's tune, despite not fitting the verse structure and therefore written for something else, was irremovable. 'Faith of our fathers' is similar. 'A Swiss Air', together with melodies by Haydn and Beethoven, is offered by Hemy; *The Parochial Hymnal* produces a completely different anonymous tune; whilst Storer in *A Catholic Tune Book* uses his own setting.[89] Hemy's 'Swiss Air', though, appears elsewhere in the book.[90] This resurfaces as the first of two melodies in *The Westminster Hymnal*. Once again Terry could not dispose of it; indeed he even discusses its proper performance in the preface.[91]

With 'Full in the panting heart of Rome' he is more assured, for different melodies had been offered by Hemy, *The Parochial Hymnal*, *The Catholic Tune Book* and Tozer.[92] Terry rejects them all, offering a choice between a tune by C.A. Cox and something from *La scala santa* of 1681 (WH 139). Here divisions in congregational taste gave Terry the opportunity to impose his preference. He does the same thing with 'Praise to the holiest in the height'. Elgar's *Dream of Gerontius* setting, Storer's tune in *The Catholic Tune Book*, 'An English Hymn Melody' and another by Arthur Somervell in *Arundel Hymns* are all discarded.[93] One melody – his own – is provided.[94]

Statistics show how much latitude Terry gives himself. Forty-eight tunes by him are listed in the back;[95] but it is when the small number of tunes from earlier hymnals are identified that something close to a break with the immediate past clearly emerges (see Table 4.8).

Behind this show of confidence, though, there are symptoms of uncertainty. First, as noted before, there was a clash in Terry's mind between the

---

89 WH 138. *Crown of Jesus Music*, ed. Hemy, no. 155; *PH* 8; *The Catholic Tune Book*, ed. Storer, no. 266.

90 *The Catholic Tune Book*, ed. Storer, no. 305.

91 WH, p. vi.

92 *Crown of Jesus Music*, ed. Hemy, no. 157; *PH* 160; *The Catholic Tune Book*, ed. Storer, no. 267; *Catholic Hymns with Accompanying Tunes*, ed. Tozer (London: Burns & Oates/ Novello, Ewer & Co., 3rd edn, 1898), no. 157.

93 Elgar's *Dream of Gerontius* setting, of which an adaptation was made by Elizabeth Poston (see *The Cambridge Hymnal*, ed. David Holbrook and Elizabeth Poston (Cambridge: Cambridge University Press, 1967), was not apparently in use before the First World War.

94 *The Catholic Tune Book*, ed. Storer, no. 88; *Arundel Hymns*, ed. Howard and Gatty (1905), no. 6; WH 56.

95 WH, p. 414.

Table 4.8   The number of hymn tunes found both in
The Westminster Hymnal and in earlier Catholic collections

Date of publication	Title of hymnal	Number of tunes also in *The Westminster Hymnal*	Total quantity of numbered items in the hymnal[a]
1864	*Crown of Jesus Music* (Parts 1–3)	9	377
1883	*The Parochial Hymnal*	23 (8 with significant variations in the tune)	633
1886	*Catholic Hymns*	14	79
1892	*The Catholic Tune Book*	21 (17 with English texts, 4 with Latin texts)	319
1898	*Catholic Hymns* (both editions)	29	186

a In some cases more than one tune is offered under each numbered item.

claims of the choir and those of the congregation. In *Catholic Church Music* he did 'not think it desirable that the people should sing in Mass where a really good choir is in existence'.[96] Clearly his interest in Renaissance polyphony, which could be sung only by choirs, had something to do with this. Similarly he had reservations about plainsong, especially Solesmes-style chant. Outwardly he supported the official line – 'The Pope has spoken and matters which were regarded as subjects for discussion have been removed from the region of controversy to the region of obedience';[97] but Andrews noted that he developed his own style of chant singing, and from 1903 he reduced the proportion of plainsong masses sung at Westminster Cathedral in favour of Renaissance polyphony.[98] Such reservations were shared by Burge, who was especially critical of Mocquereau's methods.[99]

This helps explain the small role played by plainchant in *The Westminster Hymnal*, even after its extra-liturgical function has been taken into

---

[96] Terry, *Catholic Church Music*, p. 122.
[97] Ibid., p. 39.
[98] Andrews, *Westminster Retrospect*, pp. 69–70, 74.
[99] Anselm Burge, 'An Examination of the Rhythmic Theories of Dom Mocquereau', *Ampleforth Journal*, 10 (1904), pp. 301–24; id. and S.H. Sole, 'Letters to the Editor: "Solesmes Plainsong"', in *The Tablet*, NS 73 (Jan.–June 1905), pp. 20–22.

account. There are only 13 Latin texts with a total of 16 melodies, six of which are not in plainchant, though this could be due to traditional Catholic taste. Moreover, although claiming to follow the Vatican and Solesmes antiphoners, the layout, combining neumes on four-line staves for the voices with an accompaniment in modern notation, is similar to that of *The English Hymnal* (1906). Even the typography is virtually the same. With the accompaniment Terry uses his own system, keeping in view four points: 'simplicity, directness, due regard to the accentuation of the notes, and strict adherence to the Mode in which the melody is written'.[100] He was even accused of using a Mechlin version discarded by the Vatican typical edition for the 'Stabat Mater'.[101]

With the exclusion of Protestant material there is a similar dichotomy. Here again Terry endorsed official policy: 'It has been deemed advisable that the tunes, like the hymns, should be by Catholic authors, or from Catholic sources.'[102] Indeed he had openly advocated it in the memorandum of 1910. Moreover, during the 1930s when the hymnal was being revised, he took this much further, as an annotated copy of the 1932 edition sent to Dom Gregory Murray at Downside Abbey shows. For example, under 'Hail to thee! True Body sprung!' he wrote 'as the composer has apostatised and is returned to Anglicanism (and is still alive) I think it best to scrap this ...'.[103] Yet such behaviour is proof that he had been insufficiently rigorous in 1912. Moreover in the 1930s, at that very time he was editing Calvin's 1539 Psalter and the Scottish Psalter of 1635, three items from which appeared in the revised *Westminster Hymnal* of 1940. One of these is even paired with a Faber text – 'Dear Angel! Ever at my side'.[104] Andrews also noted that when at Westminster Cathedral Terry commissioned works from non-Catholics, such as Vaughan Williams, Arnold Bax and Herbert Howells.[105]

How then did Terry 'square the circle'? One argument was that 'In the case of Continental tunes the authorship is sometimes difficult to fix, since many are sung by Catholics and Protestants alike. The presence of such tunes in Catholic chorale books and their constant use amongst Catholic congregations has been deemed sufficient warrant for their inclusion here.'[106] Even so, it is extraordinary that in two cases he used tunes attributed to Claude Goudimel, whose *Les Psaumes mis en rime françoise*,

---

100 *WH*, p. x.
101 'P.L', 'Letter to the Editor', 3 August 1912, in *The Tablet*, NS 88 (July–Dec. 1912), pp. 184–86. Actually Terry claimed it was 'French: Possibly 17th century'; *WH*, p. 409.
102 *WH*, p. ix.
103 *WH* (1932 edn), no. 70. The composer in question was S.E.L. Spooner-Livingstone.
104 *The Westminster Hymnal: a New and Revised Edition*, ed. Bainbridge (1940), no. 184.
105 Andrews, *Westminster Retrospect*, pp. 133–34.
106 *WH*, p. ix.

published in 1565, was co-edited by Théodore de Bèze, John Calvin's successor as leader of the Protestant theocracy of Geneva.[107] Another argument was to take the 'recovery of Catholic heritage' line used with Renaissance polyphony. Catholic music performed in Anglican cathedrals 'was written by Catholics for the services of the Catholic Church. It is our heritage – our birthright.'[108] It is the same concept of re-establishing links with the past as understood by Guéranger, Hedley, Burge and other Benedictines. It meant that 'Catholic hymns' could be 'recovered' from Protestant hymnals. Thus *The Westminster Hymnal* shares five texts and music with *The English Hymnal* (1906);[109] nine items have identical or near identical texts with different music[110] and a further eight are related in some way.[111] Such sophistry did not pass unnoticed in *The Tablet*'s review.[112]

The use of Continental material referred to above is a particular feature of *The Westminster Hymnal*, affecting 59 English and two Latin texts. Terry named his sources in 45 cases.[113] Twenty-eight out of the 32 collections are German.[114] Table 4.9 lists his Continental sources by period. A rather greater emphasis on the early modern period, compared with the medieval and nineteenth-century bias in the texts, is apparent. Terry must have felt that this was justified by the need to bring English Catholics into closer contact with the culture of their European co-religionists.

In reality, one Continental tradition was being substituted for another. A striking feature of *Crown of Jesus Music* is the number of tunes by established 'Classical' – especially Viennese – composers (see Table 4.10). In *The Westminster Hymnal* this number is cut to nine, but with a small compensatory increase in the number of Renaissance composers, reflecting Terry's personal tastes (see Table 4.11).

---

107 *WH* 15 and 134. Paul-André Galliard/Richard Freedman, 'Goudimel, Claude', in *The New Grove Dictionary of Music and Musicians*, 2nd edn, ed. Stanley Sadie and John Tyrrell (London: Macmillan, 2001), vol. 10, pp. 209–11.

108 Terry, *Catholic Church Music*, p. 198.

109 *EH* 40/*WH* 18; *EH* 99/*WH* 95; *EH* 161/*WH* 53; *EH* 28/*WH* 5; *EH* 71/*WH* 24.

110 *EH* 5/*WH* 1; *EH* 512/*WH* 59; *EH* 471/*WH* 56; *EH* 341/*WH* 52; *EH* 419/*WH* 19; *EH* 638/*WH* 246; *EH* 390/*WH* 245; *EH* 382/*WH* 145; *EH* 381/*WH* 64.

111 For example, four had the same Latin source but a different translation. (e.g., *EH* 153/ *WH* 4 'Come Holy Ghost, our souls inspire/Come Holy Ghost Creator come', based on 'Veni Creator Spiritus'.

112 Anon., review of *The Westminster Hymnal*, 26 June 1912, in *The Tablet*, NS 87 (Jan.– June 1912), p. 968.

113 Elsewhere he just refers to an 'Italian Melody', an 'English Melody', and 'Irish Melody' or 'German', *WH*, p. 413, nos. 126, 12, 53, 153, 166, 211, 222, 235, 201, 203, 18, 73(ii), 133, 169.

114 This includes the *Strasbourg Gesangbuch* of 1697, as the city was then part of the Holy Roman Empire although already under French occupation.

Table 4.9 Continental hymnals in
The Westminster Hymnal divided by period

Period	Number of hymnals used	Title of hymnal as given by Terry (*WH*, pp. 403–409)
1500–99	4	From Vehle's *Gesangbuchlein*, 1537
		Leisentritt's Gesangbuch, 1567
		Catholicum Hymnologium Germanicum, 1587
		Speier Gesangbuch, 1589
1600–99	13	*Andernach Gesangbuch*, 1608
		M. Praetorius, 1609
		(therefore his *Musae Sioniae*)
		Catholische geistliche Gesange, 1608
		Koln Gesangbuch, 1622
		Geistliche Kirchengesange (Cologne), 1623
		Korners Gesangbuch, 1631
		Psalteriolum Harmonicum, 1642
		J. Cruger, 1658 (therefore the *Psalmodia Sacra*)
		Mainz Gesangbuch, 1661
		Nurnburg Gesangbuch, 1676
		La Santa Scala, 1681
		Strassbourg Gesangbuch, 1697
		Katholisches geistliche Gesange, 1698
1700–99	5	*Mainz Gesangbuch*, 1725
		Tochter Sion (Cologne, 1741)
		Katholisches geistliche Gesangbuch (Vienna, 1744)
		Paderborn Gesangbuch, 1765
		Landshut Gesangbuch, 1777
1800–77	6	Adapted from [X.L.] Hartigs *Siona* (1832)
		Limburg Gesangbuch, 1838
		Caspar Ett (*Cantica Sacra*), 1840
		Koln Gesangbuch, 1852
		Rottenberg Gesangbuch, 1865
		Trier Gesangbuch, 1872
Undated	4	*Cantuarium S. Galli*
		La Feillée
		Miltenburg Processionale
		Tours Breviary
Total no. of hymnals	32	

Table 4.10   Tunes by 'Classical' composers in
Crown of Jesus Music (Parts 1–3)

J.S. Bach	1	Handel	14	Purcell	1
Beethoven	43	J. Haydn	47	Romberg	1
Cherubini	1	M. Haydn	1	Rossini	1
Cimarosa	1	Himmel	2	Spohr	1
Clementi	1	Mendelssohn	11	Tallis	1
Farrant	1	Mozart	37	Weber	3
Gluck	3	Pleyel	4		

Total: 175 out of 377 in the collection

Table 4.11   Classical and Renaissance composers in
The Westminster Hymnal (pp. 413–14)

Composer	Number of melodies	Hymn numbers
Renaissance composers		
T. Tallis	6	4, 13, 42, 47, 50 and 227(iii)
C. Tye	6	131, 142, 157, 221, 224 and 237
H. Isaac	3	32, 49 and 205 (all reharmonised by J.S. Bach)
Total	15	
Classical composers		
[J.S. Bach]	[2]	[16 and 266] (these are reharmonisations of earlier melodies)
C. Ett	2	204 and 261
M. Haydn	1	71
J. Haydn	3	156, 197 and 210
I. Pleyel	1	65
Total	7 [+2] = 9	

Table 4.12   Tunes by established 'Classical' and
Renaissance composers in Catholic hymnals

Hymnal	Renaissance composers	18th-century composers	19th-century composers
The Catholic Hymn Book (1892)	O. Gibbons (no. 273) G. Palestrina (no. 167)	J. Haydn (no. 145)	F. Mendelssohn (nos. 56, 201)
Catholic Hymns (1886)	—	—	J. Stainer (no. 22) [V. Schulthes (nos. 27, 264)]
Catholic Hymns (1898)	—	J. Haydn (no. 164)	F. Mendelssohn (no. 92) J. Stainer (no. 170)

However, in fairness to Terry, 'Classical' composers had already been largely removed from earlier hymnals, as Table 4.12 shows, the gap being filled by English tunesmiths. What Terry did was to substitute his Continental sources for these native composers, in a sense bringing the wheel round in an overlapping circle.

Whatever his doubts on these matters, Terry showed no uncertainty about uniformity of performance:

> It has been felt that the chief defect in Catholic hymn-singing today is the lack of uniformity in the melodies of even the most popular hymns. Each congregation is a law unto itself, and variants of almost every popular tune are so numerous, that chaos is the result when … different congregations unite in singing.[115]

This passage was lifted straight from the memorandum of 1910; and the parallel with the bishops, obsessed with creating a uniform collection of texts, is unmistakable. Terry goes on to cite 11 detailed examples where hymn tunes were commonly distorted in this fashion.[116] Moreover –

115 p. v.
116 'Faith of our fathers', 'Hail Queen of heaven', 'Sing, Sing ye angel bands', 'Mother of mercy', 'Full in the panting heart of Rome', 'To Jesus' heart all burning', 'Kind angel guardian, thanks to thee', 'Tyburn's days are long forgotten', and Webbe's settings of 'Veni Sancte Spiritus', 'O salutaris' and 'Tantum ergo', the last two of which do not even appear in the collection.

Ex. 4.2 'Sweet Sacrament divine'

Source: *The Parochial Hymnal*, 1883, no. 285

Source: *The Westminster Hymnal*, 1912, no. 78

ironically enough, given Terry's suspicions of Solesmes – a similar passion for accurate performance lay behind Mocquereau's development of rhythmic signs for the singing of plainchant. Both assumed there was but one authentic original to be followed. The trouble was that this was no more true with hymnody than for plainchant. For example, Hemy provides a largely three-part harmonisation of 'Adeste fideles' with the chorus for everybody starting four bars before the 'Venite adoremus'.[117] Similarly, there are differences between *The Westminster Hymnal* and *The Parochial Hymnal* in F. Stanfield's setting of 'Sweet Sacrament divine'. Here Terry's decision to use minims instead of crotchets for the basic pulse, his double bar after 'home', and the transposition into E major accentuate the gravity and slow down the speed of performance, even though there is no tempo indication (see Ex. 4.2).

Each parish, then, may have been 'a law unto itself' through adherence to different printed versions of the same tunes. The examples given above also show a difference in taste between a faster style of execution used earlier and the more stodgy, slower, more even and more 'square' style adumbrated by Terry and perhaps deriving from his experience with editing Renaissance 'white note' music.

---

117 *Crown of Jesus Music*, ed. Hemy, p. 200. The treatment of the chorus in this fashion follows Vincent Novello's setting, first published in his *A Collection of Sacred Music* (London: Phipps & Co., 1811), vol. 2.

Such differences also raise questions about his scholarship. At the time great play was made about the qualitative improvement achieved in this respect by *The Westminster Hymnal*. Hedley's preface declares that 'the musical setting is, on the whole, far more satisfying and scientific than anything that has hitherto appeared'.[118] The word 'scientific' is particularly interesting, for it was precisely this quality that characterised Solesmes's plainchant researches.[119] It was also the watchword for the 'scientific' school of history, relying on the meticulous study of documents in state archives, proclaimed by Lord Acton in *The Cambridge Modern History* in 1902 and by other followers of Leopold von Ranke.[120] It is tempting to view Terry's work in the same light. Yet Hedley inserts the vital words 'on the whole', implying that he may have had doubts, especially since he must have known how Terry got the job as musical editor back in 1910. Richard Turbet has recently shown that in the late 1910s Terry was displaced as chief editor of the prestigious Tudor Church Music Series of publications precisely because he was found wanting in the scholarly and administrative skills that were required.[121] *The Tablet's* correspondence shows that such deficiencies may apply to *The Westminster Hymnal* as well. Britten thought it scholastically inferior to *Arundel Hymns*, a charge that might be justified when one considers the enormous amount of genuine original research Charles Gatty undertook, especially into Italian 'Laudi spirituali' and the entire output of De Pearsall. There cannot have been anything comparable behind *The Westminster Hymnal*, given the circumstances and timing of Terry's 1910 memorandum.[122] 'P.L.' attacked the 'mangling' of Burge's hymns; Francis Edward Gladstone, the ex-Anglican former organist of Norwich Cathedral, remarked on 'the inattention to the rules of prosody shown (not infrequently) by the Musical editor', citing nos. 110, 180 and 229 as examples.[123] Most tellingly of all, Mary Simpson, daughter of George Herbert, the composer of the tune 'Sunset' for 'Sweet Saviour bless us ere we go', originally written for the hymn 'Jesus! My Lord, my God, my all', stated that Terry had, as in other

---

118 *WH*, p. iii.

119 Bergeron, *Decadent Enchantments*, pp. 192–97.

120 Arthur Marwick, *The Nature of History* (London: The Macmillan Press Ltd. for The Open University, 1970, repr. 1976), pp. 34–40, 46–49, 52–54.

121 Richard Turbet, 'An Affair of Honour: "Tudor Church Music", the Ousting of Richard Terry, and a Trust Vindicated', *Music & Letters*, 76 (1995), pp. 593–600; id., 'A Monument to Enthusiasm and Industry: Further Light on "Tudor Church Music"', *Music & Letters*, 81 (2000), pp. 433–37.

122 See the Charles Gatty papers: Downside Archives: Boxes 1267–69 and 1274–78.

123 Britten, 'Letter to the Editor', 10 August 1912, pp. 222–23; 'P.L', 'Letter to the Editor', 3 August 1912, pp. 184–86; and Francis Edward Gladstone, 'Letter to the Editor', 20 July 1912, p. 104 respectively in *The Tablet*, NS 88 (July–Dec. 1912).

Catholic adaptations, mistakenly used a 'g#' in the fourth bar. Moreover she claimed that Terry had failed to reply to her letter, written before publication, warning him of this fact.[124]

This example confirms that what mattered in the final analysis was Terry's musical taste, because his published setting makes good musical sense. As he himself stated: 'This book is intended for immediate practical use; and while a reversion to the original form of ancient tunes is possible in a country with an unbroken Catholic tradition, it is *at present* [Terry's italics] in England ... rather a counsel of perfection than a practicable idea.'[125]

The effects of *The Westminster Hymnal*

It remains now to consider the effects of *The Westminster Hymnal*. Was it a break with the past? Did it improve Catholic singing? Did it establish a uniform repertoire?

The answer to the first question is mixed. Statistically, the paucity of tunes from earlier hymns signals a considerable break, as does the intrusion of numerous melodies from Continental sources. The attempt to produce one official list of hymns, and exclude all others, may have been new, but not necessarily unforeseen. The development of a standardised textual repertoire, together with the continuing influence of Faber and Caswall, is a feature of earlier hymnals. A stress on uniformity, and with it exclusivity, was inherent in the Catholic Church at that time. The removal of so many tunes by Classical composers like Mozart and Haydn before *The Westminster Hymnal*, or even the 'Motu Proprio', was published was symptomatic. Hemy's choice of Papageno's tune for 'I am a faithful Catholic', intended for children, would have been inconceivable by 1912, precisely because it was secular. The 'Motu Proprio', by distinguishing between secular and sacred music, articulated the idea that in music, as with other things, Catholics should be insulated from corrupting worldly influences.

It has been shown that in many areas Terry tried to alter Catholic taste, most notably by sidelining, if not removing, popular tunes that he disliked, hoping that in the long run they would fall by the wayside. This itself is evidence of continuity, for in several instances he failed to achieve his long-term end. *The Parish Hymnal*, published in 1966, has many *Crown of Jesus* tunes that Terry had tried to remove from the repertoire. For example, with 'Hail, Queen of heav'n, the ocean star', his alternative

---

124 Mary Simpson, 'Letter to the Editor', 27 July 1912, in *The Tablet*, NS 88 (July–Dec. 1912), p. 146. *WH* 215. Note, though, that here it has been transposed into E flat major.
125 *WH*, p. x.

melody is discarded, leaving Hemy's version in undisputed possession.[126] The same thing happens to 'Mother of mercy, day by day';[127] while with 'This is the image of the Queen' Hemy's tune, which Terry eliminated altogether, is restored.[128]

Turning to congregational singing, it is clear that standards often remained low. Terry's opinion, expressed in 1907 and 1931, was damning: 'Whatever may be the case in other countries, it is a certain fact that congregational singing is not cultivated in the Catholic Churches of England as it deserves to be.'[129] Similar strictures appeared from time to time in *The Tablet*. The previous discussion throws up five reasons for this. Two are general, namely the fact that Renaissance polyphony was confined to choirs and the failure to persuade congregations to learn plainchant.[130] Three are specific to *The Westminster Hymnal*. It was not designed for the Mass; at its heart there is uncertainty about the 'balance of power' between congregational and choral hymnody; and Terry's attempts to impose new tunes and sideline those he disliked were likely to have fallen foul of popular taste.

Such factors help explain the partial failure of the bishops to impose uniformity through the hymnal. It was not simply that prescribed lists were criticised; new hymnals continued to be introduced. For example, *The Daily Hymnal* was published in 1931; and John Driscoll produced a series of *Cantionales* for the great Jesuit establishments at Wimbledon, Stonyhurst, Beaumont and Manresa in the 1930s.[131] On the other hand, in 1922 the Catholic Truth Society published *The Catholic Schools Hymn*

---

126 WH 102. *The Parish Hymnal*, ed. John Rush (London: L.J. Cary & Co., 1966), no. 139.

127 WH 102. *Parish Hymnal*, ed. Rush, no. 102.

128 WH 119. *Parish Hymnal*, ed. Rush, no. 153. For other variations see:
'I'll sing a hymn to Mary'. Both Terry and Rush used Hemy's tune; but as an alternative Rush substituted a melody by Crüger for Terry's own composition. WH 112. *Parish Hymnal*, ed. Rush, no. 140.
'Jesu, my Lord, my God, my all', where Rush removed the last five verses along with Terry's own tune but retained the rest along with the 'Traditional' melody used in *The Westminster Hymnal*, no. 72. *Parish Hymnal*, ed. Rush, no. 110.
'Daily, daily sing to Mary'. Here Rush reversed the order of melodies, giving first place to Hemy's tune over Terry's choice of a spurious version of 'Maria zu lieben'. WH 100. *Parish Hymnal*, ed. Rush, no. 137.

129 Terry, *Catholic Church Music*, p. 121, and id., *The Music of the Roman Rite*, p. 106.

130 For example, in *The Tablet* 'Perplexed' asked 'why Gregorian Vespers sung for many years by a decent choir … should empty our Church here into which no-one … enters until Vespers are known to be over?' 'Letter to the Editor', 31 August 1929, NS 122 (July–Dec. 1929), p. 277.

131 *The Beaumont Cantionale, The Wimbledon Cantionale, The Stonyhurst Cantionale, The Manresa Cantionale*, ed. John Driscoll. Text versions were printed at Roehampton: Manresa Press in 1937. The status of Organ copies is more confused. That for Wimbledon is dated 1927. Stonyhurst's has the date 1936, but the Preface makes it clear that printing was not undertaken till 1940.

Book specifically, as its preface points out, to overcome congregational apathy. By the end of the year 140 000 copies had been sold.[132] Twenty-seven out of its 28 hymns are from *The Westminster Hymnal*, the remaining items being mainly plainchant settings. Yet the very fact that such a collection was produced shows that, at least as far as schools were concerned, Terry's volume was too unwieldy an instrument. The defining moment came in 1940. The revised version of *The Westminster Hymnal* retains only 59 texts, 35 hymn tunes and 8 plainsong chants from the 1912 edition amongst its 275 items. Terry's quota of original settings was cut to six; Faber and Caswall texts were reduced to 18 and 17 apiece.[133] Meanwhile 29 Protestant tunes were introduced and the number of plainchant settings rose to 36.

Thus although Terry's hymnal must have exerted a substantial influence, its impact was not as all-embracing and decisive as might be supposed from its official status and the number of its editions. As T.H. Knuckley remarked when it first came out, it was generally an improvement on what went before, 'but we are as yet far from possessing a hymn book which may be regarded as final, as worthy of unconditional authorisation'.[134]

---

132 This is the figure given on the copy held by St Cuthbert's Catholic Church, Durham.
133 *The Westminster Hymnal: a New and Revised Edition*, ed. Bainbridge (1940), pp. 441–42.
134 T.H. Knuckley, 'Letter to the Editor', 26 June 1912, in *The Tablet*, NS 87 (Jan.–June 1912), p. 1022.

CHAPTER FIVE

Ancient and Modern in the Work of Sir John Stainer

Nicholas Temperley

Few Victorian composers have had such a bad press as John Stainer (1840–1901). He died well respected in the musical world.[1] Yet only six years after his death, Ernest Walker passed unfavourable judgement on his music, which he lumped with that of John Bacchus Dykes (1823–76) and Joseph Barnby (1838–96) under the general stigma of 'sentimentalism'.[2] Taking his cue from Walker, Edmund Fellowes was very hard on them in his authoritative study of English cathedral music. As a leader in the revival of Elizabethan and Jacobean music, he placed what he called the 'mid-Victorians' at the other end of the scale. Though praising Stainer's choice of texts, he took the trouble to print two rather weak passages to demonstrate that the anthems were written 'too easily' – as if a composer was to be judged by his poorest work.[3] Kenneth Long, whose book *The Music of the English Church* could be called 'Fellowes plus prejudice' (even to the point of using many of the same examples), repeated Fellowes's views of Stainer in less restrained language.[4] He added a gratuitous attack on Stainer's *Crucifixion* (not, strictly, within the scope of his book), which he called 'squalid music', and he even criticised those who venture to perform it, calling them 'a hard core of organists and choirmasters who are ignorant and self-satisfied'. Recent commentators are more mildly negative. John Caldwell says that Stainer's anthems and services 'are often weakened by an enervating chromaticism and a static movement of the vocal parts'.[5]

---

1 See the many tributes quoted in Peter Charlton, *John Stainer and the Musical Life of Victorian Britain* (Newton Abbot: David & Charles, 1984), pp. 169–75.

2 Ernest Walker, *A History of Music in England* (Oxford: Clarendon Press, 1907), p. 308.

3 Edmund H. Fellowes, *English Cathedral Music from Edward VI to Edward VII* (London: Methuen & Co., Ltd., 1941), pp. 222–26. Jack Westrup made no relevant changes in this section when revising the book for the 5th edn (1969).

4 Kenneth R. Long, *The Music of the English Church* (London: Hodder & Stoughton, 1971), pp. 364–65. He also singled out for disdain a passage from Barnby's *Jubilate* in E which he had copied from Fellowes, who, in turn, had taken it from Walker.

5 John Caldwell, *The Oxford History of English Music*, vol. 2 (Oxford: Oxford University Press, 1999), p. 308.

The accepted twentieth-century view among critics and scholars was that Stainer was an excellent man and musician, who did much for musicology and music education, and for Magdalen College, Oxford, and St Paul's Cathedral; but as for his compositions, the less said the better. At mid-century Jack Westrup summed it up in a passage added to Walker's *History*: 'Fortunately Stainer's reputation depends not on his music but on his services to scholarship. Musicians today have no use for *The Crucifixion* but *Dufay and His Contemporaries* and the volumes of *Early Bodleian Music* are still valued.' It was almost as if Stainer were being given a consolation prize.[6]

This critical consensus had little to do with the views of the public, which knew and loved Stainer largely as a composer and arranger. *The Crucifixion* continued to be a great favourite, and still is, no matter what the critics think;[7] the services and anthems lingered on cathedral lists; and several of the hymn tunes, chants and carol harmonisations have survived both the general anti-Victorian reaction and the rediscovery of older music.[8]

Before attempting to reassess Stainer's church music, I will first discuss the perception that he was primarily an important musicologist. (I pass over his importance to music education, which is probably considerable, and his activities at St Paul's, which have been thoroughly described by Timothy Storey.[9])

In 1940, to mark the centenary of Stainer's birth, an unsigned article appeared in the *Musical Times*.[10] It had little good to say about Stainer's compositions, and reserved its enthusiasm for his scholarly work, saying that 'his book, "Dufay and His Contemporaries", is still a standard work on 15th-century music'. George Guest picked up this idea in a later issue of the same journal: 'It is probably true that as an all-round scholar and musician, Stainer was unrivalled in this country. His many papers published in the Proceedings of the (now Royal) Musical Association are proof of the former – as is his book on Dufay, which is still a classic.'[11]

In fact there is no such book. *Dufay and His Contemporaries*, published in 1898, is not a 'book on Dufay' by Stainer but an edition of selected songs from Bodleian MS Canonici misc. 213 by Stainer's son and

---

6   Walker, *A History of Music in England*, 3rd edn, rev. J.A. Westrup (Oxford: Oxford University Press, 1952), p. 330.

7   Long in 1971 admitted that 'each year hundreds of performances continue to be given'.

8   Fourteen of his tunes are in *Hymns Ancient and Modern Revised*, [2nd edn] ([London]: William Clowes & Sons, Ltd., 1972), and five of the most popular carols still carry his harmonies in *The New Oxford Book of Carols*, ed. Hugh Keyte and Andrew Parrott (Oxford: Oxford University Press, 1992).

9   Timothy Storey, 'The Music of St. Paul's Cathedral' (M.Mus. thesis, University of Durham, 1998), pp. 1–40.

10   'John Stainer, 1840–1901', *Musical Times*, 81 (1940), pp. 300–301.

11   George Guest, 'Counsel from the Console', *Musical Times*, 100 (1959), pp. 104–5.

daughter. The palaeographical expertise was supplied by E.W.B. Nicholson, then Bodley's Librarian. Sir John contributed only a chapter of the introduction, in which he did not discuss the manuscript or its provenance, but analysed the music. He also probably went through the musical text, adding editorial suggestions. It was much the same with the 1901 publication, *Early Bodleian Music*. In that case Stainer's contribution remained unfinished at the time of his death, but the editors acknowledged that he was responsible for the added *musica ficta* accidentals.

It is true that Stainer became interested in fifteenth-century music in the last few years of his life, apparently as a direct result of the historical lectures he organised at Oxford after his appointment as professor in 1889. The texts of these lectures are lost, but their titles and the names of the lecturers are preserved, and have been printed as an appendix to Peter Charlton's book.[12] At first Stainer spoke on such subjects as 'The present state of Music in England', 'Mendelssohn's oratorio, "Elijah"', 'Mozart's Requiem', and certain theoretical topics, leaving the early history to Hubert Parry. In 1893 he gave his first 'early music' lecture, on 'Palestrina's Mass, Aeterna Christi Munera', and in 1896 he spoke on 'The secular compositions of Dufay, with illustrations'; later he ventured into other Renaissance topics such as Morley, Hassler, and early psalm-tune harmonisations.

Some of these topics are also reflected in his addresses to the Musical Association. It is probably true that Stainer's prestige helped to arouse interest in these earlier kinds of music, a fact for which Parry expressed his gratitude in comments following Stainer's paper delivered to the Musical Association on 12 November 1895.[13] This was entitled 'A Fifteenth Century MS. Book of Vocal Music in the Bodleian Library, Oxford' and was about Canonici misc. 213. Musical illustrations were played on three or four violas, because of the difficulty of finding singers who knew how to pronounce medieval French. No doubt the lecture was essentially the same as the one to be delivered at Oxford a few months later. Stainer's introductory chapter to *Dufay and His Contemporaries*, which he dated 'Oxford, 1898', was a revised and more comprehensive version of the same material.[14]

In the Musical Association paper Stainer reacted to the music as a musician, and a modern musician at that. He was obviously fascinated by the notation and musical style of Dufay and the ways in which they differed from his own time. In one example, shown here as Ex. 5.1, from Dufay's

---

12   Charlton, *John Stainer*, pp. 205–8.

13   John Stainer, 'A Fifteenth Century MS. Book of Vocal Music in the Bodleian Library, Oxford', *Proceedings of the Musical Association*, 22 (1895–96), pp. 1–21.

14   John Stainer, 'Chapter III', in J.F.R. and C. Stainer (eds), *Dufay and His Contemporaries: Fifty Compositions* (London: Novello, 1898), pp. 27–45.

Ex. 5.1   Dufay's 'Belles vueillies votre mercy donner', as transcribed by Stainer

'Belles vueillies votre mercy donner', there is a glaring false relation between the two lower parts. Stainer theorised that the sharp before the bass *f* was a warning to singers *not* to sharpen the note according to the rules of *musica ficta*; in other words, it meant 'sing F natural'.[15] He offered no supporting evidence. In Heinrich Besseler's edition of the same song,[16] now considered authoritative, the sharp is retained and the alto *f* is supplied with an editorial sharp as well, a rather awkward solution. Interestingly enough, Stainer's theory that a sharp might in some circumstances mean 'don't sharpen' has been revived much more recently, backed up by substantial evidence; but it is still controversial.[17] I cannot adjudicate the case, but I draw attention to the fact that Stainer's solution was prompted solely by his musical intuition, which, of course, was based on modern tonality.

Ex. 5.2a is also a musical example from the 1895 paper, taken from another song by Dufay, 'Bon jour, bon mois'. Stainer says of it: '[Dufay] clearly wishes in one place to make a cadence in A minor, but he diverts it thus, being clearly unable to reach the desired key. This frequent avoidance of definite cadences in keys into which he evidently would be glad to modulate is a sign of the peculiar and unsettled state of key-tonality in his time.'[18] But by 1898 he had changed his mind, probably under the influence of scholars who knew about *musica ficta*. When the song appeared in *Dufay and His Contemporaries,* editorial accidentals were supplied as in Ex. 5.2b,[19] and in his Introduction he said of this song: 'His [Dufay's] modulations are much superior to those by most of his contemporaries ... notice ... the smoothness of the modulation into *A minor*' (from G minor), with the example printed as in Ex. 5.2c.[20]

---

15   Stainer, 'A Fifteenth Century MS.', p. 5. This song is not included in *Dufay and His Contemporaries*.

16   *Guillelmi Dufay Omnia Opera,* ed. Heinrich Besseler, vol. 6 (Rome: American Institute of Musicology, 1964), p. 77.

17   See Don Harrán, 'New Evidence for Musica Ficta: the Cautionary Sign', *Journal of the American Musicological Society,* 29 (1976), pp. 77–98; Irving Godt and Don Harrán, 'Comments and Issues', *Journal of the American Musicological Society,* 31 (1978), pp. 385–95. Neither source mentions Stainer's anticipation of Harrán's theory.

18   Stainer, 'A Fifteenth Century MS.', p. 11.

19   Stainer and Stainer, *Dufay and His Contemporaries*, p. 134.

20   Stainer, 'Chapter III', p. 35. The same solution is offered by Besseler, *Guillelmi Dufay*, p. 66.

Ex. 5.2   Three different transcriptions of a passage from Dufay's 'Bon jour, bon mois'

Stainer's comments in these two cases are a sign that he was no musicologist, but rather a highly intelligent musician, who believed in the excellence and permanent validity of modern, that is nineteenth-century, harmony. He could understand early music only in teleological terms: 'the composers of the first half of the fifteenth century are still groping after facility of modulation and contrast of keys'.[21] That was not an unusual attitude in his time and place, and it elicited no protests in the discussion at the Musical Association, or in reviews of the edition. But it had certainly been overtaken by musicologists well before that time – mostly German, but including also such British scholars as William Chappell (1809–88), Edward Rimbault (1816–76), and the French émigré Arnold Dolmetsch (1858–1940). The contemporary edition of the *Fitzwilliam Virginal Book* (1899), edited jointly by John A. Fuller Maitland (1856–1936) and William Barclay Squire (1855–1927), also displayed a professionally musicological approach in clear contrast with Stainer's.

If we look at Stainer's life as a whole, we see that he was instinctively a modernist. In an address to the Church Congress at Leeds in 1872 he made a plea for representing the best music of all periods in the choice of music for cathedral services, including the most modern. 'There are some ancient melodies', he said, 'which lived before *harmony* (in the modern sense of the word) was invented, which have come down to our time in all their original simplicity ... The so-called Ambrosian Te Deum is one of these, and when harmonised quite simply, may claim its ... right to be heard sometimes within our cathedral walls.' But he went on: 'I do not, however, mean to say that modern chords should not be used.'[22]

This approach is borne out in Stainer's harmonisation of the Ambrosian Te Deum as printed in the *Cathedral Prayer Book* (1891), part of which is

---

21 Stainer, 'Chapter III', p. 35.

22 [John] Stainer, untitled paper, in *Authorised Report of the Church Congress Held at Leeds, October ... 1872* (Leeds: Thomas Ponsonby, [1872]), pp. 334–39, at p. 336. It was reprinted in *The Choir* (26 Oct. 1872) under the title 'The Principles on which Music should be Selected for Use in Cathedrals'.

Ex. 5.3   Stainer's harmonisation of the Ambrosian Te Deum

shown in Ex. 5.3. The melody is taken from John Marbeck's *Booke of Common Praier Noted* (1550), and is roughly in the Phrygian mode. Stainer began by using chords that he thought would have been acceptable in 1550. But when, at 'We believe', the same melody is reharmonised in C major, though each chord is still a common triad (or a 6–3 on D, perfectly respectable in sixteenth-century terms), the spirit as well as the theory of modality is lost, and the tempo and dynamic marks reveal a thoroughly nineteenth-century outlook. Later, Stainer finally yields to temptation and writes a 'modern' harmonic progression. As it happens, his setting of 'Day by day we magnify thee' is practically identical with the first phrase of that quintessentially Victorian tune 'Hollingside', by Dykes, often sung to the hymn 'Jesu, lover of my soul'.

But before passing hasty judgement let us look, for a moment, at what J.S. Bach did to a sixteenth-century tune in the Phrygian mode, 'Aus tiefer Not' (Ex. 5.4, from Cantata 38, last movement). The harmonies are more flagrantly anachronistic than anything Stainer did. If Bach, who can do no wrong in the prevailing view of music history, modernised modal music for his time, why shouldn't Stainer do the same for *his* time?

Having, I hope, cleared away the illusion that Stainer was primarily important as a scholar, I would like to reconsider his position as a

Ex. 5.4   J.S. Bach's harmonisation of 'Aus tiefer Not'

composer, specifically in the area of church music, which was obviously the centre of his creative effort and achievement.

Stainer's second address to the Church Congress, at Brighton in 1874, had a significant title: 'On the Progressive Character of Church Music'. Here he took to task those who imitated ancient styles in their church music, thus firmly setting himself against not only William Crotch and the other Gresham Prize judges of S.S. Wesley's time, but also his revered mentor, Sir Frederick Ouseley (1825–89), who was present and had given the previous lecture. Indeed he explicitly criticised not only the imitation of older styles, but the styles themselves, in those cases where 'counterpoint renders confused or unintelligible those sacred words on which it should be, as it were, a commentary'. He repeated his plea: 'I only ask that modern music shall have its proper place assigned to it, side by side with the old, and I only preach that those who call themselves church-composers should aim at something better than bygone styles.'[23]

Of course, modernity is relative. There is a natural tendency for the music of the church, in striving to suggest eternal truths, to resemble the general musical style of one or two generations earlier, so that the oldest worshippers present are not shocked by a sense of disruption or decay. Stainer's compositions show that his idea of modernity was founded on music of the Classical period, especially Mozart's. It is significant that he played Mozart's *Ave verum corpus*, a very Staineresque piece, as an illustration of the 1874 lecture. He was himself a master of Classical melody and harmony, to which he added decorative chromaticism from time to time – another trait for which he has been condemned with astonishing venom, although his chromaticisms can all be paralleled in Mozart's work.

---

23 [John] Stainer, 'On the Progressive Character of Church Music', in *Authorised Report of the Church Congress Held at Brighton, October … 1874* (London: William Wells Gardner, [1874]), pp. 530–38, at p. 531.

To a Mozartian base he added a few touches of Schubert, Mendelssohn, and Spohr, expanding, but not disrupting, the Classical tonal
system to encompass keys such as the flat submediant that had become
part of the normal tonal range by 1830. But Stainer did not embrace the
'Music of the Future': there are no hints of Wagner, Liszt, or even Brahms.
In his inaugural address as professor at Oxford, he expressed a fear that 'a
too plentiful use of that descriptive and sentimental colouring which we
derive from the modern "romantic style" should tempt our church musicians into a striving after picturesque and dramatic effects not consistent
with the dignity and repose of worship'.[24] He must have been thinking of
Gounod, and his English disciples such as Barnby, who were willing to
throw off the inhibitions of cathedral tradition.[25] He went on, 'Three
centuries ago the musician, quite regardless of the meaning of the words,
revelled in the intricacies of counterpoint: now, our church composers
watch narrowly every shade of meaning in the words in order to represent
it in a tone-picture. Is this a legitimate form of Church music?'[26]

Thus, in using terms such as 'modern' and 'progressive' in the context
of church music, Stainer was taking a moderate stance. Between two
undesirable extremes he forged his own style, which was based on his
ability to write an attractive and singable melody and to enrich it with the
full resources of early nineteenth-century harmony. Both counterpoint
and word-painting were available tools, but they were used with
conscious restraint, especially in his later works.

The first, and so far the only, serious and unprejudiced study of
Stainer's church music is the work of an American scholar, William
Gatens.[27] Americans have never suffered from the hang-up about the
Victorians that afflicted British musicology and criticism for much of the
twentieth century; an earlier American work is also free of this particular
bias in its treatment of Stainer.[28] Gatens points out that 'Stainer obviously
recognizes the pitfalls on each side of the controversy: the danger of irrev-
erent theatricality on the one hand, and of frigid antiquarianism on the
other. The tenderness and expressive understatement may be seen as a

---

24 John Stainer, *The Present State of Music in England* (Oxford, 1889), p. 11.
25 Walker, *Music in England* (1907, p. 308), states that Gounod was Stainer's chief model,
and has been followed in this view by the later commentators. I would dispute this as regards
the church music, though Gounod's theatrical manner is present in *The Crucifixion* and is
occasionally found in the anthems and services. It is much more strongly evident in some of
Barnby's anthems.
26 Stainer, *The Present State of Music in England*, p. 12.
27 William Gatens, *Victorian Cathedral Music in Theory and Practice* (Cambridge:
Cambridge University Press, 1986), chap. 9.
28 Elwyn A. Wienandt and Robert H. Young, *The Anthem in England and America* (New
York: The Free Press, 1970), pp. 268–79.

possible solution.' He exonerates Stainer from the charge of easy superficiality: 'Stainer's own church music is thus an attempt to put into practice deeply considered issues and theories exhibited in this and other essays. His compositions are not a contradiction of his principles, as some later critics have suggested, but a confirmation of them.'[29]

As an example of a work in which these principles were successfully deployed, though not on a consistently high level, I have chosen the Evening Service in B flat major.[30] It was written for use in St Paul's, but not by the cathedral choir: it was for the London Church Choir Association, a combination of parish church choirs of several thousand voices, at its fifth festival in 1877. For this reason, and also no doubt with an eye to publication, it is confined mostly to four-part writing and makes no use of antiphonal effects.

In this service Stainer made his boldest step towards the 'symphonic' type of setting later developed by Stanford. He planned it with a strong and clearly 'modern' polarisation between the keys of B flat and D, which he extended to the Morning Service in B flat composed a few years later. When the combined service was published in 1884, it was conceived as a whole. The title was *The Morning and Evening Service together with the Office for the Holy Communion set to music in the key of B flat*. But the Benedictus is wholly in the key of D, while the Communion Office is in F, with one of its movements (the Sanctus) set in A. The overall key scheme of B flat – D – F/A/F – B flat resembles that of some of Schubert's sonatas and chamber works.

In 1877 the Evening Service had been conceived as a self-sufficient piece, consisting, of course, of only two canticles: Magnificat and Nunc Dimittis. But even within this smaller scheme there is a strong polarisation between B flat and D. The Magnificat begins on a D major chord for the organ, followed by a seven-bar thematic build-up to the choir's entrance in B flat on a robust unison melody. There is an episode in D major with a sweeter and more reflective melody ('and Holy is his Name'), then the organ opening returns as a transition back to B flat, where there is a repeat of the first tune ('He hath shewed strength'). More remarkably, the Gloria Patri quickly moves to the key of D. When it returns to B flat, Stainer provides a full fugue on the subject shown in Ex. 5.5a (the descending fourth is derived from the main melody). It has exactly the same rhythm and unfortunate word repetition as the subject of a similar fugue in Barnby's Service in E (Ex. 5.5b), which was later ridiculed by Tovey as a 'strange theological

29   Gatens, *Victorian Cathedral Music*, p. 172.
30   This work was performed at a special Victorian choral evensong associated with the conference, at Holy Trinity Church, Prince Consort Road, on Wednesday, 18 July 2001.

Ex. 5.5   Comparison of fugal subjects in the Gloria of (a) Stainer's Magnificat in
B flat (1877) and (b) Barnby's Magnificat in E (1864)

dogma, that of the Chorister's 40th Article of Religion'.[31] Tovey has a
point. Though this is an extreme case, Stainer too frequently weakens the
sense of the text by adhering to Classical phrase structures.

The development of the fugue is vigorous, if somewhat routine, and
leads to an exciting climax. Here Stainer, having conceded on the one side
to the 'contrapuntal' school, makes a move towards theatricality (Ex.
5.6). Then the main theme returns in the organ over a dominant pedal,
during the final repetition of 'Amen'.

Ex. 5.6   Gloria from Stainer's Magnificat in B flat

---

31 Donald F. Tovey, *The Main Stream of Music* (London: Humphrey Milford, 1938),
reprinted in *The Main Stream of Music and Other Essays*, ed. Hubert Foss (Oxford:
Clarendon Press, 1949), pp. 330–52, at p. 339.

Fellowes said that 'the B flat service was written with special reference to the acoustic conditions of St Paul's cathedral. It sounds ineffective and vulgar in most other buildings.'[32] Ex. 5.6 is the only passage I can find that gives any support to this sweeping statement, for it exploits the unusually long reverberation of the great cathedral.

The Nunc Dimittis begins with one of those tender melodies that Stainer wrote so well, and that clearly exemplify his 'middle way' (Ex. 5.7). Like many predecessors, he begins this Song of Simeon with male voices only. Again, as in Ex. 5.5a, he makes the phrase regular by word repetition, as Mozart often did; but in this case the repetition is harmless. The decorative chromaticism and the smooth part-writing, stretching at times to six voice parts, show Stainer at his best and most confident. A second, more ordinary melody (8 + 9 bars) is for trebles answered by the full choir, ending on the dominant; one more phrase completes the canticle text.

For the Gloria Patri Stainer could have simply repeated the one that followed the Magnificat, as most Victorians did, or written a completely different one, which was the habit of a minority of his contemporaries

Ex. 5.7   Stainer, Nunc Dimittis in B flat

32   Fellowes, *English Cathedral Music*, p. 225.

including George Garrett (1834–97). He did neither. The first part, modulating to D major, is the same as before; but when the theme of Ex. 5.5a enters, it is sung as a choral unison, treated as the bass of organ harmonies. There is new counterpoint, but no fugue. The final amens are shorter and less dramatic, and the whole doxology is in proportion to the shorter text and quieter character of this canticle.

These considerations show Stainer thinking on a larger scale, and using techniques derived from modern secular music to provide a broad structure. Another development from the same source, shared with many Victorian cathedral musicians, was his management and variation of texture. He used unison passages, staccato organ chords, varied spacing of chords, careful dynamic shading, and contrasts of tempo with a skill that had built up in Anglican music since the choral revival got under way in the 1840s, but in which he surpassed his rivals.

At this point I would like to examine a conversation that Stainer had with Fellowes, which has often been quoted. Dr Fellowes told the story twice in print; he also recounted it to me when I went to see him at Windsor Castle on 24 July 1951 to ask him about Victorian church music, but I took no notes. Here is the 1941 version:

> He did in fact know that he had written most of his earlier anthems too easily. Within a year of his death he confided to the present writer that he regretted deeply that so many of them had been published, adding that they had been written in response to pressure put upon him in early days by the clergy and others, who assured him that they were 'just the thing they wanted'.[33]

In 1951 Fellowes put it in this way:

> He suddenly stopped me in the Magdalen walks and said he wanted me to know that he regretted ever having published most of his compositions; that he knew very well they were 'rubbish' and feared that when he was gone his reputation might suffer because of his inferiority … He was then a poor man and gave way to demand, and he now deeply regretted it.[34]

The most significant difference between the two printed texts is that the first refers only to 'his earlier anthems' while the second is about 'most of his compositions'. In both, however, it is clear that Stainer was looking back to the early part of his life; this is reinforced by 'early days' in the 1941 text and 'He was then a poor man' in the 1951 text. And this is in itself a remarkable fact, because most commentators, including Walker, Fellowes, Westrup, Long, Charlton and Gatens, consider that his earlier anthems are his best works. The very first to be published, 'I saw the Lord'

---

33 Ibid., p. 224.
34 Edmund H. Fellowes, 'Sir John Stainer', *English Church Music*, 21/1 (1951), pp. 4–7, at p. 7.

(1858), is the only one praised by Walker, Westrup and Long, and is 'generally considered ... Stainer's best anthem', according to Fellowes.[35] The early anthems, it is agreed, are more in the traditional form and style of cathedral music, and they have less of the 'mid-Victorian' characteristics that some find objectionable; as Gatens says, 'they follow much the same pattern as the larger anthems of Goss and Ouseley' (p. 173).

In contrast, most of the later anthems were published by Novello & Co., often as supplements to the *Musical Times*, and were evidently intended for parochial use.[36] They are short, technically undemanding, and generally sweet and melodious. One of the last is the little-noticed 'O bountiful Jesu', which appeared as a supplement to the *Musical Times* of 1 February 1900. This was near in time to the remarks Stainer made to Fellowes 'within a year of his death', which occurred on 31 March 1901. We must assume, then, that 'O bountiful Jesu' is not one of those 'early anthems' that the composer told Fellowes he considered to be 'rubbish'. On the contrary, it is a mature specimen of the style that he had long cultivated as most appropriate and edifying for church music, the style which, in my opinon, brought out his best qualities.

Always resourceful in his choice of texts, Stainer took this one from a prayer that he found in a primer of 1553:

> O bountiful Jesu, O sweet Saviour, O Christ the Son of God, have mercy upon us, mercifully hear us, and despise not our prayers. Thou hast created us of nothing; Thou hast redeemed us from the bondage of sin, death, and hell, neither with gold nor silver, but with Thy most precious body offered once upon the cross, and Thine own blood shed once for all for our ransom; therefore cast us not away, whom Thou by thy great wisdom hath made; despise us not, whom Thou hast redeemed with such a precious treasure.

Its content is not unusual, being nothing other than the central tenet of Christianity, but in the Anglican world of 1900 it was unfamiliar in diction and in image, for instance in its reference to gold and silver. It is fervent, intimate, and beautiful in form and phraseology. Stainer strove to match its quality in his setting.

The anthem is in four vocal parts throughout, and 'May be sung without accompaniment'. There is no attempt at word-painting, except for well-placed climaxes at the words 'sin, death, and hell' and 'whom Thou hast redeemed'. Instead, Stainer evokes the mood and overall

---

35 Ibid. Long loosely extended the story to embrace his nemesis, *The Crucifixion* (1887) – hardly an 'early' work or one written when Stainer was a 'poor man', and certainly not an anthem – claiming that 'Towards the end of his life Stainer bitterly regretted having published it'; *The Music of the English Church*, p. 365.

36 There is a useful list in Gatens, *Victorian Cathedral Music*, p. 185.

Ex. 5.8   Stainer, 'O bountiful Jesu'

feeling of the prayer. The first sentence is formed into a tender, regularly phrased 12-bar tune (Ex. 5.8), which modulates to the dominant key. The voices are mostly kept to the lower part of their range, where amateur singers can most easily modulate their tone for expression and follow the careful dynamic markings. Slightly higher notes (the alto g' in bar 2, the tenor e' in bar 3) make a disproportionate effect, and so does each dissonance, whether passing or accentual. One is made aware of the individual vocal lines, not by counterpoint, but by harmony and spacing. Even the notoriously static Victorian alto part, as in the repeated notes of bars 7–10, draws the ear's attention to itself when other parts move around it.

The sentence is then sung again, with the same music subtly transformed by different dynamics, beginning *pianissimo* (after the end of Ex. 5.8), and by a change of spacing at 'have mercy upon us', the trebles rising to e''. The repeat of bars 9–12, instead of passing through E minor to D major, passes through A minor to G major, so that a miniature sonata form is the result, followed by a little coda referring back to the opening (Ex. 5.9).

Ex. 5.9   Stainer, 'O bountiful Jesu'

Ex. 5.10   Stainer, 'O bountiful Jesu'

Continuing to follow late-Classical models, Stainer changes key to E flat, where the first climax takes the voices to a higher range. A modulation to the dominant of G minor prepares for the return of the first tune. It is now carefully adapted to new text, 'therefore cast us not away', requiring a double upbeat and some compression of the musical phrase. This time, after the cadence on the dominant (bar 8 in Ex. 5.8), new material (Ex. 5.10) leads quickly to the second and principal climax.

A few elements of Stainer's craft may be mentioned here: the soprano/tenor imitation during the sequential rise in bars 1–6; the climax itself, where all four voices join to sing the same text, and the trebles and basses are on their highest notes; the way the expected 6/4 chord on the first beat of bar 10 is avoided, slightly prolonging the tension; then the interrupted cadence in bar 12, as the well-spaced voices at last subside to the awaited repose on the chord of G. Then the anthem ends with a repeat of Ex. 5.9 and an Amen.

By the simplest of means Stainer has achieved a truly devotional effect. It is easy to see why this sort of anthem was welcomed by parish congregations, who looked to their choir music not for intellectual challenge but for beauty, consolation and reassurance – all of which call for a high degree of predictability, but also a high level of art. The master knew exactly when and how to provide them, deploying a kind of skill that has since eroded almost to vanishing point in 'serious' music, though it is still practised in some species of popular music. Stainer's emphasis on pleasant, regular melody and rich harmony was not due to ignorance or bad taste, still less to 'enervation' or 'effeminacy', but was a principled acceptance of the resources of Classical music as suitable for the needs of the contemporary church. Some, including Fellowes, have likened his anthems to Victorian part songs, as if this in itself placed them automatically beneath serious consideration. The parallel is apt, but the implied stigma is not.

Nobody has suggested that Stainer was a great composer, or that he made important contributions to the profound changes in musical style that were taking place in his time. I am not advancing such claims now. I do maintain that he was a consummate artist. Of course anyone may like or dislike his music as a matter of taste, but it is time to give up the sweeping and uninformed condemnations of his modernisation of plainsong, and of his secularisation of church music, as if these were crimes by definition. He should be restored to his proper place in English musical history.

CHAPTER SIX

'The highest point up to that time reached by the combination of Hebrew and Christian sentiment in music'

Peter Horton

To what could these words, written at the turn of the twentieth century by a distinguished musician of German parentage, educated in Leipzig and renowned for his devotion to the music of Bach, Beethoven and Brahms, and his championship of Wagner, refer? No doubt a composer at the forefront of European musical life, perhaps Mendelssohn, Schumann, Liszt, Franck or another luminary of the Romantic period. But Edward Dannreuther's eulogy was directed at none of these, but at the anthems of a provincial English organist, Samuel Sebastian Wesley (1810–76) – and what makes his remarks all the more remarkable is that there was nothing in his background to predispose him towards cathedral music. Intriguingly, too, he saw Wesley not as a member of the minority sect of English church composers but as a fully paid-up member of the European Romantic mainstream, and it is at this aspect of Wesley's work, exemplified by the group of anthems he wrote while organist of Exeter Cathedral in the late 1830s, that I wish to look. Dannreuther wrote:

> There is nothing in the range of modern religious music more sincerely felt and expressed than, for example ... *Wash me throughly* – neither in Spohr, with whose practice certain chromatic progressions seem to coincide, nor in Mendelssohn, with whose oratorio style there is a certain resemblance in phraseology. S.S. Wesley's way of expressing religious emotion appears more individual than either Spohr's or Mendelssohn's, and it is for that very reason better worth hearing ... The sheer musical invention in ... *O Lord, thou art my God*, in the Credo belonging to the Morning Service, and in *Wash me throughly*, is that of a virile genius who knows his J.S. Bach not only contrapuntally but emotionally, and loves him ... it is not possible to convey in a few bars an adequate idea of the persistent strength of this contrapuntal music, that ought to be studied and recognised as masterly wherever the English language is spoken [and] ... the best examples of S.S. Wesley contain an expression of the highest point up to that time reached by the combination of Hebrew and Christian sentiment in music. They are well worthy of comparison with

Mendelssohn's psalms, with the best things in Spohr, and with the
Beatitudes of Liszt and César Franck ...[1]

Despite a continuing misconception that England was a musical desert
during the first half of the nineteenth century, the London of Wesley's youth
was one of Europe's foremost musical centres, albeit largely foreign-domi-
nated. While native composers struggled to gain a hearing in the more
exalted fields of orchestral and chamber music, or all-sung opera, there was
no shortage of first-rate contemporary music to be heard, much of it
performed by the leading musicians of the day. As a result a generation of
English composers grew up immersed in the works of Mozart, Beethoven,
Weber, Spohr and Ries and their Italian contemporaries, fully conversant
with their styles and with the confidence to attempt something similar themselves. John Barnett (1802–90), for example, had taken lessons from Ries,
but was also indebted – as were Wesley and Henry Smart (1813–79) – to the
works of Spohr (who had made the first of several visits to the capital in
1820). Sterndale Bennett (1816–75) took Mozart as his model – though his
piano music is often reminiscent of Schumann's – while the operas of
Michael Balfe (1808–70) demonstrate remarkable fluency in the current
French and Italian idioms. Indeed, with several of these being written for
performance in France and Italy, and Bennett enjoying the advocacy of both
Mendelssohn and Schumann (and being offered the conductorship of the
Leipzig Gewandhaus orchestra on the death of the former), it began to look
as though English music had finally overcome the inferiority complex under
which it had laboured for so long, and that its composers would again take
their place on the European stage. But it was not to be. A combination of
circumstances contrived to thwart their efforts and the brief flowering of the
1830s and 1840s passed all too quickly. As Stephen Banfield has noted, a sea
change seemed to affect British society – and music – in the immediate after-
math of the Great Exhibition of 1851, marking the end of what he aptly
described as the 'phase of militant romanticism in English music'.[2]

In the midst of all this activity Wesley initially played a seemingly insig-
nificant part, beginning to make a mark as an organist and composer in
London in the early 1830s, but abruptly turning his back on the capital and
the opportunities it offered when he was appointed organist of Hereford
Cathedral in 1832. But his experience of acting as repetiteur at the English
Opera House – where his music for the melodrama *The Dilosk Gatherer*
was performed in July 1832 – and playing the organ for the Lent Oratorio
Concerts stood him in good stead, and within a few months of his arrival in
the town he had produced his first unquestioned masterpiece, the anthem

---

1   Edward Dannreuther, *The Romantic Period* (Oxford: Athlone Press, 1905), pp. 290, 297.
2   See Stephen Banfield, 'The Artist in Society', in Nicholas Temperley (ed.), *The Romantic Age 1800–1914* (London: Athlone Press, 1981), p. 21.

'The wilderness'. Bridging the gap between concert hall and cathedral, introducing orchestral sonorities to the organ loft and above all infusing church music with a sense of drama, it heralded a new era. During the next two to three years he produced a further three works – the anthems 'Blessed be the God and Father' and 'Trust ye in the Lord' and a setting of the Creed – which deviate even further from the well-trodden path and emphasise the contemporary, secular character of his harmonic language. But it was an idiom whose appropriateness for church use he soon began to question and by 1840 his views had changed sufficiently for him to refer disparagingly to 'two little anthems and a creed' – probably the works mentioned above – as being 'fitter for the drawing room than the church'.[3] At the same time one can identify the growing influence of the music of Bach and the English cathedral school, not least through the increasing prominence of contrapuntal textures. Seen against the background of his career, this development acquires a new perspective. In 1835 Wesley had been appointed organist of Exeter Cathedral, even further from London than Hereford and without the bonus of the annual Three Choirs Festival. Denied the opportunity to hear and participate in a wide range of recently composed music and with no realistic chance of getting any large-scale non-church works of his own performed, for the first time in his career he began to concentrate almost exclusively on church music. And it can surely be no coincidence that this was accompanied by a parting of the ways between his music and that of the Romantic mainstream. The result was an idiosyncratic blend of ancient and modern, forward-looking in its imaginative use of harmony, but curiously conservative in its contrapuntal textures. This duality was recognised by Spohr with his comment that Wesley's sacred works were distinguished by 'their dignified and, frequently, antique style, by rich and choice harmonies, and by surprizing [sic] modulations',[4] and by H.J. Gauntlett, who considered that his style was 'founded on a union of Purcell, Bach and Beethoven'.[5] Significantly, these were also the characteristics admired by Dannreuther, who noted the 'persistent strength' Wesley's music derived from its contrapuntal textures and ready use of diatonic dissonance. Conversely, these qualities were most notable by their absence from the works of the majority of Wesley's Continental contemporaries. Why?

'One of the enduring features of English music', John Caldwell has suggested, 'is its tendency to adopt technical developments only after they

---

3   Letter dated 29 January 1840 to Vincent Novello (British Library Add. MS 11730, fol. 227).

4   See Royal College of Music MS 3071. containing two translations of Spohr's original German testimonial.

5   H.J. Gauntlett, 'The Gresham Prize', *Musical World*, 2 (1836), p. 84.

have been tried and tested elsewhere, but then to put them to new and inter-esting uses.[6] A consequence of this has been that while native composers have rarely kept abreast of their Continental counterparts, they have nonetheless produced some highly original, if anachronistic, works. One thinks of the florid vocal writing of such early sixteenth-century composers as John Sheppard or John Taverner, or the contrapuntal viol fantasias of Henry Purcell, and I would suggest that the English fondness for Bachian counterpoint, whether in the works of Samuel Wesley, Thomas Adams or Samuel Sebastian, belongs in the same category. Indeed, with counterpoint remaining an important ingredient of English music – and particularly church music – long after it had ceased to be so elsewhere, it can be argued that native composers would have been natu-rally predisposed towards Bach's music. In Samuel Sebastian's case this influence manifested itself both directly and indirectly. Examples of the former include obviously Bach-inspired textures in some numbers from *A Selection of Psalm Tunes, Adapted Expressly to the English Organ* (partic-ularly in the second edition of 1842), the organ Fugue in C sharp minor (published 1836) and the last movement of 'O Lord, thou art my God' (*c*.1836), but these are ultimately of less significance than those works in which Wesley re-interpreted the legacy of Bach and his contemporaries in his own terms. One can recognise this in the increasingly contrapuntal nature of his music, whose dependence on harmonic (or contrapuntal) tension between individual parts can only be understood in terms of horizontal rather than vertical musical thought. Whether through imitative counter-point, free contrapuntal writing or pedal points, this resulted in textures of great vitality, liberally sprinkled with strong diatonic dissonance and frequently with a powerfully independent bass line. Suspensions, passing notes and appoggiaturas all contribute to the overall effect, and nowhere is this better illustrated than in the three large-scale double-choir anthems Wesley wrote at Exeter between 1836 and 1840, 'O Lord, thou art my God', 'Let us lift up our heart' and To my request and earnest cry'. In outward form direct descendants of the eighteenth- or early nineteenth-century full-with-verse anthem, with a succession of movements for full choir, verse (solo) ensemble, or solo voice, they nonetheless far outclass their models in scale and seriousness of purpose. Here indeed one can see an embodiment of Wesley's later comment that 'if it is decided that music *should* be employed in our worship of the Divinity, that it *is* our duty to see that the best efforts and those alone, are devoted to an object which is perhaps among the most important it ever falls to the task [of] humanity to execute'.[7]

---

6   John Caldwell, *The Oxford History of English Music* (Oxford: Oxford University Press, 1999), vol. 2, p. 554.
7   Royal College of Music MS 2141f, fol. 48v.

The opening movements of both 'O Lord, thou art my God' and 'Let us lift up our heart' are particularly fine, and the latter also demonstrates Wesley's characteristic method of building up a long through-composed structure around its carefully shaped text. Opening with a broad passage for men's voices in unison, it gradually builds up to the incisive block harmony of the powerful statement for full (double) choir, 'Doubtless thou art our father' and a sudden and unexpected plunge into C minor for a striding imitative subject whose dissonant accented passing notes and appoggiaturas clash with the underlying harmony and maintain the harmonic and dramatic tension (see Ex. 6.1). It is at moments like this that one becomes most aware of the difficulty of placing Wesley's mature music in a wider context. Who among his European contemporaries would have written anything quite like this? Possibly only Anton Bruckner, whose striding melodies and bass lines and willingness to step outside the confines of the accepted stylistic idiom share something with Wesley's.

The comparison with Bruckner is apt because both possessed a thorough grounding in contrapuntal technique – in Wesley's view a prerequisite for success as a composer[8] – and a willingness to combine old and new, Classical (contrapuntal) dissonance treatment with contemporary Romantic harmony; it was this which made their mature idioms so distinctive.[9] In Wesley's case it had involved a conscious move away from the early Romantic lingua franca and Spohr-like, essentially decorative, chromaticism found in such works as 'Blessed be the God and Father' and his setting of the Creed, but not, however, a total repudiation of an up-to-date harmonic style. Indeed, his slightly later *Morning & Evening Cathedral Service* (1843–44) – another work praised by Dannreuther – was seized upon by the critic Edward Taylor as 'giving a *carte blanche* admission into the English cathedral-service of the modulations and transitions of the modern school',[10] and both here and in the contemporary anthems we can see him using chromatic harmony in an increasingly individual way. He also employed it more sparingly but more systematically than hitherto, whether as a means of modulation or for introducing tonal colour into an extended paragraph. Both can be seen in the bass aria 'Thou, O Lord God' which forms the centrepiece of 'Let us lift up our heart'. One of the finest examples of Wesley's writing for solo voice, it opens in B minor with a

---

8   Wesley was later to tell Hubert Parry 'that the reason why Beethoven & more especially Spohr were sometimes (frequently) so unsatisfactory was because that [*sic*] lacked the necessary, and beneficial basis of hard work at Counterpoint; and ... the reason why Mendelssohn so excelled was entirely because he had that instruction, and went through that preparation thoroughly' (Parry's Diary entry for 5 January 1866; MS at Shulbrede Priory).

9   It should be noted that the strongest influence on the Protestant Wesley was that of Bach, while that on the Catholic Bruckner was that of the Palestrina school.

10 See *The Spectator*, 17 (1844), p. 234.

Ex. 6.1   S.S. Wesley, 'Let us lift up our heart' (first movement)

typically wide-ranging theme spanning a rising tenth but thereafter, making extensive sequential use of third-related keys to build up its emotional power, it runs through almost the whole gamut – G major, E flat major, C minor, G minor. The *coup de théâtre*, however, is reserved for the coda, which opens with a dramatic restatement of the opening subject in the Neapolitan key, C major. For a dozen bars the tonality fluctuates between this key and the tonic before a characteristic tritone shift in the bass (G–C♯) and enharmonic change (F♮ = E♯) leads back to a dominant pedal and extended cadence (see Ex. 6.2).

Ex. 6.1 (*cont.*)

The occasional novelty – one might almost say naivety – of Wesley's handling of chromaticism must surely owe something to his physical isolation in Exeter.[11] Whereas he had previously merely incorporated some of Spohr's mannerisms into his own works, he now sought to develop a more individual voice, largely independent of what was happening elsewhere. The

---

11 Even in works written in the early 1830s Wesley had displayed a strongly independent streak and both his incidental music to *The Dilosk Gatherer* (1832) and the first edition of *A Selection of Psalm Tunes* (published in 1834) contain examples of what can best be described as experimental chromatic harmony.

Ex. 6.2   S.S. Wesley, 'Let us lift up our heart' (third movement)

means, centred on enharmonic change, interrupted cadences and those multi-faceted chords, the diminished seventh and augmented sixth, might be similar, but the results, as in 'Let us lift up our heart' or 'Wash me throughly from my wickedness', were very different. The latter, a short full anthem setting verses from Psalm 51 and probably written *c*.1840, represents his most concentrated use of chromatic harmony. Unlike 'Let us lift up our heart', in which chromaticism was reserved for specific effects, 'Wash me throughly' is characterised by restless movement from key to key in a manner reminiscent of that later employed by César Franck. The opening phrase, for example, moves from the tonic (D minor), via the subdominant (G minor) to the Neapolitan key (E flat major), and thence enharmonically to the dominant (A major) and back to the tonic (the harmonic outline is given in Ex. 6.3a). A similar tonal fluidity accompanies the entry of the full choir (bar 13), with an effective use of an enharmonically modulating sequence (see bars 17–20) (Ex. 6.3b). While such writing might not be particularly adventurous in comparison with what Chopin, Schumann or Wagner were doing at this time, it was quite remarkable in the highly conservative field of English cathedral music. And Wesley adds a personal twist through his use of diatonic dissonance – for example the close-position dominant thirteenth in bar 16 – to provide a welcome note of astringency.

While much of the impact of Wesley's church music is due to the uncompromising rigour of his harmonic language, it is equally dependent on his ability to build up convincing extended musical structures. Dannreuther particularly admired the long opening and closing movements of 'O Lord, thou art my God', the first a largely through-composed structure bound together by a thrice-appearing ritornello, well-planned tonal scheme and carefully compiled text, and the last a tightly organised triple fugue. Tonal scheme and text also impart a logical sense of progression to the lengthy through-composed opening movement of 'Let us lift up our heart' and to another movement unknown to Dannreuther, the massive finale of 'To my request and earnest cry'. But before examining these more closely, it is worth

Ex. 6.3   S.S. Wesley, 'Wash me throughly': (a) harmonic outline of bars 1–8;
(b) bars 9–21

looking at Wesley's compositional method and in particular the relationship between his written works and his improvisations. Like other organists noted for their improvisatory skill – and Bruckner again comes to mind – he wrote comparatively little for the instrument and by all accounts reserved his best efforts for his extemporaneous performances. Indeed, all the evidence suggests that he found large-scale composition a struggle and this doubtless explains the lack of extended choral works in his output – a solitary, largely solo *Ode to Labour* (1864), but no cantata or oratorio. But it is surely significant that many of the works he did complete, whether for the organ or another medium, are either episodic or through-composed – formal patterns which would have come naturally to an experienced extempore player – and that those which set words are frequently shaped by their texts. And herein lies part of the secret of his sacred music. Unlike many composers who chose a group of verses and set them, or a pre-selected text, with the minimum of alteration, Wesley invariably compiled his anthem texts from a variety of sources, rearranging and intermingling them until he had the perfect vehicle for his purpose. He had no scruples about omitting anything which would distract or disrupt the flow of his argument, with the result that his compilations are always concise and free of 'dead wood'. Two examples, from the first and last movements of 'O Lord, thou art my God', setting verses from Isaiah 25, illustrate his method:

Original	*As set by Wesley*
v. 1. O Lord, thou art my God; I will exalt thee, I will praise thy name; for thou hast done wonderful things; thy counsels of old are faithfulness and truth.	v. 1. O Lord, thou art my God; I will exalt thee, I will praise thy name; thy counsels of old are faithfulness and truth; for thou hast done wonderful things.
v. 4. For thou has been a strength to the poor, a strength to the needy in his distress, a refuge from the storm, a shadow from the heat, when the blast of the terrible ones is as a storm against the wall.	v. 4. For thou has been a strength to the poor and needy in his distress.
v. 9. And it shall be said in that day, Lo, this is our God; we have waited for him, and he will save us: this is the Lord; we have waited for him, we will be glad and rejoice in his salvation.	v. 9. And in that day it shall be said, Lo, this is our God; we have waited for him, and he will save us: this is the Lord; we have waited for him, we will be glad and rejoice in his salvation.

Even something as apparently insignificant as the alteration of 'And it shall be said in that day' to 'And in that day it shall be said' in verse 9 produces a sense of greater directness, better suited to a musical setting, and on this foundation Wesley proceeded to build his musical structure. In this, as surely in his improvisations, his approach was instinctive, a direct response to the words he was setting, in which changes of sentiment were reflected by the thematic material, variations of texture, vocal scoring or predominant note values. And even the frequent absence of an obvious (thematic) formal scheme is no drawback, given the invariable presence of a well-considered tonal plan. But important as they are, none of these techniques can account for the quite exceptional fervour of those works in which Wesley transcended his limitations to produce music which blazes with sincerity – and here too one must step back and consider wider aspects of his life and career. As a member of one of the best-known clerical families in the country, an erstwhile chorister and, from the age of twenty-two, a cathedral organist, Wesley had been immersed in the beliefs, teaching and language of the Christian faith for most of his life. For him the Anglican choral service was an art-form in its own right, with the church composer – himself – an artist in the service of God:

> must we not agree in the principle that whatever forms a part of our National worship should be the best of its kind. That our Architecture, our Music and all the details of religious establishments as well as the more important matter of our liturgy itself should possess a degree of merit and excellence unattained to in things designed merely for our own uses and gratifications, that they should be the most cared for, the objects of our highest and wisest and most enduring solicitude, that they should be objects of the unceasing thought of men most remarkable for intellectual thought, or genius, in their several branches, that no beauty with which they can be endowed or which *could be* desired, in these particulars should be wanting.[12]

Perhaps more than almost any other contemporary composer of note, though Bruckner again comes to mind, he lived and breathed the life and world of the cathedral and tried to re-create it through his compositions. Without sufficient compositional skill to support it, such a vision would have been worthless, but allied with a rare sensitivity to words and a vivid, well-developed musical imagination it could, and in his case did, result in works of great emotional power. And it was surely this which so struck Dannreuther and led to his comment that there was 'nothing in the range of modern religious music more sincerely felt and expressed' than such works as 'Wash me throughly' and 'O Lord, thou art my God'.

---

12 Royal College of Music MS 2141f, fols 48v–48r.

Such a spirit pervades all the music Wesley wrote at Exeter, but perhaps nowhere more powerfully than in the long concluding movement of 'To my request and earnest cry'. A sonata form-fugue hybrid framed by chorale-like sections, it combines ancient and modern elements, with the influence of Bach rarely far away. But whether in the two chorale statements, the running countersubjects in the organ part, or such moments as the slowly rising chromatic bass line under a chain of suspensions (see Ex. 6.4), it is Bach refracted through the lens of Wesley's own individuality. Indeed, his handling of this bass line, which underpins the approach to the sudden move to the flat side of the tonic – the *minor* flat seventh, D minor – and the final climactic Neapolitan harmony, is masterly. Note how the treble part gradually rises up to the final top g'', the similar use of the top of the register in the bass part, and the continuation of the fanfare-like pattern in the accompaniment while the voices sustain their thrilling harmonies. The return to the tonic, via an enharmonic modulation ($B^\flat = A^\sharp$), is handled no less masterfully and a short coda, based on the opening chorale melody, provides a peaceful, and ultimately serene, conclusion.

It is in movements like this that one is inevitably drawn to a comparison of Wesley's music with Mendelssohn's, and to Dannreuther's comment that the former's 'way of expressing religious emotion appears more individual than either Spohr's or Mendelssohn's'.[13] How do their works compare? The question had first been posed by Henry Smart in 1840:

> That Wesley and Mendelssohn should fall on similar trains of ideas and similar modes of arranging and working them out, is in nowise astonishing, if the parity of their musical education and likings be considered. Both early imbibed a reverence for the grandest kind of ecclesiastical music and the severest style of organ performance; into both was the wisdom of old Bach instilled at the earliest periods of their musical existence, and both prove by their writings that their love for his sublime compositions is, at this day, in no degree diminished. Thus it is evident that the striking similarities to which we have referred cannot be rightly viewed otherwise than as kindred inspirations of like minds, journeying towards the same object and lighted by the same guide-star.[14]

Smart's opinion notwithstanding, there are significant differences. Wesley's was a cruder, less finished voice, and he lacked the versatility and fluency of his German colleague. Yet anything his music might lack in polish it more than made up for in rugged strength. Take, for example, the passage from 'To my request and earnest cry' shown in Ex. 6.5, with its harshly dissonant double $^{9-8}$ appoggiaturas, or the manner in which the

---

13 Dannreuther, *The Romantic Period*, p. 290.
14 *Musical World*, 14 (1840), p. 233.

Ex. 6.4   S.S. Wesley, 'To my request and earnest cry' (last movement)

continued overleaf

inner part in the accompaniment pursues its own independent course (bar 317). One could search long and hard for anything comparable in Mendelssohn's music, and it is precisely here, in their attitudes towards diatonic dissonance – and more broadly the music of the past – that the two composers reveal their true individuality.

Ex. 6.4 (*cont.*)

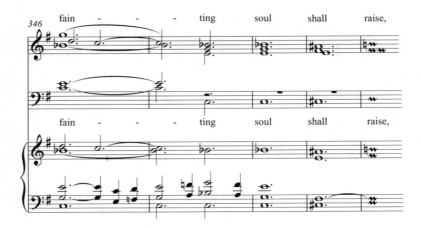

Why, given the similarities between their early musical experiences, did their mature voices diverge? The answer is to be found, I believe, in a fundamental difference in the position of English and Continental composers: the former stood almost alone in possessing no strong native tradition of serious musical composition. During the early years of the nineteenth century there were virtually no symphonies, chamber music or operas to compare with those of Austria, France, Germany or Italy, and when aspiring composers sought to write in these forms, they had perforce to adopt foreign models. And it was surely for this reason that the music of Bach made such a strong impact. Here was a composer of real stature whose admirably 'scientific' music ideally suited not only the national predilection for contrapuntal textures, but also the English love of all things old.[15] In these circumstances it is surely no coincidence that his influence on contemporary composers was as great in England as anywhere, or that Wesley should fall more deeply under his sway than his German counterpart. Even at its most overtly Bachian, Mendelssohn's music rarely loses sight of its roots in the classical tradition of Mozart, Beethoven and Weber or becomes so inextricably linked with the dissonant contrapuntal procedures of a past age as Wesley's. Wesley, however, had no English composers of such distinction to emulate and therefore

---

15 This national characteristic struck the Belgian music historian François-Joseph Fétis, who noted 'the attachment which is shewn to ancient institutions and Gothic usages' and could not understand why 'in the finest city in Europe, the king continues to inhabit a pile of brick, misnamed the Palace of St James, merely because the said pile of brick was raised by Henry VI' (*The Harmonicon*, 7 (1829), p. 184).

Ex. 6.5 S.S. Wesley, 'To my request and earnest cry' (last movement)

sought inspiration in the timeless music of the Leipzig cantor. Given his delight in strong dissonance – an increasingly old-fashioned feature in the 1830s – and real instinct for counterpoint, it was an entirely natural process and resulted in that curious combination of old and new noted by Spohr. That such a hybrid idiom should develop in the conservative field of English cathedral music was not inappropriate, but that it should, in Dannreuther's words, represent the 'highest point up to that time reached by the combination of Hebrew and Christian sentiment in music – a combination, it may be noted, essentially romantic',[16] is nonetheless remarkable. With Wesley's inability to work harmoniously with the Dean and Chapter thwarting his career at Exeter he had no real opportunity to build on these foundations, and by the time he returned to anthem composition at Leeds Parish Church in the mid-1840s, the surroundings and ethos of his position were very different. No less importantly, the various setbacks he had encountered had taken their toll on his earlier determination to succeed, come what may.[17] But in the handful of works in which he was inspired to true greatness we can recognise the voice of a small but nonetheless distinctive contributor to the sacred music of the Romantic era.

---

16 Dannreuther's full text is to be found only in the annotated typescript of *The Romantic Period* (Royal College of Music Library, Dannreuther Collection).
17 For a full discussion of Wesley's career at Exeter see my *Samuel Sebastian Wesley* (Oxford: Clarendon Press, forthcoming).

PART THREE
National Identity

CHAPTER SEVEN

English National Identity and the Comic Operas of Gilbert and Sullivan

Derek B. Scott

The crew of *H.M.S. Pinafore* (1878) praises the young sailor Ralph Rackstraw because, 'in spite of all temptations to belong to other nations', he is an Englishman. William Schwenck Gilbert and Arthur Sullivan themselves, however, were tempted several times to dress their comic operas in the fashions and musical styles of other nations, Japanese (*The Mikado*, 1885), Italian (*The Gondoliers*, 1889), and German (*The Grand Duke*, 1896). Their operas were produced during 1875–96,[1] a period that witnessed the second wave of British imperialism and the growing threat to English national identity posed by imperial federation. In them can be found older myths about what it means to be English (*The Yeomen of the Guard*, 1888), as well as newer constructions of Englishness (*Utopia Limited*, 1893). They also contain satire directed at the rise of jingoism and of racial prejudice. This essay explores what they tell us about the attitude of Gilbert and Sullivan, and that of the Victorian middle class as a whole, towards the vexed question of English national identity.

After the end of the Napoleonic Wars in 1815, the Continent was again open to British travellers and, once more, the Grand Tour, taking in France, Germany and Italy, was thought necessary for a proper aristocratic education. The growing ease of travel would also have encouraged interest in lands overseas. However, many would concur with David Cannadine's argument that whatever the locations of the Savoy operas are supposed to be they are all, in fact, about England.[2] So, perhaps the main attraction of a foreign locale was that it provided an opportunity for allegorical satire. Arthur Jacobs calls the setting of *The Mikado* 'a licensed disguise for action and characters as English as they can be'.[3] Indeed, the names of characters sometimes derive from English colloquial expressions: for example, a lip-smacking 'Yum-Yum' for the heroine, and the contemptuous sounds

---

1   *Thespis* was 1871, but only two songs survive.
2   'Gilbert and Sullivan: The Making and Un-Making of a British "Tradition"', in Roy Porter (ed.), *Myths of the English* (Cambridge: Polity Press, 1992), pp. 12–32, at pp. 19–20.
3   *Arthur Sullivan: a Victorian Musician* (Oxford: Oxford University Press, 1984), p. 205.

'Pooh' and 'Bah' joined together to produced a name for the haughty Pooh-Bah. The Mikado's entrance song is entirely English in its detail and, when Gilbert moves from Japan to Italy for *The Gondoliers*, he provides content no less English for Giuseppe's 'Rising early in the morning'.

The years during which Gilbert and Sullivan collaborated were witness to European struggles for power, the 'scramble for Africa', the Sudan War 1882–98, and the Great Depression. The 'second wave' of British imperialism that began in the 1880s was motivated largely by the fear of losing markets in a period of economic depression. Independence movements in the colonies were crushed, and the description 'British' was found useful in cementing new relationships abroad, as it had done following the Act of Union between England and Scotland in 1707. At that time, the flags of St Andrew and St George had been superimposed to create the Union Jack, and the figure of Britannia placed on coins. The celebrated patriotic song 'Rule, Britannia!' dates from 1740, thus falling between the Jacobite Rebellions of 1715 and 1745. During the 1745 Rebellion, the song existed in several reworded versions in Scotland, since that country felt just as able to call upon Britannia. This provided an early warning of how Britishness might not be equated with Englishness. In the 1880s, the label 'British' was again used to make claims on the loyalties of different countries, and it was an effective means of suggesting an imperial unity.[4] After the Golden Jubilee of 1887, Queen Victoria became the symbol of that unity.

In addition to the growing concern about how to cope with the expanding empire, there was the Irish Home Rule issue: King Paramount in *Utopia Limited* qualifies his reference to 'that glorious country called Great Britain' with the caution, 'To which some add – but others do not – Ireland.'[5] There were also social problems to be tackled in the expanding English cities. The astonishing effect the invocation of Queen Victoria's name produced on lawbreakers in *The Pirates of Penzance* (1880) was not likely to be duplicated in London's East End. Equally remote was the possibility of repeating the scene in Act II of *Ruddigore* (1887) when Richard Dauntless, by suddenly waving the British flag, causes all to fall to their knees and the wicked Sir Murgatroyd to cry, 'Foiled – and by a Union Jack.'

Several vital questions now had to be answered. What claims could be made on the loyalty of the Queen's English subjects? If the working class did not feel there was something English that bound them in a common

---

4   See Derek B. Scott, *The Singing Bourgeois: Songs of the Victorian Drawing Room and Parlour*, 2nd edn (Aldershot: Ashgate, 2001; orig. pub. Milton Keynes: Open University Press, 1989), pp. 169–70.

5   Recitative following his song 'A King of Autocratic Power' in Act I. In the Act II Finale, a reference to Britain is qualified in a similar fashion: 'Great Britain is that monarchy sublime, To which some add (but others do not) Ireland.'

cause with their rulers, what would follow – especially since they were now acquiring education and voting rights? Was English identity being diluted by imperial expansion? Was English identity being eroded by socialist and republican ideas? What *was* English identity? For years, 'English' and 'British' had been treated as if they were synonymous terms. Those fighting for Britain in the Crimean War, who included large numbers of Scottish and Irish soldiers, were described as 'sons of England' in the subtitle of a patriotic song of 1854, 'To Arms!' (Wrexford / Glover). A consequence of the colonies being encouraged to feel British, however, was that it created problems for anyone equating Britishness with Englishness. After all, Americans were more English than those in many countries where the Union Jack was flying. So much was evident when an American impresario assured Gilbert that all he had to do in order to make an even 'bigger pile of dollars' in New York was to change the H.M.S. of *H.M.S. Pinafore* to U.S.S., the song 'He is an Englishman' to 'He is American', exchange flags, and substitute the American 'Navy Boss' for the First Lord of the Admiralty.[6] Though Gilbert failed to take this advice, the operatic extravaganza *Ship Ahoy* given in New York in 1890 showed how readily imitations of his and Sullivan's work resonated with the American market.

The rise of jingoism can be interpreted, in part, as an aggressive response to insecurity about what it was to be English. The 'War Song' (words and music by G.W. Hunt) of the popular music-hall entertainer the Great Macdermott was the source of the word 'jingoism' – taken from the opening of its chorus, 'We don't want to fight, but by Jingo if we do.' Macdermott first sang it in 1877, the year before *H.M.S. Pinafore*. However, boastful songs were nothing new, and melodramas depicting patriotic 'Jack Tar' sailors abounded in the 1870s.[7] Even earlier, in the 1850s, it is possible to find a song like 'Stand to Your Guns' in which sailors gloat about blood trickling down the side of a foe's stricken ship and cheer as it sinks to the bottom.[8] That song remained popular for many years, and appeared in *The Songs of England* published by Boosey in the 1870s.[9]

---

6   See François Cellier and Cunningham Bridgeman, *Gilbert and Sullivan and Their Operas* (New York: Blom, 1914, repr. 1970), excerpted in Harold Orel (ed.), *Gilbert and Sullivan: Interviews and Recollections* (London: Macmillan, 1994), pp. 151–65, at p. 154.

7   See Penny Summerfield, 'Patriotism and Empire: Music-Hall Entertainment 1870–1914', in John M. Mackenzie (ed.), *Imperialism and Popular Culture* (Manchester: Manchester University Press, 1986), pp. 17–48, at pp. 31–33.

8   Lest it be presumed that such sentiments belong to a more barbaric age, it is instructive to recall the headline 'Gotcha' on the front page of the *Sun* newspaper following the sinking of the Belgrano in the Falklands War.

9   Charles Carter, 'Stand to Your Guns' (1854), in *The Songs of England*, ed. J.L. Hatton, 3 vols (London: Boosey, 1873–92), vol. 2, pp. 183–89.

Hesketh Pearson refers to 'the satire on blatant patriotism' in *H.M.S. Pinafore*,[10] and Arthur Jacobs comments on the 'absurd mock-patriotic context' of 'He is an Englishman', in which 'portentous music is harnessed to dramatic triviality'.[11] Leslie Ayre calls it 'splendidly mock-Jingo'.[12] Englishness is used here as part of a personal appeal. He is an English man not a British man; the latter description became increasingly reserved for the broader context of empire.

> For he might have been a Roosian,
> A French, or Turk, or Proosian,
> Or perhaps Ital-ian!
> (Chorus: Or perhaps Ital-ian!)
> But in spite of all temptations
> To belong to other nations,
> He remains an Englishman!

The tune, as James Day remarks,[13] bears a resemblance to the Norfolk folksong 'Ward the Pirate' – even more so in Vaughan Williams's later arrangement of that song for male voices. If Sullivan did use that melody as

Ex. 7.1   'Ward the Pirate' (Anon.)

10   *Gilbert and Sullivan: a Biography* (London: Hamish Hamilton, 1946, orig. pub. 1935), p. 108.
11   *Arthur Sullivan*, p. 118.
12   *The Gilbert and Sullivan Companion* (London: Pan Books, 1974, orig. pub. W.H. Allen, 1972), p. 158.
13   *'Englishness' in Music: From Elizabethan Times to Elgar, Tippett and Britten* (London: Thames Publishing, 1999), p. 147.

Ex. 7.2   Sullivan, 'He is an Englishman', *H.M.S. Pinafore*: (a) beginning; (b) final cadence

(a)

from dominant down to tonic and back

For   he him-self has   said   it,   And it's great-ly to his   cre - dit,   That he

from dominant up to tonic and back

is   an   Eng - lish - man!   That   he   is   an   Eng - lish - man!

(b)

He   re - mains   an   Eng - - - - - - -   lish - man!

a departure point, he must have relished the irony of its having been origi-nally the vehicle for words about 'the biggest robber that ever you did hear'. A basic four-to-the-bar crotchet movement is common to both, and melodic similarities between the two are indicated in Examples 7.1 and 7.2.

Note that the eighteenth-century style melisma in 'He is an English-man' could easily have emphasized 'remains' and, by drawing it out, would have served a word-painting function; instead, it extends the mean-ingless syllable 'Eng'. The resulting prominence of the vowel sound 'i' – so close to turning into 'hee-hee-hee' when sung – seems to mock at the gran-deur of the tune's final flourish (and reminds us why this vowel sound is not a common choice for a melisma). Sullivan rarely uses a melisma and, when he does, is usually being satirical – think of 'Long life to you' in *The Mikado*. That he probably considered it an outworn and banal device seems confirmed by his use of a melisma on the word 'bland' at the end of the duet 'In every mental lore' in *Utopia Limited* (see Ex. 7.3).

David Cannadine, however, sees 'nothing disingenuous' about this song,[14] and seems resistant to the ironic techniques of both Gilbert and Sullivan (for

Ex. 7.3   Sullivan, 'In every mental lore', *Utopia Limited*

So   bland,   -   -   -   -   -   -   so   bland!   -   -

---

14 'Gilbert and Sullivan', p. 20.

example, Gilbert's carefully chosen words 'in spite of all temptations to belong to other nations' and Sullivan's absurdly exaggerated melisma). In maintaining that 'the prevailing assumption of the operas is that foreigners … are mildly comical and profoundly unfortunate', he comes close to parodying Gilbert as a high Tory chauvinist.[15] It is just such a character that Giovanni Ruffini, the librettist of Donizetti's *Don Pasquale*, introduced into his English novel *Doctor Antonio* of 1855. Ruffini describes his character as being possessed of 'An unbounded and exclusive admiration for all that was, and an abhorrence of all that was not English', which 'enclosed his mind and perceptions as within a Chinese wall'.[16] Yet, Gilbert never endorses such views and, on the contrary, himself parodies this type of person – sometimes, indeed, by dressing him in the costume of a foreign country. At other times, he makes play with stereotypical ideas about foreigners to satirize English racial prejudices: when he has Yum-Yum say 'Sometimes I sit and wonder, in my artless Japanese way', his purpose is to stimulate awareness of racial stereotyping through the use of irony. Irony is a sharp satirical tool, but one that always involves the risk of being taken literally. In the case of the Japanese nobles who exclaim 'Our attitude's queer and quaint', a clue to Gilbert's intentions is the slangy banality of the following line, 'You're wrong if you think it ain't'. And the three little maids in *The Mikado* are treated more kindly than the English girls described in Nekaya and Kalyba's duet in *Utopia Limited*. You only have to read some of the reviews of *The Mikado* or descriptions of the Japanese village in Knightsbridge to realize how deliberately Gilbert avoids what we would now regard as racist language in this opera. That is not always the case, for example, in the musical comedy *The Geisha* (1896), which actually exceeded *The Mikado* in popularity.[17]

There is a determination to avoid stereotypes, too, in *The Gondoliers*. In fact, Gilbert is at pains to explain that the character of the patriotic Englishman embraces a variety of international virtues. The recipe for a Dragoon Guard, according to Colonel Calverley in *Patience* (1881), includes French, Italian, Spanish, German and Austrian qualities.[18]

Cannadine finds further evidence for Gilbert's national chauvinism in *Ruddigore*, where the Union Jack is described as a 'flag that none dare

---

15 An insight into the complexity of Gilbert's character is provided by Jane W. Stedman, *W.S. Gilbert: a Classic Victorian and His Theatre* (Oxford: Oxford University Press, 1996).

16 John [Giovanni] Ruffini, *Doctor Antonio* (Leipzig: Tauchnitz, 1861, orig. pub. Edinburgh, 1855; repr. Arma di Taggio: Atene Edizioni, 2000), p. 48.

17 Libretto by Owen Hall, lyrics by Harry Greenbank, and music by Sidney Jones.

18 'The Dash of a D'Orsay', Victor Emmanuel, 'The Family Pride of a Spaniard from Aragon', the 'Genius of Bismarck Devising a Plan', and 'The Keen Penetration of Paddington Pollaky' (a reference to the Austrian detective Ignatius Pollaky who lived at Paddington Green in the 1860s; see Ayre, *The Gilbert and Sullivan Companion*, p. 258).

defy'.[19] Yet, the opera offers evidence elsewhere that challenges this boast. In Richard Dauntless's narrative song, the 'sturdy British' make for a French ship, but when they are fired upon they decide that 'to fight a French fal-lal – it's like hittin' of a gal' and choose, instead, to show compassion by turning about and disappearing quickly. There was a mixed reception for this song: those who recognized the irony accused Gilbert of slighting the British Navy. It was a given truth that British sailors did not fear the cannon's roar. Nelson said of his men: 'They really mind shot no more than peas.'[20] Gilbert, however, also managed to offend some of those who *failed* to see the irony, and he received 'several challenges to duels from Frenchmen who felt their country had been insulted'.[21] The London correspondent of the Paris *Figaro* was deeply offended.[22] Though humour rarely survives explanation or translation, Gilbert wrote a letter in French to the editor of *Le Figaro* and enclosed a copy of the song, but the editor chose to print instead a garbled translation by the paper's outraged London correspondent.[23] It was not the first time, either, that Gilbert had satirized English boasts about their superiority over the French. In *La Vivandière*, a burlesque of Donizetti's *La figlia del regimento* written in 1867, an Englishman brags about thrashing the French, but has to admit: 'In fact, my friends, wherever we have placed ourselves, I may say we have thoroughly disgraced ourselves.'[24]

In 'When Britain really ruled the waves' from *Iolanthe* (1882), we find a typical emphasis given to Britishness rather than Englishness within an imperial context. The opening of the song makes a specific reference to the words of 'Rule, Britannia!', and Britain is the focus throughout (see Ex. 7.4). Remarkably, we are reliably informed that 'Britain won her proudest bays in Good Queen Bess's glorious days', even though Queen Bess was never Queen of Britain, only Queen of England.

---

19 'Gilbert and Sullivan', p. 20.
20 Robert Southey, *Life of Nelson*, chap. 4, quoted in Ralph Waldo Emerson, *English Traits*, ed. Howard Mumford Jones (Cambridge, Mass.: Belknap Press, 1966, orig. pub. Boston, Mass.: Phillips, Sampson, 1856), p. 85.
21 See Pearson, *Gilbert and Sullivan*, p. 175.
22 H.G. Hibbert, *A Playgoer's Memoirs* (London: Grant Richards, 1920), pp. 260–61; excerpted in Orel, *Gilbert and Sullivan: Interviews and Recollections*, pp. 149–50.
23 See Stedman, *W.S. Gilbert*, p. 243.
24 See David Eden, *Gilbert and Sullivan: the Creative Conflict* (Cranbury, NJ: Associated University Presses, 1986), pp. 149–50. Eden mistakenly assigns the date 1868 to *La Vivandière*; the piece was first performed in Liverpool on 15 June 1867 (see Stedman, *W.S. Gilbert*, p. 39). Eden offers an absorbing account of the indebtedness of Gilbert's satire to the work of Thackeray; see pp. 146–54.

Ex. 7.4   Sullivan, 'When Britain really ruled the waves', *Iolanthe*

Cannadine describes Sullivan's 'broad, stately, majestic tune' as having a soothing effect upon Gilbert's words, failing to see how the po-faced grandeur of Sullivan's music increases the satiric bite.[25] The metre, tempo and harmonic rhythm are indebted to 'God Save the Queen' rather than 'Rule, Britannia!', a parody of which must have struck Sullivan as too obvious. Sullivan is here doing something he does so well elsewhere in the Savoy operas, treating Gilbert's absurdities with deadpan seriousness. Perhaps the *locus classicus* is the song 'Tit Willow' from *The Mikado*. Gilbert and Sullivan inscribe and subvert at the same time, something we are familiar with today as a postmodernist strategy. Without invoking postmodernism, we can see how closely this practice approaches the gestic music found in the collaborative stage works of Bertolt Brecht and Kurt Weill (especially *Aufstieg und Fall der Stadt Mahagonny*).

English identity old and new

We now need to consider how the Savoy operas relate to what it meant to be English in the late nineteenth century. Philip Dodd writes of 'the remaking of English identity' that occurred in these years.[26] He cites as examples the rise of English literature and history as academic disciplines, and the production of the *Dictionary of National Biography* (1885–1900). The equating of Englishness with venerable institutions like the Anglican Church and the Universities of Oxford and Cambridge effectively cast issues relating to class and gender to the margins, and served what were perceived as national needs by the dominant social order.

---

25 'Gilbert and Sullivan', p. 20. A hundred years later, Bruce Springsteen faced a similar misconstrual of meaning among those who failed to notice that the words of 'Born in the USA' were at odds with the music.
26 Robert Colls and Philip Dodd, *Englishness: Politics and Culture 1880–1920* (London: Croom Helm, 1986), p. 1.

Dodd comments, 'during 1880–1920 the conviction that English culture was to be found in the past was stabilised'.[27]

Where Gilbert and Sullivan are concerned, older myths of Englishness are most prominent in *The Yeomen of the Guard*, the period and location of which is seventeenth-century London. In the presentation of myth, historical accuracy is never an essential prerequisite. Here, a casual approach to history is found even in the title, which was chosen in preference to Beefeaters or Tower Warders (the authentic names for the guardians of the Tower of London) on the grounds that it sounded better. The linking of English culture with the past dovetails neatly with a pride in ancestry. Sir John Davenne in Ruffini's *Doctor Antonio* takes enormous pride in being able to trace his ancestry back to the nobles involved in the Crusades. Satirizing this attitude, Gilbert has Pooh-Bah dig much deeper into the past; he tells us, with a post-Darwinian assurance: 'I can trace my ancestry back to a protoplasmal primordial atomic globule.'

However, there is recognition of a new as distinct to old English identity when Captain Corcoran, reintroduced into *Utopia Limited* from *Pinafore*, explains, 'Though we're no longer hearts of oak, Yet we can steer and we can stoke.' In the same opera, Zara introduces the Company Promoter with reference to the 'stupendous loans' he has advocated 'to foreign thrones', and of the gold mines he has floated on the Stock Exchange. He explains to the Utopians how the law may be used to reduce financial risk, and advises that their entire country should be registered as a limited liability company along the terms of the Act of 1862. Britain, he claims, is 'tending rapidly in that direction'.

At the end of *Patience*, it is the modern English everyday young man who is the subject of satirical eulogy. The poet Grosvenor, in his newly adopted guise as a 'commonplace type', tells of the everyday pleasures of his stick and pipe and his delight in bottled beer and chops. Everyday young men and women are 'celebrated' by the chorus with reference to fashionable drapers, furriers and milliners. The music hall 'swells' of the 1870s had stimulated an interest in 'slap-up toggery' that crossed classes.

Victorian notions of English qualities

The American writer Ralph Waldo Emerson, in *English Traits* of 1856, interpreted Englishness for the most part in terms of the urban bourgeoisie

---

27 Ibid., p. 22.

or, in his words, 'the educated and dignified man of family'.[28] To some extent this has remained an American perspective, as the popular TV situation comedy *Frasier* demonstrates (Frasier and his brother Niles being, for the most part, caricatures of English middle-class dandies).

English bourgeois values, such as 'character', 'duty', 'prudence' and 'composure', did become a common means of asserting English identity in the later nineteenth century. English freedom was associated with parliamentary democracy and the rolling back of arbitrary powers of monarchy and state from Magna Carta onwards. The slow achievement of this freedom became the narrative of Whig historians. Pragmatic principles were favoured as a guide to action. Bunthorne knows that most of those who sigh for the Elysian fields would, if they possessed them, only sell them out on leases for building. The English preference for the practical over the intellectual[29] motivates the satire Gilbert aims at Sir Joseph in *Pinafore* and Major-General Stanley in *Pirates*, neither of whom has the practical experience required for his position.

Where individual behaviour was concerned, there was dislike of excess, whether in emotion, manner or dress. Composure, the stiff upper lip or, to borrow from Rudyard Kipling, the ability to 'keep your head when all about you are losing theirs',[30] has long been thought of as a typical English quality. 'No other nation sets such store by composure', wrote a German journalist in May 2001[31] in attempting to explain why, despite being 'tortured, humiliated and abused' as a consequence of the transport chaos then afflicting the UK, an attitude of 'friendly fatalism' had been adopted. Composure is as important to English women as to English men; we learn in *Utopia Limited* that if they discover they are rivals for the same man's affections, they do not quarrel, they toss a coin. Gilbert satirizes composure by revealing it to be a pose, as in the self-contradictory quartet 'In a Contemplative Fashion' from *The Gondoliers*, or by showing it at its heartless extreme: the Mikado, learning his son has been executed by mistake, sighs 'Dear, dear, dear! This is very tiresome.'

Respectability and decorum were paramount Victorian virtues,[32] and those who did not possess them learned to disguise the fact. The Pirate King comments, 'I don't think much of our profession but, contrasted

---

28 *English Traits*, 83. He devotes a special chapter to the aristocracy, but concludes, 'an untitled nobility possesses all the power without the inconveniences that belong to rank' (p. 127).

29 This preference is discussed in Emerson, *English Traits*, p. 52.

30 The opening lines of Rudyard Kipling's poem 'If—' are: 'If you can keep your head when all about you / Are losing theirs and blaming it on you.'

31 *Stern* article on Britain by Bern Dörler, May 2001, quoted in the *Sunday Times, News Review*, 27 May 2001, p. 4.

32 'A severe decorum rules the court and the cottage.' Emerson, *English Traits*, p. 72.

with respectability, it is comparatively honest.' An air of respectability was crucially important for women. The English governess in *Utopia Limited* suggests that the 'well-known blush', the 'downcast eyes' and 'famous look of mild surprise' need to be practised before the mirror:

> English girls of well-bred notions
> Shun all unrehearsed emotions.

On the subject of women, Jane Stedman has long argued that Gilbert used his middle-aged corpulent dame roles to satirize 'the premium which Victorians placed on youthful beauty as the most desirable personal quality in marriage'.[33]

Sometimes one senses an irritation at the censorship that stage entertainment was subjected to at this time. Sullivan provides an austerely elegant tune for the dance interludes of Despard and Margaret's duet in *Ruddigore*, heightening the po-faced humour of the line 'That is one of our blameless dances'. It is not just the individual characters who bow to the rules of propriety: Stedman argues that the chorus is 'important to the air of decorum so often significant in Savoy staging'.[34] Fastidious behaviour makes an effective springboard for Gilbertian surprises.

Not least of what may be perceived as English qualities in these operas is the quirky, topsy-turvy and often eccentric humour. There are lots of original humorous moments: some examples chosen at random from *Pirates* are: the echoing of words and even half-words in the Policeman's song; the supposed words of solace from the female chorus that serve merely to increase the fears of the police, but which are nonetheless accepted politely as being 'well meant';[35] the pirates' supposedly covert entrance when they sing loudly about their 'cat-like tread'; and the forced rhymes, such as 'You shall quickly be parsonified, Conjugally matrimonified'.

Music and the embodiment of an English national character

Napoleon Bonaparte in one of his discourses in exile (1820) claimed that the English 'have no music, or, at all events, no national music',[36] a point

---

33 Stedman, *W.S. Gilbert*, p. 231; see also 'From Dame to Woman: W.S. Gilbert and Theatrical Transvestism', in Martha Vicinus (ed.), *Suffer and Be Still: Women in the Victorian Age* (Bloomington: Indiana University Press, 1972).

34 Stedman, *W.S. Gilbert*, p. 220.

35 A similar scene occurs in the film *Monty Python and the Holy Grail*, when Brave Sir Robin's minstrels sing of his courage and ability to endure pain.

36 Quoted in Anon., 'English Music', *Musical World*, 24 Aug. 1861, p. 584.

to which he gave additional though somewhat unintentional weight by declaring that the only good English tune was 'Ye Banks and Braes o' Bonnie Doon'. Bonaparte's sentiments were widely shared. A correspondent in *Dwight's Journal of Music* in 1861, however, takes issue with an American writer's claim that there was no national English music and that what was described as English music had 'no distinctive character'.[37] She gives a short list of songs as proof that a national music exists, which includes 'God Save the Queen' and 'Rule, Britannia!' (note that English is conflated with British in both these cases), and she refers to the 250 or so national English songs published by Chappell (*Popular Music of the Olden Time*, 1855–59). She praises Macfarren's arrangements for being better suited to the material than those of Haydn or Beethoven. She ends with the suggestion that if English composers turned to these songs and allowed them to give national colour to their compositions, 'there might be some hope for England to possess, not only a rich national song music, but also an original and characteristic school of opera and oratorio'.[38]

When, more than a decade later, Arthur Sullivan and Henry Leslie gave three concerts of English music at the French Exhibition of 1878 in Paris, it was the ritual playing of the national anthem at the beginnings and ends of the English concerts, and the rising of the audience, that made a great impression upon the French critics.[39] Yet, the anthem was not free of confusion: Beethoven used its melody in his Battle Symphony (1813) for the British, but Brahms had used it more recently in his *Song of Triumph* (1870) for the Germans (coincidentally, both pieces celebrated victories over the French). The existence of a German patriotic song 'Heil dir im Siegerkranz' to the same tune as 'God Save the Queen' was the cause of much confusion during state visits between Britain and Germany. The tune was also used for the American patriotic song 'My country 'tis of thee', as well as for patriotic songs of other nations.

The idea that the roots of Englishness might be found in the countryside among people once thought not typically English did not gain ground before imperial federation posed its threats to English national identity. It also relied upon the growing notion that Englishness was to be found in the past. The countryside was seen as important to Englishness only when England had become a predominantly urban society. Whereas German, French and

---

37 F.M.R., 'English National Music', *Dwight's Journal of Music*, 20, pt. 2 (1861), pp. 293–94, at p. 293. The source of her displeasure is Richard Grant White's work on national hymns.
38 Ibid., p. 294.
39 Anon. [Our Special Correspondent], 'British Musical Art in Paris', *Musical Times*, 19, no. 426 (1 Aug. 1878), pp. 428–32, at p. 429.

Russian folksong researchers had begun their work in the 1840s and 1850s, the English were upbraided by Carl Engel in 1878, the year of the English concerts at the French Exhibition, for having 'hitherto done the least in this field of enquiry'.[40] In the next decade, however, folksong collectors like Frank Kidson and Sabine Baring-Gould were looking for Englishness among the 'sons of the soil' in the English countryside.

A folksong character can be found in the duet 'I have a song to sing, O!' from *The Yeomen of the Guard*. Sullivan worked for two weeks trying to set the words to music, but to no avail. He knew that Gilbert often took inspiration from old airs when writing lyrics, but preferred not to know which, so as to avoid reminiscence. This time Sullivan was compelled to ask him to hum a few bars of his model.[41] Gilbert claimed it was a sea shanty, beginning:

> Come, and I will sing you –
> What will you sing me?
> I will sing you one, O!
> What is your one, O?[42]

The shanty has, as far as I am aware, not been traced, but the words quoted by Gilbert and the augmenting verses of 'I have a song to sing, O!' resemble closely the folksong 'Green Grow the Rushes, O':

> I'll sing you one, O!
> Green grow the rushes, O!
> What is your one, O?
> One is one and all alone,
> And evermore shall be so.
> I'll sing you two, O!
> Green grow the rushes, O!
> What are your two, O?
> Two, two the lily-white boys,
> Covered all in green, O!
> One is one, etc.

40 'The Literature of National Music [continued]', *Musical Times*, 19, no. 429 (1 Nov. 1878), pp. 587–89, at p. 587. Carl Engel had already published *An Introduction to the Study of National Music* (London: Longmans, 1866).
41 The anecdote is told in Pearson, *Gilbert and Sullivan*, pp. 185–86, and also recounted in Young, *Sir Arthur Sullivan*, p. 171. The most comprehensive source is William Archer, *Real Conversations* (London: Heinemann, 1904), pp. 123–25, excerpted in Orel, *Gilbert and Sullivan*, pp. 42–44.
42 See Orel, *Gilbert and Sullivan*, p. 43.

Ex. 7.5   Sullivan, 'I have a song to sing, O!', *The Yeomen of the Guard*

The Mixolydian elements, however, are Sullivan's own, and must have been employed with the intention of suggesting an old English song (see Ex. 7.5).[43] The folk-like quality is further emphasized by a drone bass.

The folksong collector Sabine Baring-Gould relates that during one of his visits to the British Museum for the purpose of researching old published music, a librarian told him that Sullivan often visited, 'doing much the same as you. But he is searching for musical *ideas*.'[44] It seems, though, that Sullivan was mainly interested in eighteenth-century sources.

An Englishness suggesting the influence of Anglican anthems is found occasionally in Sullivan: for example, 'Hail Poetry' from *Pirates*. There are also instances of the more direct influence of the English madrigal: for example, 'Brightly dawns our wedding day' from *The Mikado*, and the three-voice glee 'A British Tar' from *Pinafore*. The strong contribution of the chorus can be related to the English fondness for choral music. The role of the chorus is considerably more important than that found in contemporary Continental operettas. Gilbert's innovative use of the chorus, 'tied to plot and satire by its leaders', as Jane Stedman puts it,[45] has made the operas perennially popular with amateur music and dramatic societies.

In his early career, Sullivan was much indebted to German musicians in England as well as in Germany.[46] He makes use of German and Italian styles in the Savoy operas and is frequently indebted not only to

---

43   Sullivan had already introduced a song of folk-like character and with Aeolian features in the duet 'The Merry Maiden and the Tar' in *Pinafore*, but a 'learned' style intrudes in its pseudo-canonic refrain.

44   S. Baring-Gould, *Further Reminiscences, 1864–1894* (London: Bodley Head, 1925), p. 214; excerpted in Orel, *Gilbert and Sullivan*, pp. 108–9, at p. 108.

45   *W.S. Gilbert*, p. 220.

46   See Percy M. Young, *Sir Arthur Sullivan* (London: Dent, 1971), p. 35.

Offenbach, but also to other French composers like Charles Lecocq. The technique the latter uses for his chorus of conspirators in *La Fille de Madame Angot* (1872) is not dissimilar to the chorus 'Carefully on tiptoe stealing' in *Pinafore*. They are both, of course, parodies of the conspiratorial choruses found in Verdi (for example, in *Un ballo in maschera* of 1858). There is an unmistakable Viennese element in the duet 'Pretty Lisa' in Act I of *The Grand Duke*. Had death not intervened, it seems likely that Sullivan would have gone on to collaborate with Ignaz Schnitzer (1839–1921), the librettist of Johann Strauss's *Der Zigeunerbaron* (1885).[47] However, the subject position is always that of the English middle-class listener, the person Sullivan expects to recognize a madrigalian technique, a Handelian manner, or a traditional English air. It is the English audience for comic opera that he expects to amuse with the 'serious' fugato passages representing the law in *Iolanthe*. As James Day observes, they would probably have bored a nineteenth-century French audience.[48] Moreover, Cecil Forsyth has argued that the 'charming intimacy of words and melody' in the Savoy operas is based 'on a purely English foundation', by which he means it results from the necessity of making audible the consonants that conclude many English words as well as the varied vowel sounds of the English language.[49]

During the D'Oyly Carte Company's tour of Austria and Germany in 1886, Siegfried Ochs, writing in the *Allgemeine Musik-Zeitung* (Berlin), found traces of Suppé, Millöcker, Auber and Offenbach in *The Mikado*, but also singled out numbers that bore no relation to other operettas, such as Yum-Yum's 'The sun whose rays' and the madrigal 'Brightly dawns our wedding day' (which he linked to the music of Morley and Dowland). He also recognized that *The Mikado* was about the political and social condition of England, not of Japan.[50]

Nevertheless, nobody at the time would have considered the works of Gilbert and Sullivan to be national operas. That was, in the main, because they were thought of in less dignified terms as entertainment (something like the Mikado's 'innocent merriment'), even though, as Forsyth notes, Sullivan was from *Iolanthe* onwards trying to develop 'a higher and more complex type' from the popular form of opera.[51] For related reasons, commercial song did not count as national music: the cry that the English are 'not a musical nation' is 'dinned into our ears constantly' complained

---

47 See Jacobs, *Arthur Sullivan*, p. 352.
48 *'Englishness' in Music*, p. 4.
49 *Music and Nationalism: a Study of English Opera* (London: Macmillan, 1911), p. 191.
50 *Allgemeine Musik-Zeitung*, 13 (2 July 1886), pp. 276–77; quoted in Young, *Sir Arthur Sullivan*, p. 144.
51 *Music and Nationalism*, p. 244.

one writer, even though publishers great and small 'deluge the land every day with new songs by English living composers'.[52]

In February 1895, Sir A.C. Mackenzie gave three lectures on 'The Traditional and National in Music'. In the first, he discussed *Hänsel und Gretel*, praising the 'union of the national element with the latest and most intricate methods of composition'.[53] He remarked that musicians in England looked upon the development of national opera wistfully, since they had come to regard an English national quality as unattainable. In the second lecture, with reference to Bohemia and Russia, he argued: 'The beginning of a national school of composition had to be found in a complete knowledge (not a superficial appreciation) and a love of the people's music.'[54]

It was only in this decade that the idea of there being something English in the music rather than the words of a song gained ground, although the debate about what constituted an English musical style was not to reach any settled conclusion. Yet, anyone seeking an English alternative to the prevailing Mendelssohnian character of English concert music during this period would have found its first flowering in some of the music composed for the Savoy operas by a former student of the Leipzig Conservatorium whose father was Irish and mother half-Italian.

52 Anon., 'English Music', *Musical World*, 24 Aug. 1861, p. 584.
53 Anon., 'Sir A.C. Mackenzie on National Music', *Musical Times*, 36, no. 625 (1 Mar. 1895), pp. 164–65, at p. 164.
54 Ibid., p. 165.

CHAPTER EIGHT

'Unfurl the Flag and Federate'

Flags as a Representation of Patriotism and Nationalism in Australian Federation Songs, 1880–1906

Peter Campbell

For all of the nineteenth century (and even for much of the twentieth), Australia's composers were European-trained, if not European-born. Beginning in mid-century, there was a gradual move towards a united Australian nation, formed from the existing six independent British colonies, but this process was not completed until 1 January 1901. The period from 1880 saw the most concerted efforts to effect a federation, and the popular songs that accompany this push reflect a variety of moods and perspectives. Chief among the differences in outlook is an apparent distinction between the primarily patriotic and the predominantly nationalistic songs that were published as sheet music and which received widespread performance in music halls and around the piano at home. The poems, brought into the consciousness of the general populace by being set to music, thus raise issues of Britishness and Empire as well as nationhood and unity, largely through the pointed use of imagery. While the musical idiom of these songs is not differentiated, their sentiment is, and it is this aspect that will be examined here, taking the representation of flags as an obvious and frequently employed connecting theme.

Only thirty songs relating to Australia's Federation seem to have survived; all but one were identified by Georgina Binns in her 1989 study of Australia's early patriotic and nationalistic songs.[1] Most date from the period 1898 to 1901, at the very moment of Federation, although there are several that were written as early as 1891 (when the most concerted push towards the creation of a Commonwealth, the First National Australasian Convention in Sydney, occurred),[2] and a scattering of songs

---

[1] Georgina Binns, 'Patriotic and Nationalistic Song in Australia to 1919' (M.Mus. thesis, University of Melbourne, 1989). See especially chap. 5, '"Lead on, Advance Australia": Songs of Federation', pp. 108–34.

[2] It should be noted that throughout the preliminary discussions about a new Commonwealth, the colony of New Zealand was invited to send representatives and was

from as late as 1906, concerned more with the continued unity of the by-then federated nation than with the mechanics of its unification per se.[3]

The songs served the joint tasks of raising awareness of the Federation debate – a nationalistic aim – and giving vent to more patriotic notions such as honour, justice and freedom. The songs discussed here are drawn from the repertoire of sheet music. They fall happily into the category of popular song, each being a setting of newly composed, strophic verse, and furnished, on the whole, with simple, melody-supporting piano accompaniments. They are also overwhelmingly pro-federation; the sentiments of the anti-unionists are more likely to be found in folksong collections. Although the song collector Warren Fahey notes that 'songwriters sat on both sides of the boundary fence',[4] it seems clear, in general terms, that the wealthy and better-educated sector – those with the means to purchase sheet music and the pianos to play it on – favoured federation and might, perhaps, have some better under-standing of the legal and commercial benefits offered by it, while the poorer labour classes, largely from whom the unpublished folksongs emanated, saw only complications and a new layer of politicians growing fat.

One feature of the poems that were set is their authors' oft-repeated invocation of the flag as a powerful symbol of identity, unity and inde-pendence, and it is this vexillological preoccupation that is elaborated in the following excursion through several of the published songs. It will be seen that this attempt to highlight the general similarities of the genre and point up the major concerns of composers of the era is not quite as straightforward as might at first be thought, owing largely to the fact that the composers have chosen texts that mix patriotic and nationalistic symbolism, producing similar songs with rather mixed messages.

'Australia for Ever', with words and music by Henry Rix (1848–1906), was published by Sutton Brothers in Melbourne at 6d., probably some time during the 1890s, while Rix was a school inspector for the Victorian department of education.[5] The song is subtitled 'A Federation Song' and is

---

given treatment equal to that of the 'mainland' colonies. In fact, in the late 1890s, it seemed that New Zealand was more likely than Western Australia to form part of the new nation. WA actually joined the Commonwealth in June 1901, six months *after* Australia was proclaimed.

3   A large amount of occasional music in the form of songs, piano pieces and marches was also written. As just two examples, see Ezra Read's piano piece 'Australia Grand March: In Commemoration of the Federation 1901' (London: London Music Publishing Stores, [1901]) and W.R. Furlong's vocal work 'Australian Caledonian Welcome Song' (Melbourne: W.R. Furlong, [1901]), dedicated to Australia's inaugural Governor General, the Earl of Hopetoun, and his wife, the Countess.

4   Warren Fahey, *The Balls of Bob Menzies: Australian Political Songs 1900–1980* (Sydney: Angus & Robertson, 1989), p. 20.

5   Henry F. Rix, 'Australia for Ever' (Melbourne: Sutton Bros., n.d.). The copy examined for this essay is held in the McLaren Collection, University of Melbourne.

dedicated to the Australian Natives' Association, of which Rix was a prominent member. The simple cover shows an outline of Australia underneath a prototypical Australian flag with the Union Jack in canton and the five stars of the Southern Cross in the fly (see Fig. 8.1).

The cover artwork clearly and literally illustrates the imagery of the opening lines of the song, with its references to a flag and to a single, federated country under it:

Fig. 8.1   Henry Rix: cover of 'Australia for Ever'

On high let fly the Southern Flag,
Australia united.
Ring out the shout when on each crag
The Union Flag is sighted.

The reference to the 'Union Flag' must surely be read as meaning the Union Jack, for the two terms were then, and remain today, interchangeable. Furthermore, at this time, the British Union Jack was still the official flag of each of the individual colonies. But what then, could Rix mean by the 'Southern Flag', which he seems to equate with the Union Flag? We must presume that it is a new flag for the newly unified country, and this is what has been represented on the cover. Similar ambiguity can be seen in Samuel McBurney's setting of J. Ecclestone Walker's 'The Flag of Union' where

Morning dawns for Federation,
Austral brothers now arise,
Wave the joyous flag of union
'Neath our bright and sunny skies.[6]

There would seem to be little point in brandishing the Union Jack as a symbol of the new nation when it was already the flag for the old colonies, so perhaps the phrase 'flag of union' was used specifically in contradistinction to 'Union Jack' in order to signify the new flag. The capitalisation (or rather lack thereof) in the poems as printed in the songs is perhaps significant here. While in the title of McBurney's song the phrase 'Flag of Union' is capitalised, in the song itself it is not, a fact that suggests, albeit inconclusively, that it was not a specific flag that was being spoken of. Rix's poem, however, supported by the designer of the cover for 'Australia for Ever', was clearly illustrating a specific flag, the still-imaginary national standard that he poetically called the 'Southern Flag'. The poem is not complex and, apart from the references to flags, is rather devoid of allusion, although it speaks frankly and forthrightly of a people 'strong-souled and free', members of a 'brotherhood of liberty' whose souls 'No feuds shall sever'. The repetitious iambic metric structure is lightened by an additional syllable at the end of the short lines of each verse, giving them a strong–weak, inconclusive feeling that contrasts well with the more powerful certainty of the chorus.

As is noted by Binns, Rix's 'Australia for Ever' bears more than a passing similarity to P.D. McCormick's 'Advance Australia Fair', the current Australian national anthem. Melodically, ten of the first 14 notes are identical, and the rhythm is the same for all but one note – which becomes dotted (see Ex.

---

6   Samuel McBurney, 'The Flag of Union' (Melbourne: Spectator Publishing Co., [1890s]), copy held in the National Library of Australia.

8.1). The tonic–dominant harmony and triadic tune are hardly inventive, and the song is tiresomely repetitive in its use of the same upward-leaping fourth at the beginning of every line; yet the piece is effective, easy to sing and rousingly martial enough to do well as a popular call to unity.

But what significance can be drawn from this one example? Henry Rix was an amateur musician, a mathematics teacher who also published numerous books of mathematical tables and on mental mathematics methods, as well as a 1905 pamphlet discussing the proposed introduction of decimal coinage in Australia.[7] 'Australia for Ever' is, perhaps, not great art, but that is not likely to have been the intention. While Rix's setting suggests at least a passing acquaintance with 'Advance Australia Fair' (for that work certainly cannot claim a monopoly over tonic-chord arpeggios or tonic–dominant-laden harmony), it is well written and workmanlike, and obeys the accepted rules of melodic and harmonic movement. In short, it is a good effort from a competent amateur, and one that was no doubt popular, albeit melodically staid and harmonically unadventurous.

But perhaps staid and unadventurous was the mood of the times. There were some in Australia, the composer and conductor G.W.L. Marshall-

Ex. 8.1   Melodic and rhythmic similarities between (a) Rix's 'Australia for Ever' and (b) McCormick's 'Advance Australia Fair'

7   Henry F. Rix, *The Proposed Australian Decimal Coinage: a Criticism and an Alternative Proposal* (Melbourne: Whitcombe & Tombs, [1906?]). Decimal currency was not actually adopted in Australia until 14 February 1966.

Hall for one, whose music and poetry was called everything except staid. Quickly the establishment, through the agency of the newspapers, accused him of writing lewd poetry and making 'improper suggestions', and he, along with his advocacy of Wagner, was banished from the university.[8] Thérèse Radic states of Marshall-Hall that 'neither the sober disciplines of the conductor nor those of the academic were ever applied by the new professor to what he wrote'; of the inappropriateness of his actions and views for polite Australian society around 1899 she notes that he made

> enemies everywhere in a society devoted, at that time, to a narrow imitation of constricted middle-class, late Victorian English mores and morals. In an effort to cast off the dual taints of convict ancestry and gold lust, Melbourne had become a society determined to display solid virtues, solid wealth, respect for the law, the state and the church. An incipient bohemian let loose in the midst of the most sombre and sedate of institutions, the University of Melbourne, was bound to cause trouble.[9]

It was in this climate of conservatism that the push for federation was taking place. By the time of Marshall-Hall's banishment, precisely at the point of Federation, the colonies, or rather, individuals such as Henry Parkes, had been campaigning for an Australian nation for nearly 50 years. Although the percentage of Australian residents born in the United Kingdom had been falling rapidly as the native-born population increased, most people still thought of themselves as British. Australia sent significant armed forces to the Sudan conflict in 1885 and, more immediately, between 1899 and 1901, to the Boer War. National defence certainly lent impetus to the federation push, yet even the centennial celebrations of 1888 had sparked only passing thoughts of union and more songs were written about the Boer War than about federation itself.

Throughout the 1890s, Australia was gripped by the twin hardships of drought and depression – hardly a supportive environment for joyous professions of national unity, but oddly providing the right atmosphere for change, an opportunity to work together to achieve something beyond the reach of the states individually, and an objective that would instil a sense of optimism in a largely apathetic populace. What need had they for complex governmental arrangements for expediting such matters as trade and excise of which they had little understanding and even less direct experience?

---

8   Marshall-Hall (1862–1915) was the first Ormond Professor of Music at the University of Melbourne, 1891–1900, and was appointed as Professor again in 1915. He was responsible for establishing and promoting a fine orchestra in Melbourne and, after his appointment was not renewed in 1900, continued teaching at his private conservatorium. His surviving compositions consist of six operas, two symphonies, string quartets and vocal works.
9   Thérèse Radic, *G.W.L. Marshall-Hall: Portrait of a Lost Crusader* (Nedlands, WA: University of Western Australia, 1982), pp. 13–14.

What was important, what truly affected them, was sentiment: they wished to be moved by the beauty and poignancy of the poetry and have their emotions stirred by the strength and vigour of the songs they heard.

Rix's federation song had been written for the Australian Natives' Association, a friendly society established in Melbourne in 1871 for native-born, white Australian males of good character.[10] In a setting of his own words, Rix espouses friendship, liberty, honour and justice. His other published literary effort on the subject of federation, the poem 'Australians! Rise and Federate!', was printed on the back cover of the sheet music for 'Australia for Ever' and also separately as a single sheet by the Scrutineer Printing Works in Moss Vale, New South Wales.[11] This poem (no musical setting has yet been discovered) is a strong and grand plea for federation. Rix continues his theme of flags, both in the chorus ('Australians, rise! No longer wait, / Unfurl the Flag and Federate') and in the second verse, where

> Before the eyes of all the world
> The Union Flag must be unfurled
> That we may claim our destiny.

Here we see some similarity to the words of Francis Hart as set in another federation song, Sir William Robinson's 'Unfurl the Flag', subtitled a 'Patriotic Song', written some 20 years before Federation and sung at Robinson's installation as Governor of South Australia in 1883 (see Fig. 8.2).[12] Robinson had previously been Governor of Western Australia and had had popular success with several songs and a comic opera – another triumph for the gentleman amateur. Hart's chorus is in the same metre as Rix's poem:

---

10 Membership was also open to men who had lived in the colonies for at least 20 years. The Australian Natives' Association was a major pro-federation force, with 90 branches in five states. The first five of Victoria's delegates to the 1897–98 Federation Convention (Turner, Quick, Deakin, Peacock and Isaacs) were all ANA members. See Aedeen Cremin (ed.), *1901 – Australian Life at Federation: an Illustrated Chronicle* (Sydney: UNSW Press, 2001), p. 112.

11 Fahey, *The Balls of Bob Menzies*, p. 20, also records an unattributed version published in the *Bega Free Press* of 1898 under the title 'Australia Rise' (he renders it 'Australia Arise') that notes that the poem was a 'rousing and widely published chorus'. The first two lines are given as 'Australia rise. Why no longer wait / While wrangling politicians prate', whereas the Atlas Press edition gives them as 'Australians, rise! Why longer wait / While parliaments prolong debate'. The provenance and tighter scansion of the latter suggest that it is more likely to be the original.

12 William Robinson, 'Unfurl the Flag' (Melbourne: W.H. Glen, n.d.), copy held in State Library of Victoria. See F.K. Crowley, 'Robinson, Sir William Cleaver Francis (1834–1897)', *Australian Dictionary of Biography*, vol. 6, 1851–1890 R–Z (Melbourne: Melbourne University Press, 1976), pp. 50–51.

Fig. 8.2   Sir William Robinson: cover of 'Unfurl the Flag'

Unfurl the flag that all may see
Our proudest boast is liberty.

As with 'Australia for Ever', Rix's second poem is perhaps overstuffed
with word repetition – shore to shore, strength to strength, man to man –

yet contains some more finely wrought verse, including what seems likely to be another passing reference to 'Advance Australia Fair': 'With nature's gifts more rich and free'.[13]

The ubiquity of 'Advance Australia Fair' (or perhaps the paucity of poetic phrases available to that generation of poets) is further evidenced by Hart's poem, which – with yet another reference to flags – begins 'Australia's sons your flag unfurl'. Verse 5 includes the words 'Rejoice, Australia's sons' and verse 2 talks about soil and fruits of manly toil. While this is perhaps drawing a long bow, the likelihood of even subconscious referencing cannot be discounted entirely. 'Advance Australia Fair' had been popular ever since it first appeared publicly around 1878, and by 1901 it was accepted widely enough for it to be sung by massed choirs around the country as a national song.[14]

The verse of 'Unfurl the Flag' that talks most obviously about Federation proclaims confidently:

> In visions hopeful, fair and bright,
> Our country's future shines afar;
> When as a nation we unite
> 'Neath freedom's blest and beaming star

This brings the words 'Beneath our radiant Southern Cross', which is the first line of verse 3 of 'Advance Australia Fair', easily to mind. For all the references to 'our nation', ties to Britain are never far from the surface. The following verse begins with the exhortation

> Rejoice, Australia's sons, but ne'er
> Forget your father's native land,
> Dear England, glorious and fair,
> She claims your heart and willing hand.

In fact, numerous songs of the period are less about a united Australia than about it being part of a united British Empire. While certainly a post-Federation song, written about 1906, Georgette Peterson's 'Australia's

---

13 The first verse of 'Advance Australia Fair' is:
  Australia's sons, let us rejoice, For we are young and free,
  We've golden soil and wealth for toil, Our home is girt by sea;
  Our land abounds in nature's gifts Of beauty rich and rare;
  In hist'ry's page, let ev'ry stage Advance Australia fair,
  In joyful strains then let us sing Advance Australia fair.
14 See Warren Bebbington, 'Who Wrote "Advance Australia Fair"?', *Canberra Times*, 26 Jan. 1985, p. 15.

Song of Empire' is typical.[15] A setting of words by Annie Rentoul, the poem tells how Australians are

> Bound by bonds of friendship. Sundered by the sea
> Dear and precious Motherland distant though we be ...
> True in life and death to thee, staunch to play her part
> Proud and free but one with thee in hope and heart.

With the copy in the State Library of Victoria is a page containing the handwritten poem. While the published song is titled 'Australia's Song of Empire' and dedicated to the Victoria League of Victoria, the poem is titled 'An Australian Song for Empire Day', and the last line, 'Take our loyal love', is written in pencil, in another hand, above the original words, 'Give we thou our love'. Without tracing and comparing samples of handwriting, it may be surmised that the manuscript is Rentoul's fair copy used by Peterson when setting the poem. Peterson may have altered the last line to remove the anacrusis and make it conform to the rhythm of the other verses.

The first Empire Day in Australia was celebrated on 24 May (Queen Victoria's birthday) 1905, although the Queen's Birthday had been a special date on the social calendar for a number of years before Federation, and was the day on which the Governor's Ball was held. Peterson's song, therefore, is likely to have been written specially for the 1906 commemorations, which, as usual, would have included concerts of patriotic music. Empire Day was vigorously promoted by the British Empire League, a largely Protestant movement established in 1901 to counter the actions of the Anti-War League, opposed to sending troops to what seemed like irrelevant conflicts such as that in South Africa. Many Catholics, especially those recalling the struggles in Ireland, saw no profit in celebrating connections with Britain and pushed a 'dissident, republican nationalism' that tried to claim Australia for Australia, not Empire. The tug-of-war between patriotism and nationalism was not really decided until after the First World War, when Anzac Day began to take precedence over an increasingly unimportant Empire Day that was first renamed Commonwealth Day in an attempt to prolong its life, and, in the 1960s, reverted to a celebration of the Queen's Birthday (on a new date in June), itself a national holiday unlikely to be observed for many more years.[16]

---

15 Georgette Peterson, 'Australia's Song of Empire' (Melbourne: George Robertson, n.d.), copy held in State Library of Victoria.

16 The ideas presented in this paragraph are based on Stewart Firth and Jeanette Hoorn, 'From Empire Day to Cracker Night', in Peter Spearritt and David Walker (eds), *Australian Popular Culture* (Sydney: Allen & Unwin, 1979), pp. 17–38.

Of more apparent relevance to Australia's Federation is Chevalier Fittipaldi's 'For Britain, One and Whole', which Binns identifies definitely as a federation song, but which may have sidetracked the cataloguers by the presence of the dedication 'Written and Composed for the Imperial Federation League of Victoria'. The aims of the League, detailed on the back cover of the sheet, were to 'secure by Federation the permanent unity of the Empire' so as to 'maintain the unity of the British Dominions'.[17] The words of the song were written by H. D'Esterre Taylor, who was, according to the copy, the Honorary Secretary of the League. The cover of the sheet music lists the various parts of the Empire that the League was designed to encompass – 53 countries, dominions, colonies, protectorates, possessions and settlements in all. The objective of the Imperial Federation League, as its name rightly suggests, was not the federation merely of Australia, then, but of the entire British Empire. It is this ambiguity, this mixture of nationalistic and 'empirical' notions that characterises the popular songs of the period.

In Fittipaldi's song itself, Australia is not mentioned specifically, although there is a form of the Australian flag depicted on the cover. A large number of the cover illustrations contain representations of flags and other devices, yet an official Australian flag was not assented to until 1903. A public competition was held during 1901, closing in May that year, and winners were announced the following September, yet royal assent took two more years to make it official. Prior to 1903, the only official national flag was the Union Jack, although each colony had a flag based on the British blue ensign, that is, a dark blue flag with the Union Jack in canton, with a state seal or badge on the fly.[18]

There was in existence, however, a very popular design, known as the Australian Federation Flag, that had been designed in 1831, when it had been suggested as the New South Wales Ensign, that is, a new colonial flag of NSW. Such was the popularity of the design that it was adopted by the Australian Natives' Association and the Australian Federation League, proposed as the new national flag in 1898, and featured on many official documents for inauguration events (see Fig. 8.3).

This is the flag proudly displayed on the cover of George Sampson's 'A Federal Song', published in 1899 (see Fig. 8.4).[19] The poem, by the well-

---

17 Chevalier Ed. Fittipaldi, 'For Britain, One and Whole' (Melbourne: G. Tytherleigh, [1898?]), copy held in State Library of Victoria.

18 See Carol A. Foley, *The Australian Flag: Colonial Relic or Contemporary Icon?* (Sydney: Federation Press, 1996), pp. 22–32; G.H. Swinburne, *Unfurled: Australia's Flag* (Melbourne: Sirius, 1969).

19 George Sampson, 'A Federal Song' (Brisbane: Gordon & Gotch and Nicholson, 1899), copy held in State Library of Queensland.

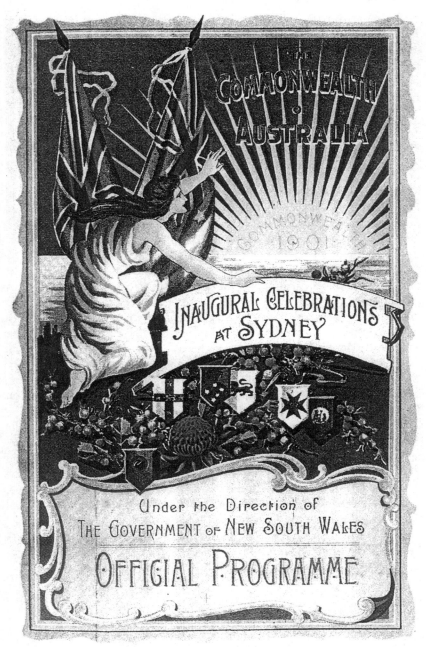

Fig. 8.3   Cover of Official Programme of Inaugural Celebrations, Sydney, 1901

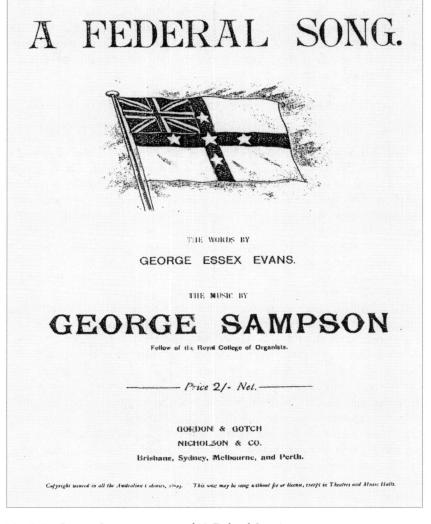

Fig. 8.4   George Sampson: cover of 'A Federal Song'

known Queenslander George Essex Evans, won its author £50 in a Federation competition, but was adjudged by some to be trite, uninspired and a statement of the obvious.[20] One of the few Federation songs in compound

---

[20] A.G. Stephens, reported in M.D. O'Hagan, 'Evans, George Essex (1863–1909)', *Australian Dictionary of Biography*, vol. 8, 1891–1939 Cl–Gib (Melbourne: Melbourne University Press, 1981), pp. 446–47.

time, its verses are more reflective – in the 'greyness of the dawning' and the 'whisper of the morning' can we 'break the land asunder God has girdled with the sea?' (as distinct from the well-known yet lexically unusual 'girt by sea' from 'Advance Australia Fair') – than those of most of the other songs of the period, and only the chorus really invokes the chest-swelling sentiments of federation:

> For the flag is floating o'er us from the desert to the sea ...
> Uplift the mighty chorus for Australian Unity!

This flag is also depicted on the much more intricate cover of John H. Nicholson's 'Sons of Britannia', subtitled 'A Federation Song' (the only item not included in Binns's list) (see Fig. 8.5). Here, all those who 'speak the stirring English tongue' are asked to unite to fight for peace and freedom so that the 'dungeons of doom' might be unbarred. There is no mention of Australia specifically, and the reference to federation may again be to a unified British Empire rather than the country. The cover depicts the Union Jack, the Australian Federation Flag and, surprisingly, the American Stars and Stripes (with its then 45 stars). What the US might have thought of being instated in a Federated British Commonwealth is difficult to imagine.

So what of other music covers? Four of the sheets examined in researching this article showed representations of a national flag, yet none dates from later than 1903. Rix's 'Australia for Ever', as noted above, shows a flag very similar to the current Australian flag but without the federal star. Amati's 'Song of Young Australia', dating from around 1894, has a similar representation although the Southern Cross is on a different angle and the field of the flag appears to be a paler colour (probably blue) than that used in the Union Jack.[21] Fittipaldi's 'For Britain, One and Whole' depicts both the Union Jack and the same Australian flag with Southern Cross as for Rix and Amati. Robinson's 'Unfurl the Flag' (Fig. 8.2) appropriately depicts two flags which, while we cannot see the fly, certainly carry the Union Jack in canton and might also be presumed to be similar. The beautifully crafted cover artwork contains many other symbols of nationhood: a coat of arms with a rather awkward emu and quizzical kangaroo as supporters, and a figure, presumably Austral herself, wearing a crown of sovereignty and carrying a sword of strength and wreath of victory or perhaps peace, all surmounted by four stars.

These four depictions of a national flag are all similar to the design chosen late in 1901, and are not representations of any flag in official (or even semi-official) use at the time of their publication. The fact that the judges had to

---

21   M. Amati, 'The Song of Young Australia' ([Melbourne?]: Troedel & Co., [1894?]), copy held in State Library of Victoria.

Fig. 8.5 John H. Nicholson: cover of 'Sons of Britannia'

announce five winners for the flag design competition because their submissions were all so similar suggests that the important elements of the design may have been in broad circulation at the time. Representations such as those on popular sheet music covers may well have contributed to this wide coverage, and to the ultimate success of the push for federation itself.

One final federation song whose title has a vexillological flavour is Augustus Juncker's 'The Flag of the Commonwealth'.[22] Neither Arthur Lennox Palmer's poem nor the setting has yet been given a date, but a rather late one is suggested, certainly well after Federation itself, unless the author was taking extraordinary poetic liberties. It is quite unclear which flag Palmer means, and it is possible, owing to the many mentions of war, that the song dates from around or after the First World War.[23] Furthermore, although Australia was proclaimed a Commonwealth, the term seems little used in common parlance in the early years of the century, and appears in the title of only one other federation song, E.A. Musico's 'God Bless our Commonwealth' (Sydney: Nicholson's, 1901).

Three elements especially point to a later dating of the song. If written soon after the announcement of the new national flag in September 1901, then the mention of Australia's navies carrying a 'star crossed flag' is plausible – it may even refer to the Australian Federation Flag with its stars placed on a cross – until it is realised that there was no navy until 1911 and, in fact, until 1966 all RAN ships were required to fly the British White Ensign![24] Verse 3 notes that a 'seven-rayed star gleams brightly afar / As the emblem of unity'. It is difficult to imagine that this refers to anything but the Federal or Commonwealth Star, which did not appear on any flags before 1901, but until 1908 it had only six points (one for each state), with the seventh then being added to symbolise all of Australia's territories and dependencies. Finally, everyone attending Federation celebrations in 1901 was acutely aware that there was not yet a national flag. It would only be after a number of years (or perhaps by an unknowing foreigner) that a mistake such as the following could be made:

> 'Tis the glorious flag of the Commonwealth
> Unfurled at the century's birth!

---

22 Augustus W. Juncker, 'The Flag of the Commonwealth' (Sydney: W.H. Paling & Co., n.d.), copy held in State Library of Victoria. Juncker (1855–1942) came to Australia in 1883. His most popular song published in Australia is probably 'I was Dreaming' (Sydney: H.J. Samuell, 1894).

23 Another Juncker setting, this one certainly dating from the war years, is 'Britannia's Jewels: An Australian Patriotic Song' (Sydney: W.H. Paling & Co., 1914). Note the continued reliance on empire and patriotism as a source of inspiration for popular song during the war. As Australian soldiers were essentially fighting in Europe as part of the British war effort – the troops were known as the Australian Imperial Force – patriotism far outweighed any thoughts of nationalism, although the resultant reputation of Australians, through the achievements of its soldiers, was to play a significant part in Australia's search for its own identity and sense of national unity.

24 Foley, *The Australian Flag*, pp. 132–34.

The music about Australia's Federation is characterised by four-square, march-like solidity that mirrors the sentiment of the words, which speak of a united country under a proud flag, whichever particular incarnation it might be. They were popular songs, melodically straightforward, harmonically supportive and easily learnt and sung along to, at the very least in the chorus. The nationalistic views expressed in earlier examples did not, in the words of Binns, 'last in such a concentrated form, but [were] weakened by the continued presence of physical ties with Britain'.[25] This apparent weakening of will, or rather, simply the failure to continue a fervent nationalism – revelling in the moment but acknowledging that once the spectacle of the actual event has passed we can return to our own quiet existence – has echoes in the failure to convert to reality the promises of an Australian Republic, and (to invoke my theme a final time) in the often stalled moves to create a new national flag. As the Sydney poet Jamie Grant noted recently, 'The role of poetry in the success of the movement for Federation was as crucial as that of the mass media in some more recent political campaigns. Perhaps that is why the recent republic campaign was unsuccessful: nobody wrote poems to support it.'[26]

And even fewer people wrote songs. Poetry and popular song were the twin weapons in the late nineteenth century's arsenal. Popular song provided the means of getting the message heard in every living room in the land. While the message might have been mixed, with nationalism and patriotism vying for supremacy, the fact was that everyone knew about Federation, and could probably even sing a song about it. Poetry and music were used in tandem to distribute propaganda, rally supporters and eventually overcome political indecision. In the words of J. Ecclestone Walker, as set by Samuel McBurney:[27]

> Rise Australians, mark your day,
> Seize the standard, bear the sway,
> Drive the clouds of sloth away,
> And advance! Still advance! … Advance Australia!

---

25 Binns, 'Patriotic and Nationalistic Song', p. 133.
26 Jamie Grant, 'Girt by Verse', *Age* [Melbourne], 5 Jan. 2001, p. 9.
27 Samuel McBurney, 'Advance Australia' (Geelong, Vic.: Troedel & Co., [1899?]), copy in private collection of Jennifer Hill, Melbourne.

CHAPTER NINE

Singing the Songs of Scotland
The German Musician Johann Rupprecht Dürrner and Musical Life in Nineteenth-Century Edinburgh

Barbara Eichner

'Indeed, during almost the whole of the [nineteenth] century, both Edinburgh and Glasgow were the Mecca for German musicians who, as was only natural, were open advocates of Germany and its music. Even some of the Scottish music critics had a pronounced Teutonic outlook.'[1] With these words, Henry George Farmer, in his *History of Music in Scotland*, states his deep disapproval of the time of the 'Relapse', when, 'apart from the lack of specialized teaching in this country, both Scotland and England were positive slaves in what Fuller-Maitland called the "foreign domination"'.[2] For a variety of reasons, however, little is known about the ways and the actual extent to which these foreigners were alleged to dominate musical life.

While German historiography seldom feels responsible for German emigrants who entered another cultural circle – Carl Halle alias Charles Hallé is one exception – British music history has been constructed in marked antagonism to a foreign and especially a German hegemony, which was to some extent held responsible for the 'Dark Age' of English music between the death of Purcell and the advent of the 'English Musical Renaissance'. Once the cultural equality of the former *Land ohne Musik* seemed established, the leading figures of this movement tried to dissociate themselves from both the German musicians who had lived in or visited Britain and the German 'masterworks' that had dominated the orchestral and partially the operatic repertoire.[3] Increasing political tension between the two countries as a result of Kaiser Wilhelm II's naval policy, the Boer War and the imperial aspirations of the German Reich

---

1   Henry George Farmer, *A History of Music in Scotland* (London: Hinrichsen, 1947), pp. 484–85.

2   Ibid., p. 484.

3   See Meirion Hughes and Robert Stradling, *The English Musical Renaissance 1840–1940: Constructing a National Music*, 2nd edn (Manchester and New York: Manchester University Press, 2001). An entire section, 'Being beastly to the Hun', pp. 115–63, is devoted to the discussion of the difficult relationship between English national music and German *Kultur*.

added further strain to cultural relations. However, discourse about the aesthetic hegemony of German *Kultur*, threatening the emergence of a national English music, often remained rather abstract. Significantly, it overlapped with more pragmatic, economic concerns:

> But whereas in Germany the enriched middle class supports German music, in England the enriched middle class supports everything except English music. And a large section of it, being infected with German ideals, supports no music that is not approved by German *Kultur*. ... All English musicians ask is fair play and fair pay, for though it is, perhaps, impossible to define nationalism satisfactorily in aesthetic terms, it is not only possible, but easy, to express it in terms of economics.[4]

A history of Scottish music has to deal with one more problem: Most surveys are devoted to the traditional or folk music, leaving little room for the discussion of 'art music'. Consequently, the recent edition of the *New Grove Dictionary* dedicates only three pages to classical music, compared to fifteen dealing with traditional music.[5] As early as 1894 David Baptie observed that 'as a nation, [the Scots] prefer melody to harmony', but this should not prevent 'acquiring a more catholic taste in music'.[6] But surveys, however detailed they may be, have to acknowledge the obvious lack of 'great composers' between 1780 and 1880.[7] As traditional music historiography tends to concentrate on the history of great works and their creators, the impression arises that there has not been a musical life meriting description in Edinburgh or Glasgow during much of the nineteenth century. For example, the article 'Schottland' in the second edition of *Die Musik in Geschichte und Gegenwart* mentions only John Thomson as a composer of some distinction – obviously for the reason that Felix Mendelssohn Bartholdy recommended him to his family.[8] Only Farmer's *History of Music*

---

4   Francis Toye, 'German Culture and English Music', *English Review*, 12 (1914), pp. 106–11, at p. 111.

5   Kenneth Elliott, 'Scotland. I. Art Music'; Peggy Duesenberry and Francis Collinson, 'Scotland II. Traditional Music', *The New Grove Dictionary of Music and Musicians*, 2nd edn, ed. Stanley Sadie and John Tyrrell (London: Macmillan, 2001) (hereafter *New Grove II*), vol. 22, pp. 906–8, 908–22. Similarly, Betsy Marlene Ross's 'Writings about Scotland's Music: an Annotated Bibliography' (Ph.D. diss., Claremont Graduate School, 1993) counts 993 entries on folk music and 430 on art music in the broadest sense.

6   David Baptie, *Musical Scotland Past and Present* (Paisley: J. & R. Parlane, 1894, repr. Hildesheim and New York: Georg Olms, 1972), pp. iii–iv.

7   Cedric Thorpe Davie, *Scotland's Music* (Edinburgh: Blackwood, 1980), pp. 43–44. See also John Purser, *Scotland's Music: A History of the Traditional and Classical Music from the Earliest Times to the Present Day* (Edinburgh and London: Mainstream Publishing Co., 1992). This detailed and beautifully illustrated history provides very valuable information, but in the 'classical' chapters concentrates largely on the history of composition.

8   'Schottland', ed. John Purser, in *Die Musik in Geschichte und Gegenwart*, 2nd edn, ed. Ludwig Finscher (hereafter *MGG²*), *Sachteil*, vol. 8 (Kassel: Bärenreiter, 1998), cols. 1123–37.

Fig. 9.1   Johann Rupprecht Dürrner, lithograph after a portrait by
A. Ossani (1858)

in Scotland, with its explicit sociological approach, and David Baptie's not
entirely reliable encyclopedia provide a starting point for research if one
wishes to discover the impressions a German musician – himself of limited
creative powers and little reputation among his German contemporaries –
left on the musical life of mid-nineteenth-century Edinburgh.

A case in question is Johann Rupprecht Dürrner (for a portrait see Fig.
9.1). He was born on 15 July 1810 in Ansbach, a small town of around
10 000 inhabitants in northern Bavaria.[9] He received his first musical
instruction from his father, an oboist in the local military band, and soon

---

9   For a list of works and bibliography see Barbara Eichner, 'Dürrner, Johannes (Rupprecht)', *MGG*[2], *Personenteil*, vol. 5 (2001), cols. 1700–1702.

showed remarkable talent as a pianist, violinist and clarinettist. But his parents destined him for the safer and less ambitious career of elementary school teacher, and in 1827 Dürrner entered the teachers' training college at Altdorf near Nuremberg.[10] In contrast to the English educational system, music played a significant role in Bavarian elementary schools. The teachers were expected to act as organists at the local churches and to direct – especially in rural communities – choral societies and amateur orchestras;[11] therefore, singing and singing pedagogy, violin, organ and piano playing and thorough bass, along with choral and orchestral rehearsals, formed a great part of the college's curriculum.[12] Dürrner's talent caught the attention of the headmaster and some members of the Nuremberg upper class, among them Gottlieb Freiherr von Tucher,[13] who encouraged and supported Dürrner's professional musical training. Friedrich Schneider, then a celebrated composer of oratorios,[14] had set up a conservatoire at Dessau, where in 1829 Dürrner became one of the first students at the newly founded institution, one with a marked emphasis on compositional skills.[15] His impressions of Dessau's manifold cultural activities remained unforgettable, and when after two years of study he took up the position of *Kantor* at his native town of Ansbach, he tried to organise a similarly varied musical life. Of course, as part of the German

---

10 August Enderlein, 'Johann Rupprecht Dürrner', Sunday insert of the *Ansbacher Morgenblatt*, no. 28 (10 July 1859), pp. 110–11, at p. 110. Reprinted in the *Niederrheinische Musikzeitung*, 7 (10 Dec. 1859), 396–98, and in the *Musical World*, 37 (17 Dec. 1859), pp. 807–8. Enderlein's biography is especially valuable, as he was not only a good friend during Dürrner's time in Ansbach, but kept in close contact with him after his emigration to Edinburgh (no letters are extant today) and even visited him in 1856 (see below).

11 See Eckhard Nolte, 'Außerschulische musikalische Tätigkeiten des Volksschullehrers im 19. Jahrhundert, ihre Voraussetzungen und deren Abbau', in *Volksschullehrer und außerschulische Musikkultur: Tagungsbericht Feuchtwangen 1997*, ed. Friedhelm Brusniak and Dietmar Klenke (Augsburg: Wißner, 1998), pp. 31–54.

12 Georg Friedrich Merz and Christoph Wilhelm Götz, *Mittheilungen über den äußern und innern Zustand des Königl. Bayer. protestantischen Schullehrer-Seminariums zu Altdorf verbunden mit pädagogischen Miscellen, I. Heft* (Altdorf: Riegel & Wießner, 1828). See pp. 62–68 for a detailed timetable.

13 Johannes Zahn, 'Tucher, Christoph Karl Gottlieb Siegmund', *Allgemeine deutsche Biographie* (Leipzig: Duncker & Humblot, 1894), vol. 38, pp. 767–70. This is still the most detailed account of Tucher's life and his activities as an editor of sixteenth- and seventeenth-century music.

14 A comprehensive study on Schneider is Helmut Lomnitzer, *Das musikalische Werk Friedrich Schneiders (1786–1853) insbesondere die Oratorien* (Diss., Univ. Marburg, 1961).

15 No survey of this conservatoire's development has yet been undertaken. Friedrich Schneider's advertising articles provide an introduction: 'Errichtung eines theoretisch-praktischen Institutes für Musik, vom Herzogl. Dessauischen Kapellm. Hrn. Fr. Schneider', *Allgemeine musikalische Zeitung*, 31 (1829), cols. 100–101, and 'Nachricht und Ankündigung wegen meines theoretisch-practischen Musik-Instituts', *AMZ* 33 (1831), cols. 112–15.

Protestant tradition dating back to the sixteenth century, Dürrner had time-consuming duties at the two main churches and in teaching music at the local *Gymnasium*.[16] Beyond that, he introduced modern musical institutions by founding the male choir *Liederkranz*,[17] by conducting touring opera companies and by setting up an annual series of subscription concerts from December 1833.[18] The latter enterprise faced considerable obstacles, as hardly any professional musicians lived in Ansbach, so that Dürrner had to recruit the orchestra from music teachers, the military band and willing amateurs. Despite these unpromising conditions he managed to perform such large-scale works as Louis Spohr's opera *Jessonda*,[19] Haydn's *Seasons* and Beethoven's Fifth Symphony.[20] From time to time the concerts featured famous artists like the violinist Bernhard Molique, a member of the court orchestra in Stuttgart, the clarinettist Carl Baermann jun. from Munich[21] and, in 1839, Clara Wieck.[22]

Young and ambitious, Dürrner was not content with the limited prospects his native town could provide. During his summer vacations, he tried to broaden his mind and travelled to cultural centres like Munich, Stuttgart, Berlin and Leipzig. There he could refine his technical skills and creative taste, renew old and make new acquaintances with colleagues and organise performances of his works. He also had the opportunity to further their publication, mostly of his Lieder and part-songs; the symphonies and other orchestral works remained in manuscript and are (with the exception of one overture) lost today. It might have been in Leipzig, centre of the German book market, that Dürrner picked up a copy of Robert Burns's poems and songs in the translation of Heinrich Julius Heintze.[23] Inspired by the sonority and imagery of the poems, he composed thirteen songs, which were published in 1843 and 1844 as Opp. 4, 5 and 10/3 (see Table 9.1). As an unnamed critic from the influential journal *Neue Zeitschrift für Musik*

---

16 Luise Meyer, *Es begann 1831 … Ein Beitrag zur Geschichte der protestantischen Kantoren und der kirchlich-bürgerlichen Musikpflege in Ansbach* (Ansbach: Selbstverlag, 1982); see esp. the chapter devoted to Dürrner, pp. 33–48.

17 Joseph Bürzle, *100 Gesangverein Jahre Liederkranz Ansbach* (Ansbach: Brügel, 1933), pp. 5–8, 39–48.

18 *Intelligenzblatt für den Rezatkreis*, 18 Dec. 1833, cols. 2078–79.

19 *Intelligenzblatt für den Rezatkreis*, 14 Mar. 1840, col. 446.

20 *Drei Festreden, gehalten bei der Säcular-Feier des Königl. Gymnasiums zu Ansbach am 12. Junius 1837* (Ansbach: Brügel, 1837), p. 50.

21 *Intelligenzblatt für den Rezatkreis*, 12 Nov. 1836, cols. 2569–70, 7 Jan. 1843, cols. 27–28.

22 Letter to Robert Schumann, 10 Oct. 1840. Robert-Schumann-Forschungsstelle Düsseldorf, Corr. vol. 10, no. 1679.

23 Heinrich Julius Heintze, *Lieder und Balladen des Schotten Robert Burns* (Braunschweig: Westermann, 1840). For a survey of the various translations see Rosemary Anne Selle, *The Parritch and the Partridge: The Reception of Robert Burns in Germany. A History* (Diss., Univ. Heidelberg, 1981).

Table 9.1   Dürrner's songs on poems by Robert Burns

Opus no.	Place and year of publication	German title	German incipit	English incipit	Tonality
4/1	Leipzig: Breitkopf & Härtel, 1843	Der Eine	Mein Herz ist krank	My heart is sair – I darena tell	E minor
4/2	ibid.	Du hast mich verlassen	Du hast mich verlassen, Jakob	Thou hast ever left me, Jamie	A minor
4/3	ibid.	O wärst du auf dem Feld	O wärst du auf dem Feld	O wert thou in the cauld blast	G minor
4/4	ibid.	Der Abschied	Für unsern rechten König nur	It was a' for our rightfu' king	A minor
4/5	ibid.	Montgomery Gretchen	Wär auch mein Lager jenes Moor	Altho' my bed were in yon muir	E minor
4/6	ibid.	Was nützt einem Mädchen	Was nützt einem Mädchen	What can a young lassie	G major
5/1	Leipzig: Klemm, 1844	Der Sommer ist so schön	Der Sommer ist so schön	Simmer's a pleasant time	B flat major
5/2	ibid.	Dein bin ich, mein treues Lieb	Dein bin ich, mein treues Lieb	Thine am I, my Chloris fair	G major
5/3	ibid.	Die schöne Maid von Inverness	Die schöne Maid von Inverness	The lovely lass of Inverness	G minor
5/4	ibid.	Mary	Himmlische Mäche	Powers celestial	A flat major
5/5	ibid.	John Anderson	John Anderson, mein Lieb	John Anderson my jo, John	G minor
5/6	ibid.	O schwer ist mein Herz	O schwer ist mein Herz	Wae is my heart, and the tear's in my e'e	A minor
10/3	Leipzig: Peters, 1844	Wie mag ich frisch und munter sein	Wie mag ich frisch und munter sein	O how can I be blythe and glad	B minor

pointed out, it had not been a difficult task to find the appropriate tone for
Burns's poetry, as many composers had turned to Scottish sources before
Dürrner. Nevertheless, he credited Dürrner for giving these songs the perfect
aspect of original Scottish folk tunes, despite their new melodies.[24] In
contrast to the often somewhat trivial style of his Lied oeuvre, nine of the
thirteen Burns songs show a very dense, even ascetic idiom. They employ a
pentatonicising minor mode to create an archaic effect, evoking the noble
simplicity and unadulterated naturalness the German Romantics had sought
in Scottish and other folk traditions since Johann Gottfried Herder's *Volks-
lieder* edition of 1779.[25]

In 1843 Dürrner was granted a sabbatical year, which he spent in
Leipzig, studying with Felix Mendelssohn Bartholdy and Moritz
Hauptmann – probably the happiest time in his life. Here he met David
Hamilton,[26] an organist, organ-builder and music publisher from Edin-
burgh, whose brother Adam had, like Dürrner, been a pupil at Friedrich
Schneider's conservatoire.[27] According to Robert A. Marr, *Kantor*
Dürrner came to Edinburgh expressly to teach at St John's Episcopal
Church's School of Music, founded by David Hamilton in 1838.[28] If we
can trust his own writing, Dürrner, frustrated by the increasing difficulties
in maintaining a flourishing concert life in Ansbach and suffering from an
unhappy love affair, expected to find a wider and more challenging sphere
of activity in the Scottish capital.[29] His aspirations were not unrealistic.
Despite the decline of the Edinburgh Musical Society in 1798, which
during the eighteenth century had provided a platform for local talent and

24 *Neue Zeitschrift für Musik*, 20, nc. 37 (6 May 1844), p. 145.

25 See Roger Fiske, *Scotland in Music: a European Enthusiasm* (Cambridge: Cambridge
University Press, 1983), esp. 'A Myth Captivates Western Europe', pp. 31–54.

26 Enderlein, 'Johann Rupprecht Dürrner', p. 111.

27 David Hamilton (1803–63), a native of Edinburgh, was organist at St John's
Episcopal Church 1833–53 and inventor of the 'pneumatic lever', and founder of the
School of Music attached to the Chapel. Adam Hamilton (1820–1907), a composer and
organist, was conductor of the Edinburgh Harmonic Society since 1847 and of the
Edinburgh Choral Union 1866–83. He gave organ recitals on the organ of St John's
improved by his brother. With his wife, a sister of his fellow student Louis Drechsler, he
had three children, who showed remarkable talent (*Musical World*, 40 (23 Aug. 1862),
p. 536). Most biographical information is provided by the respective entries in Baptie's
Musical Scotland Past and Present, pp. 73–74, and Farmer's *History of Music in
Scotland*, pp. 401, 479–80.

28 Robert A. Marr, *Music for the People: a Retrospect of the Glasgow International
Exhibition 1888, with an Account of the Rise of Choral Societies in Scotland* (Edinburgh
and Glasgow: Menzies & Co., 1889), p. lxviii.

29 Letter to Friedrich Schneider, 10 Aug. 1844, printed with three earlier letters in Julius
Meyer, 'Zur Geschichte der Musik in Ansbach', *Unterhaltungsblatt der Fränkischen
Zeitung*, 44/45 (1913), pp. 175–76, 178–79, at p. 179.

attracted virtuosos from abroad,[30] Edinburgh was by no means devoid of music. Although the dominating Presbyterian church prohibited more elaborate church music, all denominations were interested in improving the standard of choral singing, especially after the German Joseph Mainzer[31] had opened a singing school in York Place, and the Association for the Revival of Sacred Music in Scotland was established in 1844.[32] Higher education in music was much harder to obtain: once a pupil had exhausted the various offers of private tuition, he or she had to move to London or to the Continent – the University of Edinburgh (the Reid Professorship in Music was established in 1839) offered degrees in music only after 1863.[33] The annual memorial concerts, however, had played an important part in Edinburgh's concert life since 1841.[34] They complemented the Edinburgh Festival Concerts, held in 1815, 1819, 1824 and 1843, which were an important spur to the establishment of regular concerts on a professional basis.[35] The most influential was the Professional Society of Musicians, founded in 1819 'for the purpose of improving the state of vocal and instrumental music in the city'. To secure its financial support, the Edinburgh Musical Association joined the Professional Society in 1835,[36] and this combination of professional and amateur music-making shaped the musical life in Edinburgh until the advent of great choral societies, beginning with the establishment of the Edinburgh Choral Union in 1858/59.[37] In addition, many virtuosos like Franz Liszt in 1840 or Frédéric Chopin in 1848 paid visits to Edinburgh, and publishers and private entrepreneurs catered for the popular taste.[38] Not only a large population of music teachers provided the basis for these activities, but also the professional orchestras of the Theatre Royal, the Caledonian and the Adelphi, which brought the highlights of international opera to the Scottish capital.[39]

---

30 Isobel Preece and Stuart Campbell, 'Edinburgh', *MGG*[2], *Sachteil*, vol. 2 (1995), cols. 1649–56, at col. 1653.
31 Joseph Mainzer (1801–51), a native of Trier in Germany, ex-priest, teacher and organiser of free singing classes for the working classes first in Paris and from 1841 onwards in London and Edinburgh. See Bernarr Rainbow, 'Joseph Mainzer', *New Grove II*, vol. 15, p. 642.
32 Farmer, *A History of Music in Scotland*, pp. 382–83.
33 Ibid., p. 395.
34 Ibid., p. 471.
35 Preece and Campbell, 'Edinburgh', col. 1654.
36 Farmer, *A History of Music in Scotland*, p. 470. This double structure explains why Dürrner is sometimes mentioned as conductor of the Professional Society, sometimes of the Musical Association.
37 Preece and Campbell, 'Edinburgh', col. 1654.
38 Farmer, *A History of Music in Scotland*, p. 472.
39 Ibid., pp. 415–16.

Thus Dürrner found a large field of activity on his arrival in autumn 1844. It was very different from his permanent position in Ansbach, for in Edinburgh he had to find his place in a free and rapidly developing market. Private tuition offered a solid basis for prosperity. As Alexander Campbell Mackenzie remembered, 'our characteristic predilection for foreign teachers steadily increased'.[40] Judging from his regular advertisements in various newspapers, Dürrner taught singing, violin, music theory and even psalmody. This was undoubtedly not the glorious career he might have expected. But he soon found colleagues and friends who invited him to participate in their musical activities. Among them were Adam Hamilton, Louis Drechsler, another student of Friedrich Schneider,[41] the singer and singing teacher Edmund Edmunds and his wife,[42] Finlay Dun[43] and especially Alexander Mackenzie senior, violinist and leader of the Theatre Royal orchestra.[44] Together, these musicians set up a series of chamber music concerts in the season 1844/45, and Dürrner received a cordial welcome from press and audience. He also joined a private chamber music circle that gathered weekly at the home of Lady Murray, an old friend and pupil of Chopin,[45] and he is reported to have

---

40 Alexander Campbell Mackenzie, *A Musician's Narrative* (London: Cassell & Co., 1927), p. 14. For his role in the 'English Musical Renaissance', see Hughes and Stradling, *The English Musical Renaissance*, esp. pp. 33–34, 38–39, 61–62.

41 Louis Drechsler (1823–60), son of the cellist Carl Drechsler (member of the Dessau court orchestra) and himself an able performer, was founder of the Edinburgh Singverein (1846), a male choir dedicated to German part-song, and of the Society of Musical Amateurs (1848). See William Saunders, 'A Byway of Musical History', *Scottish Musical Magazine*, 2 (1921), pp. 102–3, 125–26, 149–51, 173–75, 197–98, 218–20, 239–41, 258–60. Dürrner's relations to these two ensembles are still unclear.

42 Edmund Edmunds (born 1809, date of death unknown), from Worcester, was a singer and teacher of singing at St John's Singing School, and since 1830 resident in Edinburgh. Mary Giovanna Cawse (1809–50), his first wife, was a renowned soprano. See Baptie, *Musical Scotland Past and Present*, p. 51.

43 Finlay Dun (1795–1853), a native of Aberdeen, was a viola player, composer and teacher and editor of various collections of Scottish music. His two symphonies, today apparently lost, are the only Scottish contributions to the modern large-scale forms, apart from the works of John Thomson. See W. Hume, 'Dun, Finlay', *Grove's Dictionary of Music and Musicians*, 5th edn, ed. Eric Blom (London: Macmillan, and New York: St. Martin's Press, 1954), vol. 2, p. 802; John Purser, *Scotland's Music*, p. 211.

44 Alexander Mackenzie (1819–57). The *New Grove II* dedicates only a couple of lines to him in the article on his famous son (Duncan J. Barker, 'Mackenzie, Sir Alexander Campbell', vol. 15, pp. 500–503, at p. 500). Baptie remarks of him: 'As a soloist his pure tone and fine manipulation were all that could be desired ... Alike as editor and executant Mr. Mackenzie did much to foster musical taste in Scotland' (*Musical Scotland Past and Present*, p. 111).

45 Fiske, *Scotland in Music*, pp. 151–52.

been the stimulating centre of this circle.[46] At the end of 1845, Dürrner and Drechsler became members of the Edinburgh Musical Association, as the Minute Book shows.[47] When James Dewar, the conductor of the Musical Association, suffered from continued indisposition,[48] in December it was proposed to invite Dürrner as interim conductor. After initial reservations against calling in an 'outsider',[49] he conducted his first rehearsal on 3 January 1846 and the first concert one week later. The music critic of the newspaper *The Scotsman* was impressed with the new conductor and concluded:

> From what we witnessed last Saturday, he seems to us an excellent conductor; cool, steady, determined and knowing his score thoroughly. No conductor can manage any band rightly, unless he know every note of his score, and keep the whole performance in order. Strict discipline in a well-organised orchestra, is as necessary as strict discipline in a military band. This is not yet *understood* by British musicians, but will be understood very soon under such men as Mr Durrner ...[50]

In Alexander Mackenzie Dürrner had a most experienced and reliable leader. According to the Minute Book, he invested more time for rehearsals than his predecessor Dewar, rehearsed very carefully, and regularly brought new scores back to Edinburgh from his summer trips to Germany. During Dürrner's time as conductor – which was admittedly rather short, lasting from 1845 to 1849 and again from 1852 to 1853 – the Musical Association premiered many works hitherto unheard in Scotland, among them Mendelssohn's symphonies, Niels Gade's tone poem *Efterklange af Ossian*, Op. 1, Beethoven's *Egmont* overture, Op. 84, and Berlioz's overture *Le Roi Lear*.[51] This ambitious repertoire cannot exclusively be attributed to Dürrner's influence; he acted in accordance with the general policy of the Musical Association, which a programme note from 1843 defines as follows: 'The Performances will consist chiefly from the Works of the most Classical Masters, occasionally interspersed with the lighter Compositions of the Modern School; and it will be the Object

---

46 Richard Müller, 'Johannes Rupprecht Dürrner', *Johannes Dürrners sämmtliche Männerchöre* (Leipzig: F.E.C. Leuckart, 1890), p. iii–viii, at p. v.

47 Today preserved in the Edinburgh City Library. The Minute Book documents committee meetings, rehearsals (sometimes mentioning the rehearsed works) and concerts beginning on 28 September 1844, finishing with the first concert of the 1847/48 season on 8 January 1848. At the end of the book membership lists from 1844 to 1852 are added.

48 James Dewar (1793–1846), a native of Edinburgh, was deputy leader at the Theatre Royal, a founding member and conductor of the Professional Society, and a composer and arranger of Scottish melodies. See Baptie, *Musical Scotland Past and Present*, pp. 42–43.

49 Minute Book, 13 Dec. 1845, 3 Jan. 1846, 10 Jan. 1846.

50 *The Scotsman*, 14 Jan. 1846.

51 *Edinburgh Evening Courant*, 25 Jan. 1847, 10 Jan. 1848, 20 Jan. 1852, 8 Feb. 1853.

Table 9.2   Concert programmes of the Edinburgh Musical Association
in the 1847/48 series

8 January 1848

Niels Gade	*Efterklange af Ossian*, Op. 1
Elias Parish Alvars	Grand Solo for Harp, played by Henry Dibdin
Ludwig van Beethoven	Symphony no. 4
Boisio	Waltz *Jenny Lind* (first performance in Scotland)
Karl Gottlieb Reissiger	Overture *Die Felsenmühle zu Estalieres*

22 January 1848

Ludwig van Beethoven	Ouverture *Egmont*, Op. 84
Henry Vieuxtemps	Fantasie-Caprice
Felix Mendelssohn Bartholdy	Symphony no. 3 *Scottish*
Boisio	Waltz *Isabella*
Carl Maria von Weber	*Jubilee* overture

5 February 1848

Felix Mendelssohn Bartholdy	Overture *Die Hebridean*
Louis Spohr	String quartet
Ludwig van Beethoven	Symphony no. 6 *Pastoral*
Charles Coote	Quadrille
Adrien Boieldieu	Overture *Jean de Paris*

19 February 1848

Ludwig van Beethoven	Overture *Leonore*
Friedrich August Krummer	Solo for bassoon
Wolfgang Amadeus Mozart	Symphony no. 41 *Jupiter*
Matthew Locke (?)	Incidental music to *Macbeth*
Joseph Labitzky	Galop *Karlsbad Sprudel*

4 March 1848

Niels Gade	*Efterklange af Ossian*, Op. 1, 'by desire'
Alexandre Goria	Grand Fantasia for piano solo
Louis Spohr	Symphony *Die Weihe der Töne*, Op. 86
I.I.	Waltz *Rivulet*
Carl Maria von Weber	Overture *Der Freischütz*, 'by desire'

16 March 1848

Felix Mendelssohn Bartholdy	*Meeresstille und glückliche Fahrt*
Henry Dibdin	Potpourri for harp
Ludwig van Beethoven	Symphony no. 5
Joseph Labitzky	Waltz *Victoria*
Daniel François Auber	Overture *La Muette de Portici*

of the Directors to diversify the Programmes as much as possible.'[52] The
programmes of the season 1847/48 give a good idea of the high standard

---

52 Programme note from 25 Nov. 1843, included in the Minute Book of the Musical
Association.

and the great variety of the repertoire (see Table 9.2). This concept of mixing popular music with more demanding works proved very successful. Most concerts were attended by a 'large and fashionable audience', and many music critics pointed out the educational value of the concerts:

> The support given to a society like this, which, much to its credit, disdains the glitters of quadrilles and polkas, big drums and cymbals, and confines itself exclusively to the noblest creations of a great and beautiful art, may at all times be taken as test of the state of musical taste in a community. ... The performance of such models as the works of the great masters afford, is the way to bring out so desirable a result, and as the ear becomes familiarised with those masterpieces, it will soon learn to feel their beauty, and loose [sic] the relish for the meaningless trifles with which it used to be satisfied. Believing that the Association may do efficient service in this matter, we are glad to see the present season commence under such favourable auspices. The orchestra has been augmented to upwards of forty performers, among whom we observed a sprinkling of amateurs. This is as it ought to be; for there is no good reason why amateurs and professionals should not [join] their efforts in promotion of the good cause.[53]

It is frequently observed that the Musical Association well served the promotion of the 'good cause', bringing the established and contemporary repertoire to Edinburgh, thus connecting the Scottish capital to the major European centres. Far from feeling overruled by the predominance of non-British compositions and a German conductor (and probably many foreign performers as well), the critic G.F.G., possibly identical with George Farquhar Graham,[54] the eminent music historian and collector of traditional Scottish music, commented in 1846:

> The concerts of this Association are calculated ... to render classical music more familiar to the public of our metropolis, and thus to advance the knowledge of really good music, and the love for it, throughout Scotland. Having an ancient musical tradition of our own, peculiar in our national melodies, we must not lag behind our neighbours who are exerting themselves to extend the knowledge of classical instrumental music.[55]

From this contemporary vantage point, the rich and vital Scottish tradition functions as a stimulus to broaden the musical horizons. Graham

---

53 *North British Advertiser or the Ladies' Own Miscellany*, 29 Jan. 1853.
54 George Farquhar Graham (1789–1867), a native of Edinburgh, was a musical scholar, composer and editor. In 1815 he was joint secretary of the first Edinburgh Musical Festival and published an account of it. He contributed the article 'Music' to the 7th edn of the *Encyclopedia Britannica*, edited the Skene Manuscript and *The Songs of Scotland* (see below). See William H. Husk, 'Graham, George (Farquhar)', *Grove's Dictionary*, 5th edn, vol. 3, p. 744.
55 *The Scotsman*, 14 Jan. 1846.

voices no concern about a possible exclusion or disheartening of native talent, but sees a modern, metropolitan concert life as a prerequisite for future development. The impression that foreign musicians and their skills and culture were not only tolerated in Edinburgh, but highly welcome, is strengthened by the memoirs of Alexander Campbell Mackenzie, who remembers his childhood in Edinburgh:

> Among our family's best friends were several admirable men: the burly, jolly Bavarian, Johann Dürrner, a partsong writer of deserved popularity in his own country, who became my guardian, but only survived my father by less than a couple of years. The lanky, grotesque-looking Hanoverian 'cellist, George Hausmann (uncle of the better-known Robert of the Joachim Quartet).[56] Unlucky in love, our good friend made a voluntary exit from this world. The amiable Küchler,[57] and others, who *via* opera companies, found their way to where better luck awaited them. The genial old Frenchman Théophile Bucher (once a flautist of renown before becoming a teacher of singing) ...[58] Tom M. Mudie – in the first brick of R.A.M. [Royal Academy of Music, London] students[59] – the Hargitts[60] etc., all worked companionably together.[61]

And when Dürrner's friend August Enderlein paid a visit to the Scottish capital, his journal explicitly emphasised the friendly atmosphere he experienced. Bucher and Mackenzie, above all, treated him with a cordiality he would have expected only from lifelong friends, and they even presented

---

56 Not even Baptie's *Musical Scotland Past and Present* provides any information about this performer. An obituary from the *Edinburgh Daily Courant*, reprinted in the *Musical World*, 38 (21 July 1860), p. 459, mourns the 'sudden decease of Mr. Hausmann', who had played the cello in 'Mr. Costa's unrivalled band' and conducted the Musical Association very successfully in the 1858–59 and 1859–60 seasons.

57 Heinrich Küchler (1815–73). Like Dürrner a native of Ansbach, the baritone came to England with an opera company and settled in London; later he worked in St Andrews as a music teacher, before moving to Edinburgh in 1858, where he conducted the Scottish Vocal Association and other choirs. See Baptie, *Musical Scotland Past and Present*, pp. 95, 240 (there with the wrong first name Hermann).

58 Theophilus Bucher (c.1802–71), a French flautist; in Edinburgh he was a teacher of singing and a publisher of vocal exercises and 'several highly artistic art songs'. See Baptie, *Musical Scotland Past and Present*, p. 24.

59 Thomas Molleson Mudie (1809–76), an English composer and teacher of Scottish parentage. He was student at the Royal Academy of Music since 1823, a pupil of Crotch and Cipriani Potter, in 1832–44 professor of pianoforte at the RAM, and from 1844 onwards a teacher in Edinburgh. See G.A.M., 'Mudie, Thomas (Molleson)', *Grove's Dictionary*, 5th edn, vol. 5, p. 986.

60 Charles Hargitt (c.1785–1889), an organist in Edinburgh for some years. Charles John Hargitt (1833 to after 1894), a native of Edinburgh, was organist at St Mary's Church, and in 1858–62 conductor of the Edinburgh Choral Union. See Baptie, *Musical Scotland Past and Present*, p. 75.

61 Mackenzie, *A Musician's Narrative*, p. 14.

him with precious gifts for his family at home.[62] This contrasts strongly with the statement Philipp Körber gave in Dürrner's obituary. He was another friend of his youth who obviously never visited him in Edinburgh: 'He died far from his friends among strangers, of whom he himself told me that they never approached him otherwise than as subordinates.'[63] Körber's chauvinism, which makes him perceive his friend as a lonely exile in an underdeveloped, even hostile country, is rather obvious. Dürrner's Edinburgh friends and colleagues were less possessive. After his surprising and untimely death on 10 June 1859, following an evening entertainment at his house, a 'large circle of friends' was reported to mourn his loss.[64]

This is not to say that Edinburgh was an easy place for native or foreign musicians. Apart from labouring under ill-health and homesickness, Dürrner felt constantly overworked. Two years before his death he wrote, alluding to the political situation in Germany: 'Despite being in a free country, I'm working as hard as any slave.'[65] As in Ansbach, he became very irritable when organisation and rehearsals for a concert did not turn out as expected. Prior to a charity concert he complained: 'I think they never had such a good orchestra in Edinburgh … But what a nuisance to rehearse with these conceited amateurs!'[66] The competitive conditions of the market for private tuition, publication and concert-giving further added to the strain. As a permanently employed *Kantor* in Ansbach he never had to face any professional rivalry, while his experiences in thriving Leipzig were transfigured in nostalgic retrospect. In a letter to a friend living in Leipzig he judged the business-dominated way of life in Edinburgh very sarcastically:

> The entire life in this country is just business. I'm up to my ears, not in debt, but in business, as the Scots are pleased to call life in art. Because I took over the conducting post at the subscription concerts, my workload

---

62 August Enderlein, *Reisetagebuch* (MS), Stadtarchiv Ansbach, H 4.

63 Philipp Körber, 'Joh. Rupprecht Dürrner, Musikdirektor', *Erinnerungsblätter für die Mitglieder des Nürnberger Sängertags* (Nuremberg, 1859), pp. 114–20, at p. 120: 'er starb ferne von seinen Freunden unter Fremden, von denen er mir selbst sagte, daß sie ihm nie anders denn als Untergebene nahe getreten'. Körber's account of Dürrner's life is on the whole not very reliable and in some passages quite obviously tinted by his conception of the Romantic artist.

64 *The Scotsman*, 11 June 1859.

65 Thomas Stettner, 'Dürrner, Johannes, Tondichter', *Lebensläufe aus Franken* (Erlangen: Palm & Enke, 1936), vol. 5, pp. 71–76, at p. 74: 'Obwohl in einem freien Land lebend arbeite ich härter als ein Sklave'.

66 Letter to an unknown friend, *c*.1849, Staatsbibliothek Berlin, Stiftung Preußischer Kulturbesitz. 'Ich glaube, sie haben nie ein so gutes Orchester in Edinburgh gehabt. … Aber welche Plage, die eingebildeten Amateure einzuüben!'

> has increased many times ... And additionally these tedious music lessons,
> which would alone suffice to kill a man in six years' time![67]

Dürrner's claim to a life purely in and for his art, although typical for his generation, was nowhere reconcilable to the demands of everyday life – neither in Germany nor in Scotland. Not even greater creative powers than his would have sufficed to ensure an existence independent of economic pressure.

Despite these complaints, some of Dürrner's most interesting works were created in Edinburgh. Drawing-room ballads such as 'The Kelpie's Bride' (1857) and a set of Sacred Songs (1855) were clearly aimed at the British market, while his song collections Opp. 16 (1848), 18 (1851) and 23 (1854) provide both German and English text. Similarly, adaptations and arrangements of traditional Scottish airs for voice and piano were popular both on the Continent and in Britain. Dürrner, however, decided to set six melodies as part-songs for male voices. By choosing this genre and dedicating the collection to the German *Liedertafeln*, he clearly intended to serve the German music market, where a growing number of male choirs waited eagerly for new, melodious and not too demanding pieces. Dürrner had already built up a good reputation as composer of such part-songs; therefore, when he started on the 6 *Schottische National-gesänge* in summer 1851,[68] he readily found a publisher. Breitkopf & Härtel issued the set in October 1852,[69] with both English and German words as well as background information about the melodies. For all of these, Dürrner relied on George Farquhar Graham's edition *The Songs of Scotland*,[70] and on his personal contacts with this expert of Scottish music, duly acknowledged in the notes preceding no. 4 of the collection, 'The blue bells of Scotland'. The composers of the piano arrangements of Graham's collection – T.M. Mudie, J.T. Surenne,[71]

---

67 Letter to Ferdinand Böhme (?), 17 Mar. 1846, Staatsbibliothek Berlin, Stiftung Preußischer Kulturbesitz. 'Das ganze Leben in diesem Lande ist hald [?] ein Geschäft. Ich stecke hier bis über beide Ohren, nicht in Schulden, aber im Geschäfte, wie die Schottländer das Leben in der Kunst zu nennen belieben. Dadurch, da mir zu meinen [be]stehenden Funktionen noch die Leitung der abonnirten [sic] Konzerte übertragen worden sind [sic], hat sich meine Arbeit um Vieles vermehrt. ... Zu allem kommt noch das lästige Stundengeben, was allein hinreicht, hier einen Menschen in sechs Jahren umzubringen.'

68 The collection is first mentioned in a letter to an unknown lady, 18 June 1851, today Staatsbibliothek Berlin, Stiftung Preußischer Kulturbesitz.

69 Johann Rupprecht Dürrner, 6 *Schottische Nationalgesänge* (Leipzig: Breitkopf & Härtel, 1852).

70 George Farquhar Graham, *The Songs of Scotland Adapted to their Appropriate Melodies Arranged with Pianoforte Accompaniment by G.F. Graham, T.M. Mudie, J.T. Surenne, H.E. Dibdin, Finlay Dun etc. Illustrated with Historical, Biographical and Critical Notices by George Farquhar Graham*, 3 vols (Edinburgh: Wood & Co., 1848–54).

71 John Thomas Surenne (1814–78), a native of London and there a pupil of Henri Herz, was later editor of collections such as *The Dance Music of Scotland* (1841) and *Songs of Scotland without Words* (1852–54). See Baptie, *Musical Scotland Past and Present*, p. 182.

H.E. Dibdin[72] and Finlay Dun – must have been well known to Dürrner, since they appeared in concerts their German colleague conducted or in which he participated. In the preface, Dürrner gives a clear account of his intentions.[73] He claims first-hand experience from his extended stay in Scotland, which had provided him with ample opportunity to become familiar with its national music. To test whether he had handled the melodies properly, he had some of them sung in Edinburgh, and despite some deficiencies in the execution of the unfamiliar genre, the result was encouraging.[74]

For the German public, he supplied the arrangements with extensive dynamic indications and exact metronome markings to ensure an authentic performance, crucial in rendering Scottish songs. To stress this point, he relates how Paganini and a famous German singer tried to flatter a Scottish audience with the performance of traditional tunes. Both failed, because the highly political 'Charlie is my darling' was rendered as coquettish love song and the solemn march 'Scots wha hae wi' Wallace bled' as lighthearted galop. If the collection finds a warm reception, Dürrner promises further volumes with Irish or English melodies. Yet, this project was never carried through, and no other arrangements are known. Lack of response cannot have been the reason for giving up these plans: soon after their publication, the part-songs became very popular in Germany, not only because of their dedication to the German choral societies, but also for their 'high artistic and historical value', as Otto Elben, a leading figure of the German male-choir movement, stated.[75] Dürrner's sensitive, evocative, yet not too demanding settings were equally attractive to smaller and more ambitious clubs. Universal topics like love and nature – in translation – appeal to any international public, as in 'Das Mädchen von Gowrie' ('The Lass o' Gowrie', no. 2), 'John Anderson' (no. 3), 'Die blauen Blumen Schottlands' ('The blue bells of Scotland', no. 4), and 'Schwarz ist die Nacht' ('The night is dark', no. 6). On the

---

72 Henry Edward Dibdin (1813–66), from an English family of professional musicians, was grandson of Charles Dibdin; he studied the harp under Challoner and Bochsa. After 1833 he lived in Edinburgh as organist of Trinity Chapel and music teacher and performer; he was the compiler of the *Standard Psalm Tune Book* (1857). See Alfred Loewenberg, 'Henry Edward Dibdin', *Grove's Dictionary*, 5th edn, vol. 1, p. 696.

73 Dürrner, *6 Schottische Nationalgesänge*, pp. 3–4.

74 For instance, the 'Scots ballad "John Anderson my jo", arranged by Durrner [*sic*] for four voices' was performed by the Musical Association on 7 February 1846. Whether this piece was an earlier version of no. 3 of the *6 Schottische Nationalgesänge* is not clear from the short review in the *Edinburgh Evening Courant*, 9 Feb. 1846.

75 Otto Elben, *Der volksthümliche deutsche Männergesang*, 2nd edn (Tübingen: Laupp, 1887; repr. Wolfenbüttel: Möseler, 1991, ed. Friedhelm Brusniak and Franz Krautwurst), p. 436. 'Die von ihm für Männerchor herausgegebenen schottischen Lieder haben gleichermaßen künstlerischen, wie geschichtlichen Werth'.

other hand, a song like 'Schotten, deren edles Blut' ('Scots wha hae wi' Wallace bled', no. 5), with its slogan 'death or victory', could easily be read and sung as incitement to nationalist feelings in Germany, but without provoking censorship, which after the revolution of 1848 became more severe.

Despite the ample notes accompanying each song, reception in Germany sometimes differed significantly from the Scottish under-standing of a song. 'Die Blumen vom Walde' ('The Flowers of the Forest', no. 1) bears special connotations for a Scottish audience, as this song is part of its cultural memory, recalling the disastrous defeat of the Scots in the battle on Flodden Field in 1513.[76] Almost word for word, Dürrner uses Graham's explanation in *The Songs of Scotland*, the 'Forest' in question meaning 'a favourite resort of the Scottish kings and nobles for hunting. The Forest boasted of the best archers, and perhaps the finest men in Scotland.'[77] Some German friends of Dürrner, however, to whom 'Floddenfield' did not have any special meaning, preferred to detect biographical references. The melancholy mood of both text and melody in D flat major were thought to refer to the sad and mysterious love story in Dürrner's past, or to his professional disappointment, that is that he could not return to his beloved native country for want of an adequate position (see Ex. 9.1). A touching anecdote relates that in 1855 a group of students from the University *Singverein* St Paul in Leipzig began singing 'Die Blumen vom Walde' at the Wartburg inn. A stranger, sitting quietly in a corner, suddenly started crying when the full chorus joined in the line 'Wie war ich selig'. Afterwards, he introduced himself as Dürrner, thanked them for the beautiful rendering of his composition and explained that he had just returned from his second home Scotland to see his beloved homeland once again before his death.[78] In fact, Dürrner visited Germany at least once more in 1857, but mysterious foreboding is a favourite part of biographical story telling. However, it is remarkable how this explicitly Scottish song receives a completely different meaning by linking it with the putative sad fate of a German exile on the one hand, and the Wartburg castle on the other hand, a place of unique importance to the nationalist movement because of its association with St Elisabeth, the legendary singing contest and Martin Luther. In Scotland, listeners were somewhat surprised that the national melodies had been turned into the unfamiliar form of part-songs, but on the whole the reviewer appeared

---

76 Purser, *Scotland in Music*, p. 90..
77 Graham, *The Songs of Scotland*, vol. 1, p. 159.
78 A.H. Gensel, 'Pauliner- und andere Jugenderinnerungen', *Pauliner-Zeitung* 1928, pp. 61–63, 74–76, 85–86, at p. 62.

Ex. 9.1   Johann Rupprecht Dürrner, 'Die Blumen vom Walde', from 6 *Schottische Nationalgesänge* (1852). Printed by permission of Breitkopf & Härtel

Ex. 9.1 (*cont.*)

continued overleaf

Ex. 9.1 (*cont.*)

very content with Dürrner's exact and reverent treatment of the national treasures:

> But Mr Dürrner has, in the work before us, thrown the Scotch songs into the form of part-songs for men's voices – an entirely new form as regards Scotch songs; and has arranged them in such an able and judicious manner as will, no doubt, render them more acceptable, and disseminate them more extensively throughout Germany, where part-singing is so much relished and cultivated. Mr Dürrner's residence for several years in Edinburgh has afforded him an opportunity to study the peculiar character and style of Scotch music; and, in his treatment of the Scotch melodies, he has shown that he has turned that opportunity to good account. He has judiciously preserved the characteristic features of the airs intact; has given great variety of effect to his arrangement, by skilful employment of the voice-parts – now making them sing two at a time, now three at a time, sometimes in half chorus, and sometimes in full chorus; and, what is perhaps rare in a *modern* German, he wisely abstained from using chromatic and farfetched harmonies and cramp forms of accompaniment; so that the *principal* melody stands out, as it should do, clear and well defined, while the simple and suitable vocal accompaniment blends harmoniously with it, adding an agreeable richness to the effect of the whole.[79]

One can hardly wish for a clearer example to demonstrate how much Dürrner had by then, six years after his arrival in Edinburgh, become an integral part of musical life in the Scottish capital. His Continental training and his experiences in European centres like Leipzig were very welcome in a community still struggling with inadequate means of musical education and performance and trying hard to attain a metropolitan level of music-making. At the same time, Dürrner – and like him probably many of his non-British colleagues – was able to absorb specific local and national traditions, treat them with respect and make them, as arrangements, accessible to a wider circle of interested musicians in both Britain and Germany. The preface of the 6 *Schottische Nationalgesänge* concludes with the sincere wish that the German choirs should embrace the Scottish melodies as warmly as the Scots had welcomed German songs.[80] Foreign musicians found a competitive yet stimulating atmosphere and a warm welcome in nineteenth-century Edinburgh, but they also found ways to repay the hospitality and the companionable spirit they experienced.

---

79 *Edinburgh Evening Courant*, 24 Mar. 1853.
80 Dürrner, 6 *Schottische Nationalgesänge*, p. 4.

PART FOUR
National and Local Institutions

CHAPTER TEN

Another String to his Bow
The Composer Conducts

Duncan James Barker

Like many British musicians of his day, Alexander Campbell Mackenzie (1847–1935) led not one but several musical careers simultaneously. In addition to his ongoing work as a composer, he was also conductor of the Philharmonic Society's orchestra and Principal of the Royal Academy of Music. It is hardly surprising, at least for anyone connected with the multifaceted world of musicians and music-making, that there was a great deal of synergy between these various roles. As conductor of the Philharmonic Society, Mackenzie held a prestigious musical position that was often in the public eye. Among other responsibilities, he could influence, in consultation with the Directors of the Society, which works by which composers would appear during the Philharmonic's London season, thus promoting certain styles and schools of composition over others. Similarly, as Principal of the Royal Academy of Music, he took on the role of conductor of the student orchestra, again exerting a direct influence on the nature of the music performed by the student musicians. This was not an inconsiderable responsibility, given the heady world of professorial politicking that accompanied the Academy's public concerts, and bearing in mind that the students would ultimately form the backbone of the performing musical profession when they left the conservatoire's courses of study. Previous research on Mackenzie has been based almost exclusively on biographical work contextualising his compositions.[1] Consequently, it seemed natural to investigate some of the composer's other activities during his most productive period of composition between 1880 and 1900, since a study of the other parts of his life can give a greater insight into his musical work as a whole. Although this brief examination of Mackenzie's conducting is by no means exhaustive – much of the data-crunching, percentage comparisons and analysis of repertoire, for example, has been left to one side in favour of pen portraits and first-hand reminiscences – it will go some way to providing a more rounded picture of his musical views and preferences that ultimately influenced his own compositions.

---

1 Duncan J. Barker, 'The Music of Sir Alexander Campbell Mackenzie (1847–1935): a Critical Study' (Ph.D. diss., University of Durham, 1999).

It will be no surprise to anyone who has closely charted the life of a Victorian musician to learn that Mackenzie received a varied apprenticeship in conducting drawn from both direct and indirect experience. Before the age of 30 he had taken his place as a rank-and-file violinist in various orchestras in Germany, in the cities of Edinburgh and Glasgow in his native Scotland, in London and at various provincial festivals, the most prominent being the Birmingham Triennial Festival. As a result he had played under some of the best-known conductors and composers of the period, including such luminaries as Liszt, Costa and von Bülow.[2] This performing experience gave Mackenzie, as a young musician eager to get on in the profession, the opportunity to play and hear from the inside a long procession of the great orchestral and choral works from the mid-nineteenth century, not forgetting some of the more significant premieres of music by men in the preceding generation of composers.

Mackenzie also held some conducting posts early on in his career, including for one season a choral society in Edinburgh which employed John Hullah's system of tonic sol-fa. However, he soon relinquished the post after being given 'a hint that an examination for a qualifying certificate from head-quarters must be passed'.[3] Also, at the beginning of October 1870 he was appointed to the position of Precentor at St George's Church, Charlotte Square, where he was in charge of the provision of music for services with a choir of 25–30 voices.[4] Though he was never to write as extensively in the genre of sacred choral music as did his later contemporaries, he enjoyed the challenge of this post and raised the standards of singing so much that after his ten years' service the church authorities were very reluctant to let him go. Lastly, he took charge of another, larger choir, the Scottish Vocal Society, three years after his St George's appointment, and with them introduced a great deal of mid-century and contemporary European music to the city. This period of activity soon ended. As the 1870s drew to a close the pressure of teaching and performing in Edinburgh had proved too much for him and he was sent abroad under doctor's orders to recuperate. Much of the next decade was spent in Tuscany, where he composed many of his larger scores, such as the lyrical dramas for Rosa at Drury Lane and a succession of choral

2   A.C. Mackenzie, *A Musician's Narrative* (London: Cassell, 1927), pp. 37–38 (Liszt), pp. 56–57 (Costa), and pp. 91–92 (von Bülow). Hereafter referred to as *MN*.
3   *MN*, p. 78.
4   See 'Scottish Composers and Musicians: II. A.C. Mackenzie', *Scottish Musical Monthly*, 1/6 (1894), pp. 82–84. This includes the reminiscences of Mr P. Glencourse, a chorister under Mackenzie at St George's.

works for festival performances.[5] He did, however, return to England intermittently to direct his own works from the rostrum as well as to take on the post of conductor of the reinstated Novello Oratorio Concerts for a few years in the mid-1880s.

All this changed when Mackenzie was elected Principal of the RAM in February 1888. He firmly asserted his authority as head of the institution and its members. Despite the work of Macfarren, who had also been Professor of Music at Cambridge, the Academy still continued to be a 'professor's club'. He soon overcame some of the more arcane rituals in general practice, such as the segregation of the male and female students on all occasions unless they were engaged in ensemble playing, deservedly winning the approbation of his students for this move. Furthermore, he also reorganised the courses of study available at the school together with the help of some of the younger and more forward-thinking professors.[6]

'Recognising that much of the prevailing unrest had been constantly arising at rehearsals when students tried their wings to orchestral accompaniment', he wrote in *A Musician's Narrative*,

> I stipulated that my duties should include the conductorship, as that office provided the only artistic link between pupils and Principal, and the best opportunity for observing talent and its progress. Furthermore, the professorial habit of interference at rehearsal by instructing the conductor as to *tempi*, etc. – in public – had to come to an end. Too many cooks had been stirring the broth and for much too long a period.[7]

As Mackenzie points out, the orchestra had long been a point of conflict within the professorial circle and often disagreements between staff concerning the technical interpretation of concertos and other artistic matters rankled for years after the performance had been long forgotten. The sheer number of opinions voiced over the direction of the orchestra made it imperative in his view for the ensemble to be directed by one man alone. Amply qualified for the post of conductor through his experience in directing the Novello Choir and other ensembles prior to his RAM election, Mackenzie was pleased to define his new position as Principal by the active role he could take in his students' development.

---

5   One of his greatest successes during this period was the oratorio written for the 1884 Norwich Festival, *The Rose of Sharon*. See Duncan J. Barker, 'Mackenzie's *The Rose of Sharon*: Continental Prima Donna or Norfolk Lass?', in *Nineteenth-Century British Music Studies*, vol. 2, ed. Jeremy Dibble and Bennett Zon (Aldershot: Ashgate, 2002), pp. 101–13.

6   See *MN*, 165. Mackenzie recognises the work of Frederick Corder, the Curator of the Academy and Mackenzie's 'trusted lieutenant', Oscar Beringer, Tobias Matthay, Emile Sauret and Hans Wessely in this area of modernisation.

7   *MN*, p. 162.

Almost all of the instrumental students played under Mackenzie in the orchestra, and some of the more famous among the institution's alumni have left interesting and humorous accounts of their Principal's attitude to music. Perhaps the most detailed was written by Eric Coates, composer and then pupil of the violist Lionel Tertis, who spent many a rehearsal in the viola section under Mackenzie's direction:

> The orchestral practices with the Principal took place on Tuesdays from two till five, with a welcome break for tea at four, and on Fridays from three till five. Tuesday was the 'star turn', for on that day only the most advanced students were permitted to perform to the accompaniment of a full orchestra. The Friday practices, in which a smaller orchestra was employed, were reserved for those students who were in a lower grade and from whom not so much was expected. Hence the innumerable ruses resorted to by both professors and pupils to get their names down on the list for the most important occasion, as appearing at the 'Fridays' had the result of stamping one as a mere beginner. You can imagine with what scant respect the Friday rehearsals were treated when a facetious pupil, on being asked at one of the examinations at end of term to give an example of a discord, replied, 'The RAM Orchestra on a Friday.' The examiners were evidently in agreement with this unexpected sally and I believe the remark was long chuckled over in the Principal's room after-wards.[8]

Rather than the orchestra being an ensemble made up of only current students, Coates points out that many of the sections were led by members of the profession who had often passed through the care of the Academy. These professional musicians were also responsible for the majority of the solo passages in the performances and only reluctantly gave up these moments in the limelight when they felt that the students with whom they shared desks might benefit from the exposure or, more truthfully, when 'a more than usually difficult solo presented itself, prob-ably quite glad to be relieved of the responsibility'. As is the way with student orchestras, the balance of instruments was never quite right and Coates, for instance, bemoans the fact that there was the inevitable lack of violists and surfeit of second violins. He continues:

> I found these rehearsals instructive on the whole, though I fear I derived more fun from them than anything ... The Principal was in his element at the head of an orchestra, and when he was not raging at some wretched singer or harpist who, through sheer nervousness, would keep making an entry before the beat, he would entertain the company with every conceivable kind of joke, very often at the expense of some unfortunate member of the ensemble. ...

---

8   Eric Coates, *Suite in Four Movements* (London: William Heinemann Ltd, 1953), pp. 64–65.

The Principal of the RAM was not an inspiring conductor, for, like most composers, his tempi were very much on the slow side; in fact, so slow would they sometimes become that it was difficult, if you entered the Concert Hall during the performance of a symphony or some such work, to come to any definite conclusion as to what movement was being played. I do not think the make-up of the orchestra improved matters, particularly in the string section, where the lack of balance was deplorable. It was a question of quantity rather than of quality. Between fifteen and twenty first violins, hundreds of seconds, six to eight violas (when you were lucky), a fair body of cellos and three or four basses. The woodwind on the whole was good, the horns fair, and the brass bad. The unfortunate percussion instruments went through a trying time, being pulled about by students whose fingers were itching to have a whack at the inviting-looking bass-drum; the kettle-drums, although presenting just as inviting an appearance as the bass-drum, wanted a bit more managing, and besides, the tuning was such an infernal nuisance. And so, between the slowness of the Principal and the unbalanced and cumbersome body of instrumentalists, most of the performances gave the listener an impression of one of the larger denizens of the forest awakening from slumber.[9]

Despite a century's distance, the feel and atmosphere of Mackenzie's orchestra at the Academy does not sound that unfamiliar in comparison with most school or college orchestras of today. One of the main differences is the type of repertoire that would have been performed by students under Mackenzie. Coates reports that the Principal 'had a passion for digging up unknown overtures by long-forgotten French composers or the lesser-known works by composers such as Dvořák, and would spend hours plodding through some of the duller compositions of Sterndale Bennett or Walter Macfarren'.[10] Mackenzie also took the opportunity to try out some of his own compositions with his young charges, works that, on reflection, Coates felt pleased to have become acquainted with. However, although the Principal was fully in command of the orchestra and its rehearsals, despite his admission in his autobiography, he was still not able to shake off the demands of the professors who insisted on the inclusion of particular concerto movements, various scenas and arias in order to exhibit their star pupils before the London public. In his recent essay, 'Miscellany vs. Homogeneity: Concert Programmes at the Royal Academy of Music and the Royal College of Music in the 1880s',[11] William Weber explores the repertoire of the student performances given by the two conservatoires. He demonstrates that, as in many things, the

---

9   Ibid., pp. 65–66.
10 Ibid.
11 Chap. 14 in Christina Bashford and Leanne Langley (eds), *Music and British Culture, 1785–1914: Essays in Honour of Cyril Ehrlich* (Oxford: Oxford University Press, 2000).

two royal schools were completely different in their approaches to programming. In general, the Academy favoured the 'miscellaneous concert' with a large number of different musical items, following in the tradition established well over a century previously. Conversely, the College tended to promote 'homogeneous concerts', concentrating on a smaller number of linked items, with a preference for works from the Austro-Germanic canon of 'great' composers. An examination of some of the programme books of student concerts in the RAM archive demonstrates there is little evidence to show that the tradition of the 'miscellaneous concert' at the RAM had disappeared in the 1890s under the direction of Mackenzie.

In addition to broadening the repertoire of those instrumental students who performed in the Academy's orchestra, Mackenzie and the ensemble also had the unenviable responsibility of playing through certain new works produced by the composition students. 'The composer-students generally had a raw deal when they appeared at the side of the Principal for a run-through of a new work', admits Coates.

> I can still see Montague Phillips scowling at the members of the orchestra while his cherished manuscript was being ruthlessly turned by Sir Alexander from a sparkling Scherzo into a sober Moderato, and the latter, on being requested to 'hot-up' the proceedings, turning furiously on the composer, telling him it was quite fast enough and that if he thought he was going to take it any faster he was wrong.[12]

Though hardly a fan of Mackenzie during his time at the Academy, Arnold Bax, too, found the Principal's attitude to student composers less than satisfactory. 'Mackenzie from the first regarded me as a thorn in the flesh', Bax explains in *Farewell, My Youth*, 'and when rehearsing one of my tentative and irritatingly difficult efforts was wont to fling down his stick and ejaculate my short name with the effect of an imprecation.'[13] It seems that Mackenzie often exhibited his temper in front of the orchestra, although, as he himself admits, these outbursts were 'not always real'.[14] 'To argue with Mackenzie was more than useless, nay, it was fatal', records Coates;

> The only thing to do was to approach him with every artifice of diplomacy that you had at your command and put yourself completely in his hands, always making your request in a low voice. After all, you cannot very well criticise the Head in front of the whole school (at any rate not out loud), which is what it amounted to.[15]

---

12 Coates, *Suite*, p. 66.
13 Arnold Bax, *Farewell, My Youth* (London, 1943), pp. 19–20.
14 *MN*, p. 162.
15 Coates, *Suite*, p. 67.

With competition from Stanford and his composition pupils in Kensington, it is no surprise that, with support such as this, very few composers of any true standing – with the exceptions of Coates, Bax and Bantock – emerged from the Academy during the 1890s.

Although Mackenzie was extremely busy with his work at the Academy during his period in office, he did make time for other conducting engagements. During the 1890s he renewed his acquaintance with the Philharmonic Society, for which he had written the orchestral ballad *La Belle Dame sans merci* in 1883. Taking the baton from Frederic Cowen, whose contract with the Society had been ended owing to differences with the orchestral personnel, Mackenzie became conductor of the Philharmonic orchestra for seven of its concert seasons beginning in 1893. This was hardly the most auspicious situation in which to commence his tenure as artistic director and, of course, it did not go unnoticed by the critical press. '[Mackenzie], in accepting the post, practically declared against Mr Cowen', reported George Bernard Shaw, 'a course which he has now to justify by producing better results than Mr Cowen, with no better preparation.'[16] Each season consisted of seven long orchestral concerts, with the first in late February or early March and the last in June. Under Mackenzie's direction almost every concert programme included some work by a native composer, among which numbered some of his own compositions. The most celebrated of these was the *Scottish Concerto* for piano and orchestra, commissioned by the Philharmonic Society for performance by Paderewski in its 1897 series. The Continental repertoire was not neglected and, in his first season as conductor, Mackenzie was fortunate enough to delegate some of his conducting duties to the succession of musical dignitaries who were passing through London to receive honorary doctorates at the Cambridge University Musical Society's Fiftieth-Anniversary Jubilee celebrations in 1893.[17] However, in subsequent seasons Mackenzie personally conducted the notable British premiere of Tchaikovsky's *Pathétique* Symphony as well as other works.

In his recent book on the Philharmonic Society Cyril Ehrlich points out that during his time as conductor Mackenzie was meticulous in his planning of programmes for the orchestra: 'His efforts on behalf of the Philharmonic had been prodigious and unceasing. He read a wide range of scores, and reported on them with zest.'[18] As chief music adviser to the

---

16 George Bernard Shaw, *Music in London* (London: Constable & Co. Ltd, 1932), vol. 2, pp. 268–69. Article dated 15 Mar. 1893.

17 Chronicled in Gerald Norris, *Stanford, the Cambridge Jubilee and Tchaikovsky* (Newton Abbot: David & Charles Ltd, 1980).

18 Cyril Ehrlich, *First Philharmonic: a History of the Royal Philharmonic Society* (Oxford: Oxford University Press, 1995), p. 175.

Board of Directors, Mackenzie had to deal with the large number of compositions submitted to the Society for possible inclusion in the programmes. Continuing his appraisal of the conductor's work, Ehrlich states, 'Mackenzie's adjudications ... were generally enlightened and stimulating. His advocacy of new music was often accompanied by a scepticism towards past masters.'[19] Indeed, the Philharmonic archive, Loan 48 in the British Library, boasts numerous letters from Mackenzie to Francesco Berger, the secretary of the Society, demonstrating the Scotsman's open-mindedness to new music from both Britain and the Continent, and further afield – in Ehrlich's estimation, 'he was no organ-loft pedant'. Mackenzie was constantly on the lookout for works that could be considered 'up to Philharmonic pitch'.[20] In one letter, he reported on no fewer than eight new works by British composers, qualifying his comments by stating, 'I can't tell you how I dislike to sit in judgment upon others; but I take it as a duty to the Directors of the Society and so I perform it.'[21] During his employment by the Philharmonic, he appraised scores from Chadwick, Holmès, Borodin, Tchaikovsky, Maclean, Foote, German, Smetana, Aston, Matthay, Fanning, Bunning, Barnett, Barclay Jones, Corder, Wallace, MacDowell and Doctors Hiles and Allenby of Manchester and Cambridge respectively. Although the traditional repertoire of the Philharmonic had to retain its place in the programmes, Mackenzie was particularly interested in performing music from eastern Europe, including works by Smetana, Borodin and Tchaikovsky, his interest in the latter obviously fuelled by the Russian's visit to London at the start of Mackenzie's Philharmonic reign. It was also on the subject of east European music that Mackenzie was later to give lectures at the Royal Institution.[22]

One aspect of the Philharmonic seasons that worried Mackenzie was the length and format of the programmes offered to subscribers. Although the programmes were not as long as those of the Academy in the 1880s as described by Weber, nor as short as the RCM model, the Philharmonic concerts always verged on the lengthy side. Furthermore, as a result of the selection of soloists chosen by the Directors for certain concerts, the format of the programmes would be adversely affected when various shorter pieces were appended to show off the soloists in their best light. Again, Shaw manages to capture the predicament of the permanent conductor of the Philharmonic Society orchestra in one of his columns:

---

19 Ibid., p. 176.
20 Philharmonic Collection, British Library (Loan 48.13/21, fol. 50).
21 Ibid., fol. 130.
22 'The Bohemian School of Music' at the Royal Institution, 4, 11 and 18 Feb. 1905.

This is an old story; but it remains true to the present hour that whenever anything is well rehearsed for a Philharmonic concert, nothing else thereat is rehearsed at all. For the last season or two we have seen certain composers – Grieg, Moszkowski, Benoit, etc. – all engaged to conduct their own compositions. At the rehearsals, they were of course accorded the first turn; and they naturally kept the band at their works until they had got the effects they wanted. Then there was the concerto player to be attended to: he or she, an artist of European reputation, was not going to be kept waiting for anybody. By the time composer and virtuoso were half satisfied, the men were hungry, impatient and due at other engagements: in short, the rehearsal was virtually over. Mr Mackenzie or Mr Cowen could at most approach the Society's illustrious guest with a polite request for just five minutes at the end to run through Beethoven's Ninth Symphony, or any other trifle that might have been announced. The effect of this was of course to make the unfortunate official conductor in contrast with the composer who had appropriated all his opportunities of rehearsing, seem only half as competent and conscientious as he really was.[23]

This state of affairs was never going to make life easy for the poor conductor. Ever the reformer and having had his position as conductor renewed directly after the end of the 1896 season of concerts, Mackenzie replied to the Directors through Berger with the following recommendations:

> I accept the position, in the hopes that the Directors will share with me the view that certain conditions, until now adhered to, might be seriously reconsidered. Without wishing in the smallest degree to dictate to the Directors, I feel that I must bring to their notice the following facts, a continuance of which are in my judgment highly detrimental to the stability of the Society's Concerts.
>
> I.   The great length of the programmes (involving much fruitless labour on my part, as well as on that of the orchestra)
> II.   The selection of the vocalists and the want of supervision over their pieces.
> III. The 'encores' taken by the soloists and singers.
>
> If these important points are duly considered and altered, I believe that the Concerts might take rank with the very best orchestra concerts in Europe. On the other hand, a continuance of the present system prevents them keeping pace with the success of the ever increasing number of similar enterprises in London.[24]

Although Mackenzie was not reticent in expressing his views on certain subjects, as this letter demonstrates, he did acknowledge in his later writings the particular artistic difficulty which faced the Directors of

---

23 Shaw, *Music in London*, vol. 1, pp. 144–45. Article dated 11 Mar. 1891.
24 Philharmonic Collection, British Library (Loan 48.13/21, fols 121–22).

the Philharmonic. 'Little is known and less is understood of the constant anxiety which fell – must always fall – to the lot of the Honorary Direc-tors', he wrote, 'whose efforts were then often rewarded by more blame than encouragement – sometimes quite unjustly, I thought.'[25] Between the Scylla of the cognoscenti and the Charybdis of the concert-going audi-ence, the Philharmonic Society sailed a difficult artistic course. There is little doubt that he was able to strike a happy medium during his tenure as conductor. Indeed, as even a cursory glance at the appendices to Ehrlich's survey of the Philharmonic will testify, during the seven years that Mackenzie was conductor of the orchestra, there were significantly greater numbers of world and London premieres. In his own way and in comparison with his contemporaries, Mackenzie was a true advocate of new music and widened the orchestral repertoire.

After he resigned from the Philharmonic Society in 1899, Mackenzie never took another permanent conducting engagement outside his work with the student orchestra at the Academy. The 1880s and 1890s had been periods of considerable creative activity for him and during these years he had had to decline various other opportunities to conduct outside London. For example, in 1895 Dan Godfrey tried to lure his colleague down to Bournemouth to present his own music and received a polite reply:

> While I thank you most cordially for your kind intentions in asking me to come down and conduct some of my pieces, I deeply regret to say that it is impossible. Frankly and honestly, I have been so much overworked with all this thing, travelling, conducting, composing, etc. etc., that my health and strength begin to fail me at far too early a period. Therefore, I have been obliged to decline all offers to leave London, or do anything beyond my own work (which is heavy enough) during the next twelve months at least.[26]

However, his new-found freedom from the restraints of the Philhar-monic's concert season in London meant that Mackenzie was more than happy to visit Bournemouth from 1900 onwards. Unlike many of his contemporaries, Godfrey was one of the early 'career conductors' in this country. In his memoirs he devoted a not inconsiderable amount of space to the 'Art of conducting', noting that the 1880s had brought on the advance of the 'composer conductor', a group into which Mackenzie, Stanford, Corder and Cowen all fell, and a necessary evolutionary step towards the establishment of the role in the twentieth century. Writing of this sea change in the musical profession, Godfrey isolates Henry Wood

---

25 *MN*, p. 182.
26 Letter from Mackenzie to Godfrey dated 9 Aug. 1895. Reproduced in Stephen Lloyd, *Sir Dan Godfrey: Champion of British Composers* (London: Thames Publishing, 1995), pp. 29–30.

and Landon Ronald as pre-eminent in their sphere. However, he qualifies this assessment with an interesting 'Darwinian' observation:

> In a measure the way has been prepared for them by the spadework of musicians like Cowen and Mackenzie. There is a good deal of the poet in Cowen and, poet-like, he is inclined to linger on the beautiful while everyone waits. Mackenzie is one of those who bore the brunt of the fight in days when it was generally said – if anything was said about him at all – that the British conductor was 'no good'. He brought the valuable technique of the orchestral player – he was one at ten – to bear upon his work.[27]

He was still, of course, welcome down in Bournemouth with Godfrey's orchestra and often went to provincial music festivals where a performance of his own music called for the composer's own baton. Possibly his greatest conducting achievement after his stint at the Philharmonic was the tour of Canada he undertook in 1903, which had been organised for him by Charles Harriss.[28] During the six weeks of this tour, Mackenzie visited 15 concert centres and performed with three professional and semi-professional orchestras. Furthermore, the repertoire was almost entirely British and 14 new choirs were brought into existence specifically for the performances.[29] This was no mean feat by any conductor's standards.

What effect, then, did Mackenzie's conducting career have on professional musicians and, more importantly, the concert tradition? At the Academy he managed to knock the orchestra further into shape and free it from the interference of the more conservative of his professorial colleagues. He gave young composers at the Academy opportunities – albeit laced with his own inimitable reactions – to hear their works performed by their contemporaries. At the Philharmonic he gave a fair appraisal of all of the manuscript scores submitted to the orchestra and also managed to take a good proportion of them through to public performance. In conclusion, Mackenzie was by no means the greatest conductor of his generation working in this country – that status was fought over by others such as Manns, Richter and Wood – but he was above all sympathetic to both performers and composers, taking as a starting point his own practical experiences of performance early in his career.

---

27 Sir Dan Godfrey, *Memories and Music* (London: Hutchinson & Co., 1924), p. 120.
28 'Dr Charles Harriss', *Musical Times*, 50 (1 Apr. 1909), pp. 225–29 (and photograph).
29 Mackenzie, *MN*, chap. 26: 'A Canadian Tour', pp. 208–19; id., 'To the Editor of The Musical Times' [series of three letters written *en route*], *Musical Times*, 44 (1 May 1903), pp. 317–18; 1 June 1903, pp. 385–88; 1 July 1903, pp. 456–59; commemorative photograph of those involved, 1 July 1903, p. 453 and opp. p. 452.

CHAPTER ELEVEN

Vincent Novello and the Philharmonic Society of London

Fiona M. Palmer

They all lived happily ever after. This much can be said of the epony-mous heroine Rosalba, her husband Licida and their friends and family.[1] The story is encapsulated in the dramatic cantata *Rosalba* (1833) written by Vincent Novello in response to a commission from the Phil-harmonic Society. It was first performed on 17 March 1834 in the Hanover Square Rooms at the second concert of the Society's twenty-second season.[2] Novello, now in his fifties, conducted, Domenico Dragonetti played the obbligato double bass part, and François Cramer led the band. The young Clara Novello sang the part of Rosalba and was joined by Mrs Henry Bishop, Messrs Horncastle, Bennett and Chapman, and her brother Alfred.[3]

These facts are easily retold. What is more difficult is to assess Novello's involvement with the Philharmonic Society as performer, Director, composer and decision maker. This article considers the impli-cations of Novello's relationship with the Society for our understanding of his status among the movers and shakers of the English musical world. An appraisal of the critical reception, not only of his *Rosalba* but also of many of the other works which resulted from the Society's burst of commissioning, illuminates aspects of Novello's career and also the expe-riences of his colleagues. It offers an insight into the state of native

---

1   British Library (hereafter BL) Loan 4.469**, autograph manuscript orchestral score of *Rosalba*. Novello summarises 'The Argument' as follows: 'Rosalba, the wife of Licida, mourns the loss of her husband, whom she supposes to have been killed by a secret Enemy during his absence abroad: Her friend, Costanza, endeavors [*sic*] to console her, and Rosalba tries to resign herself to her fate, but is gradually sinking into languor and insensibility – when her father, Uberto, arrives with his friend, Silvestro, to inform her that her Husband has escaped from the treacherous designs of his Enemy, and still lives for her sake. Rosalba, at first, can scarcely believe in the joyful intelligence; but the appearance of Licida, accompanied by her Brother, Orlando, dispels her fearful doubts, and the scene ends with a Sestetto by all the Characters, expressive of their restored happiness and general felicity.'

2   BL Loan 48.10/11, *Classified Vocal Works*, fol. 30r. Note that Henry Bishop's cantata *The Seventh Day* was performed in the first concert of the season. William Horsley's motet *Exaltabo Te* was performed in the third concert [fol. 30v].

3   See the BL printed edition of the vocal/piano reduction, shelfmark: H. 2831. j (21), p. [1].

composition (not least the nepotistic selection of authors), and the preparation, planning and programming of these commissions in London.

In 1832, when Mendelssohn was the apple of the Philharmonic Society's eye, the Directors simultaneously commissioned instrumental and vocal works by 'resident' composers. It is fair to say that Vincent Novello is seldom remembered for his original compositions. His legacy found its greatest impact through his editorial work and collecting activities. By the time of *Rosalba*'s premiere in 1834 his editions and arrangements were numerous and were primarily of vocal and organ music.[4]

On 6 February 1813 Novello signed his name as a founder member of the Philharmonic Society. He was the twenty-seventh man to do so.[5] If anything is said about Novello in passing it is usually that he was one of the founder members of the Society. What is not often said is that he came roughly half-way down the list and that he served as Director for only one season: 1818.[6] When elected again, 24 years later in 1841, he declined to serve.[7] Regular Directors, such as William Ayrton, Henry R. Bishop, Muzio Clementi, F. and J.B. Cramer, William Dance, Cipriani Potter, William Shield and Sir George Smart, were, in consequence, among the most influential musical men in the metropolis. The *Minute Books* reveal that Novello tended to attract very few votes when elections occurred – he frequently tied for bottom place. Scattered within the Society's archive[8] are scraps of evidence which show that Novello was more a 'hanger-on' than a VIP. The ups and downs of everyone's success in these directorial ballots defy easy analysis since fortunes inevitably fluctuated according to who was in attendance at a particular meeting and any prevailing issues surrounding their popularity or outside activities. Novello's energies were

---

4   For example, he had recently completed his 72-part, five-volume set of *Purcell's Sacred Music* (1828–32).

5   BL Loan 48.1, *Foundation Book*. Ries, Watts, Potter, Calkin, Wesley, Mori, Weichsel, Spagnoletti, Klengel and Dragonetti came further down the list. See also George Hogarth, *The Philharmonic Society of London: From its Foundation, 1813, to its Fiftieth Year, 1862* (London: Bradbury & Evans, 1862), p. 6.

6   1817–18. BL Loan 48.3/1, *General Minute Book 1813–54*, Annual General Meeting, 16 June 1817. Results of the ballot (following which 12 Directors were appointed) were as follows: Attwood 14; Ayrton 14; Neate 14; Griffin 13; Weichsel 13; Ries 13; Bishop 13; Lindley 12; Spagnoletti 12; Novello 10; Webbe 6; P. Meyer 4; Sir G. Smart 4; Braham 3; Clementi 2; Dr Crotch 2; Horsley 2; Shield 2; H. Smart 2; Viotti 1; Welsh 1; Ashe 1.

7   BL Loan 48.3/1, General Meeting, 26 July 1841 (Novello was absent). Moscheles declined the post of Director and a further ballot was held. Novello gained 8 votes against Joseph Calkin's 3 and P. Meyer's 3. He was elected a Director in his absence. At the General Meeting on 9 August it is recorded that: 'A letter [was] read from Mr. Novello declining to serve as a Director.' The Society had fallen on hard times and announced a loss of £533 9s. 6d. for the season on 13 July 1842 at an adjourned AGM.

8   BL Loans 4 and 48. Royal Philharmonic Society Manuscripts.

channelled into his work as organist, editor and teacher in the years prior to his retirement to Nice in 1849.

Nevertheless, it is important to emphasise that Novello took an interest in the Society's affairs and attended General Meetings – fairly regularlyp early on, sporadically in later years – until November 1844.[9] In 1815 he was elected to a 'Committee of six persons ... for the revisal of the Library, and the examination of all the works copied for performance at the Concerts' together with Potter, Burrowes, Carnaby, Walmisley and Williams.[10] Because of his role as a Director that season, Novello 'presided at the pianoforte' at the sixth concert on 11 May 1818 – a programme which included Beethoven's first symphony.[11] In 1846 he played the organ for Beethoven's *Missa Solemnis* as a favour to Michael Costa.[12] Thus his services as a performer were called upon infrequently – it was to be his daughter Clara who advanced the family name in this respect.[13] In 1830 he was included among a proposed committee charged with revising the laws of the Society – a committee that never materialised.[14] Having seconded a proposal that Clementi's funeral be overseen by the Society in March 1832, he went on, in November that year, to second Thomas Attwood's motion that Mendelssohn should be requested to compose 'a Symphony, an

---

9   BL Loan 48.3/1, *passim*. His name featured in ballots for Directors for the last time at the AGM on 12 July 1847, when he attracted 2 votes.

10   BL Loan 48.3/1, 11 December 1815. On 26 February 1816 the Committee was extended to eight members by the addition of Shield and Tousse. See also *The Letters of Samuel Wesley: Professional and Social Correspondence 1797–1837*, ed. Philip Olleson (Oxford: Oxford University Press, 2001), pp. 258, 265–66.

11   Myles Birket Foster, *The History of the Philharmonic Society of London 1813–1912: a Record of a Hundred Years' Work in the Cause of Music* (London: John Lane, 1912), p. 36.

12   See BL Loan 48.13/25, *Original Letters MOU–NOV*, letter from Novello to Watts dated Tuesday, 3 March 1846, fol. 230r. See also BL Add. MS 65839, Karl F. Curshmann's 'Ti prego o Padre eterno', trio for three voices and orchestra in Michael Costa's hand, 'Scored for the Philharmonic Society' 1846 with an inscription to Novello. It was performed at the Philharmonic Society concert on 16 March 1846. See BL Loan 4.788* for the Society's copy.

13   She was elected unanimously as a Female Professional Subscriber on 10 November 1834. See BL Loan 48.3/1. Foster accounts for her involvement in 22 concerts between 25 March 1833 and 13 June 1859. See Foster, *History*, pp. 121–258. For further information on Clara's career see Averil Mackenzie-Grieve, *Clara Novello 1818–1908* (London: Geoffrey Bles, 1955).

14   BL Loan 48.3/1, Annual General Meeting, 30 June 1830. 'It was Moved by Mr. Neate and Seconded by Mr. Ayrton that a new Committee be formed for the purpose of revising the Laws of the Society, and that no Member of the former Committee be named for the above. It was Moved by Mr. Ayrton and Seconded by Mr. Dance that Messrs. Neate, Bishop, Novello, Sherrington and Weichsel be requested to form the above Committee. Carried.' At the following General Meeting, Horsley, seconded by Dance, 'asked that the New Committee be now rescinded – carried by a show of hands'.

Overture, and a Vocal Piece'.[15] This commission initiated the process that was to include Novello himself as a composer on the Society's books.

Despite his comparatively low public profile in Philharmonic Society affairs Novello refused to be treated as an inferior. He pressed to be rewarded with complimentary tickets for his work on the Correcting Committee,[16] and his exasperation at the treatment of a nomination he put forward in 1837 became a bone of contention. As a full member of the Society, Novello exercised his privileges and recommended the Russells as subscribers to the Philharmonic. This simple recommendation turned into a saga. The Directors refused to accept it without further supporting evidence. Novello felt that his judgement and standing within the musical world had been called into question, along with the quality of the brother and sister whom he had recommended. In an unusually candid letter, he made no secret of his wounded pride:

> Mr. & Miss Russell are the Son & Daughter of a most respectable Brother Professor,[17] the late excellent Organist at the Foundling, and in that capacity I consider them perfectly eligible as Subscribers to the Philharmonic, especially as that Concert was instituted expressly for the gratification of Professors and their families.
>
> I knew the father to be a very estimable man in every respect, & I never heard the slightest imputation upon the character of either the Son or the Daughter, or I should not have sent in their names. Indeed I cannot but feel hurt that the Directors could for a moment suppose me capable of wishing to introduce any improper persons to the Concert.[18]

The Directors, probably still reeling from the criticisms of their ticket-transfer system during the 1836 season,[19] remained unsatisfied[20] and wrote to Novello again asking him to furnish them with details of the 'occupation or profession' of the Russells.[21] Novello forwarded a letter sent to him by Mr Russell and permission was finally granted.[22] Despite

---

15 BL Loan 48.3/1, Annual General Meeting, 5 November 1832.

16 See *Letters of Samuel Wesley*, ed. Olleson, pp. 265–66.

17 William Russell (1777–1813), son of the London organ builder Hugh Russell. See his letter to Novello [1811] in BL Add. MS 11730, *Letters to Vincent Novello from Eminent Musicians*, fols 174r–175v.

18 BL Loan 48.13/25, autograph letter from Novello, dated only 'Sunday Eve[nin]g' and written from 69 Dean Street, Soho Square, fol. 232r.

19 Cyril Ehrlich, *First Philharmonic: a History of the Royal Philharmonic Society* (Oxford: Oxford University Press, 1995), p. 54.

20 See letters dated 11 and 18 February 1837 written to Novello by Watts. BL Loan 48.6/1, *Letter Book 1831–44* [From the P. Soc.], unfoliated.

21 BL Loan 48.2/2, *Directors' Minute Book 1822–37*, 18 February 1837.

22 Ibid., 25 February 1837, 'Letter read from Mr. Russell to Mr. Novello. Resolved that he be informed his Letter is quite satisfactory to the Directors, and that his Ticket will be made out on applying at 201 Regent St.'

his annoyance over the officious grinding of the Society's bureaucratic machine, Novello must have known that he had not been singled out for such treatment. In 1836 his friend Ignaz Moscheles had been moved to pen a heartfelt paragraph to the Directors. He was outraged by their refusal to supply him with an additional ticket for a concert at which he was to play Beethoven's Piano Concerto No. 5 in 1836: 'My feelings at the Directors refusal are of too unpleasant a nature, entirely to suppress them and I shall therefore feel obliged by your communicating this to them either privately or at their next meeting.'[23]

As early as January 1815 the Society had accepted a motion proposed by William Horsley and seconded by Thomas Attwood that a sum 'not exceeding Two Hundred Pounds' should be used to allow trials of pieces written in England and placed before a committee of seven Society members on or before St Cecilia's Day each year.[24] Simon McVeigh has shown that the need to nurture British talent found its advocacy through the *Quarterly Musical Magazine & Review* in the 1820s and 1830s but that this campaign was not one supported by, for example, William Ayrton – a key Philharmonic Society figure.[25] A brief glance at the tables in Ehrlich's *First Philharmonic* or in Foster's *History* speaks volumes. The founding of the Society of British Musicians in 1834, and the new exclusively British focus it offered, came after Novello's inclusion as composer in a Philharmonic Society Concert. He became a member of that new committee.[26]

The buoyancy of the Philharmonic Society's funds in the early 1830s, coupled with Mendelssohn's popularity in England and the views of the Directors, may have led to the surge of commissioning. *The Spectator*'s candid dismissal of many of the resulting works indicates a marketing failure on the part of the Society. The rationale behind the commissions was not made explicit. By the time that Horsley's vocal work had been publicly performed in the wake of those by Bishop and Novello, *The Spectator* unleashed its frustration in no uncertain terms:

> It is one part of the Directors' duty to feed the public appetite for novelty; and on this occasion it was not neglected: how far excellence

---

23 BL Loan 48.13/24, *Original Letters MI–MOS*, fol. 114r, letter from Moscheles to Watts, dated 20 February 1836, evening.

24 BL Loan 48.3/1, pp. 35–36. General Meeting, 28 January 1815 (Novello absent). An advertisement was worded and included the lines: 'But to prevent mortification and disappointment it must be observed, that, as a considerable portion of the Society's fund will be extended in the prosecution of this desirable object, it is expected that no composition will be presented which has not been first carefully studied and digested.'

25 Simon McVeigh, 'The Society of British Musicians', in Christina Bashford and Leanne Langley (eds), *Music and British Culture 1785–1914: Essays in Honour of Cyril Ehrlich* (Oxford: Oxford University Press, 2000), pp. 148–49 *et passim*.

26 Ibid., p. 150.

was joined to novelty, may in some instances be questioned. The whole affair of bespeaking compositions of certain members of the Society, instead of proceeding upon clear, intelligible principles, appears to have been dictated by mere caprice. If the Society had desired to do an act of justice to the English vocal writers of the present day, it would have selected their best works for occasional performance; but from this it has systematically refrained. It manifests the waywardness of a child, which values nothing unless allowed to call it 'its own'. What need is there to adventure in a lottery for the chance of a prize, when so much wealth is within reach? Did it never occur to the minds of these adventurers, that there are blanks as well as prizes in lotteries? The third of the new vocal pieces appears in the scheme of the present concert – the Motet by HORSLEY. Now one, at least, of this author's Motets is known to the public, and known only to be admired. Why was not this taken? Here was no risk of failure – no doubt – no uncertainty. But the Society could exercise no ownership over it: they could not place it on their shelves as an unique copy: they could not lock it up from the rest of the world, and allow it to grow venerable with dust and cobwebs. Has the spirit of HASLEWOOD descended on the Philharmonic, or is Dr DIBDIN admitted to its councils?[27]

The response of the critic in the *Morning Post*, following the same concert, echoed these sentiments.[28]

The letter from the Philharmonic Society commissioning Sigismund von Neukomm, Bishop, J.B. Cramer, Griffin, Potter, Moscheles, Attwood, Horsley, Thomas Cooke and Novello is undated and falls between a letter to William Dance dated 13 November 1832 and a letter to Mendelssohn dated 11 December 1832.[29] As a result of a General Meeting resolution each of these ten men was sent an identically worded letter, which offered:

a third portion of one hundred Guineas namely, the sum of thirty five pounds for a composition which shall be the property of the Society for the term of two years from the time of its delivery, after which the Copyright shall revert to you, the Society reserving to themselves the privilege of performing it at all times, and with the

27 *The Spectator*, no. 302, for the week ending Saturday 12 April 1834, p. 346, cols 1–2.
28 *Morning Post*, no. 19761, Wednesday, 9 April 1834, p. 3, cols 3–4.
29 BL Loan 48.3/1. Novello was not included in the first list of names proposed as recipients of a commission. Bishop, Cramer, Potter and Griesbach were confirmed on the same day as Mendelssohn (5 November 1832). After an intervening General Meeting, Neukomm, Moscheles, Griffin, Attwood, Horsley, Novello and T. Cooke were selected as recipients (19 November 1832). Goss was subsequently 'engaged to write an instrumental composition' after some wrangling (see General Meeting minutes 4 January–13 April 1833). Moscheles' letter accepting the commission is dated 6 December 1832; see BL Loan 48.13/24, fol. 106r. Correspondence from John Goss relating to his acceptance and the progress of his instrumental piece can be found in BL Loan 48.13/14, *Original Letters GOS–GR*, fols 16 (dated 11 January 1833) and 17 (dated 21 December 1833).

understanding that you shall be allowed to publish any arrangement
of it, as soon as you may think proper after its first performance at
their Concerts.[30]

These men were paid the same fee as Mendelssohn, money which
resulted from the sale of £600 stock.[31] The result was instrumental
works, including a Quintet by Cramer, Septet by Moscheles, 'Fantasia
Drammatica' by Neukomm and a Symphony by Potter.[32] All these were
performed during the 1833 season.[33] The 1834 season boasted
Bishop's *The Seventh Day*, Novello's *Rosalba*, Moscheles' *Concerto
Fantastique*, Horsley's *Exaltabo Te*, both Mendelssohn's *Melusine*
overture and his Scena 'Ah ritorna', and J. Henry Griesbach's overture
to *Belshazzar's Feast*.[34] It seems that initially not everyone chose to
understand the terms of this commission. The Society found itself
obliged to spell it out patiently for Neukomm, who sent his answer to
the commission by early January 1833. It was returned to him via
Moscheles and he was carefully reminded that the composition was
required to be original.[35]

Novello must have felt full of confidence as he completed the commission in April 1833. His pen had recently found its outlet, to public
acclaim, through the ever-popular glee. In 1832 his 'Old May Morning'
had won the Manchester Glee Club Prize for 'best Cheerful Glee'.[36] It is an
ATTB setting of words by Charles Cowden Clarke.[37] Henry Bishop won
the serious glee prize[38] and wrote rather charmingly to Novello following
their shared victory:

---

30 BL Loan 48.6/1, n.f. Letter from William Watts.
31 BL Loan 48.3/1, General Meeting. 13 April 1833. 'It was moved by Sir George Smart,
and seconded by Mr. Attwood that the Trustees be empowered to sell out six hundred
pounds Stock by Power of Attorney, to defray the expences [*sic*] incurred for Compositions
Copying &c. to be paid into the hands of the Treasurer.'
32 BL Loan 4.1021, J.B. Cramer, Quintet for piano and strings, 1832; autograph
manuscript dated 12 December 1832. BL Loan 4.1194, Ignaz Moscheles, Septet, Op. 88,
autograph manuscript. BL Loan 4.805, Sigismund von Neukomm, Fantasia Drammatica for
orchestra 'on some passages of Milton's Paradise Lost', autograph manuscript.
33 Hogarth, *The Philharmonic Society*, pp. 62–63.
34 Ibid., pp. 63–64.
35 BL Loan 48.6/1, n.f. Letter from Watts to Neukomm dated 16 January 1833.
36 Henry Watson, *A Chronicle of the Manchester Gentlemen's Glee Club from its
Foundation 1830 to the Session 1905–6* (Manchester: Charles H. Barber, 1906), p. 41.
37 Charles Cowden Clarke had married Vincent and Mary Novello's eldest child, Mary
Victoria, on 5 July 1828.
38 Bishop's glee, 'Where shall we make her a grave?', was also sung at the meeting on 7
February 1833. BL Add. MS 65384 is a copy of Bishop's glee in Novello's hand. See
Nicholas Temperley and Bruce Carr, 'Bishop, Henry R.', in *The New Grove Dictionary of
Music and Musicians*, 2nd edn, ed. Stanley Sadie and John Tyrrell (London: Macmillan,
2001), vol. 3, p. 634, which gives 327 glees as Bishop's total.

> With much sincerity I return my congratulations on your success at
> Manchester. And I assure you that when I learned that you had been
> not only my 'companion in arms' but also in Victory, I felt the value
> of the prize was doubled; as it was at once a proof to me that our
> judges possessed discernment![39]

Novello had triumphed over 20 other entries to win his prize.

Careful to keep the Directors abreast of his progress, Novello wrote to
them on 16 January to let them know that he had not had time to prepare
his manuscript but that he hoped to do so shortly.[40] Three months later he
submitted the full score and parts.[41] The letter he enclosed included the
offer of Clara's services as Rosalba as a cheaper alternative to those of
Madame Malibran.[42] The Directors resolved that Maria Malibran should
be asked to sing the principal part of Rosalba; Horncastle and Henry Phillips were to be engaged for the principal tenor and bass parts. Novello
should be asked for his choice regarding the other three singers.[43]
However, time had run out for the season and, at their meeting on 15
May, the Directors agreed that both Bishop and Novello should be
informed that their works could not be performed until 1834, when they
would also be put on trial.[44] Bishop had explained to the Directors that his
involvement with 'business of the Theatre, of very immediate import …
has prevented my attending to my composition for the Philharmonic as I
could have wished'.[45] Just before the twenty-second season and the trials
for it began, Novello added a postscript to his nominations for
subscribers. It tells us much about his views on performers in the marketplace (or at least his wish to further his daughter Clara's career). He
states:

> P.S. I take this opportunity of requesting you will present my
> Comp[limen]ts to the Directors, & say that as the Piece (Rosalba)
> wh[ich] I had the pleasure of writing for the Society is, I understand, to

---

39 BL Add. MS 11730, letter from Henry Bishop, dated only 'Wednesday morning', fol.
29r.

40 BL Loan 48.13/25, fol. 220r, autograph letter from Novello to Watts dated 16 January
1833.

41 BL Loan 48.2/2, Directors' Meeting, 27 April 1833, 'Letter read from Mr. Novello
presenting the score of his New Composition.'

42 BL Loan 48.13/25, fol. 224r–v, autograph letter from Novello dated Friday 19 April
1833.

43 BL Loan 48.2/2, Directors' Meeting, 27 April 1833.

44 Ibid., Directors' Meeting, 15 May 1833, 'Letter read from Mr Bishop. Resolved that
Messrs Bishop and Novello be written to stating that in consequence of their Compositions
having been Completed so late in the Season the Directors must postpone the performance of
them to next Season when they may appoint a Trial Night for them.'

45 BL Loan 48.13/4, *Original Letters BERI–BOY*, fol. 96r. Letter from Bishop to Watts
dated 17 January [1833]. Note that Foster calculates that Bishop made 39 appearances 'at
the piano' and as conductor between 1817 and 1845 (Foster, *History*, p. 535).

be rehearsed on the 2d. trial night. I shall be obliged if they will have
the goodness to let it be performed entirely by *English* Singers, as I wish
to shew that we can do very well without the assistance of *Foreigners*.

If there be no objections on the part of the Directors, I should prefer
having my little Composition performed by the following singers

2 Soprani—Miss Clara Novello & Miss H. Cawse
2 Tenors—Messrs. Vaughan & Bennett (or Mr. Horncastle)
2 Basses—Mr. H. Phillips ('Uberto'—Principal Bass) Mr Alfred
Novello.

I mention my son Alfred, as I know that he will be happy to give his
gratuitous services to the Society on the occasion, unless the Directors
sh[oul]d think proper to gratify him by an admission to the Concerts
this Season, for one of his Sisters, as a token of their approbation.[46]

Arrangements for the two trial nights, between which the remaining
commissions were to be divided, were finalised on 16 January 1834.[47] *The
Spectator* made its feelings clear in what it omitted from its comments about
Novello's new piece following the trial night on Thursday 13 February 1834:

three of the new vocal pieces were rehearsed, and English musicians,
after having suffered a twenty years' exclusion from this orchestra,
were suffered to exhibit either their strength or their weakness. The
first piece was a Sestetto by NOVELLO, in which the soprano voices
sustain the prominent parts; the second a Motet, chiefly choral, by
HORSLEY. We believe (but we speak with some hesitation) that the
language of the first was Italian, and the second Latin. To these
succeeded a Cantata by BISHOP, entitled 'The Seventh Day', the
words selected from *Paradise Lost*. As these compositions have sever-
ally to want the decision of the Directors, we had intended, as before,
to abstain from giving any opinion on their character and merits; but
it would be an act of injustice to BISHOP to withhold the expression of
our admiration at the masterly way in which he has treated a theme of
such matchless grandeur, and demanding such a varied combination
of vocal and instrumental power. We reserve a more detailed examination of this composition for a future occasion, when a second
hearing will enable us to analyze [*sic*] and describe it as it deserves.
The instrumental pieces subjected to the ordeal of a trial were Overtures by LATOUR, RITTER, and GRIESBACH. Whether they were all of
sterling ore, and worthy to be issued from the Philharmonic mint,
remains to be seen. Like other great judges, we may be allowed to
doubt.[48]

---

46 BL Loan 48.13/25, fol. 225r–v, autograph letter from Novello dated 29 January 1834.
47 BL Loan 48.2/2, 16 January 1834. 'Resolved that the following Pieces be tried on the 6th
Feb viz: Mr Potter's Symphony, Mr Lucas' Overture, Mr Mendelssohn's Overture,
Romberg's Overture, and Berlioz Overture. ... Resolved that the Vocal Compositions be
rehearsed on the 2[n].d Trial Night.' 30 January 1834, 'Resolved that the 2d Trial Night be
fixed for Thursday the 13th Inst. Resolved that Mr Horsley and Mr Bishop be written to
acquainting them of it.'
48 *The Spectator*, no. 294, for the week ending Saturday, 15 February 1834, p. 155, col. 1.

So it was that the first three concerts of the 1834 season each included at least one of the flood of home-grown commissions. Bishop's *The Seventh Day* initiated the process on 3 March.[49] This was, of course, neither his first nor last taste of compositional glory at the Philharmonic. His cantatas *Paradise* (6 June 1836) and the *Departure from Paradise* (16 May 1853) featured, along with some recitatives and arias, over the next 20 years.[50] By dint of gushing compliments, Bishop tried to gain permission to have *The Seventh Day* performed at Worcester in 1833 before its Philharmonic premiere. We can only admire his doomed efforts in this regard since he must have known that the rejection of his petition was a foregone conclusion:

> You have already, Gentlemen, by your vote, in employing Professors to write for your Concerts, evinced a liberality which, as regards the principle, I must warmly applaud, and which, as regards myself, individually, I acknowledge with every sentiment of pride and gratitude: and, I should hope, that your generous aid of the Musical Art would not consider itself bound to stop at that point, but, that when it is in your power ... as in the present case, still further to assist in the possible chance of doing some service to the Professional reputation of a Brother Professor (and it is that alone, in this instance, not pecuniary gain, he seeks) you will not reject the petition I now make to you.[51]

It was, however, not until after the *Seventh Day* concert that Novello's cantata was formally scheduled for the next one, held a fortnight later.[52] Novello wrote to William Watts asking whether *Rosalba* would indeed be included in the next concert and saying that Clara would otherwise accept an alternative engagement.[53] Following the trial nights, each composer was asked to appoint the leader he preferred for his concert.[54] It appears

---

49   Performed on 1 March 1834 as the result of a resolution made at the Directors' Meeting of 17 February 1834, when it was 'Resolved that Mr Bishop's Cantata be performed on the first night' (BL Loan 48.2/2).
50   BL Add. MS 41779, *The Philharmonic Society Extracts from 1813 to 1860*, fols 4r, 13r, 23v, 25r–26v *et passim*.
51   This obsequious letter (BL Loan 48.13/4, letter from Bishop dated 26 June 1833) and the Society's refusal (BL Loan 48.3/1, Annual General Meeting, 26 June 1833) are evidence of Bishop's nerve.
52   BL Loan 48.2/2, 5 March 1834, 'Resolved that Mr. Novello's Cantata be performed at the 2[n]d Concert.'
53   BL Loan 48.13/25, fol. 228r–v, autograph letter from Novello dated 4 March 1834. '... Can you let me know when my Piece is likely to be brought forward? or whether the Directors will want Clara for the second Concert? My reason for asking is – that she has been offered an engagement for the 17th of this month but I will not allow her to accept it until I know whether her attendance will be required at the Philharmonic, as I wish to give the latter engagement the preference. Accept my best acknowledgements for your polite and kind behaviour to my little Daughter, yesterday Evening ...'.
54   BL Loan 48.2/2, 10 February 1834, 'Resolved that the Authors of the new Compositions be written to requesting them to appoint leaders as they may prefer.'

too that the hurdle of the trial, frequently an insuperable barrier to public performance, was a formality for these commissioned works – having paid for them, the Directors had to include them.

Novello's final preparations were stressful. In his letter to Watts (undated but following one dated 12 March) he said that he would do his best to meet the deadline with the help of his own copyist.[55] The Account Book shows that Novello received the £35 promised and his copyist got five shillings.[56]

By 1899 *Rosalba* was gathering dust in a cupboard labelled 'obsolete music' in the Society's library; it appears to have had no further public performances after its premiere.[57] The text is taken from a 'manuscript dramatic sketch' by Guarini.[58] Three main sources are extant: the original autograph manuscript score, the obbligato bass part in Dragonetti's hand, and the printed edition.[59] The last was produced and published by J. Alfred Novello in 1840 in a piano reduction with the announcement that orchestral parts could be obtained from the publishers, along with 'the whole of V. Novello's Musical Works'.[60] Figure 11.1 shows the title page of the printed edition.

Novello engaged in a revision process between trial and first performance.[61] It is unclear whether the modifications were made of his own volition or strongly suggested to him by the Directors. His request for the return of his score from the Society in order to put some amendments into effect demonstrates his keenness to take on board suggestions detailed in a letter from Moscheles dated 16 February 1834.[62] Moscheles' inventory of

---

55 BL Loan 48.13/25, fol. 222r (follows a letter about Clara dated 12 March 1833).

56 BL Loan 48.9/1, *Account Book 1813–66*. Listed in 1833 under 'Compositions'.

57 BL Loan 48.11/6, *Catalogues of Music: Incipits of Vocal Works in the Royal Philharmonic Society's Collection,* fol. 1v. Reads: 'Memorandum/As there is not room in the "Vocal" cupboard I have moved some of the music into another cupboard calling the cupboard "obsolete" music as it is very seldom used – Alfred Mapleson 1899.' *Rosalba* was allocated number 1763 in this catalogue. For details of the cataloguing history of the Society's library see Alec Hyatt King, 'The Library of the Royal Philharmonic Society', *British Library Journal*, 2/1 (Spring 1935), pp. 1–24.

58 BL Loan 4.469**, in Novello's hand, fol. 1r.

59 Ibid., oblong folio 30cm × 26cm. Autograph manuscript of Novello's *Rosalba*. Published vocal/piano reduction of which a copy survives as part of the British Library's printed music collection. Shelfmark: H. 2831. j (21). The manuscript double bass part in Domenico Dragonetti's hand, annotated by Novello in 1846 after his friend's death, can be found in the collection at Queen's University, Belfast.

60 Available for 6 shillings from 67 Frith Street, Soho.

61 See BL Loan 48.13/25, autograph letter from Novello to Watts, dated Tuesday Morning 4 March 1834. 'Will you be so obliging as to tell Mr. Goodwin to send me the Score and Parts of my "Rosalba"? as I think I can improve the effect of the first Air and Recitative, – by a few curtailments. I will make what little alterations I may consider adviseable [*sic*], & return the Copies to you directly they have been made to correspond with the Score.'

62 BL Add. MS 11730, letter from Moscheles to Novello, dated 16 February 1834, fol. 135r.

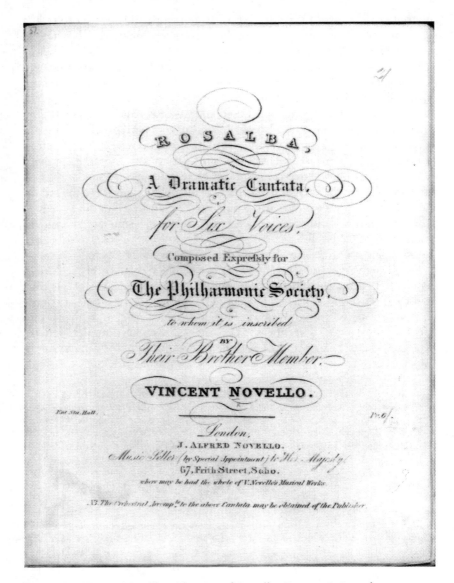

Fig. 11.1   Vincent Novello: title page of *Rosalba*. By permission of the British Library

small changes was prefaced by an endorsement of the composition that must have filled Novello with pride: 'I feel much flattered by the contents of your note and can only express the general opinion of the best judges in our profession by saying that your Rosalba is a Composition of distinguished merit as regards unity and chasteness of Style.'[63]

Amusingly, despite the fact that he had been commissioned as part of a drive to acknowledge local composers, and his own desire to use English soloists, Novello made great play of his Italian heritage not only in the inscription on the autograph orchestral score,[64] but also in his choice of libretto. The cantata comprises five sections (recitative–aria–recitative–aria–sextet) and involves six characters: Rosalba (soprano), Costanza (soprano), Licida (tenor), Orlando (tenor), Silvestro (bass), Uberto (bass). Tonally, the cantata shifts from the opening G minor (mirroring Rosalba's despondent belief at the outset that her husband is dead) to the B flat major of the denouement in which her fears prove to be unfounded. The leading ladies, Rosalba and Costanza, share the same voice range and each sings a recitative and aria, but Rosalba has the dominant role – not least in the length of her solo contribution. The musical language employed by Novello is generally simple and reveals a vocabulary strongly influenced by Mozart and Haydn. Example 11.1 gives an example of the melodic lines typical of the work.

Scored for an orchestra of double woodwind (no oboes – despite their availability in the Philharmonic line-up), four horns (2 in B♭, 2 in G) and strings, it includes a piano part intended for rehearsal use only.[65] The orchestral version of the opening to Rosalba's aria shows Novello's conservative use of the woodwind – for example, the flutes simply reinforce the violins at cadence points. The closing Sestetto requires the additional forces of trumpets in B♭, trombones and timpani in B♭ and F.

Ex. 11.1   Vincent Novello, *Rosalba* (Aria di Costanza, bars 5–12)

63   Ibid., fols 135r–136v.
64   BL Loan 4.469**, oblong folio, fol. 2v, 'La Musica composta da Vincenzo Novello'.
65   See Novello's proviso ibid., fol. 6v.

Ex. 11.2   Vincent Novello, *Rosalba* (double bass obbligato from the final movement, bars 150–56)

Novello's inclusion of an obbligato part for Dragonetti in the closing sextet is no surprise. The role given to the double bass is one of momentum and drive – the line draws on the range available from Dragonetti's three-stringed instrument and the rhythmic punctuation natural to his bowing style (see Ex. 11.2). Novello continued in this vein in his aria 'Thy Mighty Power', written for Clara and Dragonetti and performed at the Hanover Square Rooms on 24 April 1837.[66]

We know that the concert on 17 March began at 8 pm and involved a 30-minute rendition of Beethoven's Eighth Symphony in Act 1.[67] *Rosalba* premiered as the penultimate piece in Act 1, sandwiched between Spohr's *Nonetto* and Weber's overture *The Ruler of the Spirits*.[68] *The Spectator* was unimpressed and concluded that the instrumental works had stolen the show:

> Mr. NOVELLO'S new Cantata contains some agreeable traits, with one striking feature – a Sestetto with an obligato part for DRAGONETTI: and any thing that calls *him* into more than usual activity is sure to be welcome to the audience. The subject of this piece is not very happily chosen; as two long recitatives and airs for soprano voices of the same character follow in immediate succession, necessarily producing a monotonous effect. Is it possible for GUARINI (who is said to be the author of the words) to have written this kind of doggerel?[69]

The *Morning Post* both agreed and disagreed with this review:

---

66 Fiona Palmer, *Domenico Dragonetti in England 1794–1846: the Career of a Double Bass Virtuoso* (Oxford: Clarendon Press, 1997), pp. 198–99. Note that the review stated, rather damningly, that 'the chief merit in this song lies in the accurate knowledge the composer has displayed of the genius and resources of the double-bass'.

67 See BL k.6.d.3, *Sir George Smart's Annotated Programmes* (5 volumes), vol. 3, no. 29, Second Concert, Monday 17 March 1834.

68 'Musical', *Morning Post*, no. 19745, Friday, 21 March 1834, p. 5, col. 4.

69 *The Spectator*, no. 299, for the week ending Saturday, 22 March 1834, p. 275, cols 1–2.

> The dramatic cantata savoured too strongly of MOZART to pass for a very original composition; its counterpoint was figurative and smooth, the vocal parts well suited to the voices, and the subject of the drama well conceived. The obligato part for the double bass was, to our taste, totally ineffective and superfluous.[70]

To add insult to injury, the review ended by putting the programme as a whole into perspective: 'The instrumental pieces were selected with judgement and afforded a striking contrast to each other. The vocal music was dull.'[71] Sadly for Novello, *The Atlas* also found his work derivative:

> Mr. NOVELLO'S dramatic cantata evinces an intimate acquaintance with the styles of MOZART and GLUCK – but it is deficient in originality; while the excellent taste of the passages must be confessed – it must also be confessed that they have all been heard before. Of compositions made out of other compositions, there are already more than enough, what is wanted in our composers is something of original thought, and this we appear to look for in vain. The cantata consists of a *recitative* and *aria agitato*, in G minor (most admirably performed by MISS NOVELLO); a *recitative and air* in the major (tastefully sung by Mrs BISHOP), and a concluding movement for six voices, with *contra basso obligato*, in B flat. The music, formed as it is on two excellent schools of composition, was heard with complacency, and received the degree of approbation which it deserved.[72]

Bishop's *Seventh Day*, on the other hand, had launched the season to plaudits, not least because of the source of its text – the seventh book of Milton's *Paradise Lost*.[73] Indeed, in an outburst of praise, *The Times* declared:

> This is a composition every way calculated to do honour to the state of the art in this country, and has seldom been surpassed in any other for variety of effect, splendour, and even, in some passages, sublimity. Mr Bishop displays his knowledge, without servilely copying them, of all the great masters of his day.[74]

We must remember that these commissions from local composers were heard for the first time by those who regarded a concert whose programme limited the number of works by the great German masters as dull and inadequate.[75] Horsley's effort was to provoke even less praise than Novello's –

---

70 See above, n. 68.

71 Ibid.

72 'Music and Musicians', *The Atlas*, no. 410/ix, Sunday, 23 March 1834, p. 188, cols 2–3.

73 For example, *The Spectator*, no. 297, for the week ending Saturday, 8 March 1834, pp. 225–26.

74 'Philharmonic Society', *The Times*, no. 15418, Thursday, 6 March 1834, p. 5, col. 5.

75 'Musical', *Morning Post*, no. 19761, Wednesday, 9 April 1834, p. 3, cols 3–4, review of the third Philharmonic Society concert.

how disappointed he must have been to find himself written off by *The Spectator* for his motet *Exaltabo Te*,[76] performed in the third concert just before Mendelssohn's latest overture, *Die Schöne Melusine*. And all the more so when we consider his active promotion of awareness of the sad lot of British composers during the 1830s.[77] Griesbach's overture, as the finale of the concert, was only pitied: 'MENDELSSOHN'S new Overture is full of originality and beauty, and of those felicitous groupings of the wind instruments which always distinguish his compositions, while they equally evidence the skill as the genius of their author. GRIESBACH'S Overture ought to have had a better situation.'[78]

In conclusion, it is worth remembering that, in general, Novello was on the sidelines and not a leader in the direction of a Society which both mirrored and shaped the musical tastes and expectations of the metropolis. As a composer he demonstrates little originality – his voice is not distinctive. Paradoxically, it is clear that *Rosalba* could only have emanated from his pen. With both his daughter and his friend Dragonetti in mind he wrote for people he knew in styles that he favoured. The libretto furnished a story founded on family values and the power of good over evil. His diffidence in referring to his 'little cantata' is telling.[79] Bishop, by contrast, saw himself, and was seen, as a possible ambassador for English composition and accorded far greater attention than Novello.

Novello's seemingly unquenchable thirst for editing and antiquarian pursuits together with his life as an organist mean that his songs, glees and *Rosalba* are evidence of only brief interludes in a career notable for its single-minded and relentless effort to share his discovery of the music of the past with a wider audience. The fact that he never quite found a niche in the running of the Philharmonic Society may or may not have grieved him. There is no questioning that the organisation provoked heated debate both internal and external. The politics of Directorial election were multilayered in their complexity.[80] Not all the pieces of the jigsaw

---

76 BL Loan 4.277**, original manuscript full score 'Composed by Wm Horsley. M.B.Oxon'. 'Exaltabo te Deus', motet no. 4 for six voices and orchestra, 1834. Loan 4.2148* is the same work, vocal score copy. Griesbach's Symphony No. 2, Op. 23, 1832 'Composed expressly for the Philharmonic Society of London', survives as Loan 4.112. Loan 4.643 is his overture 'Titania', Op. 33, 1848 'Dedicated to the Philharmonic Society of London'. See BL Loan Catalogue.

77 McVeigh, 'The Society of British Musicians', pp. 148–49 *et passim*.

78 *The Spectator*, no. 302, for the week ending Saturday, 12 April 1834, p. 346, cols 1–2.

79 BL Loan 48.13/25, autograph letter from Novello to Sir George Smart, dated Monday evening, 10 March 1834, fol. 229r–v. Concludes: 'I will also send the <u>words</u> of my little "Dramatic Cantata" – to Mr. Watts ready for the Printers of the Phil[harmoni]c. Society.'

80 See, for example, BL Loan 48.13/24, fols 131r–132v. Letter from Moscheles dated 5 April 1841 in which he details the reasons behind his refusal to perform that season.

are available despite the riches of the Society's archive. However, reflected in Novello's story are the struggles of all musicians determined to carve themselves a niche and sustain an income from freelance work under-pinned by labyrinthine networks of contacts. The enterprising musician in the marketplace undoubtedly walked a perilous tightrope where rumour and speculation, unfavourable critical reception and the views of the press in general were crucial factors.

When the acidity of the criticisms levelled at his *Rosalba* had dimin-ished, Novello knew that his creative association with the Society assured him a place in the history books alongside many of his idols.

An AHRB Small Grant in the Creative and Performing Arts (2000–2001) made the research for this article possible. A critical biography of Vincent Novello (1781–1861) is planned for completion in 2004.

CHAPTER TWELVE

The Oxford Commemorations and Nineteenth-Century British Festival Culture

Susan Wollenberg

In his recent edition of the *John Marsh Journals*, Brian Robins notes: 'Large[-]scale festivals became an increasingly familiar part of provincial music making during the 18th century, particularly in cathedral cities.'[1] The musical festival, not exclusively but very characteristically an English phenomenon, had developed a varied and widespread profile by 1800, and continued to evolve thereafter. Some of the connotations of the festival genre included a religious or sacred element, as with the St Cecilia Festivals[2] and the Three Choirs;[3] and a specific charitable purpose (as with these, and also the annual Festival of the Sons of the Clergy at St Paul's),[4] the religious and the charitable elements often being combined. Further, they evoked a strong sense of corporate effort, as Roger Fiske observed apropos of the Three Choirs at 'Gloucester, Worcester and Hereford, whose geographical proximity – they are all within 30 miles of each other – made it practicable for their choirs to combine once a year to present for charity more ambitious music than any one of them could have achieved on its own',[5] and a focus on particular musical genres or specific pieces – *Messiah*, and the oratorio in general, spring to mind – which became enshrined in the festival tradition.

---

1   *The John Marsh Journals: the Life and Times of a Gentleman Composer (1752–1828)*, ed., introd. and annot. Brian Robins (New York: Pendragon Press, 1998), p. 58 n.

2   From the late seventeenth century onwards the Cecilian tradition was established in London and the provinces: see especially Tony Trowles, 'The Musical Ode in Britain *c.* 1670–1800' (D.Phil. diss., University of Oxford, 1992).

3   The meeting of the three choirs was founded as early as *c.*1713. See H. Watkins Shaw, *The Three Choirs Festival: the Official History of the Meetings of the Three Choirs of Gloucester, Hereford and Worcester, c. 1713–1953* (Worcester and London: E. Baylis & Son, 1954).

4   On this 'annual service to raise funds for the relief of distress among the families of clergy' see 'Festival', 3, in *The New Grove Dictionary of Music and Musicians*, 2nd edn, ed. Stanley Sadie and John Tyrrell (London: Macmillan, 2001), vol. 8, pp. 735–36.

5   H. Diack Johnstone and Roger Fiske, *The Eighteenth Century*, Blackwell History of Music in Britain, vol. 4 (Oxford: Blackwell, 1990), p. 20.

Further ingredients of the genre included the periodic injection of visiting talent into the local concert scene, which was a characteristic of the various annual festivals; and the integration of the musical performances into the larger festival context, alongside diverse entertainments and observances; together with, obviously, an association with particular dates or times of year, perhaps linked with special occasions in the calendar. All these ingredients – and more – were seen in nineteenth-century Oxford. Clearly all this represents a distinctive culture, and its widespread adoption and development created a plethora of subcultures. Among others, festivals are documented in Birmingham from 1768; in Chester from 1772; Norwich from 1788; and Salisbury and Winchester.[6]

From the late seventeenth century, with the opening of the Sheldonian Theatre as the University's Assembly Room, and the inception of the Encaenia (originally the ceremony for the dedication of the Theatre, later connected with the giving of honorary degrees), the Oxford commemorative and degree ceremonies developed as a festive occasion combining ceremonial and music. The Commemoration celebrations had acquired the distinctive character of a musical festival from the early eighteenth century onwards. The 1733 'Act', when Handel was invited to lend musical lustre to the proceedings, and his *Athalia* was premiered in the Sheldonian Theatre – and when various other works by him were performed in Oxford over a period of several days in a variety of locations – set a standard against which subsequent celebrations were judged.[7] The 1733 Act also set the enduring fashion for Handel's music in Oxford, which thus turned from a fashion into a tradition.[8] The nineteenth-century Commemorations, descended from the legendary 1733 occasion, derived their richness of character partly from a combination of continuity and change. Another landmark event, Haydn's visit to Oxford for the Commemoration festivities in July 1791 ('as the University of Oxford

---

6   See Douglas Reid and Brian Pritchard, 'Some Festival Programmes of the Eighteenth and Nineteenth Centuries, iv: Birmingham', *R.M.A. Research Chronicle*, 8 (1970), pp. 1–33; Joseph C. Bridge, *A Short Sketch of the Chester Musical Festivals, 1772 to 1829* (Chester: Phillipson and Golder, 1891); Trevor Fawcett, *Music in Eighteenth-Century Norwich and Norfolk* (Norwich: Centre of East Anglian Studies, University of East Anglia, 1979); and (on Salisbury and Winchester) Robins, *The John Marsh Journals, passim*.

7   For details, see inter alia Susan Wollenberg, *Music at Oxford in the Eighteenth and Nineteenth Centuries* (Oxford: Oxford University Press, 2001), chap. 2, esp. pp. 23 ff.

8   Cf. Susan Wollenberg, 'Handel in Oxford: the Tradition c. 1750–1850', *Göttinger Händel-Beiträge*, 9 (2002), pp. 161–76. The great Handel Commemorations of 1784 and following were not a totally new phenomenon but a vastly enlarged version of existing structures.

... is too great an Object for me not to see before I leave England'),[9] consolidated his position (already well established even prior to his visit) in the Oxford concert repertoire for decades afterwards.

If the Commemoration celebrations represented, academically, musically and socially, a high point in the university calendar and in the life of the city, then the occasions featuring the installation of a new Chancellor of the University (or of some other high-ranking officer) constituted a particularly notable landmark. Among the ways in which these festivities developed their own culture were the varied commercial aspects, ranging from lodgings for the many visitors[10] to the sale of fashions (a kind of equivalent to hats for Ascot nowadays). Young Betty Flippant, in the ballad-opera *The Oxford Act* (which lampooned Handel's visit in 1733), bewailed to her undergraduate friend Dick Thoughtless the dent in her funds made by the need to purchase 'fine cloth[e]s' for the occasion.[11] If her real-life counterpart had been present in 1810 to witness the Installation of Lord Grenville as Chancellor she would have had ample opportunity to disburse her savings on a range of Installation fashions, as the advertisements in *Jackson's Oxford Journal* for 30 June 1810 show (see Fig. 12.1: the notion of 'linked' merchandise is not a modern invention).

Sir Henry Bishop in 1852, defining the duties attached to the Heather Chair of Music at Oxford (which he occupied from 1848 to 1855), mentioned that – apart from examining the musical degree exercises –

> The Professor of Music at Oxford has also to be present at the Annual Commemoration, and preside at the Organ in the Theatre on that occasion ...
> ... also 'to compose for and conduct all musical performances ordained by, or connected with, the Academical regulations', such as Installation Odes, &c.[12]

The ceremonial Ode had traditionally featured in the Commemoration proceedings – the odes produced by William and Philip Hayes, for example, in the eighteenth century were partly in this specific genre – and the Heather Professors in the first half of the nineteenth century continued, as Bishop indicated, to fulfil the role of purveyor of occasional music along these lines.

---

9   Quoted from *Jackson's Oxford Journal*, 28 May 1791, in H.C. Robbins Landon, *Haydn in England 1791–1795*, Haydn Chronicle and Works, vol. 3 (London: Thames & Hudson, 1976), p. 80.

10   One visitor to the city for the Commemoration of 1763 remarked (*Gentleman's Magazine*, 33 (1763), pp. 348–49) on 'providing ourselves with lodgings, (which indeed was no easy matter to do)', on the occasion.

11   *The Oxford Act* (London, 1733), Oxford, Bodleian Library, MS Gough Oxf. 59, Act I, scene 2.

12   *Royal Commission on Oxford University. Evidence* (Parliamentary Papers 1852), p. 265.

OXFORD
Grand Musical Festival,

For the Public Reception of the new CHANCELLOR,
The Right Hon. Lord GRENVILLE,
Is fixed for the following days—JULY 3d, 4th, 5th, and 6th.

PRINCIPAL VOCAL PERFORMERS,

Madame CATALANI,
Mrs. ASHE, and Mrs. BIANCHI;
Mr. BRAHAM,
Mr. W. KNYVETT, Mr. VAUGHAN, Mr. BELLAMY,
AND
Mr. BARTLEMAN.

Instrumental Performers,
Leader of the Band, Mr. CRAMER.
VIOLINS—Messrs. MARSHALL, MORALT, MAHON, STORM, LYONS, HERSCHELL, GRIESBACH, jun, TOMLINS, TIBBET, JUNG, HARDY, WHITE, SIKES, COLE, HATTON, &c. &c.
VIOLA—Messrs. R. ASHLEY, C. LINDLEY, WOODCOCK, and CHAPEL.
VIOLONCELLOS—Messrs. LINDLEY, REINAGLE, ASHLEY, and J. MARSHALL.
DOUBLE BASSES—Messrs. BOYCE, SMART, ADDISON, and HALDON.
FLUTES—Mr. JACKSON, &c.
OBOES—Messrs. GRIESBACH and OLIVER.
CLARIONETS—Messrs. HALDON and PHILLIPS.
BASSOONS—Messrs. HOLMES, FELDON, and WILKINS.
TRUMPETS—Messrs. SCHMIDT and DROVER.
TROMBONES—Messrs. DRESSLER, FLACK, & ZWINGMAN.
HORNS—Messrs. LEANDER.
SERPENT—Mr. HATTON.
DOUBLE DRUMS—Mr. JENKINSON.

FIRST CONCERT, Tuesday, July 3.
ACT I.

OVERTURE. *Sampson.*	Handel.
RECIT.—Mr. VAUGHAN. "This day a solemn feast."	
CHORUS. "Awake the trumpet's lofty sound."	Handel.
SONG—Mrs. ASHE. "Pious orgies." *Jud. Macc.*	Handel.
SONG—Mr. BARTLEMAN. *Tempest.*	Purcell.
"Arise, ye subterranean winds."	
QUARTETT and CHORUS. *Te Deum.*	Graun.
"Te gloriosus apostolorum Chorus."	
SONG—Mr. BRAHAM. "Questo è Torso."	Zingarelli.
CONCERTO, Oboe—Mr. GRIESBACH.	
SCENA—Madame CATALANI. "Se Griselda."	Paer.
The NIGHTINGALE CHORUS. *Solomon.*	Handel.

ACT II.

Grand OVERTURE to Henry IV.	Martini.
QUARTETT—Madame CATALANI, Mrs. BIANCHI, Mr. BRAHAM, and Mr. BELLAMY.	Guglielmi.
"Perfido a questo excesso."	
SONG—Mr. BRAHAM.	Dr. Clark.
"The last words of Marmion."	
CHORUS. *Jud. Macc.* "O Father."	Handel.
MOTETT. "Methinks I hear."	Dr. Crotch.
OVERTURE and CHACONNE.	Jomelli.
SONG—Mr. BARTLEMAN. "O Lord, have mercy."	Pergolesi.
SONG—Madame CATALANI. "Ah ti nuova."	Mayer.
Grand CORONATION ANTHEM.	Handel.
"Zadock the priest."	

The Whole to be conducted by Dr. CROTCH.
The Orchestra will consist of more than a Hundred Performers.
Tickets, 10s. 6d. each, to be had of Messrs. Lock and Son, High-street, and of Mr. Thorp, Broad-street; Mr. Cooke, Mr. Parker, M. Bliss, and Robert Bliss, booksellers.
. The doors will be opened at Four, and the performances will begin at Five o'clock.

INSTALLATION.

THE Nobility and Gentry at Oxford, at the approaching ENCŒNIA, are respectfully informed, that on TUESDAY and FRIDAY Evenings (the first and last of the festival) there will be

BALLS AT THE TOWN HALL.

The Stewards will be named at the time.
Tickets to be had at the Star Inn.

INSTALLATION.
PERUKE & ORNAMENTAL HAIR MANUFACTORY,
HIGH-STREET, OXFORD.

A. ROUTLEDGE

MOST respectfully begs leave to return his sincere thanks to the Ladies and Gentlemen of the University and City of Oxford, and its vicinity, for the many favours he has experienced, and to inform them, that he has just received a large and fashionable assortment of LADIES' HEAD DRESSES, both DRESS and UNDRESS GENTLE-MEN'S PATENT PERUKES, ROYAL BANDEAUX

INSTALLATION.

MRS. GRIFFITH begs leave to return her sincere thanks to the Ladies of Oxford and its vicinity for past favours, and informs them, she is returned from London, where she has been selecting a new and elegant assortment of
Fashionable Millinery, Fancy Dresses, &c.
with which her Rooms are now open; and she trusts, on inspection, the above articles will be found worthy of their patronage.—A great variety of Black and White Lace Dress Shawls, Mantles, Scarfs, &c.
High-street, Oxford, June 30, 1810.

Mrs. ALLEN, CUTLER, &c.
HIGH-STREET, ABINGDON,

EMBRACES this opportunity of returning her sincere thanks to her Friends and the Public, for the favour and support which she has experienced, since the death of her husband, and respectfully informs them, that she has disposed of her STOCK IN TRADE to Mr. JOHN BAYNE, CUTLER, from Oxford, whom she earnestly begs to recommend to their notice as her successor.

JOHN BAYNE, CUTLER,
Successor to Mrs. ALLEN, High-street, Abingdon,

RESPECTFULLY informs his Friends, the Friends of Mrs. ALLEN, and the Public, that he has taken to her shop, which he purposes to furnish immediately with every article in the CUTLERY LINE, procured from the first manufactories and best markets, and humbly solicits a continuance of their favour and support, which will be ever gratefully acknowledged.
Cutlery in all its branches executed in the best style.
The Stock of Mrs. ALLEN, consisting of Knives, Scissor Buckles, Buttons, &c. &c. is selling off CONSIDERABLY UNDER PRIME COST.
Abingdon, June 30, 1810.

ON THE THIRD OF JULY
(Being the first day of the GRAND MUSICAL FESTIVAL, for the reception of the new CHANCELLOR)

WILL BE PUBLISHED, BY TAYLOR,
Drawing Master, Exhibitor in the Royal Academy, &c.
ALL SAINTS', OXFORD,
A GENERAL VIEW OF

THE HIGH-STREET, OXFORD.

HUMBLY DEDICATED TO
The Right Hon. Lord GRENVILLE, Chancellor;
The Right Hon. Lord ELDON, High Steward;
The DOCTORS; and other MEMBERS of the University of Oxford,

	£ s. d.	PRICE.	£ s. d.
Prints	0 15 0 each.	Coloured ditto	1 1 0
Proofs	1 5 0 ditto.		

The HIGH-STREET, of Oxford, from its peculiar and characteristic beauties, cannot fail to excite universal admiration. Mr. T. flatters himself that, as it has been his aim to exhibit a correct representation of this magnificent Street in all its most prominent features, from a point generally allowed to be the best, this View will be found not unworthy of the attention of the public.

☞ LIKENESSES taken in profile shade.
Prints lately published by TAYLOR.—The EAST VIEW of BRAZENOSE COLLEGE—the magnificent WEST FRONT of CHRIST CHURCH—a VIEW of WINCHESTER COLLEGE—a PAIR, the CANDELABRA, in the Radcliffe Library—and the ACADEMIC COSTUME of the UNIVERSITY of OXFORD, twenty-five Plates.—A Pair of CABINET PICTURES to be disposed of.

VIEW OF THE
HIGH-STREET, OXFORD,
Dedicated, by permission, to the Rev. JOHN PARSONS, D.D.
Vice-Chancellor of the University of Oxford.

JAMES WYATT,
CARVER, GILDER, and PICTURE-FRAME MAKER,
High-street, Oxford;

RESPECTFULLY informs the Noblemen and Gentlemen of the University, and the Public, that the PICTURE of the HIGH-STREET, from the pencil of that eminent Artist, JOSEPH MALLORD WILLIAM TURNER, Esq. R.A. *Professor of Perspective to the Royal Academy,* is now exhibiting in his Shop, for the inspection of the Subscribers, and those Noblemen and Gentlemen who will do him the honour to call at his house. The Picture will be engraved by the celebrated Artists, Messrs. MIDDIMAN and PYE, who have engaged to execute it in the LINE MANNER, and in their BEST STYLE.

	£ s. d.
The price to Subscribers,	1 11 6
Proof Impressions,	3 3 0

The Proprietor begs to observe, that the Prints will be delivered in the order in which they are subscribed.

Fig. 12.1 Advertisement for the 1810 Oxford 'Grand Musical Festival'. *Jackson's Oxford Journal*, 30 June 1810

Crotch's 1810 setting of the Ode for the Installation of Lord Grenville as Chancellor is apparently missing, presumed lost (notwithstanding the information printed in Rennert and in the *New Grove*, 2nd edn).[13] However, his 'Motett' *Methinks I hear the full celestial choir*, which was included in Act II of the Commemoration concert on Tuesday, 3 July, survives. Crotch's setting went through several stages. The first version in the Oxford Harmonic Society volumes is intimate in style, although scored for eight voices; a later version in the Harmonic Society source is more 'artistic' and ambitious, though for five voices only.[14] (Both these settings bear the title 'Glee', and are unaccompanied.) Finally, the five-voice version (for Canto, Alto, Tenor, and Bass 1 and 2) appeared with instrumental accompaniment, published later by the Regent's Harmonic Institution, under the title 'Motett': its opening, which starts with voices alone, is given in Example 12.1. Not only does the grandeur of this setting seem appropriate to its performance (in the Sheldonian Theatre) as part of the Commemoration programme, but also it could be seen as conveying a message about the effect of the voices (the 'celestial choir'): this was not the first time, nor the last, that such associations had been suggested in Oxford.[15]

For the 1810 occasion Crotch's participation encompassed not only performances of his compositions, but also the role of conductor, with a dazzling row of principal vocal performers and an orchestra of over 100

Ex. 12.1 William Crotch, 'Methinks I hear the full celestial choir'

13 I am grateful to Peter Ward Jones for confirming this.

14 Oxford, Bodleian Library, MSS Tenbury 598–600 ('The Compositions of the Harmonic Society of Oxford established Aug. 23rd 1796, for the encouragement & improvement of musical composition').

15 On the death of the famed Oxford countertenor Walter Powell (who sang for Handel in 1733) an obituarist claimed that now 'To sing the everlasting birth; the choir of heav'n's compleat' (from a poem by 'an Oxford scholar', printed in the *Gentleman's Magazine*, 1744, and quoted in Daniel Lysons, *History of the Origin and Progress of the Meeting of the Three Choirs of Gloucester, Worcester and Hereford* (Gloucester: Walker, 1812), pp. 17–18).

players, 'The Whole to be conducted by Dr. CROTCH' (see the advertisement partially reproduced in Fig. 12.1 for further details). The report of
the 1810 Commemoration in the local press gives an overwhelming
impression of the grandeur of the occasion, although at this stage we find
relatively little detail on the musical content (this aspect of the reporting
was to be developed considerably during the course of the nineteenth
century: see further below). Although, with the early nineteenth-century
Commemorations, the programme of events began substantially on the
Tuesday, lasting throughout the week thereafter, the build-up to this
could occupy several days beforehand:

OXFORD,

SATURDAY, JULY 7.

> The expectation of a most numerous and distinguished body of visitors
> to our University, which had been so strongly and so generally felt
> throughout the country, was abundantly fulfilled during the late week.
> The first public reception of a Nobleman so eminently distinguished
> both as a Scholar and a Statesman as Lord Grenville was a circum-
> stance in itself sufficient to raise up, in the minds of many personages,
> an eager desire of evincing their respect towards his Lordship by
> attending upon this peculiar ceremony; while the Noble Chancellor,
> anxious, on his part, to testify every impression of gratitude towards
> his Alma Mater, which has so judiciously placed him in the first and
> most honourable situation she has the power of bestowing, solicited
> the presence of his illustrious relations and more immediate friends, for
> the purpose of swelling the pageantry and of lending an additional
> grace to the grandeur of this academical celebrity. Accordingly, so
> early as Saturday and Sunday visitors were pouring into the town, and
> during the whole of Monday the roads leading to Oxford in every
> direction were thronged with carriages ...[16]

Juxtaposed with the detailed listing of recipients of the honorary degree of
D.C.L., among them Charles and Henry Watkin Williams Wynn,[17] and Rear-
Admiral Sir William Sidney Smith ('TUESDAY, JULY 3 ... About ten Sir Sidney
Smith, in a full dress naval uniform, entered the Theatre, and as soon as his
person was recognised, the intrepid Admiral was conducted to a seat, amid the
long and loudest bursts of cordial approbation'), together with detailed listings
of the prize recitations ('Compositions', here referring to Latin and English
verse and essay prize submissions: 'Each of the Compositions was, in the
highest degree, creditable to the accomplishments of its respective Author, and
they were, individually, honoured by reiterated bursts of applause'), the

---

16 *Jackson's Oxford Journal*, 7 July 1810. The quotations regarding the 1810 event that
follow here are taken from this source.
17 These awards were thus made in their uncle's 'first year of office as chancellor of the
university' (*DNB*, vol. 21, p. 1171).

comments on the musical performances convey a comparable sense of the occasion and of their correspondingly enthusiastic reception:

> The ... ODE, composed on the occasion, by the Professor of Poetry, and set to music by Dr. Crotch ... commenced with a Recitative and Air from Mr. Bartleman. Mrs. Bianchi and Mr. Braham had also solos allotted them, which they executed with their usual stile [sic] of excellence. The chorusses [sic] were grand, and the whole was rapturously applauded.

The text of Crotch's Ode is reproduced in the *Journal* in full; beginning with ancient and Classical allusions, it closes in more specifically on the occasion itself, in the fourth stanza:

> ... ours the task to guard the glittering prize.
> Still as we tend the grateful toil,
> Princes lend the cheering smile;
> And Nobles of her loftiest line
> England sends to deck the shrine
> By wisdom, worth, and learning won,
> Where Oxford seats her patriot son ...

While the commentary on the musical substance of the performances is only slight, an impression of the context in which these took place, and of their effect, is nevertheless vividly evoked:

> [TUESDAY] About five in the evening the doors of the Theatre were again thrown open for the Grand Musical Festival ... and, in a short time, every part of that gorgeous structure was filled to an overflow by Ladies and Gentlemen of the first distinction. There is, perhaps, no building in Europe better accommodated for the advantageous display of a large assembly; and on the present occasion the Theatre, studded to the very top with beauty, rank, and fashion, presented a most striking and brilliant *coup d'oeil*. The performers, both vocal and instrumental, acquitted themselves to the entire satisfaction of their audience; and in conclusion Madame Catalani electrified the house, by singing, in her unrivalled manner, '*God save the King*'.

The comment on the concerts tends to get shorter as the events of successive days are described: for Wednesday evening the *Journal* noted simply that 'Dr. Crotch again conducted a Grand Musical Concert, and the "full melody of song" was poured forth to an enraptured and most numerous audience', while for Thursday evening it was reported even more succinctly that 'A third Grand Musical Festival, to a very numerous and splendid audience, closed the ceremonies of this day'. However, in mentioning the concluding concert on the Friday, the *Journal*'s reporter expanded somewhat on this final opportunity to express due appreciation and unabated enthusiasm for the music heard, and other entertainments:

> In the evening a fourth grand Musical Festival was performed in the
> Theatre, and the whole of the celebrated band, both vocal and instru-
> mental, had the happiness of giving universal and unqualified satisfaction
> to the judges and admirers of Music. The same evening the Town-Hall
> was again fitted up for a Subscription Ball, and at an early hour the room
> was honoured with an overflow of beauty, rank, and fashion.

Among the 'many ... illustrious visitors upon this grand occasion', besides
giving a selective list of members of the nobility, the reporter noted Dr
Charles Burney, together 'with many other eminent scholars'.

The final paragraphs of the *Journal*'s extensive report set the seal of
memorability on the 1810 event: 'the inaugural ceremonies have been
conducted throughout with the most majestic dignity, and the most brilliant
eclat. Many years will pass away before the splendour and general felicity of
this occasion are forgotten'; and (after a last elaborate tribute to the distinguished personage of the new Chancellor, including mention of 'the exquisite
delicacy of his taste'), a final burst of contextual detail was added: 'During
the week the visitors have been additionally entertained with Polito's unrivalled collection of Birds and Beasts ... and many other respectable Exhibitions, which have been largely and deservedly patronized.'

Just as the 1733 occasion featuring Handel's visit had served as a reference point for Commemoration celebrations later in the eighteenth
century, so the 1810 Commemoration was referred to subsequently, as in
1813, when the *Journal*'s reporter opened his account of that year's festivities (headed 'OXFORD, SATURDAY JULY 3') with the comments that

> The powerful attraction of a Musical Festival, comprising nearly all the
> vocal and instrumental talents of the country, has given an *eclat* and
> vivacity to the Commemoration of this year, which we do not recollect
> to have been equalled since the memorable Installation of our present
> Chancellor. For although the unfavourable nature of the weather has, of
> course, operated disadvantageously, yet the University has been exhila-
> rated by a very brilliant bumper of visitors; and we will accordingly
> proceed to mention, in a concise manner, the distinguishing features ...

While an extra-long paragraph was devoted to the distinguished
honorands on this occasion,[18] still ample space was found to include more

---

18 These included 'the Most Illustrious Prince Koslovski, Envoy from the Emperor of
Russia to the King of Sardinia', the Earl of Northesk (on whom see 'Carnegie, William',
DNB, vol. 3, p. 1048; the *Journal*'s account characterizes him as 'the only remaining
member ... of that unrivalled triumvirate, who presided over the glories of Trafalgar'), and
'the celebrated Warren Hastings', apropos of whom the reporter observed that 'doubtless,
the placable, unadorned, and venerable aspect of this good old man, his cruelly protracted
and most unmerited prosecution, the incalculable value of his services in India [etc.] ... all
conspired to swell that universal note of congratulation which, both upon his entrance and
exit, was reverberated from every point of the Theatre in frequent and fervid bursts of
applause' (*Jackson's Oxford Journal*, 3 July 1813).

than cursory details of the various concert performances. But before turning to these, it was noted that, following the recitation of the Prize Compositions, 'in conclusion' at this point 'Madame Catalani sang *Rule Britannia*, in a manner that is above all praise of words, and which can be fully appreciated by those alone who have had the happiness to be electrified by this gifted enchantress'.[19]

As for the 'Grand Musical Concerts' performed in the Theatre to 'very numerous and splendid audiences' on the evenings of the Monday, Tuesday and Thursday of Commemoration week in 1813, comparison with precedent ('the Band was more select and more powerful than we ever remember to have heard in this place') generated all the greater enthusiasm: 'the principal instrumental performers exerted their high talents in the concertos allotted to them with the greatest effect. The choruses were given in a style of superior excellence.' As regards the vocal soloists, the leading notice was given to the enchantments of Catalani:

> The unrivalled talents of Madame Catalani delighted all who heard her; and whether we consider the brilliancy of her Italian Bravura, or the dignified and impressive style in which she gave her English Recitative, she fully sustained the high character which her inimitable voice and wonderful execution have so unequivocally established.[20]

The comment immediately following this typical paean of praise for Catalani introduces a more unusual slant vis-à-vis performing practice and audience reception:

> At the same time we cannot but remark upon the good sense and taste of the audience in insisting upon the Messiah being opened by a tenor voice, and in its proper key; otherwise the contrast, intended by its great Composer to be produced, would have totally failed of its effect. Mr. Vaughan's talents were fully adequate to the arduous parts assigned to him, as the applause with which he was received abundantly testified.[21]

The line-up of soloists for the 1813 Commemoration included also Mrs Vaughan (whose 'sweet' and 'chaste' style of singing 'both in her songs and glees, were never shewn to greater advantage'); Miss Darby and Master Hobbs, both of whom 'acquitted themselves with great credit'; Mr Goss, singing with 'his usual sweetness and science'; and Mr Bellamy,

---

19 Ibid. A distinct shift in the language of criticism, away from the comparative restraint of eighteenth-century comment, is clearly discernible here. It would be interesting, too, to trace the tradition of singing 'Rule, Britannia!' on patriotically charged occasions such as this (beyond the original 1745 occasion).

20 *Jackson's Oxford Journal*, 3 July 1813.

21 Ibid. On the tradition of variant vocal scorings in *Messiah* generally, see the Peters Urtext edition by Donald Burrows (1987), pp. iii–v

Conductor, Sir H. R. BISHOP, Mus. Bac. Oxon,
Conductor of Her Majesty's Concerts of Ancient Music.

PROGRAMME.

FIRST CONCERT—Tuesday, June 18.
Handel's Sacred Oratorio, the MESSIAH.
PART I.

Overture.
Recit. accomp.—Mr. Bennett. "Comfort ye, my people." }
Air. "Every valley." }
Chorus. "And the glory of the Lord."
Recit. accomp.—Mr. Phillips. "Thus saith the Lord of Hosts." }
Air. "But who may abide." }
Chorus. "And he shall purify."
Recit.—Mr. Hawkins. "Behold, a virgin." }
Air and Chorus. "O thou that tellest." }
Recit. accomp.—Herr Staudigl. "For behold darkness." }
Air. "The people that walked in darkness." }
Chorus. "For unto us a child is born."
Pastoral Symphony.
Recit.—Madame Caradori Allan. "There were shepherds." }
Recit. accompanied. "And lo! the Angel." }
Recit. "And the angel said." }
Recit. accompanied. "And suddenly." }
Chorus. "Glory to God." }
Air.—Madame Caradori Allan. "Rejoice greatly."
Recit.—Mrs. Alfred Shaw. "Then shall the eyes of the blind." }
Air. "He shall feed his flock." }
Second Part.—Miss Rainforth. "Come unto him." }
Chorus. "His yoke is easy."

PART II.
Chorus. "Behold the Lamb of God."
Air.—Mrs. Alfred Shaw. "He was despised."
Chorus. "Surely he hath borne our griefs."
Chorus. "All we like sheep."
Recit. accompanied—Mr. Manvers. "All they that see him." }
Chorus. "He trusted in God."
Recit. accomp.—Mr. Manvers. "Thy rebuke."
Air. "Behold and see."
Recit. accomp.—Madame Caradori Allan. "He was cut off." }
Air. "But thou didst not leave his soul in hell." }
Semi-Chorus—The principal Singers. "Lift up your heads."
Full Chorus. "He is the King of Glory."
Recit.—Mr. Manvers. "Unto which of the angels."
Chorus. "Let all the angels."
Air.—Miss Rainforth. "How beautiful are the feet."
Quartet and Chorus. Miss M. Marshall, Mr. Hawkins, Mr. Manvers, and Mr. Phillips. "Their sound is gone out."
Air.—Herr Staudigl. "Why do the nations."
Chorus. "Let us break their bonds."
Recit.—Mr. Bennett. "He that dwelleth in heaven."
Air. "Thou shalt break them."
Grand Chorus. "Hallelujah!"

PART III.
Air.—Mad. Caradori Allan. "I know that my Redeemer liveth."
Quartet—Madame Caradori Allan, Mr. Hawkins, Mr. Manvers, and Mr. Phillips. "Since by man came death."
Chorus. "By man came also."
Quartet. "For as in Adam all die."
Chorus. "Even so in Christ."
Recit. accomp.—Mr. Phillips. "Behold! I tell you a mystery."
Air. "The trumpet shall sound."
(Trumpet obligata, Mr. Harper.)
Recit.—Mr. Hawkins. "Then shall be brought to pass."
Duet—Mr. Hawkins and Mr. Manvers.
"O death! where is thy sting?"
Chorus. "But thanks be to God."
Air.—Miss Marian Marshall. "If God be for us."
Grand Chorus—" Worthy is the Lamb."

FIRST GRAND MISCELLANEOUS CONCERT,
WEDNESDAY, June 19.
PART I.
Grand Sinfonia (in C. Minor.) ... ... Beethoven.
Glee—Mr. Hawkins, Mr. J. Bennett, Mr. Manvers, and Mr. Phillips. "By Celia's arbour." ... W. Horsley
Air—Herr Staudigl. "Revenge!" (*Pascal Bruno.*) J.L.Hatton
Quartetto—Miss Rainforth, Mrs. Alfred Shaw, Mr. Manvers, and Mr. Phillips. "Ecco quel fiero istante." Costa.
(Harp obligato, Mr. Chipp.)
Romance—Madame Dorus Gras. "Va, dit elle."
(*Robert le Diable.*) ... Meyerbeer.
Concerto, VIOLIN—Signor Camillo Sivori. ... Sivori.
Romanza—Signor Salvi. "Ciel pietoso."
(*Uberto di St. Bonifacio.*) ... Verdi.
Terzetto—Miss M. Marshall, Mr. J. Bennett, and Herr Staudigl. "Fia grata al ciel." (*Fidelio.*) Beethoven.
Cavatina—Mrs. Alfred Shaw. "Ah! s'estinta." Mercadante.
Duetto—Madame Dorus Gras and Signor Salvi.
"Chiedi all 'aura." (*L'Elisire d'Amore.*) Donizetti.
Sestetto—Miss Rainforth, Miss M. Marshall, Mr. Bennett, Mr. Manvers, Mr. Phillips, and Herr Staudigl.
"Ciel fatтом." (*Les deux journées.*) ... Cherubini.

PART II.
Overture—"A Midsummer Night's Dream."
Dr. F. Mendelssohn Bartholdy.
Scena—Miss Rainforth. "Ocean, thou mighty monster."
(*Oberon.*) ... ... Weber.
Recit.—Mr. Phillips. "At last from Aries." }
Air—"With joy the impatient husbandman." } Dr. Haydn.
(*Seasons.*) }
Quartetto—Madame Dorus Gras, Mrs. Alfred Shaw, Signor Salvi, and Herr Staudigl. "Cielo il mio labbro."
(*Bianca e Faliero.*) ... Rossini.
Recit.—Miss M. Marshall. "Sposa, Euridice." } Gluck.
And *Air*—"Che farò." (*Orfeo.*) }
Septetto, Concertante—Flute, Oboe, Clarionet, Bassoon, Horn, Trumpet, and Double Bass—Messrs. Card, Grattan Cooke, Williams, Baumann, Platt, Harper, and Signor Dragonetti.
Neukomm.
Recit.—Mad. Dorus Gras. "Du village voisin." }
And *Air*—"De l'enfance." (*Le Serment.*) } Auber.
Quintet—Miss Rainforth, Miss M. Marshall, Mrs. Alfred Shaw, Mr. Manvers, and Mr. Phillips.
"Zemira, children, all draw near."
(*Azor and Zemira.*) ... Dr. Spohr.
Recit. and *Cavatina*—Signor Salvi. "A quest' anima."
(*Gli Arabi nelle Gallie.*) ... Pacini.
Glee—Miss M. Marshall, Mr. Hawkins, Mr. Bennett, Mr. Manvers, and Mr. Phillips.
"O bird of Eve." ... The Earl of Mornington.
Air—Herr Staudigl. "O! wie will ich triumphiren."
(*Die Entführung aus dem Serail.*) Mozart.
Finale, Sestetto—Miss Rainforth, Miss M. Marshall, Mrs. Alfred Shaw, Mr. Bennett, Mr. Phillips, and Herr Staudigl.
"Alla bella Despinetta." (*Così fan tutte.*) Mozart.

SECOND GRAND MISCELLANEOUS CONCERT,
THURSDAY, June 20.
PART I.
Grand Sinfonia (in A.) ... ... Beethoven.
Air—Herr Staudigl. "In diesen heil'gen Hallen." Mozart.
(*Die Zauberflöte.*)
Recit. and *Air*—Mr. J. Bennett. ... ... Handel.
"Love sounds the alarm." (*Acis and Galatea.*)
Ballad—Mrs. Alfred Shaw. "By the sad sea waves." Benedict.
(*Brides of Venice.*)
Trio. (Two Violoncellos and Double Bass.) Corelli.
Mr. Lindley, Mr. W. Phillips, and Signor Dragonetti.
Air—Madame Dorus Gras. "En vain j'espere." Meyerbeer.
(*Robert le Diable.*)
Quintetto—Miss Rainforth, Miss M. Marshall, Mrs. Alfred Shaw, Signor Salvi, and Herr Staudigl.
"Hm! Hm! Perche menti." (*Il Flauto Magico.*) Mozart.
Recit.—Mr. Phillips. "Angel of life." ... } Dr Callcott
And *Air.* "Poor child of danger." ... }
(Bassoon obligato, Mr. Baumann.)
First Part of Grand Concerto. (Adagio and Rondo.)
VIOLIN—Signor Camillo Sivori. (*La Clochette.*) Paganini.
Duetto—Madame Dorus Gras and Miss Rainforth. Bellini.
"Deh con te." (*Norma.*)
Aria—Signor Salvi. "O cara immagine." ... Mozart.
(*Il Flauto Magico.*)
Terzetto—Miss M. Marshall, Mr. Bennett, and Mr. Phillips.
"Tremate!" ... ... Beethoven.

PART II.
Overture, Euryanthe. ... ... C. M. von Weber.
Glee—Mr. Hawkins, Mr. J. Bennett, Mr. Manvers, and Mr. Phillips. "Discord, dire sister." S. Webbe.
Duetto—Mrs. Alfred Shaw and Herr Staudigl.
"Bella imago." (*Semiramide.*) Rossini.
Scena—Mr. Manvers. "Oh! 'tis a glorious sight to see."
(*Oberon.*) C. M. von Weber.
Recit. and Air—Madame Dorus Gras.
"O tourment du veuvage." (*Le Cheval de Bronze.*) Auber.
Quartetto—Miss Rainforth, Miss M. Marshall, Signor Salvi, and Mr. Manvers.
"Mi manca la voce." (*Pietro L'Eremita.*) Rossini.
(Harp obligato, Mr. Chipp.)
Solo, VIOLIN—Signor Camillo Sivori.
(Andante, and "Carnaval de Venise.") Souvenir de Paganini.
Ballad—Miss Rainforth. "Auld Robin Gray." Rev. A. Leeves.
Aria—Signor Salvi. "A te dirò."
(*Roberto Devereux.*) ... ... Donizetti.
Glee—Miss M. Marshall, Mr. Hawkins, Mr. J. Bennett, and Mr. Phillips. "Ye spotted snakes." R. J. S. Stevens.
Recit. and Air—Herr Staudigl.
"O ruddier than the cherry." (*Acis and Galatea.*) Handel.
Finale, The National Anthem, "God save the Queen."
First verse—*Solo,* Miss M. Marshall.
Second verse—*Quartet* (double choir), Miss Rainforth, Miss Marshall, Mrs. Alfred Shaw, Mr. Hawkins, Mr. J. Bennett, Mr. Manvers, Mr. Phillips, and Herr Staudigl.
Third verse—*Solo,* Miss Rainforth.

Fig. 12.2   Advertisement for the 1844 Oxford Commemoration. *Jackson's Oxford Journal,* 15 June 1844

who 'exerted his powerful talents in a most masterly manner throughout a very laborious part both in the Messiah and Miscellaneous Concerts'.[22]

A systematic survey of the nineteenth-century Oxford Commemorations – charting repertoire, performers, venues, ticket prices, and other arrangements – leaves no doubt as to the substantial nature of these proceedings. But the literature has for various reasons traditionally given not only slight but also negative accounts of the phenomenon. For example, Bernarr Rainbow, writing about 'The Universities' in Nicholas Temperley's *The Romantic Age*, states that Bishop regarded his Oxford Professorship as 'a sinecure, its annual salary well earned by his "appearing only at Commemoration to play the ramshackle organ"'.[23] Even just a glance at some sample advertisements from the period shows that Bishop was involved more heavily than this (see Figs. 12.2, 12.3 and 12.4, from 1844 – preceding his appointment as Professor – and 1852–53).

By the 1850s there were 'special trains' laid on for the Commemoration; additionally, among the peripheral material it is worth noting (Fig. 12.3, end column) 'Just Published' – 'THE OXFORD WALTZES' composed expressly for the Grand Commemoration' and to be had at Russell's.[24] J.H. Mee, in his study of the Holywell Music Room, provided information on the Commemoration concerts, but because of the scope of his book, his outline list of these stopped at 1844, and the entries fizzled out.[25] (It is perhaps for this reason that Douglas Reid, in his article on Oxford, entirely erroneously states that after 1844 'no further festivals were held ... for many years'.[26]) As the complete text of the *Journal*'s advertisement shows (partly reproduced in Fig. 12.2), in 1844, where Mee's entry reads simply: '"Messiah". Two miscellaneous concerts. Bishop conducted', it may be noted that Madame Caradori

---

22 *Jackson's Oxford Journal*, 3 July 1813. Miss Darby was a resident singer at the Holywell Music Room (see John H. Mee, *The Oldest Music Room in Europe* (London: John Lane, 1911), p. 160). Master Hobbs would have been a choirboy in one of the college chapel establishments, groomed as a soloist for the concerts.

23 See Bernarr Rainbow, in an unfortunately altogether somewhat inaccurate passage about Oxford, in Nicholas Temperley (ed.), *The Romantic Age, 1800–1914*, Athlone (later Blackwell) History of Music in Britain, vol. 5 (London: Athlone Press, 1981), p. 30, quoting William Tuckwell, *Reminiscences of Oxford*. Cf. Cox's dismissive claims about Crotch (quoted in Wollenberg, 'Handel in Oxford', p. 169 n.). The 'ramshackle organ' (Tuckwell), incidentally, probably is fair comment: the Sheldonian organ has had a somewhat chequered history. On Oxford organs see particularly Robert Pacey and Michael Popkin (eds), *The Organs of Oxford: an Illustrated Guide to the Organs of the University and City of Oxford* (Oxford: Positif Press, 1997).

24 This was a precursor of the music-sellers Russell Acott, sadly no longer of High Street, Oxford.

25 See Mee, *The Oldest Music Room*, p. 198.

26 Reid and Pritchard, 'Some Festival Programmes of the Eighteenth and Nineteenth Centuries, ii: Cambridge and Oxford', *R.M.A. Research Chronicle*, 6 (1966).

Fig. 12.3 Advertisement for the 1852 Oxford Commemoration. *Jackson's Oxford Journal*, 12 June 1852

Allan, Signor Salvi and others sang; the string players included Sivori, Lindley and Dragonetti; Cramer and Loder led. This imported talent was mingled, characteristically, with members of the local musical community, partly drawn from prolific musical dynasties such as the Marshall and Reinagle families.

The practice of calling in increasing numbers of reinforcements, both for voices and for instruments, is well documented for the nineteenth century, with, typically, their sources proudly proclaimed in the announcements in the papers. So with the *Journal* for 15 June 1805 (Fig. 12.5), which includes, among the individuals named, the Leander brothers on the horn, and Cramer and Lindley as 'CONCERTO PLAYERS', a note at the foot of the advertisement promises that 'the Rest of the Band will be numerous, selected from the Choirs of Worcester, Gloucester, Windsor, &c.'. A glance at the advertisement for 1852 (Fig. 12.3) shows that the performers continued to be drawn from among the varied and distinguished ranks of the profession, including, on this occasion, 'Herr

OXFORD GRAND COMMEMORATION.

INSTALLATION OF THE CHANCELLOR OF THE UNIVERSITY.

On TUESDAY EVENING, June 7, there will be

A GRAND BALL, IN THE TOWN HALL,

At which Mr. WEIPPERT, with his Band, will attend.

On WEDNESDAY, June 8th,

A GRAND MISCELLANEOUS CONCERT,

IN THE THEATRE,

TO COMMENCE AT THREE O'CLOCK IN THE AFTERNOON.

PRINCIPAL VOCAL PERFORMERS.

**Mademoiselle ANNA ZERR, Miss LOUISA PYNE, and Miss DOLBY,
Signor GARDONI & Mr. LOCKEY, Herr PISCHEK & Herr STAUDIGL.**

THE ENGLISH GLEE AND MADRIGAL UNION,

**Mrs. ENDERSOHN, Miss M. WILLIAMS,
Mr. LOCKEY, Mr. HOBBS, and Mr. H. PHILLIPS.**

INSTRUMENTAL SOLO PERFORMERS.

Herr MOLIQUE (Violin), Signor PIATTI (Violoncello), Signor BOTTESINI (Contra-Basso),
and Herr NABICH (Trombone).

LEADER OF THE BAND, MR. H. BLAGROVE.

Principal Second Violin, Mr. MARSHALL.

Conductor, Sir HENRY R. BISHOP, Prof. Mus., Oxon.

Tickets, 10s. 6d. each, to be had at the Town Hall.

On THURSDAY EVENING, June 9th,

A GRAND BALL, IN THE TOWN HALL,

At which Mr. WEIPPERT, with his Band, will attend.

THE BALLS WILL BE UNDER THE PATRONAGE OF THE

Marquis of LOTHIAN,	Lord LOUGHBOROUGH,	The Hon. L. G. DILLON,
Earl of LINCOLN,	The HIGH SHERIFF,	The Hon. E. C. LEIGH,
Viscount DUNGARVAN,	The Hon. R. T. HARRIS,	G. R. SOMERSET, Esq.,
Viscount GREY DE WILTON,	The Hon. W. BYRON,	J. W. MALCOLM, Esq.,
Viscount FORDWICH,	The Hon. C. B. FIENNES,	F. M. EDEN, Esq.,

And the STEWARDS of the Musical Festival.

GREAT WESTERN RAILWAY.

OXFORD GRAND COMMEMORATION,

On 7th JUNE, 1853.

Trains between PADDINGTON and OXFORD daily (except Sundays.)

IN ADDITION TO THE ORDINARY DAILY TRAINS, SPECIAL TRAINS WILL RUN AS FOLLOWS:—

On MONDAY, 6th June,

A Special Train will leave Didcot for Oxford at 2.45 p.m. on the arrival of the 12.40 Down from Paddington, which will call at Abingdon Road, and also at 1.25 and 3.15 p.m. on the arrival of the Up Trains from Plymouth, Exeter, Bristol, Cheltenham, &c. Passengers from Stations between Paddington and Didcot, at which the 6.15 p.m. Train does not stop, will be booked to Oxford by the Train leaving Paddington at 5.30 p.m., and will be taken on from Didcot by the 6.15 p.m. Train from Paddington, reaching Oxford at 8.3 p.m.—The 2.0 p.m. Train from London will stop at Abingdon Road on this day.

On TUESDAY, 7th June,

An Excursion Train will leave Birmingham at 6.30 a.m. for Oxford, calling at Warwick and Leamington, and will return the same evening from Oxford at 9 o'clock.

A Special Train will leave Oxford at 10 o'clock p.m. for Paddington.

A Special Train will leave Oxford at 10.45 p.m. for Leamington, calling at all intermediate Stations.

On WEDNESDAY, 8th June,

A Special Train will leave Oxford for Paddington at 10 o'clock p.m.

Passengers for the WEST OF ENGLAND can leave Oxford at the under-mentioned times to meet the Down Trains at Didcot:—

7.40 a.m. to meet the	6.15 a.m. Train from Paddington.	ditto.	2. 5 p.m. to meet the	12.40 p.m. Train from Paddington.	ditto.
8.42	7.40	ditto.	4.15	2.45	ditto.
9.48	9.45 Express	ditto.	5.40	4.50 Express	ditto.
10.45	6.50 3rd Class	ditto.	10.25	8.55 Mail	ditto.
11.50	10.15 Mail	ditto.			

LONDON and NORTH-WESTERN RAILWAY.

OXFORD GRAND COMMEMORATION.

ORDINARY TRAINS TO AND FROM OXFORD.

DOWN TRAINS TO OXFORD.			UP TRAINS FROM OXFORD.		
Leave Euston Station, London.	Leave Bletchley.	Arrive at Oxford.	Leave Oxford.	Arrive at Bletchley.	Arrive at Euston Station, London.
6.30 A.M.	8.15 A.M.	9.46 A.M.	7.55 A.M.	9.10 A.M.	10.30 A.M.
10.0 A.M.	11.30 A.M.	12.45 P.M.	9.50 A.M.	11.5 A.M.	12.45 P.M.
12.0 NOON.	3.0 P.M.	4.25 P.M.	12.0 NOON.	1.15 P.M.	3.15 P.M.
3.30 P.M.	5.0 P.M.	6.15 P.M.	4.10 P.M.	5.25 P.M.	7.0 P.M.
5.45 P.M.	7.30 P.M.	8.45 P.M.	5.30 P.M.	6.45 P.M.	8.30 P.M.

SPECIAL TRAINS.

A Special Train will leave Bletchley on the Mornings of **Tuesday, June 7,** and **Wednesday, June 8,** at 9.30 a.m., from the 7.30 a.m. Down Train from London, and the 7.30 a.m. Up Express Train from Birmingham.

The Return Trains to leave Oxford the same Evenings (and also on **Thursday, June 9**) at 30 minutes past 8 o'clock, arriving at Wolverton in time to meet the Down Mail Trains to the North, and the Up Express Train, arriving in London at 11.25 p.m.

A Special Train (calling at all Stations) will leave Banbury for Oxford at **9.0 a.m.** on **Tuesday, June 7.**

The Return Train to Banbury will leave Oxford the same Evening at 30 minutes past **10—after the Fireworks.**

General Manager's Office, Euston Station, May 25, 1853.   By order,   MARK HUISH.

Fig. 12.4   Advertisement for the 1853 Oxford Commemoration. *Jackson's Oxford Journal*, 4 June 1853

RADCLIFFE INFIRMARY,
June 1st, 1805.

THE Anniversary Meeting of the Governors of the RADCLIFFE INFIRMARY will be holden on Tuesday the 25th Instant, when a SERMON will be preached in the Morning at ST. MARY's CHURCH, by the Rev. Mr. BARKER, Sub-Dean and Canon Residentiary of Wells.

In the Course of the Service will be performed a TE DEUM and BENEDICTUS, by ORLANDO GIBBONS, with Instrumental Accompaniments, composed by Dr. CROTCH; an ANTHEM, suited to the Occasion; and the OLD HUNDREDTH PSALM, with Instrumental Accompaniaments.

The Governors, &c. are desired to meet at the Radcliffe Library at Ten o'Clock. The Service will begin at Eleven. After the Service a Collection will be made for the Benefit of the Charity

GEO. FRED. STRATTON, Esq. } Stewards.
HENRY C. COTTON, Esq. }

THEATRE, OXFORD.
Grand Musical Festival.

ON TUESDAY, June 25th, 1805, the SACRED ORATORIO of
THE MESSIAH,
And on WEDNESDAY the 26th, and THURSDAY the 27th,

Two Grand Miscellaneous Concerts.

Principal VOCAL PERFORMERS—Signora STORACE, Mrs. ASHE, Madame BIANCHI, Mr. BRAHAM, Mr. KNYVETT, and Mr. WELSH; Mr. BARTLEMAN having a prior Engagement for the two preceding Days, is engaged for the 27th.

Leader of the Band, Mr. CRAMER.

VIOLINS—Messrs. MORALT, MARSHALL, MAHON, HALE, SLEZACH, EVANS, BINFIELD, HOLMES, SYKES, HARDY, JUNG, &c.

VIOLAS— Messrs. J. MARSHALL, WOODCOCK, HESTER, &c.

VIOLONCELLOS—Messrs. REINAGLE, HALDON, &c. &c.

DOUBLE BASSES—Mess. BOYCE, HALE, VICARY, DRESSLER, COZIER, &c. &c.

FLUTES—Mr. JACKSON, &c.

HORNS—Messrs. LEANDER.

OBOES—Messrs. GREISBACH and SPELZBERGER.

CLARIONETS—Messrs. HALDON, &c.

BASSOONS—Messrs. HOLMES and FELDON.

TRUMPETS—Messrs. HYDE and DROVER.

TROMBONES—Messrs. DRESSLER, FLACK, and ZIVINGMAN.

SERPENT—Mr. HATTON.

DRUMS—Mr. JOY.

DOUBLE DRUMS—Mr. JENKINSON.

CONCERTO PLAYERS—Mr. CRAMER, Mr. LINDLEY, &c.

The Rest of the Band will be numerous, selected from the Choirs of Worcester, Gloucester, Windsor, &c.

The Whole conducted by Dr. CROTCH.

The Performance will begin at Five o'Clock.

Fig. 12.5   Advertisement for the 1805 Oxford 'Grand Musical Festival'. *Jackson's Oxford Journal*, 15 June 1805

Joachim', 'Signor Bottesini' and, as leader of the band, Mr. H. Blagrove. Among other famous names from England and abroad listed in the nineteenth-century Commemoration programmes, besides those mentioned earlier, were Pauline Viardot Garcia, Jenny Lind, Madame Malibran, Clara Novello, Madam Pasta, Schröder-Devrient, William Knyvett and Sims Reeves among the singers, and Thalberg, Mori, Ole Bull and Sapio among the instrumentalists. Many of the invited performers were active on the English oratorio scene, or later connected with the Crystal Palace concerts. Presumably a considerable amount of 'networking' went on, in drawing them to Oxford.

The elements of change perceivable in the nineteenth-century commemorations can be subsumed under the broad heading of 'expansion' or escalation. This process affected various parameters from early in the century onwards. For example, in some years the number of major concert events was increased from the traditional two or three to four or more, stretching over more days (as in 1810; see above). One of the performances might be a complete oratorio, as with *Messiah* in 1805 and 1813.[27] Certainly it is true that 'selections' might be substituted, as happened with the first of the three concerts advertised for the Commemoration Festival of 1823, 'in the THEATRE, OXFORD during the COMMEMORATION WEEK', which was to consist of 'a Selection from Palestine, THE SEASONS OF HAYDN, And MOZART's Requiem', and, it was added, 'The Two last will be Miscellaneous'.[28] Nevertheless, it is clear that Mee's statement that complete oratorio performances ceased after Crotch's departure for London needs to be re-evaluated.[29]

New oratorios were also included in the proceedings, sometimes in their premieres. In 1834, for the Installation of the Duke of Wellington as Chancellor of the University, the Commemoration festivities featured Crotch's oratorio *The Captivity of Judah* (billed as 'the new Sacred Oratorio')[30] on Tuesday, 10 June, as well as his Installation Ode (setting words by John Keble), and three Grand Miscellaneous Concerts on Wednesday, Thursday

---

27 A copy of the printed programme for the 1805 performance of *Messiah* on 25 June at the Sheldonian Theatre (marked by hand 'present about 1100') is in Oxford, Bodleian Library, Mus. 1 d. 64/1. The soloists included John Braham (billed here to sing 'Comfort ye' among other items), Mr Welsh, Nancy Storace, Madame Bianchi and Mrs Ashe.

28 *Jackson's Oxford Journal*, 7 June 1823. The practice persisted, for example with the 'selection from Mendelssohn's Oratorio of St Paul' performed at Commemoration in 1852: see Fig. 12.3.

29 Mee, *The Oldest Music Room*, p. 165.

30 The work was 'well received by a packed audience, many ... almost crushed to death' (see Thewlis papers: Notes on the History of Music in Oxford (unpubl., n.d.), Oxford, Bodleian Library, vol. 4, p. 866).

and Friday, 11, 12 and 13 June featuring 'Overtures, Symphonies as performed at the Philharmonic Concerts and the Royal Academy of Music', and excerpts from 'the newest Operas', all seemingly designed to inculcate in the Oxford audiences the feeling that their musical scene was *au courant*. For this event Crotch conducted; the received view, too, that his input into these occasions declined following his move to London needs modifying in the light of his extensive involvement as composer, performer, and conductor during the years that followed.

The Professor continued, also, in the nineteenth century to contribute his expertise, as was traditional, to the annual Radcliffe Infirmary service that formed part of the Commemoration week. Within the framework of this charitable event for the Infirmary (opened 1770) various musical traditions were enshrined. The advertisements for the 1805 and 1810 festivals, for instance (see Figs. 12.5 and 12.1) were preceded by an announcement of the Infirmary service: the notice for 1810 makes it clear that the concert soloists were involved in the service (thus the Boyce anthem was to be sung with verses by Messrs Knyvett, Vaughan, Braham and Bartleman; this is confirmed by the report after the event). As with other aspects, the account in the *Journal* sketches the context, in this case including the processional element and the charity sermon, that surrounded these musical performances, and within which they made their effect:

WEDNESDAY, JULY 4.

About half past nine this morning Lord Chancellor Grenville, accompanied by the Vice-Chancellor, and preceded by the Beadles, went from Balliol College to the Delegates' Room, where the Heads of Houses and Proctors were in waiting. Walking from hence to the Radcliffe Library his Lordship joined the Nobility, the Governors of the Infirmary, and other Gentlemen, and went in full procession to St. Mary's Church, where Divine Service, with a very large Choir, was performed, during the course of which were introduced the Te Deum and Benedictus, by Orlando Gibbons; the Anthem, 'Blessed is he'; and 'to swell', still more, the 'notes of praise', additional verses were given by Messrs. Knyvett, Vaughan, Braham, and Bartleman. Immediately before the Sermon the Old Hundredth Psalm, with accompaniments by Dr. Crotch, was introduced, and then the Rev. Dr. Howley, Canon of Christ Church, and Regius Professor of Divinity, delivered a most admirable discourse, for the benefit of the Infirmary, in which he ... recommended his hearers ... to plant and to cherish in their bosoms those exalted virtues and favourite attributes of Heaven, MERCY and BENEVOLENCE ...[31]

---

[31] *Jackson's Oxford Journal*, 7 July 1810.

The visiting performers were accorded critical notices for their part in these services, as well as in the Commemoration concerts; thus in 1813 it was reported:

> On Tuesday morning a Meeting of the Governors of the Radcliffe Infirmary was holden, and the assembly afterwards went in full procession to St Mary's Church, where divine service was performed; during the course of which were introduced the *Te Deum*, *Benedictus*, *Commandments*, and *Creed*, of Dr. Orlando Gibbons, and, above all, the celebrated Hymn of Martin Luther, which, in point of science and orchestral effect, was admirable, and derived an additional grace from the rich accompaniment of Mr. Vaughan's voice, whose exquisite taste, delicacy of expression, and powers of execution, are deservedly held in such pre-eminent estimation. The Bishop of Oxford then delivered, in a most luminous strain of eloquence ... a sermon ... for the benefit of the Infirmary.[32]

A special element enshrined in the Commemoration was the public performance of musical degree exercises in the Sheldonian Theatre or, as statutory, in the University Music School (or, by permission, in other locations).[33] These performances evidently took on some of the splendour of their surroundings:

> Mr. S. Wesley, whose admission to his degree of Doctor of Music appears in the academical news, performed his exercise (by the Permission of the President and Fellows, and a dispensation from the Vice-Chancellor for that purpose) in Magdalen College Chapel on Thursday last. The chapel was very numerously attended. The exercise, selected from various passages of holy writ, is written in the true cathedral manner ... abounding in the solemn melodies and harmonies which produce so deep an impression when peeling [*sic*] down the long aisles of our sacred edifices. It is written with all the science of the musician; with that deep feeling which is so indispensible [*sic*] in sacred music, and which pervades all the works of our great composers, and, above all, of Mozart. Among the passages most worthy of note was a bass solo, very ably sung by Mr. William Marshall, whom we were delighted to see assisting at the academic honours of his brother musician.[34]

That the degree exercises when performed at this time of year possessed something of the grandeur of the Commemoration proceedings into which they were absorbed is shown particularly clearly in the

---

32 Ibid., 3 July 1813. The effects of these proceedings could be most directly measured in the amount of charity gathered; on this occasion the collection 'at the doors of the Church' totalled £216 13s.

33 For the background to these events see, inter alia, Susan Wollenberg, 'The Oxford Exercises in the Eighteenth Century', *Early Music*, 28 (2000), pp. 546–54.

34 *Jackson's Oxford Journal*, 22 June 1839.

case of Charles William Corfe, organist of Christ Church, whose influence on musical life in the University during the middle decades of the
nineteenth century was of such great benefit to its development.
Corfe's doctoral exercise was heard during the Grand Commemoration week of 1852, when a star-studded group of soloists, including
Clara Novello, Sims Reeves and 'the great violinist' Joseph Joachim,
graced the festival performances.[35] Their presence was enhancing for
Corfe, too:

THURSDAY [24 JUNE]

A supplementary musical treat was afforded this morning in an exercise at the Theatre, for the degree of Doctor of Music, by Mr. C. W.
Corfe, B. M[us]., Organist of Christ Church. The performance being
open to the public the Theatre was soon filled to overflowing. The
words were selected from the 65th Psalm, commencing 'Thou, O
God, art praised in Sion', and consisted of a chorus, recitative, and
air, for tenor; recitative and air, for bass; a semi-chorus for eight
voices; duet, tenor and bass, with chorus; and concluding with a
chorus. Mr. Lockey sustained the tenor, and Herr Staudigl the bass
parts [both these contributed to the 'grand miscellaneous' concerts of
the Commemoration], and both did ample justice to this spirited
composition, for which they were rewarded with repeated bursts of
applause …

The principal instrumental performers who were engaged for the
festival assisted on this occasion, and gave increased effect to the
exercise; and the Choral Society, choristers, and others belonging to
the University choirs, combined to make a most efficient orchestra.
The composition is distinguished for its beauty, variety, and striking
passages, and among the pleasurable associations of the
Commemoration, this musical exercise will be one of the most prominent. At the conclusion of the performance Dr. Corfe was loudly
cheered; and when Sir Henry Bishop, who was present, shook the
composer by the hand, and congratulated him on his success, the
cheering was resumed …[36]

Another distinguishing element of the Oxford festival scene, one that
in this case was new to the nineteenth century, was the increasingly
important role of the colleges in providing musical and other entertainments. College, as well as university, musical societies were founded and
developed in this period concomitantly with the expansion of the individual colleges themselves, and their efforts were well represented in the
programmes of the Commemoration events. Thus, for example, during

---

35 For details of the concerts and their reception, see ibid., 26 June 1852.
36 Ibid. For programmes of the exercises performed on 24 June 1852 (which included
George Dixon's B.Mus. exercise at the Music School in the afternoon) see Oxford, Bodleian
Library, G.A. Oxon c. 68 (116–117).

the Grand Commemoration of 1852, after the 'annual procession of racing boats' on the Monday evening, 21 June (apparently witnessed by thousands), 'other attractions put forth their claims', and among these the *Journal*'s reporter singled out the concert 'given by the New College Glee Club, in the Hall, which was literally crowded, and in which a series of glees were given with excellent effect, the entertainment concluding with the celebrated "Dulce Domum" and the National Anthem'. It was also remarked that 'there is usually a number of minor entertainments previously, which serve to beguile the time, and give a foretaste of the pleasures in store'; among these was the concert given on the Friday evening (18 June) by the 'St. John's College Philharmonic Society' in the college hall, which was 'crowded to excess'; 'it is but justice to say', the reporter went on, 'that this concert was marked with a very high order of amateur talent, particularly amongst the vocalists, and that it afforded the utmost pleasure to the audience, amongst whom we observed the President of the College and party, and several other Heads of Houses and distinguished members of the University'.

Clearly, in keeping with the intensity characteristic of the festival culture, audiences were prepared to commit their time to attending a succession of events: on the Saturday evening, 19 June 1852, the University Amateur Musical Society gave a concert in the Town Hall, 'when upwards of 600 persons, including many of the Heads of Colleges and Halls with their families, Senior Members of the University, and a large number of strangers were present'.[37] By the late nineteenth century, a well-established pattern included a variety of college concerts and dramatic productions (among these were a series of Shakespeare plays in college gardens) in the build-up to the Commemoration week, as well as during the week of the festival itself:

> Commemoration proper does not begin till the Sunday, but even in the dying days of the Term there are signs of the new order. The first

---

37 Ibid. If by this time virtually all Commemorations were 'grand' in character, then the 'Grand Commemorations' were even grander, as the *Journal*'s commentator noted in 1852: 'Among the various incidents of the year there is not one more interwoven with pleasurable associations ... than the festival which marks the close of the Term preceding the Long Vacation, for then Oxford assumes an aspect different to that which it presents at any other period ... hospitality and entertainment ... are dispensed with no unwilling or niggard hand. If such is the case on ordinary occasions, it is more especially so at a Grand Commemoration, which occurs every fourth year, a circumstance that tends to increase the desire to participate in its enjoyments.' In fact, 'Grand Commemorations' occurred at other intervals, for example in 1853 with the 'Grand Commemoration, and Installation of the Earl of Derby as Chancellor' (see Fig. 12.4), and in 1863, when the festival was marked 'with more than usual *éclat*' by the Royal Visit (of the Prince and Princess of Wales); for detailed comment on this event, see *Jackson's Oxford Journal*, 6, 13 and 20 June 1863.

of these are the Commemoration concerts: we give below notes on those given by Pembroke and Keble. That at Jesus was postponed ...

The programme of the Pembroke Commemoration concert on Wednesday [i.e., the Wednesday preceding that of the Encaenia] was ingeniously arranged to suit all possible tastes, and certainly no one would complain of lack of variety in a scheme that included Brahms' 'Sapphische Ode' in amiable juxtaposition with typical specimens of the popular comic song. The crowded audience encored everything enthusiastically ...

Exceptional facilities for accommodating a large audience are present at Keble, and the annual concert is distinguished for the excellence of its programme and the relatively high standard of its performance. These features were the marks of Thursday's concert as of its predecessors, and without any sacrifice of quality the programme appealed more strongly to a mixed audience than did that of last year. Under Mr. Harwood's careful bâton both chorus and orchestra ... acquitted themselves admirably in the 'Spring' portion of Haydn's *Seasons* and Macfarren's *May Day* ... The large audience was prodigal of its applause, and indeed encored each soloist with perfect impartiality.[38]

It was also noted at this period that 'college balls seem to be growing in popularity at the expense of club and other balls'; among a whole series of these events held in the different colleges, the Magdalen College Ball acquired a particular reputation for its excellence, with consistently high musical standards among its other attractions: 'The Magdalen Ball on Tuesday night was a great and deserved success ... The Artillery Band was excellent, and Mr. Royles' new waltz, composed especially for the occasion, was vociferously encored.'[39]

At the same time as the various developments in the festivals themselves, an element in which considerable expansion can be seen is in the criticism carried in the local papers. The critical reports in *Jackson's Oxford Journal*, complementing with comments after the event the copious advertising of the Commemoration beforehand, developed from the few lines characteristic of the eighteenth-century reportage to many columns.[40] The relatively laconic style of commentary cultivated in the late eighteenth century had given way by the middle decades of the nineteenth century to an increasingly rhapsodic and effusive language of criticism:

The entrance of Signor Camillo Sivori and his violin, with which he was to perform such wonders, put all upon the tip-toe of expectation. Those who had never heard him before could not doubt from the Signor's assured air that he felt confident of success, and confidence in such matters is a great matter ... The piece selected was a concerto, Sivori's own composition. We scarcely know how to describe the

---

38   *The Oxford Magazine*, Special Extra Commemoration Number (24 June 1896), p. 2.
39   Ibid., 23 June 1892.
40   The advertisements, too, were much extended in terms of column inches in this period.

playing of this celebrated violinist – the result of that playing on the minds of the hearers is much sooner told, namely, undisguised astonishment. There is nothing in the execution which in our judgements wake[s] into life and feeling the softer emotions of the heart – nothing that 'now melts into sorrow, now maddens to pain', but by various combinations and means he has made peculiarly his own ... His performance met with unbounded applause, and he fully deserved all the honours he received.[41]

The critic on this occasion went on to provide a vivid account of the scene, when 'in the course of the piece the Signor had the misfortune to hear [sic] fly one of the strings of his instrument – Loder offered his own violin, but a string of that flew also'; finally one was found that survived, and 'the cool demeanour of the violinist at this time was such as to call forth a round of hearty applause'.[42]

The solo singers, too, attracted elaborate comment of a style unprecedented in eighteenth-century reports of performances:

In a romanza by Verdi, we could estimate the powers of Salvi as a concert singer. The person of Salvi is in his favour, and cannot fail to tell in a manner much to the advantage of the performer ... Salvi is of a commanding stature, apparently with a broad chest, and possesses the advantage of a fine open forehead. His voice is a decided tenor, and of great power and flexibility ... This piece by Verdi was not so well adapted for the display of the finer parts of Salvi's voice as a cavatina by Pacini, sung in a later part of the day; the romanza, nevertheless, was encored.[43]

Jenny Lind, appearing at the Oxford Grand Commemoration in 1856 (and billed as about to sing in Oxford 'for the last time': see Fig. 12.6 – needless to say, she returned subsequently), also attracted comments in the press concerning her reception as well as her performance; the *Journal* remarked that she 'received the most rapturous welcome' from the large and fashionable gathering in the Theatre (which, it was noted, 'comfortably' held about 1800 persons':

The doors were opened yesterday at twelve o'clock, but long before that hour they were besieged by a dense mass of human beings, who, however, upon their entrance, were not long in seating themselves. We may attribute this fact to the excellence of the arrangements ... Every seat in the Theatre was marked off and legibly numbered, and every facility was afforded by those in attendance to direct each person to the seat corresponding with the number on his ticket [the impression given here is that this was a novelty]. When all were seated, the Theatre wore a most brilliant appearance, heightened in no slight degree by the hundreds of fair forms who were present. We recognized a large array

41 *Jackson's Oxford Journal*, 22 June 1844.
42 Ibid.
43 Ibid.

LATIMER and CO. WINE MERCHANTS,
(ESTABLISHED A.D., 1797),
11 and 12, HIGH-STREET, OXFORD,

BEG strongly to recommend to the public their **CLARET**, for summer drinking, at 33s. per dozen. N.B. If three dozen be taken, 31s. 6d. per dozen. Terms, *Cash* payment.

OXFORD GRAND COMMEMORATION, 1856.

MADAME JENNY GOLDSCHMIDT
AND
MADAME VIARDOT GARCIA.

IT IS RESPECTFULLY ANNOUNCED THAT

MADAME JENNY GOLDSCHMIDT LIND

WILL SING IN OXFORD (FOR THE LAST TIME) DURING THE GRAND COMMEMORATION WEEK,

IN THE THEATRE,

On TUESDAY AFTERNOON, JUNE 3, in a

GRAND MISCELLANEOUS CONCERT,

VOCAL AND INSTRUMENTAL;

And on WEDNESDAY AFTERNOON, JUNE 4, commencing at Half-past Two,

IN HAYDN'S ORATORIO OF

"THE CREATION."

PROGRAMME OF THE MISCELLANEOUS CONCERT,
On Tuesday, June 3rd, to commence at Two o'clock.

PART I.

OVERTURE	(Der Freischütz)	C. M. v. Weber.
SONG, "The Wanderer," Mr. WEISS		Schubert.
RONDO, from "Il Rè Pastore," for Voice and Violin Obligato		Mozart.
Madame GOLDSCHMIDT.—(Accompanied by M. SAINTON.)		
FANTASIA, Violoncello, Signor PIATTI, with Orchestral Accompaniment		Kummer.
SCENA and ARIA, "Care Compagne," Madame GOLDSCHMIDT	(Sonnambula)	Bellini.
CONCERTSTUCK, for Pianoforte, with Orchestra Accompaniment		C. M. v. Weber.
Pianoforte, Mr. OTTO GOLDSCHMIDT.		
DUO, { "Ebben a te, ferisci" } { "Giorno d' orrore" }	} (Semiramide)	Rossini.
Madame GOLDSCHMIDT and Madame PAULINE VIARDOT.		

PART II.

OVERTURE	(Guillaume Tell)	Rossini.
RONDO FINALE, "Non più mesta," Madlle. PAULINE VIARDOT	(Cenerentola)	Rossini.
SOLO DE CONCERT, Violin, M. SAINTON		Sainton.
TRIO, for Voice and two Flutes, "Hörst Du," Madame GOLDSCHMIDT;		
Flutes:—Messrs. PRATTEN and REMUSAT	(Camp of Silesia)	Meyerbeer.
TARANTELLE, Pianoforte Solo, Mr. OTTO GOLDSCHMIDT		Thalberg.
SONG, "The Village Blacksmith," Mr. WEISS		W. H. Weiss.
{ BALLAD, "John Anderson my Jo"		Scotch Song.
{ THE BIRD SONG		Taubert.
Madame GOLDSCHMIDT.		

THE ORCHESTRA WILL CONSIST OF THE FOLLOWING EMINENT PROFESSORS:

FIRST VIOLINS.		DOUBLE BASSES.	BASSOONS.
Messrs. BLAGROVE, SAINTON, *Principal*, DANDO, WILLY, DOYLE, GOFFERIE, HILL, W. H. BANISTER, GRIESBACH, G. A. DEICHMANN, THIRLWALL, Sen. ZERBINI.	Messrs. WATSON (William), BLAGROVE (William) KREUTZER, PERRY, PORTER.	Messrs. HOWELL, *Principal*, MOUNT, PRATTEN, SEVERN, EDGAR, CUBITT, ROBERTS.	Messrs. BAUMANN, SNELLING.
			TRUMPETS.
	TENORS.		Messrs T. HARPER, IRWIN.
	Messrs. HILL, *Principal*, GLANVILLE, TRUST, THOMPSON, THOMAS, SCHMIDT.		HORNS.
		FLUTES.	Messrs. C. HARPER. MANN, RAE, STANDEN.
SECOND VIOLINS.		Messrs. SIDNEY PRATTEN, REMUSAT.	
Messrs. WATKINS, *Principal*, NEWSHAM, POLLITZER, MORI, N. MARSHALL, CLEMENTI,	VIOLONCELLOS.	CLARIONETS.	TROMBONES.
	Messrs. PIATTI, *Principal*, HATTON, REINAGLE, CHIPP, CALKIN, G. PHILLIPS, PAQUE.	Messrs. LAZARUS, MAYCOCK.	Messrs. COIFFE, ANTOINE, HEALEY.
		OBOES.	OPHICLEIDE, Mr. PROSPERE. TRIANGLE, Mr. GOODWIN. DRUMS, Mr. CHIPP.
		Messrs. BARRET, NICHOLSON.	

CONDUCTOR ... ... M. BENEDICT.

Reserved and Numbered Seats for the Rising Semicircle, Area, and East and West Wings of Ladies' Gallery, One Guinea. Ladies' Gallery, Semicircle (Reserved and Numbered), Fifteen Shillings. Upper Gallery, Half-a-Guinea. Reserved Seats to be had ONLY at Mr. Russell's Music Warehouse, where a Plan of the Theatre may be seen. Unreserved Seats to be obtained only at Mr. Plowman's Circulating Library, St. Aldate's.

Fig. 12.6 Advertisement for the 1856 Oxford Commemoration. *Jackson's Oxford Journal*, 24 May 1856

of the neighbouring nobility and gentry, Heads of Houses, University authorities, and their families, together with the leading residents of Oxford, and a considerable portion of our fellow townsmen.[44]

A particular draw was the performance of Haydn's *Creation*, on Wednesday, 4 June 1856. Prince Albert, Prince Frederick William of Prussia and the Prince of Baden (who were among that year's honorands) were present at this event, which reportedly allowed Jenny Lind's 'exquisitely beautiful and silvery high notes' to be 'heard to perfection in "Thy marvellous work", and "With verdure clad"; the latter was rapturously encored'.[45] Evidently beginning to run out of the superlative expressions of appreciation with which this notice is filled, the critic went on to observe that the singing of Mr Lockey and Mr Weiss in this performance was 'beyond all praise'; 'the former was loudly encored in the air, "In native worth", than which it would be difficult to find any composition more suited to the particular excellencies of this gentleman's style and voice'. At the close of the oratorio, '"God save the Queen" was sung, the solo parts being taken by Jenny Lind, Mr. Lockey, and Mr. Weiss, and the audience joining in the chorus'.[46]

Through the press notices, and the surviving programmes, it is possible to track the visiting performers, generally, at other times of the year; it seems that often they were involved in a series of concerts and were then invited back for the Commemoration. The increasingly extensive reporting of the Commemoration during the course of the nineteenth century also sets the scene and provides the detailed context in which to view the variety of musical performances which were by this time included in the festivities. Already by the mid-century, the Commemoration proceedings started essentially on the Sunday, with the arrival of the visitors to Oxford, as the *Journal* reported on Saturday 8 July 1848:

The first point of attraction on Sunday morning was, as usual, St. Mary's Church, where the University Sermon was preached by ... the newly-appointed Regius Professor of Divinity. The church was extremely crowded. In the afternoon Magdalen College Chapel

---

44 *Jackson's Oxford Journal*, 7 June 1856. (Jenny Lind's first performances in Oxford had taken place in December 1848.)
45 Ibid.
46 Ibid. That year, as the *Journal* reported, a 'General Illumination, in celebration of the return of peace, formed a fitting conclusion to the gaieties of the Commemoration'. In other years, too, happenings on the larger scene were reflected in the Commemoration: in 1887 the *Oxford Magazine* noted (15 June): 'We hear that the Vice-Principal of Jesus has written a topical Jubilee Ode in Welsh, which will be sung at the [Jesus College] Concert tonight' (p. 276); and the advertisement for the Oxford Philharmonic Society's customary Commemoration concert in the Sheldonian Theatre included in its programme Weber's 'Jubilee Cantata' (*Oxford Magazine*, 8 June 1887).

was the next point to which the visitors directed their steps. The service was here performed with that excellence which has so long distinguished this college and was listened to with the most marked attention ... In the evening a very large congregation attended at New College Chapel, which is always looked upon with deep interest. Here also the service was most ably and impressively performed, the organ being played by Dr. Elvey in his accustomed style. The next and most prominent attraction was the Broad Walk [which was] literally crammed; never do we remember to have seen a more crowded or fashionable attendance ... The weather on the whole was favourable; some slight showers, however, fell ...[47]

At this point the narrator of the adventures of Mr Verdant Green, eponymous hero of Cuthbert Bede's novel, may be allowed to take over the account of the typical proceedings:

On the Monday they had a party to Woodstock and Blenheim; and in the evening went, on the Brazenface barge, to see the procession of boats ... They concluded the evening's entertainments in a most satisfactory manner, by going to the ball at the Town Hall.

Indeed the way the two young ladies worked ... proved them to be possessed of the most vigorous constitutions; for although they danced till an early hour in the morning, they not only, on the next day, went to the anniversary sermon for the Radcliffe, and after that to the horticultural show in the Botanical Gardens, and after that to the concert in the Sheldonian Theatre, but ... they must, forsooth – Brazenface being one of the ball-giving colleges – wind up the night by accepting the polite invitation of Mr. Verdant Green and Mr. Charles Larkyns to a ball given in their college hall. And how many polkas these young ladies danced, and how many waltzes they waltzed, and how many ices they consumed ...

By ten of the clock the next morning, they appeared, quite fresh and charming to the view, in the ladies' gallery in the theatre ... [where] the proceedings ... [were] opened by the undergraduates in their peculiar way ...[48]

For the undergraduates' 'peculiar way' we should read 'riotously'. Such behaviour became *de rigueur*, and needed little specific provocation. During the 1870s Dr Corfe, playing the organ for Encaenia, became a cult figure among the undergraduates; at the Encaenia in 1873 they gave three cheers for 'Dr. Corfe *and* the organ blower'.

---

47   See also the comments in the issue of 22 June 1844: 'The Festival, for so it may be termed, must be taken to have commenced on Sunday, when the different churches were thronged with an attentive auditory.'

48   Cuthbert Bede [Edward Bradley], *The Further Adventures of Mr. Verdant Green* (London: H. Ingram, 1854), pp. 106–7.

Corfe's reputed 'unvarying use of a certain group of stops, wittily named the "Corfe-mixture"' was called for by a 'wag' at Encaenia. In 1878 'at the Encaenia Ouseley gave an organ recital to keep the Undergraduates quiet, assisted by Parratt. They were cheered.'[49]

But moving away from the pomp and ceremony of the events in the Sheldonian, we might give the last word on the Commemoration experience to Miss Catherine Lucy, who attended the St John's College Ball on 17 June 1891: the entry in her diary reminds us that the music performed, and listened to, during Commemoration week did not belong only to the public sphere:

> At 9 we started for the ... Ball ... Mr. Maxse got me a programme ... But the special thing of the evening was when Mr. Maxse took me to his rooms, which are perfectly charming, they are hung with rather dark claret-coloured brocaded silk ... He had the room crowded with plants and lighted with a pink lamp with a wonderful shade. He put me into the most comfortable chair with about 6 cushions, squirted scent over me and gave me grapes and then: played to me, he plays divinely. While he was playing Edith came in with Mr. Wilson. Soon after that it struck two and we were obliged to stop, we finished up with 'Auld Lang Syne'.[50]

My thanks are due to the staff of the following institutions: Bodleian Library, Oxford (Music Room); Centre for Oxfordshire Studies (Westgate Library, Oxford); Lady Margaret Hall, Oxford; the Oxford Union Society Library; and the Music Faculty Library, University of Oxford.

---

[49] Thewlis papers, vol. 4, p. 960. The Commemoration was implicated in the development of the solo organ recital (a genre that was developed generally in nineteenth-century Oxford): for Encaenia recital programmes from the 1880s and 1890s see Oxford, Bodleian Library, G.A. Oxon b. 138 (19–21), and *The Oxford Magazine*, Commemoration numbers, 1896 ff.

[50] Quoted from the diary of Catherine Lucy, in Malcolm Graham, *Images of Victorian Oxford* (Stroud: Alan Sutton, 1992). p. 70. Mr Maxse may well have been a scion of the Maxse family, distinguished in military, naval and colonial service, which was connected with the Cecils through the marriage in 1894 of Violet (née Maxse) to Lord Edward Cecil.

CHAPTER THIRTEEN

In Search of a Nation's Music

The Role of the Society of Arts and the Royal Academy of Music in the Establishment of the Royal College of Music in 1883

G.W.E. Brightwell

The establishment of a national music school had been on the agenda at least since the eighteenth century, when Daniel Defoe had published his thesis entitled 'A Proposal to prevent the expensive importation of Foreign Musicians, &c. by forming an Academy of our own' in *Augusta Triumphans*.[1] Later on, at the start of the nineteenth century, the dearth of indigenous musicians had been grounds for establishing the Royal Academy of Music (RAM) in 1822;[2] however, even as a private institution where students were obliged to pay fees, it had been fraught with financial difficulties, riven with bureaucracy from its inception and had faced closure on more than one occasion. It was not until 1853 that the Prince Consort, then President of the Society of Arts, had rekindled interest in a new foundation as a result of the uneven fortunes of the RAM and the nationalist *Zeitgeist* which had been gathering pace in Europe.[3] The recent triumph of the Society of Arts' international exhibition of the works of all nations in 1851 (thereafter known as the Great Exhibition) had given new impetus to its endeavours in support of the sciences and arts.[4] In 1861, upon Prince Albert's death, Sir Henry Cole, as Chairman of the Council of the Society of Arts, took over plans for the new school. Proclaimed initially as an alliance with the senior RAM in the hope of securing a government grant, the circumstances proved prejudicial to such a partnership and the National Training School for Music (NTSM) came to be established independently. Born out of a desire to provide the music

---

1 Daniel Defoe, *Augusta Triumphans: Or the Way to Make London the Most Flourishing City in the Universe* (London: J. Roberts, 1728), p. 16. This also includes articles concerning the establishment of a university in London.

2 Frederick Corder, *A History of the Royal Academy of Music* (London: Frederick Corder, 1922), p. 2.

3 Robert Stradling and Meirion Hughes, *The English Musical Renaissance 1840–1940* (London: Routledge, 1993; 2nd edn, Manchester: Manchester University Press, 2001), p. 19.

4 'The Proposed Institutions at Kensington', *Journal of the Society of Arts*, 1 (1852–53), p. 611.

profession in Britain with an indigenous workforce, like Defoe's proposal a century earlier, the Society of Arts' scheme was distinct from the RAM in so far as it championed free music education.[5] This, it was considered, could uniquely enable those from the lower orders, especially women, to acquire a profession which might secure a level of respectability often found wanting. Its pioneering mission increased its prominence and through Cole's connections drew the attention and support of the Duke of Edinburgh (Prince Alfred), and Queen Victoria, who sent two representatives: Prince Christian and her private secretary, Sir Henry Ponsonby. The NTSM's transitory disposition – it had been lauded as a five-year experiment – had motivated the Prince of Wales to begin discussions concerning the establishment of a permanent royal college of music as early as 1878, a mere two years after the NTSM had been inaugurated.[6] The NTSM's failure, by 1882, to secure its long-term future by attracting permanent government subvention ultimately paved the way for the foundation of a new college of music under the direct patronage of the heir apparent, 'who made its full accomplishment his personal concern'.[7]

Apart from the RAM, all precursors to the NTSM had failed, and Defoe's proposal of 1727 was no different, although it was certainly the result of a considered opinion.[8] It shares many of its objectives with later institutions, and Defoe makes a clear distinction between those who profess music and those for whom it is merely an acceptable pastime. While his definition of music as 'the most innocent Amusement in Life ... [which] composes the Mind into a sedateness prone to everything that's generous and good' conflicts with the nineteenth-century position which identifies musical participation at any level as the lesser of two evils, he characterises it as a 'commendable Accomplishment' once the 'more necessary parts of Education are finished'.[9] The 'accomplishment' of which he speaks is more in tune with Utilitarian principles in so far as it proclaims the ephemeral rather than the intrinsic value of music. In other words: 'it saves a great deal

---

5   'A Proposal for Founding Scholarships' (27 November 1871), Privy Purse Papers: VIC 1872/11318, Royal Archive, Windsor Castle. This proposal was issued by the Society of Arts. It states that there was to be at least one scholarship subscribed by every county, colony and dependency of the Crown to be held in connection with the National Training School for Music, for which there was to be an annual competition; hence Cole hoped to provide free education by public subscription to all those who attended the NTSM.

6   Henry Cope Colles and John Cruft, *The Royal College of Music: a Centenary Record 1883–1983* (London: Royal College of Music, 1982), p. 4.

7   Ibid.

8   Defoe, *Augusta Triumphans*, p. 16. '... what have I to do with Musick?' Defoe asks at the start of his thesis. His reply is that he has 'been a Lover of the Science from my Infancy, and in my younger Days was accounted no despicable Performer on the Viol and Lute, then much in Vogue.'

9   Ibid., p. 16.

of Drinking and Debauchery in our Sex, and helps the Ladies off with many an idle Hour, which sometimes might be worse employ'd.'[10]

Unlike the early Victorians, Defoe had advocated musical appreciation and participation as an appropriate diversion for the gentry and the 'better sort of Traders'.[11] Despite this, the title of his work clearly belies its content. In proposing an academy of music, his prime concern was not simply to amuse the upper classes, nor was it intended exclusively to save the expense and inconvenience of importing foreign musicians: it was all these things and more. In particular, it was a matter of national pride: through the establishment of a school of music, Defoe aspired to provide Britain with a worthy successor to Purcell.[12]

Defoe clearly understood the economics of institutions. His scheme's success was entirely dependent on its projected association with the substantially endowed Christ's Hospital.[13] Had this alliance been effected, he hoped that the academy would become a self-fulfilling prophecy.[14] He was confident that, after ten years, Britain would boast an indigenous 40-piece orchestra and opera chorus of 20 voices (of whom five would be soloists), and, most importantly of all, that 'in the process of time they will have even their Masters among themselves'.[15] In other words, 'a country is not musical or artistic when you can get its people to look at pictures or listen to music, but when its people are themselves composers and artists'.[16] Defoe's motivation was twofold. First, he could not see the point in engaging foreign singers (Italians in particular) at a cost of £1500 per annum each when, for £3000, 60 English musicians could be educated for a decade and 'enabled to live by their Science'.[17] There is no mention of board and lodging; however, it seems reasonable to assume that Defoe's design was for the boys to inhabit Christ's Hospital along similar lines to existing pupils. Secondly, he was concerned to inspire high standards in the students

---

10 Ibid.

11 Ibid., p. 17.

12 Ibid., p. 18. 'We have already had a *Purcel*, and no doubt, there are many latent Genius's, who only want proper Instruction, Application, and Encouragement, to become great Ornaments of the Science, and make *England* emulate even Rome it self.'

13 Ibid., p. 19. '... I humbly propose, that the Governours of *Christ's Hospital* will show their publick spirit, by forming an Academy of Musick on their Foundation. ... three Masters should be elected, each most excellent in his Way; ... and I think a 100 *l. per Annum* for each, would be sufficient, which will be a Trifle to so wealthy a body.'

14 Ibid., p. 21.

15 Ibid., p. 22.

16 Hugh Reginald Haweis, *Music and Morals* (London: W.H. Allen & Co., 1871), p. 491.

17 Defoe, *Augusta Triumphans*, p. 21. There is a misprint here: 'instead of 1500 l. *per Ann.* The price of one *Italian Singer*, we shall for 300[0] l. once in ten Years, have sixty *English* Musicians ...'. £3000 would have been the cost of employing three masters for a decade: cf. n. 13.

through the introduction of awards and prizes and by simply providing them with a first-class education.[18]

Thirty boys were to be given apprenticeships and divided into three classes: six for woodwind (two each to study the oboe, bassoon and flute), 16 to study strings, and eight to study voice, and organ or harpsichord.[19] They were to be educated by a different master in each subject and all were to be taught composition.[20] Morning and evening were to be devoted to music classes and practice, while the afternoon was to be set aside for reading and writing.[21] While there is no detailed discussion of girls' education, provision is made for it.[22] These plans were merely the first draft: Defoe had intended the institution to be expanded to 'a greater length and Grandeur' once profits allowed for it.[23]

Defoe's was not the only abortive attempt to establish a school of music in London, although it was not until a century later that a further attempt was made. Two members of London's Philharmonic Society (founded in 1813) had devised a plan for the establishment of an academy of music.[24] Livius, a member of the Society described as 'an amateur of high distinction', had vaunted the idea of an academy for vocal instruction and had even had a prospectus printed;[25] however, a school with such a limited brief could hardly have expected to win the confidence of the music profession as a whole, let alone the general public. This scheme, to which substantial amendments were made by Thomas Forbes Walmisley, suffered a fatal blow: just as the Philharmonic Society's committee had prepared its report to be discussed at a general meeting, an announcement was made, on the very day that the meeting was due to be held, that the RAM was to be established under the patronage of the king.[26] In effect, the Philharmonic Society's plans had been 'jostled off the course by the superior strength and activity of the noblemen and gentlemen originating the Royal Academy of Music';[27] however, all was not as it seemed.

---

18 Ibid., p. 21. 'There ought ... to be ... proper Prizes ... allotted, to excite Emulation in the Youths, and give Life to their Studies.'
19 Ibid., p. 19.
20 Ibid.
21 Ibid., p. 20.
22 Ibid., p. 21. 'For the greater Variety they may, if they think fit, take in two or more of their Girls where they find a promising Genius, but this may be further consider'd of.'
23 Ibid.
24 'The Royal Academy of Music', *Quarterly Musical Magazine and Review*, 4 (1822), p. 371.
25 Ibid.
26 Ibid.
27 Ibid., p. 393.

Bedevilled from its inception, the RAM had been founded 'without any consultation or co-operation with leaders of the musical profession'.[28] As an indifferent amateur composer, the qualification of the chief founder, Lord Burghersh, to head an institution which claimed to afford facilities for attaining perfection in music was questionable.[29] Indeed the inclusion of not a single musician on the Board of Directors or any of the committees did little to endear the RAM to the profession or the general public.[30] In 1823 this caused the RAM to be described in the *London Magazine* as a 'farce got up by "several persons of distinction"'.[31] Ironically, the aristocratic management of the RAM secured middle-class support as it was seen to preserve the institution from the unpredictable government and questionable integrity of 'mere professional hands'.[32]

Middle-class approbation did not last long, however. Burghersh's appointment of a foreigner, the French harpist Nicholas Bochsa, as secretary to the Board of Directors was a serious faux pas.[33] To compound matters, *The Times* had carried an article in 1826 exposing Bochsa: he had been convicted of fraud and grand theft in a French court and, in his absence, had been sentenced to be branded and sent into forced labour for 12 years.[34] In 1827 Bochsa was forced out of the RAM. As Beedell says, that he 'continued in aristocratic patronage' only goes to show to what extent the aristocracy was capable 'of maintaining its indifference to the claims not only of English musicians but of middle-class morality'.[35]

Considering Bochsa's appointment, it is particularly ironic that the primary objective of the RAM in 1822 had been to train indigenous musicians to compete successfully for employment with foreigners.[36] That this had also been Defoe's *raison d'être* indicates how little prospects for professional musicians had changed in London in nearly a century, and it clearly emphasised the need for a national conservatoire to train indigenous musicians. Indeed music was the only profession dominated by foreigners;[37] consequently, the importance given to the RAM's ability to

---

28 Ann Beedell, *The Decline of the English Musician 1788–1888* (Oxford: Clarendon Press, 1992), p. 68.
29 'The Royal Academy of Music', p. 372.
30 Ibid.
31 Quoted in Beedell, *The Decline of the English Musician*, p. 69.
32 Quoted ibid., p. 68.
33 Ibid. See also Leanne Langley, 'Sainsbury's *Dictionary*, the Royal Academy of Music, and the Rhetoric of Patriotism', *Music and British Culture 1785–1914* (Oxford: Oxford University Press, 2000), pp. 73–88.
34 Ibid.
35 Ibid., p. 69.
36 Corder, *A History*, p. 2.
37 Cyril Ehrlich, *The Music Profession in Britain since the Eighteenth Century: a Social History* (Oxford: Oxford University Press, 1985), p. 16.

rid London's musical arena of its foreign monopoly was symptomatic of the nationalist *Zeitgeist* mentioned above.

Lord Burghersh's overambitious management structures had beleaguered the RAM and brought pressure to bear on inadequate resources. As a private venture, the RAM received little or no government support, unlike its European counterparts.[38] Its only sources of income were funds raised through public subscription and student fees. While public indifference had limited the RAM's ability to attract funds through public subscription, Burghersh, absurdly, appointed yet more directors in a desperate attempt to raise capital. The RAM's main source of revenue was student fees. With few scholarships at its disposal and a student population largely from the lower orders (those who could least afford to pay fees), its influence upon the musical life of the nation was severely restricted.[39] At a time when there were a mere 20 students (as opposed to the intended 80), there were 25 directors, 13 trustees and 40 professors.[40] Corder's observation – 'truly a vast deal of machinery to very little purpose! There were as many governors as governed' – was modest.[41]

Such a management structure would have caused problems for any institution. In 1824, Lord Burghersh petitioned for government subvention. This was unforthcoming; consequently, in 1825, the directors enlarged the student population to 100, by which means they were able to increase revenue. Student expansion compelled the RAM to enlarge its premises and the lease of 5 Tenterden Street was acquired with the help of public subscription.[42] The government's decision to defray the cost of a Royal Charter in 1830 gave the institution short-term security; however, Cazalet's assertion that 'after 1834 ... the Academy settled down into a regular form and routine' was unwisely premature.[43] In 1834 William IV directed that four King's scholarships were to be created at the RAM out of the proceeds (£2250) from the Westminster Abbey Musical Festival that year, although such paltry sums were not about to secure its long-

---

38 Stradling and Hughes, *The English Musical Renaissance*, p. 33. The Paris Conservatoire, in particular, had consistently received government subvention at the equivalent of £10 000 a year.

39 Beedell, *The Decline of the English Musician*, p. 70.

40 'The Royal Academy of Music', p. 372. The RAM was founded for the 'maintenance and general instruction of a certain number of pupils, not exceeding at present forty males and forty females'. That it commenced work with only 20 students is a clear indication of the level of organisation which preceded its foundation.

41 Corder, *A History*, p. 3.

42 William Barclay Squire, rev. F. Corder, 'The Royal Academy of Music', *Grove's Dictionary of Music and Musicians,* 4th edn (London: Macmillan, 1948), vol. 4, p. 458.

43 William Wahab Cazalet, *The History of the Royal Academy of Music* (London: T. Bosworth, 1854), p. 271.

term future.[44] In an effort to resolve its financial problems and in recognition of the Kensington Estate's newly accorded cachet, following the success of the Great Exhibition of 1851, the directors applied to the Commissioners for a site there in the same year.[45]

The Great Exhibition of 1851 had enjoyed success of every kind. As a Society of Arts enterprise, with Henry Cole at the helm, it had enjoyed the support of Queen Victoria, and had been instigated by the Society's President, Prince Albert. During the course of the only year it remained open to the public at Hyde Park, it had attracted over six million visitors at a time when the census for London was a mere two million, accumulating profits in excess of £180 000.[46] The Royal Commissioners had used part of the substantial profit to acquire land on the south side of Hyde Park, which came to be called the South Kensington Estate. In 1851 and 1854 the directors of the RAM applied for land to erect a building there, as their premises, situated just off Hanover Square, were in an area of London where immigrants outnumbered natives, and where the mortality rate from diseases such as typhus, cholera and smallpox was high. As the Kensington Estate was to be used for other government projects enjoying royal patronage, the directors were convinced that government protection and subvention would surely follow the RAM's acquisition of land there.[47] In 1860, upon hearing nothing from the Commissioners, the Society of Arts was approached directly by the RAM's directors for advice on restructuring its management. They had hoped their appeal would receive the sympathetic attention of the Society's President, Prince Albert. His death in December 1861 shattered the Academy's chances of success; instead, it catapulted the irascible Utilitarian Henry Cole into a position of immense power and responsibility as the Society of Arts' Chairman of Council. His success in creating the Great Exhibition of 1851 had confirmed him as an eminent Victorian and he had been knighted. Thus it was into his hands that responsibility for certain aspects of the RAM's future now came to be placed.

It was not until May 1861 that the Society of Arts finally responded to the RAM's petition in the form of a report.[48] Cole's radical proposals were designed to transform it into an effective national institution, assured of the approbation of the music profession. To effect this, Cole's

44 Ibid.

45 'The Proposed National Institutions at Kensington', p. 611: 'it is proposed to erect certain buildings for Government objects, such as the Department of Science and Art, and for any institutions which may require them, such as the Royal Academy of Music, which has already applied for ground at Kensington for a building'.

46 Michael Musgrave, *The Musical Life of the Crystal Palace* (Cambridge: Cambridge University Press, 1995), p. 9.

47 'Music Education Committee', *Journal of the Society of Arts*, 13 (1864–65), p. 593 f.

48 Society of Arts Council Minutes (22 May 1861), Royal Society of Arts Archive.

intention was to remodel the RAM as a national institution on the Kensington Estate in connection with the Royal Albert Hall. Of the 21 recommendations, three were significant in establishing the RAM as a truly national institution. First, the Society recommended that any national school of music should put the best possible instruction, affordably priced, within the reach of those with musical aptitude, as on the Continent.[49] Secondly, it advised the RAM to reorder its management to combine distinguished professional musicians with those who fostered an interest in the art.[50] Thirdly, it recommended the establishment of a national library of music and musical literature, a museum, and a reading room to incorporate existing collections from the British Museum and the Academy's own library.[51] Successful implementation of the Society of Arts' Report was entirely reliant on solid financial management and adequate premises to accommodate the increased numbers of students, teaching facilities, libraries, reading room and museum. These were not luxuries at the Academy's disposal. Affordable instruction could only be provided on the scale of European conservatoires if government subvention were forthcoming, as it was on the Continent, and the RAM did not have the resources at its disposal to implement the Society's recommendations; in any case, the directors procrastinated and the report was deferred. Nevertheless, with the intention of submitting a report to the government, Cole established a music committee at the Society of Arts in 1865, to compare the state of music education abroad with that in England, with special reference to the RAM.[52] The Prince of Wales agreed to chair the committee so long as 'nothing should be done hostile to the Royal Academy of Music'.[53] As a result of Cole's petition, the Gladstone government acceded to the RAM's demands for a grant, and donated the magnanimous sum of £500.[54]

The RAM had more pressing matters to deliberate: in January 1866, a serious fire had broken out at Tenterden Street, making it 'barely possible

---

49 Ibid. Significantly the Society of Arts Report makes no mention of free education, rather recommends pricing it on 'moderate terms'.

50 Ibid.

51 Ibid.

52 'Minutes of the Music Education Committee', *Journal of the Society of Arts*, 13 (17 February 1865), p. 217 f. 'The Committee issued the following queries to the professors, amateurs and others interested in the subject, and desire to obtain their opinions thereon. Members willing to aid them in this enquiry are requested to communicate their views: What are the essential differences between the plan of the Royal Academy of Music in London, and the Conservatoires of the Continent, with regard to their constitution and management; their revenues ... derived from the State, annual subscriptions, fees from pupils, concerts, or other sources.'

53 Alan Summerly Cole, *Fifty Years of Public Work of Sir Henry Cole, K.C.B.* (London: G. Bell & Sons, 1884), p. 366.

54 Squire, rev. Corder, 'The Royal Academy of Music', p. 478.

to carry on the institution ... from the ... dilapidated state of the house'.[55] As a temporary concession, one of the Commissioners, Lord Granville, agreed to allow the RAM to move to the South Kensington Museum if Michael Costa, the leading conductor of the day, were appointed Professional Director.[56] Costa's view of the RAM was not complimentary: he felt it was 'no use to mend an old coat'.[57] Despite this, he accepted Cole's generous offer to become Principal at a salary of £1200 a year and a tied house on condition that the RAM was given government protection and that Lord Granville and Cole were appointed President and Vice-President respectively.[58] Regrettably, Granville reneged on his promise and Costa was never appointed. After some 18 months' negotiation, the Department of Science and Art found they were unable to 'accede to the request ... for temporary accommodation at the South Kensington Museum' as they wished to avoid giving the impression the Government shared responsibility for the RAM's state of affairs.[59]

In August of 1866 there were two important appointments at the RAM: William Sterndale Bennett (Professor of Music at Cambridge, alumnus and professor at the RAM) was appointed Principal and Otto Goldschmidt (a composer and former pupil of Mendelssohn at the Leipzig Conservatoire) was appointed Vice-Principal, to 'ensure the approbation of the musical profession'.[60] Bennett's appointment did not improve the RAM's chances of securing accommodation at Kensington. First, he had not been Lord Granville's preferred choice; secondly, it had been made clear in an interview at the Society of Arts that his views did not concur with those of the Music Education Committee; and thirdly, he was opposed to any union between the RAM and the Society.[61] While Bennett conceded that a move to South Kensington would be ideal if the RAM remained in London, he nevertheless advocated a move to cheaper premises outside the capital where students could be educated in an environment free from the distraction and inconvenience of city life.[62] He was

---

55 William Sterndale Bennett's Private Papers (13 August 1866), Royal Academy of Music Archive.

56 Elizabeth Bonython (ed.), 'Sir Henry Cole's Diaries' (unpublished edition, c.1992). Entry dated Friday, 9 February 1866.

57 'Minutes of the Music Education Committee', *Journal of the Society of Arts*, 7 (1858–59), pp. 448 and 451.

58 Cole, *Fifty Years of Public Work*, p. 367. Costa subsequently managed to negotiate a projected salary increase to £2000 even before he had embarked upon the post.

59 Ibid.

60 William Sterndale Bennett's Private Papers (13 August 1866), Royal Academy of Music Archive.

61 Cole, *Fifty Years of Public Work*, p. 369.

62 'Minutes of the Music Education Committee', *Journal of the Society of Arts*, 14 (1866–67), p. 303.

happy for financial decisions to rest with a lay committee of management, but he was adamant that all musical decisions should be undertaken solely by a board of professors chaired by the Principal. Furthermore, he was resolute that the RAM should remain separate from any attempt to found a new school of music.[63] Such differences of opinion did not augur well and Bennett was moved to resign in order to allow the RAM freedom 'to elect a principal more acceptable to the authorities of South Kensington' as he and Goldschmidt both knew that without suitable premises, it would be 'hopeless that the suggestions contained in the [Society of Arts'] Report ... could ever be put into force'.[64]

In 1867 the RAM's directors petitioned the new Tory administration for a grant. The response was not heartening: Disraeli, then Chancellor of the Exchequer, stated in the House of Commons that the 'Government were of the opinion that they would not be authorized in recommending any enlargement of the grant, the result of the institution not being in fact of a satisfactory character'.[65] This was followed by a complete withdrawal of the grant. Exasperated at the situation, Bennett attacked Cole the following year as a 'national music-master' and declared the Society of Arts report a 'deception'.[66] Disraeli's statement in the Commons had done the RAM untold harm and naturally incensed Bennett who, in a letter dated 22 June 1868, wondered 'when and where the investigation [implicit in his speech] took place, and by whom on the part of the Government it was conducted'.[67] In a reply, Herbert Murray, Disraeli's secretary, wrote that the speech had been 'simply to give effect to the opinion that it was not so expedient to subsidise a central and quasi independent association, as it was to establish a system of musical instruction under the control of some department of government'.[68] The Liberal victory in the General Election of 1868 came as a mixed blessing: on the one hand they restored the RAM's grant; on the other, they added a proviso that it had to be used for accommodation. If the RAM achieved a move to the South Kensington Museum, it would be discontinued.

The restoration of the RAM's grant had incensed the music profession. In 1868, 130 professional musicians petitioned the Department of Science

---

63 Ibid.
64 William Sterndale Bennett's Private Papers (13 August 1866), Royal Academy of Music Archive.
65 Committee of Management Minutes (24 January 1868), Royal Academy of Music Archive, p. 314.
66 James Robert Sterndale Bennett, *The Life of William Sterndale Bennett* (Cambridge: Cambridge University Press, 1907), p. 373 f.
67 William Sterndale Bennett's Private Papers (1868), Royal Academy of Music Archive.
68 Ibid.

and Art to establish a government school of music and a national opera. Their criticism of the RAM was damning:

> Understanding that the government and the commissioners of the arts exhibitions are being petitioned to contribute still further to the maintenance of the institution called the Royal Academy of Music, we, the undersigned professional musicians residing in England, realizing the fact that the Royal Academy of Music has failed to promote the highest interest of the musical art, that the late government grant has simply prolonged its existence but not extended its usefulness, and feeling, moreover, assured that any further repetition of such an attempt can only end in similar failure, and prove equally discreditable to the country and wasteful of its funds, do hereby respectfully advise the establishment of a *new school* of music, in which every advantage may be offered to musical students, to be presided over by competent professors appointed by the State, and responsible to it for the efficiency of the institution. Connected with such an academy, we would further advise, if possible, the establishment of an English national opera, believing by such agencies a genuine and useful impulse might be given to the development of musical genius in this country, and ultimately redeem it from the disgrace of being the only European nation that fails to cultivate its own national music.[69]

The musicians' petition led the Society of Arts' Committee on Musical Education to approach Parliament directly. On 20 June 1869, Sir John Pakington submitted a memorial recommending

> that certain students should receive gratuitous training, and ... be selected by public competition.
>   That your petitioners respectfully submit to your honourable House that a national training school can never be maintained by private enterprise, but only be established by the State, and supported by public funds, disbursed under parliamentary and ministerial authority.
>   That so far as your petitioners are enabled to judge from the evidence, they consider that at least two hundred students should be trained, that they should receive grants for maintenance, varying rates, in accordance with the system that is found to work so successfully in the art training schools at South Kensington.[70]

To be truly influential a national school of music would have to be run along Utilitarian lines, that is, the greatest good for the greatest number; however, the Society of Arts' attempt to gain government subvention backfired. Inspired by Benthamite principles, Cole's new school was intended to provide the greatest number of musicians (in this case 300) with the best musical instruction available. However, the government had

---

69 Extract from Appendix A to Fifteenth Report of the Science and Arts Department (1868), Royal Archives, pp VIC 1872/11318.

70 'National Training School for Music', *Journal of the Society of Arts*, 19 (1870–71), p. 448.

a different agenda: extending the Utilitarian principle further, they chose not merely to restrict their subvention to a minority group, such as would benefit from a national music school. Instead, through the implementation of W.E. Forster's Elementary Schools Education Act of 1870, they established education for all, in reading, writing, arithmetic and music. As yet another petition for a government endowment had failed, the Society's Musical Education Committee was forced to explore other means to raise capital for their projected school of music. By 1870, the Society of Arts' Council had begun to organise a series of six fund-raising concerts to be held in the Royal Albert Hall in 1871 and 1872.[71]

The invitation to Sir Michael Costa, the leading conductor of the day, to conduct the series was an indication of the level of support for Cole's scheme from professional quarters. It also attracted the support of 76 guarantors and 50 subscribers. The first concert, held on 12 April 1871, attracted an audience of some 5000 people, including the members of several foreign royal families. Initially the outlook was positive: excellent attendance and royal patronage would seem to have constituted certain success for Cole's music school. However, the concert-going public proved to be neither as sophisticated nor as appreciative as had been hoped, as the following subscriber's letter to *The Times* indicates:

> [The concerts were due to start at 8 but] ... visitors kept on coming in fully up till nine o'clock. Three or four seats in front of me were unoccupied for nearly three-quarters of an hour. The boys who vended the programmes took care that they should be heard, and were pushing their trade during the whole time. On my right two gentlemen stood for some considerable time, talking with subdued loudness. Behind me two ladies and a gentleman were talking with genteel loudness and the whole hour through, except during the *pianissimo* parts. For all the world like a drawing-room. Now, fancy the majority of 5,000 persons having a comfortable chat, and their voices going in genteel crescendo with the music, and the riddle is explained why the loud parts of the music became so often comparatively indistinct.[72]

As a result the series made a loss of £100.

Unperturbed, Cole drew up a rigorous campaign to provide funds for his national training school through public subscription.[73] The cost of providing such an education for each student was estimated at £40 a

---

71 'National Training School for Music', *Journal of the Society of Arts*, 19 (1870–71), p. 29.

72 Quoted ibid., p. 470.

73 National Training School for Music: 'A Proposal for founding Scholarships' (1872), Royal Archives, pp VIC 1872/11318.

year.[74] In order to achieve his goal to endow 300 places, he hoped to persuade the authorities in every county, colony and dependency throughout the Empire to provide the funds for at least one scholarship each.[75] Awarded for a period of five years, these scholarships were to be won by public competition held annually.[76]

Despite the Royal Academy's consistent failure to win confidence within either public or professional arenas, Cole remained committed to the idea that any new school of music should be formed as an 'outgrowth' of the senior institution, a feeling still strong in influential quarters.[77] Hence, in 1872, he made an attempt at reconciliation, offering £5000 worth of scholarships, if the RAM remodelled its administration.[78] On three occasions between July 1872 and March 1873, Cole attempted to lure the Royal Academy's authorities to Kensington with the offer of temporary accommodation at the Royal Albert Hall.[79] The directors found the spaces to be 'totally uninhabitable' and the matter was closed for the time being, Cole being forced to establish the National Training School for Music as an independent venture.[80]

Cole successfully applied for land on the Kensington Estate, this time for the NTSM. That 'temporary use of houses in the immediate neighbourhood of the Royal Albert Hall' was immediately available to the NTSM is an indication of the politics which had really bedevilled the RAM. The Commissioners subsequently extended the offer to 'a plot of land immediately adjoining [the Royal Albert Hall], to be leased on very favourable terms'.[81] In the meantime, the Royal Albert Hall Corporation had set aside rooms, including a lecture theatre, for use at a nominal rent until adequate provision could be made. Such assistance, estimated at £1000 a year, would have given the RAM new life and security. Cole secured the services of his neighbour, Charles Freake (a successful London builder), to erect purpose-built premises next to the Royal Albert Hall at his own cost.[82] Freake was said to have raised Kensington from a 'neglected suburb to a second Belgravia'.[83] The building, designed by

---

74 Ibid.
75 Ibid.
76 Ibid.
77 Cole, *Fifty Years of Public Work*, p. 369.
78 Ibid.
79 Ibid.
80 Entry in Sir William Sterndale Bennett's Daily Memorandum Book (February 1873), Royal Academy of Music Archive.
81 John Skidmore, 'The Society and the National Training School for Music', *Journal of the Royal Society of Arts*, 140 (1991–92), p. 205.
82 Ibid. The cost of erecting the building was £20 000.
83 Ibid.

Cole's son, Lieutenant H.H. Cole of the Royal Engineers, boasted 30 classrooms, professors' rooms and offices.[84] There had been a plan to link the NTSM to the Royal Albert Hall by means of a connecting bridge and to the Kensington Road by means of an arcade.[85] Cole had even contemplated building a chapel and wrote to the organist and composer H.J. Gauntlett; however, these additions were never completed.[86]

The Albert Hall Corporation's offer of temporary accommodation had come in the form of a letter expressing its approbation of 'the zealous efforts of the Society ... to promote musical education in the Queen's dominions'.[87] It had been signed by Prince Alfred, Duke of Edinburgh. Through Cole's persuasion, he was to become intimately involved with the NTSM, not merely as a figurehead, but as an active participant in its organisation.[88] In addition, his keen interest in music – he was leader of the amateur Royal Albert Hall orchestra – made him the ideal choice to chair the NTSM's Committee of Management.[89] The NTSM's accommodation and the active support and involvement of senior members of the royal family and the Society of Arts would seem to have constituted certain success; moreover, the NTSM's link to the Royal Albert Hall ensured its facilities were unrivalled by any conservatoire in Europe.

On 29 May 1873, a meeting was convened at Clarence House, the London home of the Duke, 'to discuss the founding of a national training school for music, separate from the Royal Academy of Music'.[90] It brought together some of the most influential men in England,[91] and acknowledged the fundamental principle of the new school to be 'the cultivation of the highest musical aptitude in the country in whatever station of society it may be found'.[92] In other words, from its inception, the NTSM's chief aim was to provide free instruction to musicians of limited means in order to occupy a 'field of action wholly distinct from ...

---

84 NTSM Committee of Management Minutes (June 1875), Royal College of Music Archive 001/1, p. 58a & b.

85 Ibid.

86 Bonython (ed.), 'The Diaries of Sir Henry Cole'.

87 Council Minutes (8 January 1872), vol. 14, Royal Society of Arts Archive, p. 188.

88 Skidmore, 'The Society and the National Training School for Music', p. 205.

89 Ibid.

90 NTSM Committee of Management Minutes (18 December 1873), Royal College of Music Archive 001/1, p. 18a.

91 Ibid. The Committee of those present comprised H.R.H. the Duke of Edinburgh, the Lord Gerald Fitzgerald, the Lord Clarence Paget, Mr Alan Cole, Mr Henry Cole, Major Donnelly, Mr C.J. Freake, Mr Frank Morrison, Mr Puttick, Mr S. Redgrave, Colonel Strange and General Earley Wilmot, Chairman of the Royal Albert Hall Corporation.

92 'Minutes of the Music Education Committee', *Journal of the Society of Arts*, 21 (1872–73), p. 447.

any other institution'.[93] In order to achieve this, Cole determined to raise funds for 300 scholarships through public subscription.

Candidates for the scholarships had to be nominated by their local communities, corporations and schools or by individuals, and competition was open to any subject of the Queen who was able to comply with the regulations and pay a fee of five shillings.[94] Candidates were required to provide a medical certificate, a birth certificate and two references showing them to be of good moral character.[95] Competition for scholarships, each valued at £40 per annum, was administered on a local basis. The NTSM took candidates 'having a natural disposition which ought to be cultivated for the advancement of musical art and public benefit. This musical gift may manifest itself either in vocal power, instrumental ability, or ... composition'.[96] National scholarships were to be available only to those already at the School. If successful, applicants for all scholarships could expect to have their books, instruments and music all funded by the School. For the majority of students, scholarships did not cover board and lodging; however, a few covered maintenance besides free tuition.[97] The NTSM's founders were adamant that entry to the School would not be facilitated by payment of fees alone, as had been the case at the RAM.[98]

The establishment of 300 scholarships in time for the NTSM's opening proved an impossible target. A compromise was reached whereby subscriptions for 100 scholarships for five years were to be established in order for the School to operate during its first year. Cole took his campaign across Britain, visiting Wales, Birmingham, Manchester, Liverpool, Nottingham, Sandwich, Hastings, Dover and Leeds. In 1874 the *Birmingham Post* carried an article which only served to focus attention on the need for financial support: 'Something more than a building ... will of course be needed for the successful establishment of the School; and unless the public come forward liberally with their contributions for the foundation of scholarships ... Mr Freake's munificence will have been to little purpose, and we shall be as far as ever from the accomplishment of our object ...'.[99] Cole had sent out 200 invitations for the London conference, which was opened by H.R.H. the Prince of Wales on 15 June 1875. The committee it established comprised some of those holding the highest

93 NTSM Committee of Management Minutes (June 1875), Royal College of Music Archive 001/1, p. 58a & b.
94 Ibid.
95 Ibid., p. 60a.
96 Ibid.
97 Ibid.
98 Ibid.
99 'National Training School for Music', *Journal of the Society of Arts*, 22 (1873–74), p. 376.

offices in the land: the Lord Mayor and Aldermen, the Sheriffs and representatives of the Corporation, the City Companies, the Archbishop of
Canterbury, the deans of Westminster and St Paul's, the Governor and
Deputy Governor of the Bank of England, the Chairman of Lloyds and
merchants of the City of London.[100]

It had been agreed that once the funds for 70 scholarships had been
subscribed, the Committee of Management would consider appointing a
staff of professors and examiners.[101] The NTSM did not have the complex
management structures which had afflicted the RAM and while the
Committee of Management was composed entirely of amateurs (a criticism levelled at the Academy), day-to-day administration was to be
undertaken by the professors and a registrar.[102] However, no principal
had been appointed. On 27 November 1875, Lord Paget suggested
approaching the 34-year-old Arthur Sullivan (then professor of composition at the RAM) with a view to appointing him Chairman of the Board of
Principal Professors.[103] Sullivan replied to the Duke of Edinburgh and in
his letter, dated 1 January 1876, included the following memorandum:

1. As I already hold the appointment of principal professor of
    composition at the Royal Academy of Music, I should not be
    inclined to accept a similar position at any other institution,
    unless it were accompanied by increased dignity. This could be
    accomplished by my being appointed Principal of the new
    School.

2. The appointment of Principal is an important one. He it is who is
    to direct the teaching, and to influence the whole institution – to
    encourage or admonish both pupil and teacher, and by his precept
    and example to give distinctive character to the School. The first
    exercise of his authority ought to be carefully choosing and
    recommending to Council [viz.: Committee of Management] for
    appointment of the staff of professors who are to carry on the
    work, without their cordial co-operation, he can do very little: still
    less if he has no control over them. The Principal Professors being
    already appointed, I could not simply consent to act as their
    chairman, for being chosen from among them, I might find myself
    in the position of having my decisions overruled, and my
    authority reduced to nought. This is why I strongly urge that a
    Principal be at once appointed, totally distinct from the Board of
    Professors, and that no further appointments of professors should
    be made except on his recommendation.

---

100 Ibid., p. 669.
101 Ernst Pauer was professor of piano, John Stainer was professor of organ with Dr
Frederick Bridge as his assistant, Albert Visetti was professor of singing, John Carrodus was
professor of violin and the Revd John Richardson was Registrar.
102 NTSM Committee of Management Minutes (June 1875), Royal College of Music
Archive 001/1, p. 35.
103 'National Training School for Music', *Journal of the Society of Arts*, 24 (1875–76), p. 195.

3. Under the Council, the Principal ought to be the chief authority
    in the School, and should have the right to direct communication
    with the Council.
4. I would respectfully urge that the institution be not termed a
    'training school', but simply National School of Music. The
    word 'training' would imply a school for teachers, and not for
    artists; as an artist, I have no inclination to become the head of a
    school of teachers.
5. I append a short outline of what I consider some of the duties of
    the Principal or Director.
6. As it will take a great deal of time and attention to carry out these
    duties thoroughly, I respectfully suggest that the salary should be
    one thousand pounds a year.[104]

Cole's candidate had been Sir Michael Costa, and he initially opposed
Sullivan's appointment as Principal, possibly as a result of his youth and
because he thought his private engagements would render it impossible to
make the NTSM his first consideration.[105] *The Orchestra* had carried an
article in which it was stated that Sullivan should have resisted accepting the
post of Director of the NTSM as it would distract him from his real gift for
composition.[106] Despite these differences of opinion, it was subsequently
agreed that, in the event of his acceptance, Sullivan's valuable services be
engaged.[107] By 11 January, Cole had received no word of acceptance from
Sullivan and after several visits concluded that he had 'no personal desire
whatever to be connected with the National Training School'.[108] Sullivan
had become aware of Cole's opposition to his appointment and it is not
unreasonable to assume there had been a character clash, hence his delay. A
series of meetings followed at which the two men reached a consensus.[109]
On 13 January, against his better judgement, Sullivan accepted the post of
Principal at a much-reduced salary of £400 for the first year.[110]

While the opening of the NTSM on 17 May 1876 marked a new era in
British music education, the future was by no means assured. As the
school's reputation was not yet sufficiently well established, it had
managed to attract only 51 scholars, instead of the revised figure of 100.[111]

---

104 NTSM Committee of Management Minutes (12 January 1876), Royal College of Music
Archive 001/1, p. 92.

105 Ibid., p. 94.

106 Quoted in Arthur Jacobs, 'Sir Arthur Sullivan and the R.C.M.: a Tribute to the
Composer's 150th Birthday', *Royal College of Music Magazine*, 89 (Summer Term, 1992).

107 NTSM Committee of Management Minutes (12 January 1876), p. 92.

108 Ibid., p. 93 f.

109 NTSM Committee of Management Minutes (13 January 1876), Royal College of Music
Archive 001/1, p. 95. Letter from Sullivan to the Duke of Edinburgh.

110 Arthur Jacobs, *Arthur Sullivan: a Victorian Musician*, 2nd edn (Aldershot: Scolar Press,
1992), p. 104.

111 Bonython (ed.), 'Sir Henry Cole's Diaries', entry dated Wednesday, 17 May 1876.

This naturally had serious financial implications, forcing a cut in salary on the professors before they had taught a single class.[112] There were also too few professors to teach the full complement of orchestral instruments. While the intake increased slowly but surely, the paucity of staff and students alike prompted the professors to send a statement to the Committee of Management in 1877:

> The orchestral practices, of so much importance as distinguishing a national school of music from a private venture, have been hitherto wanting and can no longer be delayed without serious injury to the career of the students, and without the danger of compromising the reputation of the school.[113]

In May 1877, the financial situation compelled the Committee of Management to send a 'memorial' to the Commissioners for the Great Exhibition requesting a grant. In the memorial, the Committee emphasised the imperative of securing funds for 300 scholarships and the students to fill them, if the school were to become financially viable.[114] In reply, the Royal Commissioner, Earl Spencer, suggested the school accept fee-paying students to remedy its financial quandary, as he doubted whether the founders' goal of establishing 300 scholarships could ever be achieved.[115] To add insult to injury, he raised the possibility of an amalgamation between the school and the RAM, the Academy already taking students exclusively on this basis.[116] This proved impossible for a number of reasons. First, the Duke of Edinburgh had expressed his opposition to any such manoeuvre on no fewer than three occasions in public and could not be seen to go back on his word. Secondly, he felt that 'the union of the two institutions could not be effected without risk of breaking faith ... with everyone connected with the School'.[117] Thirdly, he considered it unlikely that the RAM would wish to become part of a merger necessitating surrender of its charter, now that the students on its books had increased in number to 341 from 121 in over 20 years between 1855 and 1877.[118]

As to the founders' claim that the 'government ought, and are expected to take [the NTSM] completely under its own management', Spencer

---

112 NTSM: Committee of Management Minutes (17 May 1876), Royal College of Music Archive 001/1, p. 109.

113 Ibid., p. 188.

114 Ibid., p. 157.

115 NTSM Committee of Management Minutes (17 May 1877), Royal College of Music Archive 001/1, p. 172.

116 Ibid., p. 174.

117 Ibid.

118 Royal Academy of Music: Minutes of the Directors' Meetings (14 March 1877), Royal Academy of Music Archive, p. 160.

thought it a 'broken reed to lean upon and that the Treasury are not likely to undertake the charge of providing musical education if they find two institutions ... who do this work with small government assistance'.[119] He suggested that the NTSM would be more likely to attract funding from the Commissioners if it were to form an affiliation with a university for the purpose of granting music degrees or to obtain the necessary Parliamentary Faculty to award its own.[120] While no plan was matured in this regard, this innovative suggestion would have put the NTSM at the head of the musical world in providing residential music degrees, the first of their kind in Britain. In addition, the Commissioners felt that if the school could be

> united with the Royal Academy of Music, to form together the nucleus of a larger institution, which could be placed on a more permanent and extensive basis ... such an institution would fall more directly within the scope of the operations of Her Majesty's Commissioners, and might look to them for substantial help.[121]

On 13 July 1878, the Prince of Wales convened a meeting at Marlborough House at which he outlined a scheme for the new Royal College of Music: an amalgamation between the RAM and the NTSM. Prince Christian had been appointed to put it into effect.[122] On 29 July 1878 he wrote to Le Neve Foster, Honorary Secretary of the Society of Arts, seeking its support.[123] Sir Henry Ponsonby was appointed to the NTSM's Committee of Management to report to Queen Victoria on the progress of the scheme. In the hope of obtaining a grant from the Commissioners, Earl Spencer expressed his hope in a letter to Francis Knollys, the Prince of Wales's secretary, that the

> Prince of Wales will urge his views on Lord Beaconsfield. I do not think that Parliament will ever do as much for a college of music as the French do for their Conservatoire, but I quite hope that the Government will assist us very materially. Considering that now they spend nearly £90,000 a year on grants for musical education in our national schools, and this it is admitted to very little purpose, I think they might spend out of it £5,000 or more a year on our new college.[124]

---

119 NTSM: Committee of Management Minutes (17 May 1877), Royal College of Music Archive 001/1, p. 175.

120 Ibid., p. 176.

121 'National Training School for Music', *Journal of the Society of Arts*, 26 (1877–78), p. 223.

122 'College of Music', *Journal of the Society of Arts*, 26 (1877–78), p. 817.

123 Ibid.

124 Letter from Earl Spencer to Francis Knollys (12 November 1878), Royal Archives, Windsor Castle R.A.F28/160.

Lord Beaconsfield (Benjamin Disraeli) was unable to give any guarantee of government subvention, although he agreed to give the matter his full attention;[125] it is unlikely he would have favoured the subvention of an institution formed from the RAM, whose meagre grant he had removed when Chancellor of the Exchequer. Fortunately, if the merger were to prove successful, the RAM's 300 fee-paying students would secure the financial backing required, effectively subsidising scholars from the NTSM. Hence fee-paying students were to be educated alongside scholars whose instruction was to be defrayed gratuitously.

While both institutions had intimated their inclination to cooperate, any ideas for amalgamation proved fraught with difficulties. The success of the merger was entirely dependent on the Academy's surrendering its charter in favour of one drawn up by the Prince of Wales in 1878.[126] This effectively put an end, once and for all, to any chances of amalgamation, as the RAM's charter allowed it to surrender neither its autonomy nor its name.[127]

With the end of the five-year endowment period in sight, the Committee of Management had become resigned to the fact that the NTSM would form the nucleus of the new Royal College of Music. Responsibility fell to the Prince of Wales, as President of the proposed College, to persuade the NTSM's supporters to subscribe in favour of the new foundation. Hence a new charter was drawn up for the Royal College of Music in October 1880. In the final draft, it stated that there were to be three types of student: scholars, government pupils and ordinary students.[128] The scholars were to have their education and maintenance defrayed on their behalf. The introduction of Government pupils was an

---

125 Note on the back of Earl Spencer's letter in the handwriting of Sir Dighton Probyn (Comptroller and Treasurer to the Prince of Wales) indicating that he had spoken to Lord Beaconsfield on 19 November 1878.

126 NTSM Committee of Management Minutes (4 April 1879), Royal College of Music Archive 001/1, p. 190 f. Headed 'Draft Charter of the Royal College of Music (incorporating the Royal Academy of Music and the National Training School for Music)', it begins: 'Victoria, by the grace of God of the United Kingdom of Great Britain and Ireland Queen, Defender of the Faith, to all to whom these presents shall come, greeting: Whereas it has been presented by our most dearly beloved son, Albert Edward, Prince of Wales ... that it is most expedient to promote the further advancement of the art of music in the United Kingdom by the establishment of a Royal Musical Corporation of Music [sic] on a more extended basis than any existing institution'. Note that the proposed Draft Charter of the Royal College of Music of 8 October 1880 refers to a 'royal college of music ... with the inclusion as part thereof of the National Training School for Music at South Kensington.'

127 Royal Academy of Music: Minutes of the Committee of Management (30 November 1878), Royal Academy of Music Archive, p. 67.

128 'Papers relating to the Draft Charter of the Royal College of Music', *Journal of the Society of Arts*, 27 (1879–80), pp. 869–71.

innovative departure, designed to establish an effective link between the RCM and the State, in the hope of attracting financial support. Ordinary students had to find the cost of their education and maintenance themselves. Finally, the charter allowed students already enrolled at the NTSM to transfer to the new RCM as scholars.[129]

The charter broke new ground in terms of the influence the Royal College of Music was intended to exert over British music, as it was to superintend musical instruction in elementary schools and elsewhere in Britain in the interests of cultural enrichment.[130] In fact, this blatantly unworkable requirement was never implemented; however, it was undoubtedly intended as another means to attract funding for the College from the State, a prerequisite for any truly national institution.

There were more difficulties to come. The planned opening of the RCM in time for the Easter Term of 1881 was dependent on a positive conclusion to negotiations with the Government regarding financial support. In the event the timescale made it impossible to inaugurate the new institution in time; hence in a letter of 29 November 1880, the Duke of Edinburgh asked the founders and subscribers of the NTSM scholarships to donate funds for a further year in order to allow more time to institute the RCM.[131] The prospect of having to attract an entirely new group of scholars and professors was an inconvenience the founders of the new institution naturally wished to avoid. To this end, the Prince of Wales organised a royal visit to Manchester, the main aim of which was 'to rouse the Government to a sense of duty in encouraging and materially supporting the proposed Royal College of Music or National Conservatoire'.[132] George Grove, who was to become a member of the Council and Executive Committee of the new RCM in July 1881 and later its first Director, was one of the speakers at the Manchester campaign. It was Grove who, in the following year, in March 1882, undertook a six-month campaign to organise subscriptions for the Capital Fund.[133] This was a significant departure from the financial policy of the NTSM, where scholarship endowments had been subscribed as income rather than capital.

By this time, the landmark meeting, convened at St James's Palace by the Prince of Wales on 28 February 1882, had already taken place.[134] This marked the official establishment of the RCM, for the mayors of all the

129 Ibid.

130 Ibid.

131 NTSM: Committee of Management Minutes (29 November 1880), Royal College of Music Archive 001/2, letter between pp. 14 and 15.

132 Ibid., p. 24.

133 Percy M. Young, *George Grove: 1820–1900* (London: Macmillan, 1980), p. 162.

134 'The Royal College of Music', *Journal of the Society of Arts*, 39 (1881–82), p. 433 f.

cities in Britain, the Archbishop of Canterbury, members of the nobility and the Government (including the Prime Minister) were all invited.[135] At the final meeting of the NTSM's Committee of Management on 13 March 1882 the following resolution was carried: 'that the National Training School for Music be closed at the end of the present term'.[136] During the School's existence from 1875 to 1882 £21 493 had been spent, leaving £1100 which, in addition to the furniture, fittings and the building, were transferred to the RCM at Easter 1882.[137]

The desire to establish a national music school in Britain had begun in theory in the eighteenth century with Defoe's proposal of 1727. The series of circumstances which led to the foundation of the Royal College of Music at the end of the nineteenth century were entirely the result of Sir Henry Cole's determination as Chairman of the Society of Arts Council and the active involvement of every senior member of the Royal Family. The fact that the original idea had come from the Prince Consort himself and was developed by Cole undoubtedly explains Queen Victoria's personal interest. The common misunderstanding that the Prince of Wales had established the Royal College of Music in 1878 as a completely separate entity in competition with the NTSM is not borne out in the evidence found in the two draft charters and must surely be dismissed. The draft charter of 1878 clearly states that the name 'Royal College of Music' was initially intended to be applied to the organisation resulting from the merger between the RAM and the NTSM. That the Academy was unable to proceed does not alter the fact that the Royal College of Music was simply the umbrella organisation into which the NTSM, with common consent, became subsumed; consequently, a new draft charter was drawn up in 1880 to accommodate the revision. Both charters refer to Albert Edward, Prince of Wales, thus confirming his involvement (along with that of his two brothers and Queen Victoria) at both stages of the project. In addition, the Prince of Wales had supported Cole's campaign to attract scholarship subscriptions for the NTSM; he had approached the Government for a grant and worked with Cole at the Society of Arts. His involvement had ensured the RCM's establishment and the expansion of Cole's philosophy. Charles Freake's building, the creation of a capital fund at the Prince of Wales's insistence and the education of fee-paying students alongside scholars all ensured the College's future and security.

---

135 Ibid.

136 NTSM: Committee of Management Minutes (13 March 1882), Royal College of Music Archive 001/2, pp. 63 ff.

137 'The National Training School for Music', *Journal of the Society of Arts*, 30 (1881–82), p. 864.

CHAPTER FOURTEEN

The Family von Glehn

Valerie Langfield

Introduction

'She was a beautiful pianist, & lived much in musical circles, & had many friends amongst musicians both English and foreign.'[1] So was Mimi von Glehn described, to whom Sir George Grove was devoted; but it might have been said of many amateur musicians of the nineteenth century, at a time when the dividing line between amateur and professional musician was as strong as it is today, if perhaps of a rather different nature.

The amateur families, where music was understood, encouraged and played, and where the family members knew professional musicians on musically equal terms, but themselves rarely or never performed in public, formed an almost invisible backbone to the broad musical scene of the time, linking the anonymous (and comprehensively documented)[2] mass of amateur home pianists with professional musicians.[3] Between these public and the homely domains were many others: Mary Gladstone's diaries (running more or less from 1870 to her death in 1924), for example, while focusing on her life as the daughter of a Prime Minister, include frequent and casual mention of her musical activities: concert attendance (often at the Crystal Palace or St James's Hall) was regular, and Joseph Joachim was a friend of the family; she also sang in choral concerts. It is clear that she did not consider these activities special, and that they were part of her everyday life.[4] Muriel Draper's lively *Music at Midnight* (covering a later period, the few years from 1912 to 1914) describes a more concentrated musical life, the informal chamber music world of her home at Edith Grove, London,[5] but Gladstone and Draper have in common a clear knowledge and understanding of music, a strong involvement in it, and association with professional musicians, but no

---

1   Louise Creighton, *Memoir* (private archive), p. 22.

2   See Cyril Ehrlich, *The Piano: a History*, 2nd edn (Oxford: Oxford University Press, 1990).

3   See Cyril Ehrlich, *The Music Profession in Britain since the Eighteenth Century* (Oxford: Oxford University Press, 1985).

4   Mary Gladstone, *Mary Gladstone (Mrs Drew): Her Diaries and Letters*, ed. Lucy Masterman (London: Methuen, 1930).

5   Muriel Draper, *Music at Midnight* (London: Heinemann, 1929).

attempt to take the stage and be on display: Mary Gladstone's choral singing was acceptably amateur.[6]

The salon culture of the period, linking private and public concert worlds, is colourful enough to have been recorded on canvas as well as in print; James Tissot's 'Hush! (The Concert)', first exhibited in 1875, is especially evocative, with its images of rapt listeners, and those with quite different agendas.[7] Literary images of nineteenth-century concert life and the lives of professional musicians are supplied – thanks largely to the self-publicising nature of the subjects, and the natural verbosity of contemporary critics – in such volumes as Joseph Bennett's *Forty Years of Music*, Hermann Klein's *Thirty Years of Musical Life in London*, and J.H. Mapleson's *Memoirs*;[8] in consequence, the upper-class amateur with ability, who raised money for charity through concert performances, but would never dream of turning professional, is not an unknown figure. There were some, certainly, who did turn professional – Gervase Elwes and Elsie Swinton, amongst others – but in general it was not considered an appropriate activity.[9]

In the salon realms, too, much of the significance for the hostesses lay in being seen, with the consequent reporting of events in the society papers. Occasionally, however, one catches a glimpse of more philanthropic activity: in her unpublished memoir *Myself When Young*, the wealthy musical patron Mrs Wyndham Knatchbull (who, as Dora Bright, was a pianist-composer) describes her efforts to secure funding for the proposed Festival of English Music in 1904.[10]

The private music circles, however, still guard their secrets. Their contributions were valuable: their members were knowledgeable, competent amateur musicians, and did not seek publicity; music was simply an intrinsic part of everyday life. The Lehmann-Chambers family was one such;[11] the Glehn family was another, but much more shadowy, appearing

---

6   For a fuller discussion of the amateur/professional divide and the tensions it could cause, see Paula Gillett's excellent chapter 'Ambivalent Friendships: Music-Lovers, Amateurs, and Professional Musicians in the Late Nineteenth Century', in Christina Bashford and Leanne Langley (eds), *Music and British Culture, 1785–1914: Essays in Honour of Cyril Ehrlich* (Oxford: Oxford University Press, 2000), chap. 15.

7   It is owned by Manchester Art Gallery.

8   Joseph Bennett, *Forty Years of Music 1865–1905* (London: Methuen, 1908); Hermann Klein, *Thirty Years of Musical Life in London 1870–1900* (New York: Century, 1903); J.H. Mapleson, *The Mapleson Memoirs: the Career of an Operatic Impresario 1858–1888*, ed. Harold Rosenthal (London: Putnam, 1966).

9   See respectively Winefride and Richard Elwes, *Gervase Elwes* (London: Grayson & Grayson, 1935), and David Greer, *A Numerous and Fashionable Audience: the Story of Elsie Swinton* (London: Thames Publishing, 1997).

10   Dora Knatchbull, *Myself When Young* (private archives), pp. 72–74.

11   See R.C. Lehmann, *Memories of Half a Century* (London: Smith, Elder, 1908), and John Lehmann, *Ancestors and Friends* (London: Eyre & Spottiswoode, 1962).

in passing and in footnotes rather than anywhere more substantive (see the family tree in the Appendix). The Glehns were not of a class for whom a child prodigy in the family – such as the pianist Adelina de Lara (1872–1961) or the violinist Marie Hall (1884–1956) – meant an escape from poverty and labour. Nor were they amongst the wealthy patrons of the time, to whose soirées and salons eminent musicians came to perform. Rather, they were a multitalented and multifaceted family, in which music played a vital part; with such families as these, musicians and composers found themselves in relaxed, congenial and sympathetic surroundings.

The Glehn family origins

There were two centres of interest: the family home, Peak Hill Lodge, in Sydenham, and one of the daughters, Mary Emilie, always called Mimi.

The story of the family begins with Mimi's father, Robert von Glehn, an Estonian immigrant merchant. The Glehn family originated from the village of Glehn, near Cologne in the Rhineland, but they had moved away from there some generations previously, migrating via Lübeck to Reval (now Tallinn), the capital of Estonia. The family is still known there, remembered in the Glehn castle, built by Nikolai von Glehn, a relative of Robert. Robert's father, Peter von Glehn, married Elizabeth Clayhills, of a Scottish family established in Reval for several generations; her father had founded the firm of Thomas Clayhills & Son there. Robert was their second son, born 6 January 1801, and though their circumstances seem to have been somewhat straitened (owing to the 'follies of a brother-in-law'),[12] they were still genteel.

As a Russian subject, Robert spoke Russian and Estonian; the house language was German, and he also spoke English and French. He first came to London in 1828 in connection with import–export business; he visited several times more, and by the time of his marriage in 1835 to Agnes Duncan, he had settled in England, eventually becoming a naturalised British citizen (see Fig. 14.1.) He established a business, though from the end of the First World War, the family firm was owned by a partner, S.A. Spillar, and it finally ceased business in 1921.[13]

---

12 J.T. Covert, *Memoir of a Victorian Woman* (Bloomington and Indianapolis: Indiana University Press, 1994), p. 2.

13 The various business addresses, all in London, were: by 1850, 1 Birchin Lane; by 1854, 31 Nicholas Lane (D.R. Webb (Librarian, Bishopsgate Foundation) to K. Richardson, 21 May 1979); 1860–64, 6 Martins Lane; 1865–70, 27 Mincing Lane; 1871–77, 9 Fenchurch Street; 1878–1921, 7–8 Idol Lane. (D.A. Painter (the Baltic Exchange) to K. Richardson, 19 March 1979.)

Fig. 14.1   Robert von Glehn (courtesy of John de Bruyne)

Robert's future mother-in-law, Catherine Reierson, née Melville, had first married Thomas Duncan. He travelled out to India and she set out to join him there, leaving her daughter Agnes behind to be brought up in Edinburgh by her uncle, Agnes's great-uncle, David Brodie, and his sister Margaret. On her arrival in India, however, Catherine discovered that her husband had died. She was unwilling or unable to return, and instead stayed with one of her brothers; when eventually she did return, it was with a second husband, Peter Reierson, a Dane.[14]

In the meantime, she had left very detailed instructions on how Agnes was to be treated – her natural inquisitiveness, for example, was not to be suppressed, but rather encouraged. Agnes's great-uncle was not entirely in accord with the wishes, but nevertheless she grew up not only well educated,

---

14   Ernest von Glehn, *Memoir* (private archive), p. 7, and Louise Creighton, *Memoir*, p. 2.

and with the usual accomplishments, but with an open and independent
mind, a significant factor in the atmosphere of the future household.

Agnes's mother and stepfather clearly aimed for a good marriage
match for her; Robert may not have been the ideal choice, and he was also
indecisive in the matter, since it was some years before Robert and Agnes
married. He was nevertheless acceptable: though not especially well
educated he was sociable, very fashionable, good company and person-
able. He was over six feet tall and of slender build, he was musical – as
was his wife – and he was a good dancer. For their honeymoon, they went
abroad, 'travelling across Europe by road in their own carriage from
Ostend to Lübeck where they took ship for St Petersburg'.[15] Their journey
took them through Belgium and Germany and they arrived in St Petersburg in the middle of July 1835. They travelled on to Reval, meeting
Robert's family, returned to St Petersburg and left there 10 August 1835,
returning to England via Hamburg. Writing to her mother, Agnes
described Reval as 'a nice old town, so old-fashioned and primitive and
the country round is very pretty, the people too are old-fashioned, just like
what I can fancy in Scotland 30 or 40 years ago'.[16]

The house and household

Agnes's mother owned a house (now demolished, rebuilt and renum-
bered) at what was then 34 Upper Harley Street, London. Though it
suited them all to live there together, she combined poor health with a
narrow-minded and domineering manner and Robert clearly found it a
trial living with her. He decided he needed a home outside London –
where Mrs Reierson would naturally always have a room available – and
they would spend part of the year at Harley Street and the rest in the
country. In the early 1840s, he took a house in Sydenham where
Trewsbury Road is now,[17] but in 1845, after renting it for a summer,[18] he
bought Peak Hill Lodge on a 60-year lease, for £1200, from the Reverend
Thomas Bowdler, nephew of the Shakespearean Bowdler, and he
extended it twice to accommodate his growing family – there were 13
children in all, though the first was stillborn and one, Edward, died of
scarlet fever when he was 10; his name was forbidden to be mentioned
ever again.[19] The architect for the extensions was H. Currie, who was

15 Ernest von Glehn, Memoir, p. 9.
16 Agnes von Glehn to her mother, 2 August 1835, quoted ibid., p. 30.
17 1841 census.
18 Louise Creighton, Memoir, p. 6.
19 He was buried at St Bartholomew's Church, Sydenham.

later the architect for St Thomas's Hospital: a day nursery (later the schoolroom) was built over the kitchen; a bedroom or two was added; the dining room was lengthened, and 'finally the tower at the south west of the house'. When the schoolroom was no longer needed for its original purpose, 'it became the sitting room of the younger members'.[20] There was a piano there which was later moved to Mimi's room.

In the early years at the Peak, Robert and Agnes led a quiet life, and Robert even travelled third class into London, 'so as not to be disturbed by acquaintances'.[21] Catherine Reierson died in 1849, but Robert and Agnes kept the Harley Street house on. However, imprudent financial speculations by Agnes's uncle reduced the value of her inheritance, and after their son Edward died in 1854, they sold the Harley Street house and another property of Mrs Reierson's, Woodhill, near Guildford, Surrey, and made Peak Hill Lodge their only home (see Fig. 14.2). One of Robert's daughters, Louise, described it in her memoir as 'a pretty little red-gabled house standing in seven acres of land. There was a large field in the front; and the London and Brighton railway ran at the bottom of the field'.[22] Louise's concept of 'little' appears to be somewhat unusual, but

Fig. 14.2   Peak Hill Lodge c. 1880 (courtesy of Anne-Cécile de Bruyne)

20 Louise Creighton, *Memoir*, p. 8.
21 Louise Creighton, *Abstracts from the Diary of Robert von Glehn* (private archive), p. 16.
22 Louise Creighton, *Memoir*, p. 7.

she may have been influenced by her accommodation at the time of
writing, since she was by then living in a grace and favour apartment at
Hampton Court. Her brother Ernest's memory of the land was slightly
more expansive: in *his* memoir, the house stood in eight acres, and was
'surrounded by pasture and woods (in which nightingales sang loudly)
and … looked out on a charming distant view of Kentish uplands'.

Figure 14.2 shows the house, and some occupants, as it was in the time
of the Glehns, 1886 or earlier. Water was supplied from an old artesian
well to several local houses, and was pumped up by a steam engine housed
in a circular building just outside the grounds; the engine furnace would
not infrequently belch out thick foul black smoke.

Robert von Glehn was a member of the Baltic Exchange from 1860 to
1876, and his business connections brought many foreign visitors to the
house. The family had Continental ways and strong Continental links, and
they felt themselves to be a little out of the ordinary, something they clearly
rather relished; even mealtimes were sometimes conducted in French, with
the children being sent out if they refused to comply.[23] Some members of
the family married into European families, so that there were links with
France, Germany and Russia. Ida, another of Robert's daughters, married
her cousin Nicolai Koch, son of Robert's sister Molly and an old Estonian
friend Andreas Koch, and she lived the rest of her life in Estonia.

The Glehns seemed to have emerged from nowhere, with no English
social background, and there was something intriguing about them; even
the house was considered rather Gothic, its atmosphere known within the
family as 'The Gloom of the Glehn'.[24] The household was lively and unpredictable: personalities were strong and interesting, conversation likewise.
There was an informality, unconventionality and freedom that was very
attractive to visitors, at least to interesting visitors; dull ones were treated
politely enough but were probably left wondering quite what was going on.

The Glehns tended to associate more with the long-established inhabitants of Sydenham, rather than the newcomers who moved in as Sydenham
developed. Mr and Mrs Mayow Adams and their daughter Edith, for
example, lived at the Old House, a great Georgian red-brick house, on the
left-hand side of the road a short way down the hill; the Mayow Adams
were the major land-owning family of the area, their wealth deriving from
the efforts of an earlier-generation solicitor with business acumen. The
property had a wood (the nightingale wood), separated from the grounds
of the Peak by a railway cutting, and in it there was a pond, part of an
older canal which had extended to London. In the pond were muddy
tench, which the Glehn boys used to fish.

---

23 Ernest von Glehn, *Memoir*, p. 30.
24 Covert, *Memoir*, p. xi.

Robert was a shareholder in the Crystal Palace and the family went to the Saturday concerts regularly, and also to the various exhibitions which the children found fascinating, but though Robert and Agnes are spoken of in the warmest terms in contemporary reports (C.L. Graves describes Agnes as clever and well read and says that she 'shone as a conversationalist'),[25] it was their children who tended to generate the artistic circles, since they were so much younger and more energetic. The family kept open house on Sunday afternoons, keenly awaiting visitors, and excited to see who would visit – 'any number from twelve to eighteen might turn up to lunch on Sundays and more to tea'.[26] They felt that the visitors became more interesting as time went on, with the increase in the proportion of musicians to businessmen; the latter they found rather unstimulating. The household management was fairly frugal, neither luxurious or extravagant: Robert received an 'adequate income from the business in which he was engaged, at first with Russia, and later with Mauritius and India, but he was not what would be called a rich man now'.[27] In addition, 'somewhere about the year 1875 the family fortunes sank rather low owing to the failure of a Bombay House in which [the] Firm was involved, & in consequence of this a good many economies were introduced into the family life'.[28] Agnes von Glehn worked extremely hard running the house, and although naturally there were servants, she was often ill with tiredness and overwork.

Local families came to the weekly reading parties at which books of general interest were read aloud and discussed: the Scott Russells lived at Westwood Lodge, a red-brick house that they had had built, with grounds laid out by Paxton; their house was considered 'very exquisite with "Pompeian style of decoration"'. John Scott Russell was a naval architect, involved in the building of the *Great Eastern* steamship; he 'was a versatile good looking man, full of enterprise, a great talker, full of original schemes, always originating new ideas & making wonderful plans'[29] and there was a 'freedom of expenditure'[30] that was lacking at Peak Hill Lodge. The other regular visitors to the reading parties – the Davidsons (Charles Davidson was a barrister), the Rowlands (David Rowland was a solicitor) and the painter Henry Wyndham Phillips – had houses on Sydenham Hill, close to the

---

25 C.L. Graves, *The Life and Letters of Sir George Grove* (London: Macmillan, 1903), p. 41.

26 Louise Creighton, *Memoir*, p. 9.

27 Ernest von Glehn, *Memoir*, p. 45.

28 Ibid., p. 80.

29 'They had three beautiful and talented daughters & one son' (Louise Creighton, *Memoir*, p. 11).

30 Ibid.

Peak;[31] but neither the Davidsons nor the Rowlands had children, and their names fade out of the story. Another family, the Ogilvys, also figured in the family life. The Glehns were close to Westwood House, home of Henry Littleton, the proprietor of Novello's, who, though considered rather an upstart and not of the proper social background, was in a position to play host for what would be Liszt's last visit to London, in April 1886.

According to Ernest von Glehn, the family held theatricals: 'the double drawing room would be converted into a sort of theatre with footlights and an attempt at scenery [made]'. Louise von Glehn wrote that 'music from the first played a great part in the family life. My father & mother were both genuinely musical & many of the family had exceptional musical gifts. Sophie & Ida, Alick, Ernest & Harry sang & Mimi was a very fine pianist ... Willie, Oswald & I were the three of the family who were quite without musical talent, but growing up in such a musical atmosphere, we all loved music & understood at least something about it. Every evening after dinner my father called for music & there was playing & singing for an hour or two; he still himself sang when I was a child.'[32]

Mimi von Glehn

The focus of the many musical evenings was undoubtedly Mary Emilie (Mimi), her fine abilities as a pianist attracting both attention and musicians. She studied with Franklin Taylor, and also periodically in Hanover with Hans von Bülow, who thought very highly of her playing, regarding her as 'the most gifted of his amateur pupils',[33] and Graves, in his biography of Parry, described her as 'fragile, gifted and magnetic'.[34] Her sister Louise said 'she was very much admired & beloved, a tall charming looking woman, very gifted especially musically. She was a beautiful pianist, & lived much in musical circles, & had many friends amongst musicians both English and foreign. She was very quiet & reserved in her manner but every one fell in love with her and there were many love affairs, but she could never make up her mind to give herself to one man. These agitating love affairs really wore her out.'[35] She was aware of her attraction, and consequently 'often [kept]

---

31 Ernest von Glehn, *Memoir*, p. 37: Davidson and Rowland 'lived next door to one another at the Old Grange and the Cottage in Sydenham Hill ... Phillips ... lived at 24 Westwood Hill' and later at Hollow Coomb, 'near the top of Westwood Hill'; John Coulter, *Sydenham and Forest Hill Past* (London: Historical Publications, 1999), p. 112.

32 Covert, *Memoir*, p. 8.

33 Quoted in Ernest von Glehn, *Memoir*, p. 41 and recorded also in Graves, *Grove*, p. 42.

34 C.L. Graves, *Hubert Parry* (London: Macmillan, 1926), vol. 1, p. 232.

35 Louise Creighton, *Memoir*, p. 22.

herself in the background trying to get newcomers to take to [her sister] Olga, but they always ended by being attracted to Mimi'.[36]

Following the reduction in family fortunes in 1875, Mimi began to give piano lessons. Her brother Ernest wrote 'there was at the Crystal Palace a sort of high school with classes for music, drawing & literature etc, and there she taught her pupils for a good many years. To me at that time this was an unwelcome innovation, & I suppose I took the Victorian view that it was infra dig. for a girl of our class to undertake professional teaching. Mimi had before this done some literary work, chiefly in the way of translations from the German, & with this & her pianoforte lessons she was earning enough to make herself independent of an allowance from the father.'[37] Like all the family, she was a fine linguist and undertook many translations, often for publications with which Grove was connected; amongst other things, she translated Karl Mendelssohn-Bartholdy's *Goethe and Mendelssohn (1821–1831)*, of 1872, and Ferdinand Hiller's *Mendelssohn – Letters and Recollections*, of 1873, both published by Macmillan; there was translation work for *Macmillan's Magazine* and also for the *Shilling Magazine*. In April 1880, she wrote in very friendly manner to Sir Hubert Parry (a frequent visitor to Peak Hill Lodge), congratulating him on his piano concerto, from which she took 'the greatest enjoyment from beginning to end', and particularly commenting on the 'lovely [oboe] part in the slow movement'.[38] One of Mimi's closest friends was Mrs Wodehouse, who wrote the article on 'Song' for Grove's *Dictionary*. There is no doubt that Mimi's presence was an artistic stimulus to the visitors to the Peak.

The rest of the family

As a young man of 20, Mimi's brother Willie went to Le Havre to learn the world of business;[39] he was a member of the Baltic Exchange from 1860 to 1878, two years longer than his father. At one stage, he was a very frequent visitor to Westwood Lodge, and was clearly developing an attachment to the eldest daughter of the house, Louise Scott Russell; she was a great friend of Olga and Mimi von Glehn, and like Mimi, she died of tuberculosis.[40] However, she was unable to make up her mind whether or not to marry Willie (this may have been the time she was otherwise occupied with Sullivan); eventually he gave up and in Stuttgart in 1877 he

---

36 Ibid., p. 23.
37 Ernest von Glehn, *Memoir*, pp. 80–81.
38 Mimi von Glehn to Parry [7 April 1880] (Shulbrede Priory Archive).
39 Louise Creighton, *Abstracts*, p. 20.
40 In March 1878.

married Sophie Löwe, one of Julius Stockhausen's singing pupils, who then gave up her singing career for one of teaching.[41] Their daughter Rhoda was also a singer: she was with the Stuttgart Court Opera for a time, and gave a recital at the Bechstein Hall in January 1903[42] and numerous other recitals in private salons.[43] Sophie still sang occasionally after her marriage: Fuller-Maitland records (though with some doubt about the accuracy of his memory) that she sang at his house, at a benefit concert for the new College of Music.[44] Both Sophie and Rhoda's musical careers were clearly more developed than Mimi's, though both performing careers were effectively curtailed upon marriage.

Mimi was not the only musical child of Robert and Agnes: Olga – godmother to Grove's youngest son Arthur – was a music teacher, though she too undertook translation work and probably compiled the index for J.R. Green's *Short History of the English People*. Clever and affectionate, she was also rather jealous, with a bad temper, and was considered the plain one of the family, although the singer Raimund von Zur Mühlen visited the Peak frequently and was evidently fond of her, and she of him.[45] She lived at Priory Cottage, 32 Sydenham Road, from 1894 to 1915. Ernest went to Christ Church, Oxford, and later married Marian Bradley, half-sister to George Grove's wife Harriet; he was 'the moving spirit' in the celebration of Grove's sixtieth birthday.[46] He was Managing Director of the Ragosine Oil Company from 1882 to 1909,[47] but his main claim to musical fame is that he was secretary of the Bach Choir for many years.

Alfred von Glehn was, like Ernest, a practical man, an engineer, famous within railway circles for his significant design work on compound locomotives; the French Railway Museum perpetuates his name in its address, 2, rue Alfred de Glehn, Mulhouse, Alsace.[48] He lived in Mulhouse all his adult life, and Grove, on his way home from Ragatz in 1893, visited him and his wife there.[49]

---

41 Louise Creighton, *Memoir*, p. 25, and Graves, *Grove*, p. 223.

42 Wigmore Hall Archives.

43 Rhoda von Glehn's concert diary.

44 J.A. Fuller-Maitland, *A Door-Keeper of Music* (London: John Murray, 1929), p. 89.

45 After retiring from singing, Zur Mühlen became a noted singing teacher. His pupils included Mark Raphael and, very briefly, Marian Anderson.

46 Young, *Grove*, p. 155.

47 Rocol archives. Victor Ivanovitch, who founded the company in 1878, was so convinced of the worth of his company's product that he declared substantial profits even though there were none, an accounting practice that still has its adherents today. In the structural reorganisation that followed in the wake of the inevitable revelations, Ernest was brought in, and he established the oil lubricant firm on a proper business footing.

48 Covert, *Memoir*, p. 14.

49 Young, *Grove*, p. 234.

Other children showed a more artistic bent: Oswald trained at the Slade School of Art and exhibited his work in England, and although Alick showed no especial musical or artistic aptitude, his children did. He had an inclination to go into medicine, but his education was inadequate, and instead, he carried on the family business, learning the trade by working first in St Petersburg and then in Mauritius. He married Fanny Monod, of a Huguenot family of medics – thus were his medical leanings satisfied – and they had a house on Peak Hill. One of their children, the charismatic Louis von Glehn, later lived in Grantchester, Cambridge, and taught French at the Perse School nearby; he was also at King's College. Another son was Wilfrid, an artist of the English Impressionist School, who became a member of the Royal Academy in 1923. He often travelled abroad with the noted portrait painter John Singer Sargent, who was somewhat annoyed when Wilfrid married a soft-spoken American from New York, Jane Emmet, in 1904; she was herself of a highly artistic family and a fine portrait painter in her own right. She was distantly related to Henry James, and an Irish ancestor was commemorated in Thomas Moore's 'Elegy on the Death of Robert Emmet', which in transla-tion, and called 'Élégie', was set by Henri Duparc.

Although Louise, Robert von Glehn's tenth surviving child, made no claims to be musical, some of her family were, by blood or by marriage. She married Mandell Creighton, who later became Bishop of London; while staying with them at Embleton, Northumberland, in August 1883, while Creighton still had the living there, Grove attended a service at the church, commenting afterwards: 'The service to-day was one of the nicest I ever took part in.'[50] Louise was a formidable character; Mary Gladstone met her in 1885 and said of her that she was 'so handsome ... a strong, direct, trustworthy face; liked her immensely but she frightened me to death'.[51] Mandell Creighton's nephew, Basil Creighton, wrote novels and programme notes, and did numerous translations from German, including B. Traven's novel *The Treasure of the Sierra Madre*, first published in German and later immortalised in John Huston's film, star-ring Humphrey Bogart. Basil Creighton's first wife, Ursula, wrote a little book called *Music*, which has a preface by Edward Dent, whom they both knew well. One of Louise and Mandell's children, Gemma, married Cyril Bailey, author of the biography of Hugh Allen.

Louise and Mandell's fourth child, Walter (see Fig. 14.3), went up to Emmanuel College, Cambridge, to read medicine, but gave it up to study singing in Paris, Berlin and Frankfurt; his parents disapproved at first but

---

50 Louise Creighton, *Life and Letters of Mandell Creighton* (London: Longmans, Green, 1904), vol. 1, p. 161.
51 Gladstone, *Mary Gladstone*, p. 352.

Fig. 14.3   Walter Creighton (courtesy of Mrs Hugh Creighton)

eventually gave their blessing. He was greatly encouraged by his aunt
Sophie Löwe, and like her, studied with the – by then – irascible Julius
Stockhausen, in Frankfurt in 1899.[52] Creighton's debut recital – at the
Bechstein Hall – was in June 1903, at which he premiered Roger Quilter's
Bodenstedt songs, for which he had also provided translations.[53] He gave

---

52 Stockhausen was by this time very ill, in permanent pain, and dependent upon teaching
for his income. He taught on a master-class basis, and according to Creighton, his bullying
methods meant that he 'counted each day a failure should less than three girls be reduced to
tears and hysteria or two men to suicidal despair'. (Walter Creighton, *Just on Sixty*,
unpublished autobiography; fictionalised in a vain attempt to hide identities.)
53 The set was reissued in 1911, with different translations by R.H. Elkin, and given its Op.
2 number.

the first performance of Vaughan Williams's *Songs of Travel* at the Bechstein Hall on 2 December 1904.

Creighton was also an actor, performing in a wide range of plays in London before the First World War, from Shakespeare to *Snowdrop and the Seven Little Men* and *Pinkie and the Fairies*, as well as *Orpheus in the Underground* and *Trilby*; he tried his hand at writing plays too. He was awarded the Military Cross in the First World War, and developed a long-hidden ability for organisation, one that he perhaps inherited from his terrifyingly well-organised mother. As a boy, he took violin lessons from Elgar, when they were both living in Worcester (they overlapped from 1885 to 1889), and in 1924, when organising the Pageant of Empire, Walter commissioned the Empire March from him. Ten years after that, he commissioned music from his friend Quilter for the Pageant of Parliament, which Creighton devised, wrote and directed and which was held at the Royal Albert Hall from 29 June to 21 July 1934.

The visitors

If trade provided the warp of the family, music and art provided the weft, with decorative threads woven in by the many visitors. Before he retired from performing (as oratorio singer and recitalist), Julius Stockhausen would come to stay (probably in the 1870s), bringing his wife and sometimes one of his most promising pupils, Sophie Löwe (thus enabling her to meet Willie von Glehn). Stockhausen performed regularly with Brahms; he was one of the first interpreters of Brahms's songs and arranged the first London performance of Brahms's *German Requiem*, which was given at the house of the surgeon Sir Henry Thompson.[54] At Peak Hill, he would usually sing Schubert and Schumann.

Charles Stanford had first come into the circle as a boy of 12 in 1864, when he and his parents went to dinner with the Scott Russells; here they met Arthur Sullivan, Frederic Clay and George Grove,[55] but without a doubt, it was Grove who was the 'most frequent habitué'. When he was abroad, Grove wrote frequently to Olga and Mimi; he was clearly fond of Willie and Ernest too, and he introduced many literary and musical figures to Peak Hill Lodge. He called in there every day on his way to the Crystal Palace – it was only a little out of his way – and sometimes also on his way home, to his old wooden house, 'standing in its own secluded shady garden back from the road'.[56] He

---

54 Ernest von Glehn, *Memoir*, p. 51.
55 C.V. Stanford, *Pages from an Unwritten Diary* (London: Edward Arnold, 1914), p. 82.
56 Louise Creighton, *Memoir*, p. 7; and Ernest von Glehn, *Memoir*, p. 35.

would usually '[bring] with him something of interest from the outer world of literature, music, or art'.[57]

Grove, the Scott Russells and the Glehns were thought of as a triumvirate – once introduced to part of the circle, a visitor was part of it all. Sullivan first came to the Peak as a 'very young man, when just home from Leipzig after his first success with the Tempest' in 1862,[58] and he soon became a regular visitor: Ernest von Glehn claimed that the first or nearly the first performance of Cox and Box was given at the Peak, with Sullivan as Box, Freddie Clay as Cox, Norman Scott Russell as Bouncer and Franklin Taylor as the orchestra; Sullivan and Clay would often amuse themselves improvising at the piano.[59] A schoolfriend of Ernest, Lionel Lewin, wrote the libretto for Sullivan's projected opera Guinevere, though it came to nothing.

These social and artistic circles overlapped with others and provided a continuum with earlier times: Grove, Sullivan and Henry Chorley (1808–72), the critic for the Athenaeum, knew Frederick and Nina Lehmann;[60] they all (especially Chorley) knew Charles Dickens (1812–70) well, and Wilkie Collins (1824–89) too. The cleric Alfred Ainger (1837–1904), Master of the Temple, was a regular visitor to the Peak; he had been at school with Dickens's children, and had performed in theatricals with them.[61] Ainger was well acquainted with the author of Music and Morals, H.R. Haweis (1838–1901), known as Rennie; Haweis was another constant visitor to the Peak and also a fine violinist, and Mimi used to accompany him on the Broadwood grand.[62] An opinionated but whimsical and amusing little man, he was 'full of antics and tricks' despite his lameness, and used to '[hang] by one leg, head downwards from the branch of a tree in [the] garden'.[63] He was godfather to Alick von Glehn's son Rennie, and officiated at little Rennie's service of baptism, resulting in his asking himself the various questions and then listening to his own answers.

---

57 Ernest von Glehn, Memoir, p. 65.

58 Louise Creighton, Memoir, p. 10.

59 Ernest von Glehn, Memoir, p. 55 and H. Saxe Wyndham, Sullivan (London: Harper, 1926), p. 240. The programme for the Peak Hill production is dated 17 January 1868, nearly two years after the first performance (with piano only).

60 Nina was a daughter of Robert Chambers, the Edinburgh publisher (1802–71). Frederick's niece was Liza Lehmann. The Lehmanns used to hold musical soirées at their home in Westbourne Terrace, W2, near Paddington.

61 He held the readership of the Temple until he became Master. Other details from Ernest von Glehn, Memoir, p. 53.

62 Louise Creighton, Memoir, p. 8.

63 Ernest von Glehn, Memoir, pp. 48–49.

The fields of endeavour covered by visitors were wide; the artist Holman Hunt was known to the household, as was the economist Joseph Hume[64] and Emmanuel Deutsch, the Talmud scholar;[65] for the sake of stimulating argument, one hopes that perhaps he visited at the same time as the historian J.R. Green (1837–83), later the librarian at Lambeth, and writer of the *Short History of the English People*;[66] Green found the healthy intellectual society at the Peak invigorating, and though Louise von Glehn thought highly of him, she did at one stage feel that perhaps the relationship was going in a direction that she was not altogether happy about; he seemed to be partial to the company of young women and when Louise married (in 1872), he at once transferred his attentions to her sisters. He married Alice Stopford in 1877; she was a friend of Mandell Creighton and corresponded with him regularly on matters of religion. She also corresponded with Roger Quilter in the years around the First World War, and it seems probable that the links between the Quilter family and the Glehns went back at least one generation if not two: Quilter knew Mandell Creighton's son Walter very well (though neither had grown up in the Sydenham area), and a Mr Quilter had gone to Italy with Grove in 1881; this was likely to have been Quilter's uncle, Harry, the art critic who wrote regularly for *Macmillan's Magazine*, but could conceivably have been his father, William Quilter, who had a fine art collection and who had lived in Norwood, not far from Sydenham, since the 1850s.[67]

The last years at the Peak

By March 1880, Mimi was showing signs of the tuberculosis that would kill her six years later[68] and 'in December 1880 there was a consultation with Dr Andrew Clark [the renowned Scottish physician, later Sir Andrew Clark] who took a serious view of her condition & decided that she must go abroad and spend the winter of 1880–81 at Cannes, and subsequent winters at Davos'[69] though there had been talk of her going to Bournemouth rather than Cannes. 'She felt the separation from home

---

64 Ibid., p. 46.
65 Covert, *Memoir*, p. 32.
66 First published in 1874.
67 William Quilter, 1808–88; Roger Quilter, his grandson, 1877–1953; Walter Creighton, 1878–1958.
68 This is evident from letters from Louise Creighton to her mother, especially 30 March [1880]; see J.T. Covert, *A Victorian Family as Seen through the Letters of Louise Creighton to her Mother* (New York: Edwin Mellen Press, 1998), p. 280.
69 Ernest von Glehn, *Memoir*, pp. 80–81.

very deeply, but always made the best of her life with a courage & hope-fulness that rarely failed her. At Davos she found great pleasure in the friendship of the Symonds (John Addington Symonds & his wife), the Stephensons, and the Hon. & Mrs Evelyn Ashley.'[70]

Grove was devastated at the news. He wrote to Parry, 'Nobody can ever know what she has been to me during the 17 years that I have been her friend and what I shall do if anything takes her permanently away from me I really cannot tell. My eyes fill with tears every time I look at her dear figure or think of her.' He continued, 'She would like to go on with her teaching wherever she goes – do you think she would get pupils at Cannes? I know something of her method & care of pupils and she might be strongly recommended as one of the best and most thorough teachers to be found anywhere up to a certain point; & that point she would never pretend she could pass.'[71] At times she seemed to improve – while abroad on one occasion (possibly in Basle), she went to two balls and was sched-uled to perform in a concert – but hopes for her recovery were always dashed.

On 14 January 1881, Agnes von Glehn, the 'charming hostess' who had been the quiet mainstay of the family, died; she was 66. Her death left Robert bereft and later that year there was talk of letting the house and living abroad; that did not happen, though in February 1885 Alick was still trying to persuade the family that the house should in fact be sold, without necessarily waiting for Robert's death.[72] By then, it was probable that Mimi and her father were both too frail and ill to move.

Robert died on 22 July that year. Arrangements for his funeral were complex, with so many people – especially Mimi – to consider. By now, she had to be carried everywhere, and was very weak physically and emotionally. There were seven carriages in the procession, and 'a good collection of Sydenham people';[73] the music (chosen by Mimi) included the chorus from Bach's *St Matthew Passion* 'Wir setzen uns mit Thränen nieder'. The service was conducted by one of Robert's sons-in-law, Mandell Creighton, and Grove was one of the mourners.

Mimi survived Robert by a few months; she died on 8 January 1886, and was buried in the family tomb at Brockley, next to her parents; Sophie, Willie and Olga would be buried there too, in due course. Stan-ford played the organ at the service. 'Such a fine creature she seemed & so vigorous & full of life. I can hardly realise such a nature to be quenched

---

70 Ibid., p. 81.

71 Grove to Parry, 6 December [1880] (Shulbrede Priory Archive).

72 Mimi von Glehn to her sister Ida Koch, who was married and living in Reval, 8 February 1885 (Ernest von Glehn).

73 Mimi to Ida, 27 July 1885 (Ernest von Glehn).

utterly' wrote Parry in his diary.[74] Her death marked the end of life at Peak Hill Lodge and it was sold that summer.

The opportunism that Robert von Glehn had brought to business was visible from time to time in later generations. On 17 May 1917, the entire family changed its name by deed poll to 'de Glehn'. This was almost certainly a consequence of bad publicity. The family export firm had failed to ensure that exports did not fall into enemy hands: British soldiers, in overrunning enemy trenches, had found it disconcerting to discover bags of Portland cement there, and the matter was duly reported. The firm of Alexander von Glehn (though Alick was dead by then) paid a very substantial fine of £3000, and then tried to claim the legal costs against tax but lost; the case set a legal precedent.[75]

The Glehn family was strong-minded, argumentative and forthright, and some of the older members were very formidable indeed. The family archives are substantial, but widely dispersed and largely uncatalogued; nevertheless, initial investigation indicates strongly that exploration of their contents will allow the very real contribution that this talented, colourful and vibrant family made to music and the arts to be recognised and fully acknowledged, and will thereby put into clearer focus and context the part that this and, indeed, other such families played in the musical milieux of the late nineteenth and early twentieth centuries.

I am greatly indebted to Mary and Susan Bailey, Anne-Cécile de Bruyne, John de Bruyne, John Coulter, Professor James Thayne Covert, Mrs Hugh Creighton, Oliver Davies, Jacqueline Knatchbull, Jill Moss and the Hon. Laura Ponsonby for allowing me access to unpublished material, and for all their help and encouragement. My grateful thanks also to Lambeth Palace Library, London, and to Paula Best at the Wigmore Hall Archives, London.

Various family memoirs provided the substance of the material for this article, of which the major ones are Robert von Glehn's *Diary*, in the form of abstracts made by his daughter Louise Creighton; Louise Creighton's *Memoir* and *Letters*, and Robert's son Ernest von Glehn's *Memoir*. The unpublished sources are: Louise Creighton, *Memoir* (private archive); Louise Creighton, *Abstracts from the Diary of Robert von Glehn* (private archive); Letters between Louise Creighton and her mother (Lambeth Palace Library, London); Walter Creighton, *Just on Sixty* (private archive); Emmet Family Papers, Archives of American Art, Smithsonian Institution (Washington, DC); Alfred de Glehn, *Memoir* (private archive); Ernest de Glehn, *Memoir* (private archive); Rhoda von Glehn, Concert Diary (private archive); Letters between other members of the von Glehn family (Lambeth Palace Library, London; private archives); Miscellaneous letters to and from Parry, Grove and the Glehns (Shulbrede Priory Archive); Dora Knatchbull,

---

74 Parry's diary entry for 12 January 1886 (Shulbrede Priory Archive).
75 (1919) 1 Ll. L. Rep. 657; (1920) 2 K.B. 553. These are the appeal reports; the negotiation over the fine was considerably earlier.

Myself When Young (private archive). The *Memoir* of Louise Creighton and the letters between her and her mother have been edited and published, the *Diary Abstracts* providing background material, in J.T. Covert, *Memoir of a Victorian Woman* (Bloomington and Indianapolis, Ind., 1994) (edited extracts of the *Memoir*), and id., *A Victorian Family as Seen through the Letters of Louise Creighton to her Mother* (New York; Edwin Mellen Press, 1998) (edited extracts of the letters), and the *Memoir*, the *Letters* and the *Abstract* also provide some of the material for J.T. Covert, *A Victorian Marriage: Mandell and Louise Creighton* (London: Hambledon, 2000); Louise Creighton (ed.), *Letters of Oswin Creighton, C.F. (1883–1918)* (London: Longmans, Green, 1920); and Louise Creighton, *Life and Letters of Mandell Creighton* (London, 1904).

Appendix
The Glehn family tree

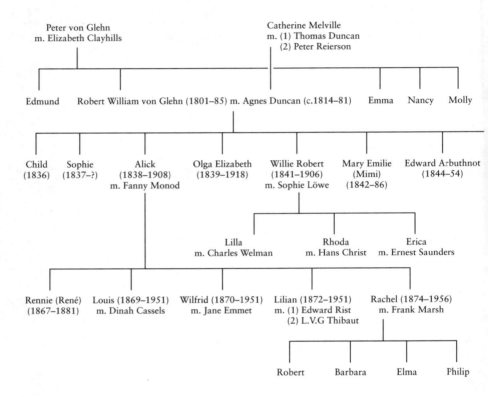

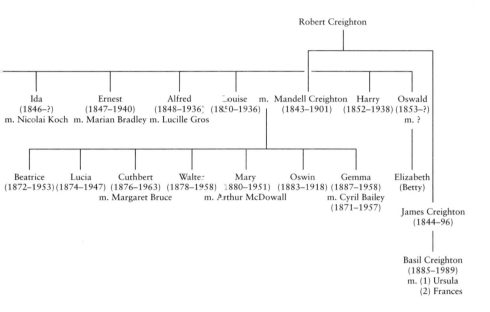

Robert Creighton

| Ida (1846–?) | Ernest (1847–1940) | Alfred (1848–1936) | Louise (1850–1936) | m. Mandell Creighton (1843–1901) | Harry (1852–1938) | Oswald (1853–?) |
| m. Nicolai Koch | m. Marian Bradley | m. Lucille Gros | | | | m. ? |

Beatrice (1872–1953) Lucia (1874–1947) Cuthbert (1876–1963) m. Margaret Bruce Walter (1878–1958) Mary (1880–1951) m. Arthur McDowall Oswin (1883–1918) Gemma (1887–1958) m. Cyril Bailey (1871–1957)

Elizabeth (Betty)

James Creighton (1844–96)

Basil Creighton (1885–1989) m. (1) Ursula (2) Frances

Index

CRACKING INTERNATIONAL MARKETS

Your Strategic Exporting Action Plan

TERRY PATRICK

FINANCIAL TIMES
PITMAN PUBLISHING

LONDON · HONG KONG · JOHANNESBURG
MELBOURNE · SINGAPORE · WASHINGTON DC

FINANCIAL TIMES MANAGEMENT
128 Long Acre, London WC2E 9AN
Tel: +44 (0)171 447 2000
Fax: +44 (0)171 240 5771
Website: www.ftmanagement.com

A Division of Financial Times Professional Limited

First published in Great Britain in 1998

ISBN 0 273 63030 X

British Library Cataloguing in Publication Data
A CIP catalogue record for this book can be obtained from
the British Library.

10 9 8 7 6 5 4 3 2 1

Typeset by M Rules
Printed and bound in Great Britain by
Biddles Ltd, Guildford and King's Lynn

*The Publishers' policy is to use paper manufactured
from sustainable forests.*

CONTENTS

Part 2
THE EXPORT BUSINESS PLAN
AND EXPORT FINANCIAL PLAN

ABOUT THE AUTHOR

Terry Patrick started his professional business career with training at IBM's business school. He has subsequently worked in some 53 countries in various executive management positions. More recently he has also developed a confidential international management consultancy business specializing in effecting export market entry into overseas markets. Terry Patrick spent the three years prior to the publication of this book engaged in business in Russia.

*This book is dedicated to
my late father, Alfred James Patrick and to
my mother, Winifred (Peggy) Patrick.*